Edward Austin Sheldon, And others

A Manual of Elementary Instruction

For the Use of Public and Private Schools and Normal Classes

Edward Austin Sheldon, And others

A Manual of Elementary Instruction
For the Use of Public and Private Schools and Normal Classes

ISBN/EAN: 9783337278083

Printed in Europe, USA, Canada, Australia, Japan

Cover: Foto ©Paul-Georg Meister /pixelio.de

More available books at **www.hansebooks.com**

A MANUAL

OF

ELEMENTARY INSTRUCTION,

FOR THE

USE OF PUBLIC AND PRIVATE SCHOOLS AND NORMAL CLASSES;

CONTAINING A GRADUATED COURSE OF

OBJECT LESSONS

FOR

TRAINING THE SENSES AND DEVELOPING THE FACULTIES OF CHILDREN.

BY E. A. SHELDON,
SUPERINTENDENT OF SCHOOLS, OSWEGO, N. Y.;

ASSISTED BY

MISS M. E. M. JONES AND PROF. H. KRUSI.

NEW YORK:
CHARLES SCRIBNER, 124 GRAND STREET.
1862.

PREFACE.

For many years there has been a growing conviction in the minds of the thinking men of this country, that our methods of primary instruction are very defective, because they are not properly adapted either to the mental, moral, or physical conditions of childhood. But little reference has hitherto been had to any natural order in the development of the faculties, or to the many peculiar characteristics of children. Memory, by no means the most important of the infant faculties, and reason, at this age but faintly developed, have been severely taxed, while but little direct systematic effort has been made to awaken and quicken the *perceptive faculties*, which are the first to develop themselves, and upon the proper cultivation of which we must depend for success in all our future educational processes. Even in schools where better views have prevailed, the want of some systematic exercises, with proper apparatus and facilities for putting them into practice, has been strongly felt.

The *design* of this work is to meet this demand: to present a *definite course* of *elementary instruction* adapted to philosophic views of the "laws of childhood."

We do not claim for it originality, either in thought or method. It is now a full half century since that distinguished educational reformer, Pestalozzi, to a great extent gave expression and embodiment to the principles and methods herein contained.

Important modifications have however been made; many errors both in principles and practice have been eradicated, and we are now able to bring to bear the suggestions of some of the most distinguished educators in Europe, based upon many years of careful study and experiment.

The work upon which this is founded, and from which, with the kind consent of its authoress, Miss Elizabeth Mayo, we have largely drawn, is, as stated in her preface, "A Manual, in two volumes, containing the essential portions of the five in which alone such help has hitherto been attainable; and this, too, with the addition of much valuable matter which is now published for the first time."

This work, entitled "Manual of Elementary Instruction," has been compiled within the past year, and brings down to us the light and experience of the best schools of Europe, where these methods have been longest and most thoroughly tested.

She further says, "The whole work has been carefully reconstructed on a plan which presents principles and practice in immediate connection, in order to illustrate their mutual dependence; all details of practice being exhibited as flowing naturally from the first truths on which they are founded."

While the general plan of this work has been followed, and some of the lessons adopted with slight changes, a large proportion of original matter has been added, and the whole arranged with special reference to the wants of our American schools.

The Lessons on Objects, Color, Moral Instruction, Lessons on Animals, and the Introduction have been made up from the original manuscripts of Miss M. E.

M. Jones, with such exceptions as are indicated, and the whole arranged by her. For more than fifteen years this lady was engaged in training teachers in these methods in the Home and Colonial Training Institution, London, and has been connected with the schools of this country sufficiently long to understand something of their wants.

Prof. Hermann Krusi* is the author of the Lessons on Form and Inventive Drawing. He has also rewritten the fifth and sixth steps in Number. His suggestions on many other points have been very valuable. We can but congratulate ourselves and those engaged in primary instruction for this timely aid from one so eminently fitted for the work.†

Of the remaining subjects, Reading has been entirely rewritten. The Lessons on Place or Geography have been slightly changed, introducing two or three original sketches of lessons in the first step, and so changing the third step as to adapt it to our American locality. Some changes have also been made in the Lessons on Sound, Size, and Weight; new matter added, and, in two or three instances, substituted for that contained in the old volumes.

While these lessons are prepared for primary schools, they are also arranged with special reference to use in

---

* At present teacher in the Oswego Training School.

† Prof. K. was born, as it were, in the very school of Pestalozzi, in which his father was for twenty years a leading and active teacher. For ten years he was engaged with his father in teaching a government school for the training of teachers in Pestalozzian principles, in one of the cantons of Switzerland, his native country. After this, he was for six years engaged in the Home and Colonial Institution, working out and adapting these methods to the English schools; and it was here that he first brought out the Inventive Drawing. In this country he has been for several years engaged in teaching normal schools and teachers' institutes. He has studied carefully the characteristics of our schools and people; and is, in every way, abundantly qualified to adapt this system to our peculiarities and wants.

Normal and Training classes. Model lessons are given, and then subjects suggested on which similar lessons may be drawn up. The models should be carefully examined and analyzed, and, in the case of classes in training, the original sketches should in every instance be submitted to the criticism of the teacher. By individual teachers, these sketches may be written out and used as lessons in their schools. In some of the lessons, general directions only are given; in others, these directions are more particular; while many are drawn out at full length, including both questions and answers. In any case, they are only designed as suggestions and models to guide teachers in working out their *own plans and methods*. Teachers who confine themselves simply to the lessons presented in this book, and to their exact minutiæ, can but fail in their work. To be truly successful, they must catch the spirit and philosophy of the system, and work it out somewhat in their *own way;* of course, always conforming to the principles upon which it is based: these we believe to be sound and philosophical, and they should never be violated.

The lessons that have been taken with no alteration, other than an occasional verbal expression, have been indicated either in the index, or in the body of the work where they occur, by the letter *M*.

It is now more than two years since these methods were practically and thoroughly introduced into the Oswego schools, and from a constant and careful observation of their working, we feel that we are in some degree prepared to judge as to what is wanted in a book of this kind for our teachers and schools; and we trust we may not be disappointed in the hope that it will meet these wants.

The subjects are arranged into steps, simply with reference to the order of time in which it is thought various portions of the work may be accomplished. All first-step lessons are designed for children from four to five years of age, or during the first year of their school life. In the same way the second step is designed for the second year, and the third step for the third year; thus covering the time usually allotted to our primary departments in towns where the schools are graded. In some instances a fourth step is added, which is designed for the next grade. The order of succession in which the various subjects are arranged, has no reference to any order in which it may be supposed they should be taken up. While it is the design that the lessons of each step, in every subject, shall be taken up at the same stage of the child's development, it is not expected that they will all be treated simultaneously. From three to five only are taken at once, and these are carried on until the interest of the children begins to flag, when they are changed for other subjects, which in their turn are to be changed, as the children weary, for others still, until we again return to the first course, to resume it, after a rapid review, where we left it. This necessity for change with little children cannot be too carefully observed; for no matter how interesting the subject is at first, they will in time tire of it; and a lively interest can only be maintained by change. Reading, spelling, and number are the only subjects that are constant. With the youngest children the programme should change fortnightly, and with the older ones monthly. In the Appendix may be seen some programmes of the Oswego schools, which will give a very good idea of the way in which these may be arranged.

In the country schools, where no such gradation and classification are possible, where the teachers find it impracticable to take up all the topics, as they usually will, they must confine themselves to those which seem to them of the most practical importance; as, for instance, Moral

Instruction, Reading, Geography, Number, Language, Form, Color, and Size.

Others might make a different selection of subjects: we only call attention to this, by way of expressing our view of the importance of doing well and thoroughly whatever is undertaken. It may seem difficult to make a selection of subjects where all are important; but it is better to leave half of them untouched than to undertake to do all, and do nothing as it should be done. Whatever is taught, let it be taught with reference to correct principles.

E. A. SHELDON.

OSWEGO, *Aug.* 25, 1862.

CONTENTS.

	PAGE
INTRODUCTION,	13
Necessity of Training,	13
Pestalozzian Plans and Principles,	14
Preparation of Sketches,	16
Criticism Lessons,	24
Reports of Model Lessons,	40
Miscellaneous Exercises,	42
COLOR,	45
FORM,	62
OBJECTS,	86
NUMBER,	138
SIZE,	200
WEIGHT,	208
SOUND,	212
LANGUAGE (M.),	219
READING,	231
DICTATION (M.),	258
GEOGRAPHY,	263
LESSONS ON THE HUMAN BODY (M.),	292
LESSONS ON ANIMALS,	310
LESSONS ON PLANTS (M.),	350
MORAL INSTRUCTION,	384
DRAWING,	419

ELEMENTARY INSTRUCTION.

INTRODUCTION.

I.—NECESSITY OF TRAINING.
II.—PESTALOZZIAN PLANS AND PRINCIPLES.
III.—PREPARATION OF SKETCHES.
IV.—CRITICISM LESSONS.
V.—REPORTS OF MODEL LESSONS.
VI.—MISCELLANEOUS EXERCISES IN METHOD.

I.—Necessity of Training.

WERE we to undertake to discuss the importance of a regular apprenticeship to the mechanic who builds houses or makes machines, or of a professional education to the artist, the lawyer, or the physician, we should expose ourselves to public ridicule. It is too self-evident to admit of sober discussion. All regard it a necessity. And even when a thorough professional education has been obtained, or a complete term of service as apprentice served, we are slow to employ them until their success has been tested by long *experience*. We are slow to trust the setting of a broken bone to one who has not given *practical* demonstrations of his skill. And yet these things are important only in a physical sense—the lowest of all human wants and necessities. How much more, then, would it seem important that those to whom we intrust the moral and intellectual destiny of the race should be carefully educated and prepared with special reference to their work!

It would seem too obvious to require an argument, that every teacher should clearly comprehend the character of the infant mind, and its mode of operation—the way in which each faculty stands related to the other, and the order of its evolution—as also the related order of appliances in the process of development, together with a knowledge of the many striking peculiarities and characteristics of children. It is clear that, without this knowledge, teachers go blindly at their work, and can but fall into many and grievous errors. One thing is certain, that with the principles and methods here discussed, no one can hope to succeed who does not carefully study and intelligently practise them.

II.—Pestalozzian Plans and Principles.

There are several different ways of giving a lesson.

EXAMPLE.—*Six ways of giving a Lesson on a Plant.*

1. Account of the plant learned by children from a book, and repeated to the teacher.

2. Description learned and repeated as before, teacher afterward explaining the meaning.

3. Piece first explained by the teacher, then learned by the children, and repeated.

4. Picture shown—parts pointed out by teacher. Description learned, and repeated as before.

5. Specimens given—parts examined first by teacher, then observed by the children.

6. Specimens distributed—parts found out by the children, who frame a description, which is put on the board and committed to memory.

Again, since all lessons should be given in accordance with correct philosophical principles, we subjoin the following, as laid down by Pestalozzi:

1. Activity is a law of childhood. Accustom the child to do—educate the hand.

2. Cultivate the faculties in their natural order—first form the mind, then furnish it.

3. Begin with the senses, and never tell a child what he can discover for himself.

4. Reduce every subject to its elements—one difficulty at a time is enough for a child.

5. Proceed step by step. Be thorough. The measure of information is not what the teacher can give, but what the child can receive.

6. Let every lesson have a point. (Except in junior schools, when more than one lesson is required before the point is reached, each successively tending toward it.)

7. Develop the idea—then give the term—cultivate language.

8. Proceed from the known to the unknown—from the particular to the general—from the concrete to the abstract—from the simple to the more difficult.

9. First synthesis, then analysis—not the order of the subject, but the order of nature.

Of course, the educational teacher, in addressing a class of students, would explain and illustrate these principles. In order to ascertain whether they are thoroughly comprehended, the following questions may be put. Answers should be given in writing.

Questions.

1. A teacher begins Arithmetic by teaching a child to count orally, 1, 2, 3, 4, &c. What principle is violated?

2. A teacher teaches multiplication by letting the children sing the tables. What principle is violated?

3. Begins Geography by use of globes, pointing out continents, &c. What principle is violated?

4. Begins Natural History by taking the children into a museum where there are specimens of all kinds, and making a classification. What principle is violated?

5. To develop an idea, begins with the definition; "Children, I am going to teach you something: 'All things through which

we can see clearly are transparent.' Look at this piece of glass." What principle is violated?

6. Having developed an idea, omits to give the term or put it on the board. What principle is violated?

7. Gives a lesson on coal, without presenting the object. What principle is violated?

8. Gives a lesson without observing any divisions either by S. R. (simultaneous repetition), or by W. B. (writing on the board). What principle is violated?

9. Teaches Reading by the name method. What principle is violated?

10. Adopts a uniform plan in her lessons, so that the children always know in what order a subject will be represented. What principle is violated?

11. Tells the children that water is a liquid, and then shows what a liquid is. What principle is violated?

12. Gives a lesson on position and distance, always measuring and representing the object herself. What principle is violated?

13. Gives a lesson on the lion, before the children have had one on the cat. What principle is violated?

14. A lesson on perching birds as an order, before any have been given on the robin, canary, and other individuals. What principle is violated?

15. Teacher, giving lesson on a tiger, refers to cat—lets one child talk of the cat at home, another of the dog, a third of the horse, a fourth of riding the horse to town. What principle is violated?

16. Undertakes to give lessons on the parts of speech to children who have had no lessons on objects. What principle is violated?

III.—Preparation of Sketches.

Too much stress cannot be laid on the importance of preparing notes or sketches in writing. It is not too much to say that no lesson ought to be given, a sketch of which has not been systematically prepared. In training students to this work it is found

PREPARATION OF SKETCHES. 17

desirable to begin with an examination and analysis of a few simple lessons.

FIRST EXAMPLE.—*Sketch on* Water.
(*See* " *Objects,*" *Second Step.*)
Directions for Analysis.

1. Matter to be separated from method.
2. Point to be found, whether definitely stated, or contained in the title, or in the head.
3. Terms and information given to be distinguished from ideas developed.
4. Ideas developed, whether
    (*a*) by addressing the senses directly.
    (*b*) by comparison.
    (*c*) by experiment.
    (*d*) by addressing the reason.
5. Illustration—Use of Board—S. R.—Ellipses—Kind of Summary.

The analysis of water as made by students should appear thus:

1. Matter. *See Summary.*
2. Point is contained in the heads, which are—
    General qualities.
    Uses, and special qualities on which uses depend.
3. Terms given—liquid and bright; information given—every country is well supplied with water.
4. Ideas developed:
    (*a*) Water is bright—has neither taste nor smell.
    (*b*) Water is a liquid—has no color—can be seen through.
    (*c*) Water is useful for washing and drinking. (Memory.)
    (*d*) Water is used for washing, on account of the absence of color and smell.
5. Illustrations—Ellipses and S. R.—Summary elliptical.

SECOND EXAMPLE.—*Lesson on Writing Paper.*

What is this? Paper. Whence do we get paper? Does it grow upon any plant? Does it come from off any animal? Do we dig it out of the ground? How do we get it then? It is made. Yes, it is made by man : but did man make it out of nothing? No; he must have something to make it from. Do you know of what paper is made? It is made of rags. Yes, the best paper is made of linen rags. Of what is linen made? Do you not know? It is made from the fibrous stem of a very pretty plant. Here is a picture of it; it is called *flax*. Repeat together, "Paper is made of rags; the finest paper is made of linen rags; linen is made from the fibrous stem of a plant called flax." Now, children, look at the paper, and tell me what you observe about it. It is white. This paper is white, but what is this? Blue. And this? Brown. What kind of paper is white? Writing paper. Try and find out why writing paper is made white. That we may see the writing upon it. Look at it and feel it. It is smooth. Put it between your thumb and finger. It is thin. Try again. It is light. Repeat together these qualities, "Writing paper is smooth, thin, and light." Now hold it toward the window. We can see through it. Can you see through it as well as you do through glass? What is the difference? We can see everything quite clearly through the glass; but through paper we only see the dim light. What did we say of glass? That it is transparent; but we say of objects through which we can see light only, that they are *translucent*. What can we say of paper? It is translucent. Try what you can do with paper. We can tear it. What more? We can bend it and fold it. Yes; on account of this quality it is said to be *pliable*. Repeat together, "Paper is *easily torn :* it can be easily bent and folded : it is *pliable*." See, I have put a part of this sheet of paper into the fire. It burns. It is *inflammable*. Why do we call paper inflammable? Because it burns readily. Tell me some other things that are inflammable. Wood, coal, &c. Of what use is this kind of paper? To write upon. Yes; and when you are grown up, and perhaps have to live very far away from your father and mother and brothers, how pleasant you will think it to receive a sheet of paper folded up, and brought to you by the postman, to tell you how they all are, and how they are getting on! What is such folded-up sheet of paper called? Yes, a letter. How glad you will then be, that when you were young you went to *school*, and learnt to *read*, so that you can understand what is written in the *letter* brought by the *postman*.

After you have told me all you have found out about writing paper, and sung a hymn, I will tell you a true little history about writing. Now all repeat together, "Writing paper is made of *linen rags;* linen is made from the fibrous *stem* of a plant called *flax:* writing paper is *white, translucent,* and *pliable;* it is *smooth, thin, light,* and *easily torn;* it is *inflammable;* and it is useful to *write upon.*"

After learning to spell any new words met with in the lesson, the children repeat the hymn—

"I thank the goodness and the grace," &c.

Now I will give you the little history I promised. It relates to one of those countries in which they worship idols of wood and stone, and where the people do not know God and Jesus Christ. The Lord put it into the heart of a very good man in England, Mr. Williams, to go over and teach these poor ignorant people how they might be saved and go to *heaven.* How do the Scriptures say that we can be saved? This good man had to cross the sea, in order to get at this *country.* How did he manage this? Yes; he went in a ship, and when he arrived at the country where the people did not know *God* and *Jesus Christ,* he began to teach them a great many things; he was very kind to them, and showed them how to build neat little cottages, and places where they might learn about *God;* and he made a ship that would sail upon the *water.* One day he was working very hard among them, when he found that he had left a tool at home of which he was in need; so he called one of the men, and taking up a chip of wood, wrote upon it the name of the tool he wanted, and desired the man to take it to his wife, and that she would give him something to bring back with him. The man looked astonished, and waited for a message. "Go quickly," said Mr. Williams; "I am in haste; show this to my wife, that is all."

Now the poor man, though he was a great man in that country, knew nothing about reading or writing, and as he went he thought, How silly it is to take this piece of wood to show. However, he did as he was bid; he was *obedient.* How great was his surprise when he had given the chip to Mrs. Williams, to see her look at it and immediately fetch the instrument. "But how do you know," said he, "that this is what Mr. Williams sent me for?" "You brought me a chip of wood," said Mrs. Williams, "and that informed me what I was to give you; you have now only to go back quickly with it." He did so, saying to himself as he returned, What a wonderful people these Englishmen are; they can make even a chip of wood speak! Now, when this chief saw how much more than he or any of his people this kind missionary knew, he became willing that he should teach them about God and Jesus Christ.

You see, dear children, how much happier we are than these poor ignorant people. Who gave us our many blessings? God. Yes; He it is who made you happy English children. What should you do? Praise Him. Is it enough to praise Him with your lips? No. How, then, should you praise Him? We should praise Him with our hearts. Yes; but when you were singing that pretty little hymn of praise, I did not see you look as if you were really thanking God in your hearts. When a kind person has given you something, I have heard you thank them, and in such a manner, too, that I am sure you *felt* they had been kind to you. Now I should like to hear you thank God as if you indeed felt all that kindness which He is ever pouring out upon you.

The analysis of writing paper, as made by the students, should appear thus:

1. *Matter of the lesson.* Paper is artificial. Writing paper is made of linen rags; linen is made of the stem of a plant called flax. Writing paper is white, translucent, thin, light; will tear easily; can be bent and folded; is inflammable; and is useful to write upon.

2. *Point* is contained in the heads, which are—nature, qualities, and uses of writing paper.

3. *Terms given:* pliable, translucent, flax; information given—that paper is made from rags (by children)—that linen is made from the stem of the flax plant, and the anecdote (by teacher).

4. *Ideas developed:*
   (a) white, smooth, thin, light.
   (b) translucent; paper is of different colors, though writing paper is usually white.
   (c) it will bend easily; pliable; it is easily torn; inflammable.
   (d) that we may see to write on it, it is white; it is made by man; artificial, but made of something that only God can make, and for which we must thank Him. Application made: the advantage of learning to write.

5. *Illustrations.* Picture of flax plant shown, and anecdote told. *Mechanical plans*—Hands out.—Ellipses—S. R.—Elliptical summary.

The students may next draw up notes on parchment as writing paper.

Third Example.

I. *Matter.* Parchment is an animal substance, and it is artificial, being the prepared skin of a sheep. It is yellowish, stiff, thick, tough, odorous, translucent. It frizzles when burning. It is durable, and therefore used to write on when the writing is to be preserved.

II. *Point.* Nature; qualities; use, and quality on which use depends.

III. *Terms given:* parchment, and refer to "*Ideas Developed,*" and supply any terms with which they are unacquainted. Information given: parchment is the dried skin of a sheep; it is used to write upon when the writing is to be preserved.

IV. *Ideas developed:*
   (a) Yellowish white, thin, smooth, **odorous**.
   (b) Stiff, translucent.

(c) Flexible, tough, frizzles when burning.
(d) Animal substance, artificial, durable.

f. Illustrations. Qualities written on the board (S. R.). Story told.—Verse given.—Summary read from the board.

It is to be observed that the preparation so often referred to consists in drawing up sketches of lessons, not in fully writing out lessons. A report of a full lesson on parchment would appear thus:

Report of Lesson on Parchment as Paper. . Do you know what this is? It is paper. It is like paper. Here is a piece of paper; see if you can find a difference between this and that. The paper is white, and this is yellow. Is it very yellow? It is rather yellow. Say it is yellowish. What did we find out in the last lesson about the color of paper? That it may be of different colors. Then paper may be yellow. I will help you to find out the real difference. What is paper made from? Linen rags. Whence come the linen rags? From the flax plant. But this was never a part of any vegetable; it is the dried skin of a sheep. Does the skin of a sheep look like this? No. What is the difference? The skin of the sheep is woolly. What has been done to it? The wool has been taken off. Yes, and it has been cleaned and smoothed. Who made the skin into parchment? Man. What do we say of things made by man? They are artificial. The dried skin of a sheep is called parchment. I will write on the board the qualities we have discovered:

Parchment is an animal substance.
" " artificial.
" " yellowish white.

Now feel the parchment and the paper. The parchment is thicker than the paper. See what you can do with them. We can fold them up. Which folds the more easily? The paper. Yes, the parchment is stiff. Do you know anything else that is stiff? Cards, a pen. Repeat together (R. T.). Things that will not bend nor fold easily are stiff (W. B.). Try once again. We can tear the paper, but we cannot tear the parchment (R. T.). Parchment is tough. Do you know anything else tough? India-rubber (R. T.). Things that will not tear easily are tough (W.B.). See, I have put it into the fire; it frizzles. But when I put the paper into the fire it burns up with a flame. Think of other things that burn with a flame. Wood, rags. What is paper made from? Rags. And rags come from the flax plant. What does wood come from? Trees. Give me another name for plants and trees. Vegetables. Try and remember what I tell you. All things that burn with a flame come from vegetables (R. T.). But how does the parchment burn? It frizzles. Name other things that frizzle. Hair, a bone. What do bones come from? Animals. Hair? Animals. Parchment itself is the skin of an animal. What can you find out from all this? That things that frizzle come from animals (W. B.). What use can we make of this? It will do to write on. It is used to write on. Can you tell me why we use it, when we have plenty of paper? Shall I help you to find out? Which can you destroy more easily; which will last longer—paper or parchment? And why? Because it is tough. Now, if you were writing a note, which would be torn up after it was read, what would do to write your note upon? Paper. But when people want their writing to last for years and years, they write on parchment. The laws of the land are written on parchment. Now, if you answer well, I will tell you a story about this, after we have gone over what is written on the board (R. T.).

Once on a time there lived a queen in England, not like the present queen, who is kind and good to all. The former queen was ignorant, harsh, and cruel. There were good people in the country, who loved to read their Bibles and to learn; but there were wicked people, who tried to prevent them from doing this, and they and the queen made a law that whoever read the Bible and worshipped God, as we are told to do, should be burned to death. Now this queen had a servant who was a clever man. He knew that such a wicked, unjust law would not last: God would not let it. So they came to him about writing out this law, and said, Shall it be written out on parchment or on paper? He answered, Take paper; for the poorest paper will last longer than the law. And so it proved; for the poor, mistaken queen died, and then the people could read and pray in peace. There is a hymn about this, beginning—

> I took the sacred Book of God,
> To keep, to fear, to read it free;
> But holy martyrs shed their blood
> To win this word of life for me.

Now, what more have I to add to what is written on the board? The Uses of Parchment.

IV. Criticism Lessons.

Many of the lessons given by the students are called criticism lessons. They are given in the presence of the members of the class, who express opinions on the various points of the lesson; enumerating those in which they think the teacher has succeeded, and those in which they think she has failed. To conduct a criticism properly, it is necessary that there should be a presiding critic, whose opinion is final. The following are the points of criticism which are given as a guide to the class:

Points of Criticism.

I. *Matter.*

1. Whether suitable to children; whether exercising observation, conception, reason, or all these.

2. Lesson—whether bearing on one point; into what heads divided.

3. Whether, in a Scripture or moral lesson, an application be made; whether the right one. In a lesson on an animal, whether the children be led to see the wisdom and goodness of God in the adaptation of parts to mode of life, and whether humane feelings be cultivated.

II. *Method.*

1. Whether the teacher clearly apprehends the distinction between what must be told and what must be given.

2. Whether she distinguishes the various mental faculties one from another; knows which should be, and how exercised.

3. Whether good illustrations are used; the specimens large enough and sufficient for distribution; whether diagrams were drawn when required.

4. Whether appropriate questions were used when general answers are wanted. Leading questions only to obtain an admission, on which another question is based.

5. Whether the board was sufficiently used—new terms written on it; also titles and heads of lessons; also, with elder children, definitions and statements.

6. Summary, of what kind; whether of the kind most appropriate to the children and the lesson.

7. Whether proper use was made of Hands Out and S. R.

III. *Teacher.*

1. Whether capable of swaying class according to her will—of awakening sympathy, including the sympathy of numbers.

2. Whether attending to all, or carrying on the lesson with a few forward children; whether taking the right standing point.

3. Manner—whether appropriate—bustling and excited—slow and languid—cheerful and energetic; whether, if a Scriptural lesson, reverential tone of voice.

4. Language—whether appropriate; syntax and correct pronunciation.

IV. *Children.*

1. Whether respectful, attentive; whether interested; if so, to what interest is owing.

2. Whether likely to carry the lesson away as a whole; if a Scripture or moral lesson, whether their hearts were touched.

As a clear illustration of the design and method of conducting these lessons, we subjoin the following remarks and sketch, taken from a paper issued by the Home and Colonial Institution of London:—

Two principal objects are always kept in view in training teachers—the first, to make them acquainted with the principles of education, as founded on the nature of children; the second, to initiate them in *the art of teaching*. One of the most successful plans for accomplishing the latter point has been that of the teachers giving a gallery lesson, before a class of the students, who criticize the matter and manner of the lesson, according to certain rules with which they have been previously made acquainted; these criticisms being summed up and commented upon by the head master or mistress. This plan acts as a strong stimulus to exertion; it gives the head master the opportunity of bringing out the principles of education, and applying them practically; and at the same time it tends to produce that self-possession so necessary to every teacher of young children.

The following is a specimen of what is called a Criticism Lesson, a sketch of which the teacher first prepares; in fact, with a few alterations, it is the report of one actually given at the Model Infant School of the Home and Colonial Institution :—

SKETCH OF A LESSON ON THE BAT.—CHILDREN FROM FIVE TO SEVEN.

The children will be required to observe :—

I. *The peculiar organization of the bat.* It has a body like that of the mouse, and wings like a bird, the latter formed by the bones being extended and the skin stretched between them, the ears extremely long; small, sharp-pointed teeth; five claws on the hind feet, somewhat like fingers and a thumb. It is also provided with hooks on its wings.

II. *Its habits.* The bat, when seeking its food, which consists of insects and small birds, flies like a bird, but always in the dim twilight. As its eyes are dazzled by glaring light, it remains during the day in old barns or houses, and suspends itself by its hind legs. In winter it falls asleep.

III. *Adaptation of the organs to the habits and propensities of the bat.* The wings and expansion of skin enable it to fly, and thus to get its food. As its prey comes out at night, it has acute feeling to guide it, instead of good sight, which would not have been so useful. It cannot rest on its legs, but is able, by means of hooks and claws, to suspend itself, with its head downward, and so get rest. Its food fails in winter; it then falls into a sleep, and requires none.

IV. *Application.* Lead the children to trace the hand of God in all this. If we see any thing beautifully fitted for some purpose, we conclude it was made for that purpose. God's wisdom, benevolence, and power to be shown in the adaptation of all the parts of the animal to its habits.

LESSON TO BE CRITICISED.

Teacher. What animal is this? (*Showing it.*)
Children. A bat.
T. Look at it, and tell me something about it. What do you see peculiar in it?
A little girl. I do not know what "peculiar" means.
T. Can any one tell her? (*A pause.*)
Another child. It means something that you see in one kind of thing, but not in anything else.
T. Well, that will do. What, then, do you see peculiar in the bat?
Several. It has wings and hands.
T. What have you at the end of your own arms?
C. Hands.
T. And what have you on your hands?
C. Fingers.
T. How many fingers have you on each hand?
All. Four, and a thumb.
T. Do you see anything in this bat that looks like four fingers and a thumb?
A little girl counted them, and said there were four bones that looked like fingers.
T. Can you tell me the difference between these bones and our fingers?
A little boy. They have no flesh on them, and they are very long.
T. What other difference do you see?

Some of the children said it had a web, others that it had a skin between the fingers.

T. Where does this skin appear to come from?

C. From the back.

T. And what does it do?

C. It stretches over the fingers.

T. What has the bat beside four fingers?

C. It has a thumb.

T. What does this thumb look like?

C. Like a claw.

T. But what kind of claw?

C. It looks like a hook.

T. (*to an active-looking but idle little boy*). Now, little boy, I am quite sure you can tell me something about this bat.

Boy. It has teeth.

T. What kind of teeth has it?

Several. Sharp teeth.

T. What kind of mouth has it?

Two or three children. It looks like a beak.

T. Would you call this a beak? What creatures have beaks?

C. Birds.

T. Well, would you call this a bird?

C. No; it is a beast.

T. What kind of ears has it?

Some of the children said, They are large.

T. Can you tell me anything about the bat's sleeping?

A little girl. It sleeps in the day, and flies about in the twilight.

T. Where does it sleep?

A boy. In a hole.

A girl. It hangs on high walls.

A boy. It hangs on trees.

T. Yes; they hang on trees, also on the walls of old houses, where nobody can live because they are so old; there they sleep all day. Do you know what they hang by?

C. By their feet.

T. If they hang by their feet, what position are they in?

C. Their heads are downward.

T. You have told me where the bat lives, and what it does by day; now tell me what it does when night comes on.

C. It goes about.

T. How does it go?

C. It flies.

T. Why can it not walk?

C. Because its legs would not bear it; they are very weak.

T. Then must it not be a very awkward animal?

C. No; because it has wings and a hook instead.

T. Now tell me what its body looks like.

C. Like a mouse.

T. Have you ever seen a mouse like this animal?

C. No; it has a skin stretched over its fingers, and a mouse has not; a mouse has four legs.

T. And what does this skin stretched over its fingers make?

C. Wings.

T. By what means does it fly?

C. By its wings.

T. Why does it fly about?

C. To get its food.

T. What is its food?

C. Insects.

T. And anything else?

A boy. Worms.

T. I don't think it eats worms, but I am not quite sure; however, I know it eats little birds. When does it come out?

C. In the twilight.

T. What do you mean by twilight?

A girl. Night. *A boy.* Evening; between day and night, when it is not quite dark.

T. What time do the insects come out?

C. At the same time that the bat comes out.

T. When it comes out at the twilight, can it see the insects?

C. Yes; because it has very sharp eyes.

T. No; you have guessed this. Look at its eyes; bats have not sharp eyes; they cannot see their food plainly, because their eyes are very small. Then, how is it they can catch their food?

Some of the children. They have little nerves.

A little boy. The food comes upon its wings.

The Head Master (*speaking to the teacher*). I do not think the children all understand how the bat catches its food; be so good as to repeat the questions.

T. Tell me how it catches its food.

A boy. The food comes upon its wings.

T. I will tell you: when the insect flies upon the wings of the bat, it shuts them up very quickly, and turns its mouth around sharply and catches it. What, then, is one of the uses of the wings of the bat?

Several. To get its food.

T. Why does it need its wings to get its food?

C. Because there is very little light, and it cannot see plainly.

T. And what are the hooks for?

C. For the bat to hang on the wall.

T. There is something else about the bat that you do not know, I think. Shall I tell you? It goes to sleep all the winter. Why should it sleep all the winter?

C. Because no insects come out.

T. What would become of it if there were no insects?

C. It would starve.

T. Now tell me again, what is the use of the wings to the bat?

C. To fly with, and to catch its food.

The teacher repeated all the questions on this point.

To the question, why the bat could not find its prey without its wings, a little girl replied, "Because its eyes *is* dull."—a fault in grammar which the teacher required the children to correct.

T. What is the use of its claws?

C. To hang on the walls.

T. When does it hang on the walls?

C. In the day.

T. If this large body (*pointing to the body of the bat*) were to walk on the ground, what would become of its delicate legs?

C. They would break.

T. And what would happen to the wings?

A little girl. They would break too.

T. Is "break" the word to use?

A boy. They would be torn.

T. Now attend to what I am going to ask you, and speak quietly: Who gave the bat these wings?

The children replied in a low tone of voice, "God."

T. What did he give the bat wings for?

C. To fly in the air.

T. And when you see this bat has wings, what are you sure it was made for?

C. To fly in the air.

T. If it looked like a mouse, and if it had not these wings, what would you think it was made for?

C. To walk like a mouse.

T. And suppose it had not these wings, what sort of eyes would it most likely have?

C. Sharp eyes.

T. When we see that God has given the bat these wings, what are we quite sure he has made it for?

C. To fly in the air.

T. What does this show you of God?

C. It shows us his power and wisdom.

T. Wisdom in what?

C. In giving the bat wings to fly.

T. How does that show his wisdom?

C. (*after a pause*). Because it would starve if it had not wings.

T. And what else does it show beside his wisdom?

C. (*after another pause*). His goodness.

T. His goodness in what?

C. In giving the bat these wings to fly in the air.

T. But why does that show his goodness?

C. Because it would not be able to get its food without them.

T. Then there is another thing that shows God's goodness;

what is it? (*No answer.*) What did I tell you it does in the winter?

C. It sleeps.

T. Well, how does that show God's goodness?

C. Because, when there are no insects, it does not require any food.

T. Can you give me a text which speaks of God's goodness to all the things which he has made?

After a short pause, a little girl said, "O Lord, how manifold are thy works! in wisdom hast thou made them all: the earth is full of thy riches."

T. Now, can you give me another short one? (*No answer.*) Well, I will repeat it: "The Lord is good to all; and his tender mercies are over all his works." Now repeat it after me.

The children did so three or four times. The lesson then closed, and the children marched out of the room singing.

THE CRITICISM OF THE TEACHERS IN TRAINING ON THE PRECEDING LESSON.

Head Master (*addressing the teachers*). You have now to exercise your judgment on the matter of this lesson, and on the manner in which it was given. Before you can give a correct opinion on a lesson, with what science ought you to be, in some degree, acquainted?

A Teacher. With the science of education.

H. M. And what are the subjects which this science acts upon?

T. Children.

H. M. What, then, should you know?

T. Something of the nature of children, and of the best method of working upon them so as to develop their faculties and form their characters.

H. M. Recollect that the object of your "criticism lessons" is not to sit in judgment upon a companion—you have nothing to do with the person; you are only so to appreciate the right and the wrong of the lesson that you may be led to imitate the one, and to avoid the other—that thus both you and the teacher whose lesson you are to consider, may learn to profit by our joint criticism. Can you tell me what ought mainly to guide a teacher in such a lesson as this—what main objects, or points, she should keep before her in a lesson on natural history?

T. The adaptation of the parts of an animal to its habits.

H. M. Be a little more general: what should be her main design?

T. To communicate information.

H. M. Would you make it the main object of such a lesson to communicate information?

Another T. Certainly not.

H. M. What, then, would be your object—what effect would you propose to produce on the children?

T. I would call forth their observation—I would require them to notice all the parts of the animal, and to examine them very minutely.

H. M. Now, suppose that repeated from day to day, what do you think would be cultivated?

T. Habits of observation.

H. M. And with young children, this is one main purpose of these lessons. The communication of information is a secondary one. Our first object is to discipline their minds, and *prepare* them to acquire knowledge. When you merely communicate information, the mind of the child is in a passive state, which is the very opposite of that in which it ought to be. No doubt, the love and the pursuit of truth are among the ultimate objects of education: but during the training of your children, you are only preparing them for these objects. As the children looked at and saw the nice and curious claw of the bat, the strangely formed wing without any feathers, the body like that of a mouse, the feet not made for walking, and were told of the fine sense of feeling given to it, did it occur to you that they did more than obtain information?

T. Curiosity was excited; and the tendency of this curiosity is to create an interest in all the objects by which they are surrounded.

H. M. Then, as it regards information, do you see anything

2*

in connection with the lesson that would, if it did not give them information, tend to the same result?

T. The children would be led to get it themselves, their curiosity having been excited.

H. M. Yes; we should not value a lesson so much for the information it gives, as for its tendency to cultivate in our children power and inclination to acquire information for themselves. We should endeavor to open to them the extensive volume of nature, and so to improve their faculties, that they may themselves investigate it.

T. You cannot call upon a child to observe anything, without, in some way, giving him information.

H. M. True. But do you not see the difference between giving information, and making him observe and examine a thing for himself?

T. Not clearly.

H. M. In the one you direct the child's own efforts—you cultivate a power in the child which must always be useful; in the other you merely pour in information, which may or may not be remembered. But it is not on the mind only that we produce effects. Do you know what is our further design in a lesson in natural history?

T. To teach the heart; to administer, it may be moral, and even spiritual good, to the children.

H. M. How is this done?

T. By showing them the goodness of God in his works: this leads them to cultivate humane feelings, and to be kind to animals.

H. M. Yes. And though the teacher said nothing about humane feelings, yet when the children were led to see how wise and gracious God has been in adapting the parts of the animal to its uses, they must have felt interested in the animal, and be less disposed to treat it unkindly, and have been taught also to admire the wisdom and power of God. I will now read the sketch of the lesson.—The Head Master having read the sketch, continued:—Now you are in possession of the general object contemplated in such a lesson as this; and you have also the teacher's written sketch, stating her special object and the manner of working it out; you are, therefore, prepared to determine how far the teacher accomplished her purpose.

The Head Master then directed the teachers to turn to page 50 of "Useful Hints to Teachers,"* and to make use of the points that are there given, confining their attention to one of the three general divisions.

First Teacher. I think the sketch is clearly arranged. The matter was well selected, and not too much for such children. There also appeared to me some attention paid to each part of the lesson, the animal itself being the chief thing in such a lesson. There was, however, a want of clearness—each point was not, as it were, *settled* as the teacher went on. I think a summary was not necessary; there was repetition, which supplied the place of a summary. The children were led to see the wisdom and goodness of God in so admirably adapting the structure of the animal to its habits.

Second Teacher. I think the teacher seemed to have command over the children. Order and attention were preserved, in part by the power of the teacher, but especially by the interest of the lesson. I do not, however, think that the interest in general was altogether so well kept up as it might have been, though many of the children seemed attentive. They saw very clearly how God had provided the animal with means adapted to the catching of its food, and with an instinct which enables it, when there is no food, to dispense with it altogether.

Third Teacher. I think the teacher's manner was kind. She did not, however, speak with sufficient firmness to the children. I thought her tone of voice was very good. She paid great attention to the pronunciation of the children, and corrected them in grammar. I thought the children might have been made to repeat with advantage some parts which they did not.

H. M. Do you suggest repetition as a means of keeping up the general attention?

T. Yes; and also of fixing the ideas gained on their minds. The questions were in general good; but she did not always work out what the first question of a series seemed to aim at.

* One of the London Society's publications.

H. M. When do you consider a question good?

T. When the children, by means of it, are led to think.

H. M. That is certainly one good feature of a question—indeed, an essential one; but your answer is general.

T. It should be a question which leads them to observe, compare, or draw a right conclusion, as the case may be. There was one point in the questioning which struck me as bad; she asked, how the bat caught its prey, and then did not wait for an answer, but went on.

H. M. Yes; this arises sometimes from want of patience, sometimes from not holding the idea to be developed with tenacity; it often defeats all the ends of questioning, and causes confusion in the gallery. A question may be good or bad, as it is, or is not, followed by another. Would you consider the question, "Do you know how the bat obtains its prey?" a good one?

T. Such a question would only bring out Yes or No.

H. M. It is therefore bad. Such a question is of no use, except to ascertain what extent of knowledge the children have; and it leads to a habit of guessing.

T. I did not observe that any of the incidental circumstances of the lesson were noticed.

H. M. What do you mean by incidental circumstances?

T. The state of the children.

H. M. Do you call their mere state, as being quiet or noisy, attentive or inattentive, an incidental circumstance? (*A pause.*) What does any one understand by an incidental circumstance?

A Teacher. Anything happening in the course of the lesson that the teacher did not expect, and that did not properly belong to it. Such incidents may often be used to give interest to a lesson.

Third Teacher (*in continuation*). I think she was right in correcting the children in grammar. The words she made use of were sufficiently plain and simple. But she did not make them hold out their hands before speaking, as much as they ought to have done.

H. M. What is the use of making children hold out their hands?

T. To prevent disorder. But she allowed them to speak without waiting till she had pointed to them.

H. M. The main use of this practice is, to ascertain what children are really at work, and to prevent the forward from answering all the questions; to secure, in short, attention and thought from as many children as practicable.

Fifth Teacher. The sketch of the lesson was not worked out in that part that spoke of the wings. I do not think the children understood how the sense of touch in the wings of the bat helped the animal to obtain its food. She appeared to confound the sense of touch with the fact of the closing of the wings; I thought she seemed rather confused about it herself. Might she not have said a little more about the eye of the bat?

H. M. Will the next teacher make her observations without referring specially to the points already noticed, but keeping in view the general objects to which I called attention before we began to make our remarks?

Sixth Teacher. I think that what the teacher proposed to do in the first stage of the lesson was well calculated to cultivate observation, and to excite the interest and curiosity of the children. She might, perhaps, have better prepared them to admire God's wisdom and goodness, by first showing them that the generality of animals with wings are birds, but that the present one was a singular case. She might have led them to see that although the animal had wings, yet that it had not another essential part of the bird, viz., a beak; that while it had wings, it had a mouth with teeth, which birds have not. And then she might have led them to see that it was most like a mammal; for although it had wings, which were the only things that it had in common with birds, yet that those wings had no feathers, and that although it appeared to be a bird, yet that in reality it had not the same parts as the bird. Then she could have shown them how adapted its parts were for procuring its food, inasmuch as it lived on insects in the air; and being a mammal, and its food being in the air, if it had no wings it could not have procured its food, and would, therefore, have starved. I have no doubt it might have brought the children to a stand, to determine whether it was a bird or a mammal; if she had shown them it had wings, they would have immediately said it was a bird; but when she drew their attention to the mouth, teeth, and body, they would have seen that it was not a bird, but that it had the appearance of a mouse; this, however, might have led to a profitable warning against hasty judgments; it might have enabled her also to lead them to see more clearly the goodness of God in supplying this creature with wings. I think the teacher was extremely kind, and able to give the children information.

Seventh Teacher. The main points of the lesson, good and bad, have been already touched upon. I thought the first part of the lesson was, upon the whole, very well given, with the exception of that spoken of by the last teacher with regard to the difference between the mammal and the bird. In the habits of the bat, and the adaptation of its parts to these habits, there was a little confusion; but there was one good proof that the children sympathized with the teacher; that is, the interest increased as she went on, and when the lesson was finished, the interest seemed to be greater than at any other period. She might sometimes have exercised their minds a little more when they gave her an opportunity, as in correcting wrong answers, and making the younger ones answer more frequently. Also, about the old walls, I think she might have got that out of the children without telling them. With respect to the bat getting its food, she told them something which I think she might have drawn from them without telling them. I think the sketch is very well written, and very clear, and, had she adhered to it, she would have given, in my judgment, an excellent lesson.

H. M. In the remarks of the teachers generally, I quite concur. On the latter part of the lesson particularly, they are very good. The first part of the lesson (that which required the children to observe) was worked out the best. Are we to suppose that the teacher had then most time on her hands, or that she excels more in cultivating the observing faculties of her children than the reflective? This is a feature I often remark among the teachers in training.

The teacher started well with the second head, the animal's

habits; but she did not keep the children so close to them as she might have done.

When any idea has been worked out, the children should always be made to *express* it clearly. The teacher several times failed in this; as when she led the children to observe the wings and the hooks. It was rather by a kind of false reasoning, or taking something for granted, than by observation, that the animal was discovered to have a mouth instead of a beak.

In the third part of the lesson, although she failed a little in holding firmly her own ideas, and in leading the children to see clearly the adaptation of the organs, yet it was fairly done. It is much to her credit, that, whilst she lost herself several times during the lesson, she rallied; a circumstance which always proves to me that the teacher has made progress in her training. She had her point before her, but stumbled in attaining it.

You gave the sketch credit for being full and clear; but did it not evince thought and ingenuity in its arrangement? There was a nice choice of parts and habits, which told well in leading the children to perceive adaptation. I hardly agree with one of you about omitting the summing up. Although there was a great deal of repetition, I do not think that repetition ought to have supplied the place of a summary; it does not answer the same purpose. Neither do I think that in such a lesson a summary is unnecessary. Whenever you want to make an impression on the hearts of the children, you should endeavor to bring before them, in a connected form, those features or ideas of the lesson by which you expect to produce such an effect.

The fourth head was to lead the children to see and feel the wisdom, power, and goodness of God. Now, to accomplish this, a summary of the points of adaptation ought to have been made and repeated by the children; such as, The body is that of an animal, but its food is in the air; therefore, to procure this food, God has given it wings. It comes out in the dusk, when its prey is abroad, and it catches it while flying; therefore God has provided it with a sense of touch so exquisite, as to be equal to sight, and also with a large mouth. These points and others, brought into one or two sentences, should have been repeated before making the application. It has often been remarked to you, that whilst the true catechetical method of teaching is admirable, yet one effect of giving lessons by questions is, that of separating it into parts or fragments, and consequently the children cannot see the matter of the lesson as a whole, or the harmony and dependence of its parts. The summary ought amply to make up for this, and after a minute and accurate examination of the parts, to present the subject as a whole.

There was a little of the same want of power in the application that I remarked under the third head; but it must be admitted that this is the most difficult part of a lesson. It requires sound judgment, very considerable clearness, and no small degree of practice. A teacher may consider herself well advanced in training when she is able to do it clearly. I like the remarks of one of the teachers on the order and attention of the children. I do not know that she required to show very much power of command, because the children were particularly steady and willing to work. The interest of several was very satisfactory, but it was not general.

Such questions as, "What time do the insects come out?" "Can the bat see the insects?" are bad, because they lead the children to guess; they imply knowledge which the children have not. With the exceptions stated, the great principle of not telling young children what they can discover by the exercise of their own faculties, was carried out; also the important one of keeping the children intellectually active during the lesson. Finally, a religious turn was given to the lesson, without any apparently forced feeling on the part of either the teacher or children.

V.—Reports of Model Lessons.

Simultaneously with the Criticism Lessons, it is of equal importance that the class should see a sufficient number of Model Lessons, *i. e.*, lessons given by teachers thoroughly trained, with the view of exemplifying the treatment of a given subject. The class should learn to draw up reports (abstracts) of these lessons while hearing them, or directly afterward, taking special notice of—

REPORTS OF MODEL LESSONS.

1. The ideas the teacher draws from the children.
2. The plan she adopts in order to draw out these ideas.

EXAMPLE.—*Report of Model Lesson on the Seal.*

MATTER.	METHOD.
I.—*Habits, etc.*	I.—1. Drawn from the children, who were led to form the sentence, which was written on the board.
1. The seal lives in water and on land. It is found in cold countries.	
2. The seal feeds on water fowl and fish.	2. Drawn from the children by asking them what food the seal would be likely to find in or near the water, and such framed into a sentence, and W. B.
3. The seal is loving and intelligent.	3. Drawn from the children by questioning on an anecdote told them. Terms *loving* and *intelligent* given. (S. R.) Sentence framed. (W. B.)
4. The hearing of the seal is acute.	4. Drawn as an inference from anecdote told. Little girl gave term *acute*. (W. B.)
II.—*Adaptation of structure to habits.*	II.—
1. The body of the seal should be light, slender, tapering, and flexible.	1. Drawn from the children by reference to the animal's food, fish; how these move rapidly, suddenly; how the seal must move rapidly also to catch them. What kind of body he must have to enable him to move and turn quickly. Teacher required the children to represent on the board such a shaped body as seal ought to have.
2. The limbs of the seal should be short and broad.	2. The necessity for breadth drawn out by reference to different things made to go in the water, as oars of a boat, fins of a fish, &c. Why the seal cannot have fins, drawn out by reference to his double habitation (land and water). Advantage of shortness drawn out by asking why the limbs of a dog would not suit the seal—they would be too narrow as well as too long.

3. The tail of the seal should be broad and flexible.	3. Brought out by reference to a rudder.
4. The seal should have sharp, strong teeth.	4. Brought out by reference to the character of its food.
5. The seal should have lungs.	5. Brought out by reference to its coming to land, and its swimming with its head above the surface.
6. The seal should have a warm covering.	6. Brought out by exercising the reason in discovering what kind of covering an animal thus situated needs. Children at first said scales. Teacher told them these would not be warm enough, but desired them to judge how it was that scales would suit the fish and not the seal. Others supposed that because the seal sometimes came out of the water; others, because the fish lived in warm countries. By referring to the sensation of feeling or touching a fish, led them to see that the fish had cold blood. Teacher told them that the seal had warm blood, and therefore needed warm covering.
7. The seal has short, thick, smooth fur.	By reference to the covering of a dog, sheep, and the effect of water, etc., on this, children decided what sort of covering an animal needs which is always swimming, or climbing rocks.
	Each point, as drawn from the children, framed into a sentence, and put on the board.
	Summary read from the board.

VI.—Miscellaneous Exercises in Method.

FIRST EXAMPLE.—*Exercise on the Fable, "The Lark and her Young Ones."*

(See "*Moral Instruction*," *last lesson of Second Step.*)

Directions for Students.

I.—State the Point.
II.—Find the Introduction.

MISCELLANEOUS EXERCISES IN METHOD. 43

III.—Find the Points on which the Conceptive Faculties should be exercised.

IV.—Find the Points on which the Reasoning Faculties should be exercised.

V.—Where the application should be made.

Students' Answers.

I. *Point.*—To teach the advantage of self-reliance.

II. *Introduction.*—To see that the children have an idea of a lark—kind of bird as to size, color, mode of life—before telling the story.

III. *Points on which the Conceptive Faculties are exercised.*—The corn field—appearance of the ripe corn—the hidden nest, with mother bird and young ones—the anxiety of the farmer—conversation in the field—should be, as it were, dramatically rendered.

IV. *Points on which to exercise the Reasoning Faculties.*—Why the lark builds her low nest amongst the corn. What danger she avoids. What danger she incurs. What the young birds would infer from the first and second conversations. What the old bird. What the young birds would infer from the third conversation. What the old bird. What she would do.

V. *Application.*—To be made after the narration of each conversation.

SECOND EXAMPLE.—*Exercise on Sketch on the Tortoise.*

(See " *Course on Animals,*" " *Miscellaneous Sketches.*")

Students examine sketch, and state:

    I.—What is told, and why.
    II.—What must be developed.
    III.—Where the Observation is exercised.
    IV.—Where the Reasoning Faculty.
    V.—Where the Conceptive Faculty.

Students' work should stand substantially as follows:—

I.—1. What is told.—The tortoise lives either on land or in water. It moves slowly on the ground, but swims beautifully.

It comes on land to deposit its eggs, of which it lays a great number—scrapes a hole in the ground, and leaves them to be hatched by the heat of the sun.

1. Why.—Because the children have no opportunity of observing.

2. What is told.—The eggs of birds become hard, those of reptiles soft, by boiling.

2. Why.—Because it would be inconvenient to try the experiment.

3. The tortoise is covered by a thick, hard, strong shell; the tail has a scaly covering of its own.

3. Because a picture is used instead of a specimen. If a specimen shell can be procured, this would not be told.

II.—What must be developed.—All that can be discovered by the observation or the reasoning faculty.

III.—Where the Observation is exercised.—The tortoise has a small head like that of a serpent, four legs, and a tail. The shell that covers the back has thirteen large pieces in the middle, and twenty-three smaller pieces round the margin. The head and legs are without armor.

IV.—Where the Reasoning Faculty is exercised.

1. Eggs of reptiles become soft by boiling. The eggs of the tortoise become soft by boiling, therefore we infer that the tortoise is a reptile.

2. Provision is made for the safety of the young of all classes of animals. The tortoise is one of a class of animals, therefore provision is made for the safety of its young (while in the egg).

3. Animals that can fight possess weapons of attack. The tortoise has no weapons of attack, therefore the tortoise cannot fight.

4. All creatures with thick horny coverings are reptiles. The crocodile has a thick horny covering, therefore the crocodile is a reptile.

V.—Where the Conceptive Faculty is exercised.—The tortoise on a bright summer day. The tortoise scraping away the sand to lay its eggs.

COLOR.

In the First Step the teacher exercises the Perceptive Faculties in distinguishing the nine Colors, also Black and White. The Memory is exercised in learning the names attached to these. Order and Taste in arranging them.

In the Second Step the Conceptive Faculty is exercised, also a more minute Perception.

The first of these, in recalling the ideas of Colors previously seen. The second, in distinguishing the Tints and Shades of the nine Colors. Names learned as before.

In the Third Step, the Reasoning Faculties are exercised on the relation of Colors and the production of Hues. As a matter of course, the subject being Color, the Perceptive Faculty is exercised still. It now distinguishes the Hues, which are named as before.

In the Fourth Step, Imagination is exercised, with the Powers of Analogy and Generalization.

FIRST STEP.

Distinguishing Prominent Colors.

1. *Lesson given to the Class. Distinguishing Blue and Yellow.*

I.—1. Point to the yellow pattern on the board. Let a child pick up a card like it; compare the yellow, placing the card beside the pattern. Let all the children present decide whether a correct choice has been made.

2. Select a yellow card; call on a child to find the corresponding color amongst all those exhibited on the board. The other children judge and decide as before.

3 and 4. Proceed with blue as with yellow.

II.—1. *Exercises.*—Select two yellow and two blue wafers; arrange them thus: B. Y. B. Let a child place other blue and yellow wafers in corresponding positions.
    Y.

2. Place the wafers Y. B. / B. Y. A child to imitate as before.

3. Thread five large beads thus—B. Y..B. Y. B. A child to imitate.

(As many children as possible are employed in this, and all the rest as judges whether the actions are correctly performed.)

The members of the class draw out sketches of lessons on Red and Green or on Orange and Purple. inventing different exercises for each sketch.

2. *Lesson on naming principal Colors.*

1. Show a red card. Let a child select one that is similar; say: "This is red." This is to be repeated by the children simultaneously while looking at the card. Let another child select all the red cards that are to be found.

2 and 3. Proceed in the same way with yellow and with blue.

4. Point rapidly to the blue, red, and yellow patterns, requesting the children to give their names as pointed to.

5. Bid a child place a yellow card on the table, a red one on the desk, and a *blue* one on the chair.

6. Select 3 children; one to find examples of blue, one of red, one of yellow; red on the furniture of the room, or the dress of any one present.

7. Let a child place the colors on a line, according to direction, as blue, yellow, red, yellow, blue.

The members of the class draw out sketches according to the pattern, on:

COLOR. 47

Distinguishing and naming Orange, Green, and Purple.
" " Citrine, Russet, and Olive.

3. *Lesson on Arrangement of Yellow, Red, and Blue.*

1. Let the children select all the yellow, blue, and red cards.

2. Form them into patterns thus:

```
      Y.             Y.
R. B. R.   or    B. R.        &c.    &c.
      Y.         R. B.
                    Y.
```

3. Let the children imitate these patterns; when they can do so readily, encourage them to invent new ones, selecting the colors in order to cultivate the eye to harmonious combinations.

Till the subject of Color is better understood, the general teacher will be found to require special preparation on this point. The class should be exercised in combining colors according to the laws of harmony; as—

1. Harmony of Primaries with Secondaries.

Yellow. | Red, Green. |
Purple, Purple. | Green, Red. | Orange, Blue, Blue, Orange.
Yellow. | |

2. Harmonies of Secondaries with each other.

	Orange.
Orange.	Green, Purple.
Purple, Green, Purple.	Purple, Green.
Orange.	Orange.

```
                    Purple.
        Orange.    Green.    Orange.
Purple. Green.    Orange.   Green.   Purple.
        Orange.    Green.    Orange.
                    Purple.
```

3. Harmony of Secondaries with Tertiaries.

| Citrine, Russet. | | Citrine, Olive. |
| Russet, Citrine. | Olive, Orange, Olive. | Olive, Citrine. |

4. Harmony of Tertiaries with Primaries.

Citrine, Red.	Yellow, Russet.	Yellow, Red, Olive.
Citrine, Blue.	Russet, Blue.	Yellow, Red, Olive.
Citrine, Red.	Yellow, Russet.	Yellow, Red, Olive.

48   COLOR.

These will suffice for examples: Class continue to form patterns with—
  5. Citrine, Russet, and Olive.
  6. Black, Red, and Olive.
  7. Black, Orange, and Green.
  8. Black, Red, Yellow, Orange, and Green.
  9. Gray, Red.
  10. Gray, Green.
  11. Gray, Red, and Green.
  12. White with Blue.
  13. White with Purple.

4. *Lesson given to develop the Perception of the most obvious Harmonies of Color.*

1. Let the children who have been accustomed to combine colors, select those they wish to place side by side. After their previous practice in arrangement, the children as a class will make good combinations. Should an individual child choose, say a green and blue, take a similar blue, and put it beside an orange. Let all decide whether blue and green or blue and orange look better together.

Even when good combinations are made, as purple and green, it is sometimes well to resort to the plan of putting a red with the purple, that all may see how much better the green looks.

2. Colors which look well together, to be placed in order before the children, who commit to memory the results of their observations and comparisons, as facts, and without reference to rules.

Colors arranged thus—
            Yellow and Purple.
            Red and Green.
            Blue and Orange.
            Orange and Purple.
            Green and Purple.
            Purple and Green.

Members of the class draw up sketches on the Harmonies of Black with Red, &c.

The Harmonies of White and Gray, &c., &c.

SECOND STEP.

I. Remembering Principal Colors.

1. *Lesson on the Color Blue.*

1. To make sure that the children have a clear idea of the color, let the youngest child select all the pieces of card that are blue, while the rest are employed in finding any objects of a blue color in the room.

2. Lead the children to compare these blues with their recollections of the color in objects not just now visible. What they see overhead is blue. Whether the sky is always blue. What other colors they have seen it show. When it is bluest. At what season of the year, &c., &c.

3. Let the children name flowers that are blue, as harebells, speedwell, forget-me-not. Where these flourish; whether in meadows and gardens, or on heaths or roadsides.

4. Let children name fruits that are blue; as the blueberry and plum. Whether these are blue, as the pattern is blue. They are rather blue. "Things rather blue are said to be bluish." (S. R.)

5. Let children name animals that have any part blue.

(a) *Birds :* Peacock, kingfisher, duck, swallow, jay.

(b) *Insects :* Some beetles, dragon fly, house fly. These, why called bluebottles; children to say what parts are blue.

6. Any other natural objects that are blue or bluish, as steel, phosphorus.

Summary.—Children name from memory: Things that have life and are blue. Things (natural) not having life that are blue.

2. *Lesson on the Color Yellow.*

1. Introduce this lesson as that on blue.

2. Lead children to name any natural objects of a yellow color. Write all the names on the board, and help children to classify.

(a) What birds with any part yellow? Canaries, yellowhammer; also the crest of the cockatoo is yellow.

(*b*) What insects are in part yellow? Some butterflies, caterpillars, wasps.
(*c*) What flowers contain yellow? Buttercups, daisies, sunflowers, &c. What part of each is yellow? When leaves are yellow.
(*d*) What fruits? Lemons, some gooseberries, green gages, apricots, apples. Whether these are yellow as the card is yellow. They are yellowish.
(*e*) Other natural objects; as, sulphur, gold, brass, sand, straw, ochre, butter, yelk of eggs, sometimes the sky; when?

3. *Summary.*—Children say what animal, vegetable, and mineral substances are wholly or in part yellow.

Members of the class draw out sketches on—

   Red. Orange and Purple.
   Green. Citrine, Russet, and Olive.

The following lesson presented to the class for analysis:

The class find where observation is exercised; where memory, conception, and imagination; where judgment.

3. *General Lesson on Color.*

1. Bring before the children a variety of pebbles, black, white, and colored. Let them select those they like best. Question on the principle of selection, and lead them to discover that they find pleasure in looking at colored things.

2. Let them say what color they can see by looking upward; sky, blue; clouds, white, black, or gray; sun, moon, and stars, yellow. The rainbow, red, orange, yellow, green, blue, purple.

What colors they can see in the fields; grass which is green. Trees with green, red, or yellow leaves, and brown stems. Flowers, which? Let each name a flower of a different color, to show that these are of all colors. What they see when they stand on the shore. Yellow sand; white, green, or black rocks; greenish sea.

What living things show the brightest colors? Tiger, leopard, redbreast, bullfinch, peacock, macaw, kingfisher, butterflies, ladybirds, &c. What parts of themselves are colored? Hair, eyes, cheeks, lips. We see colors wherever we look—the earth is full of them.

3. Lead the children to imagine the trees, flowers, and objects in general, all of one hue, as white, drab, gray. Let them trace the effect of such a state of things on their minds. It would make people feel dull. Bright colors make us feel cheerful. (S. R.) Suppose a gray rosebush, trained against the wall of a gray house, springing from a gray soil, under a gray sky, all the surrounding objects being gray. Were they sent to gather it, how near must they come before they would see it? "Color helps us to distinguish objects." (S. R.)

Draw a similar picture, representing every object as red; how painfully exciting! as blue; how cold and forbidding! Refer to the effect of green; soothing, cheerful, refreshing. Whether it would be better if everything out of doors were green, and why not.

Who has furnished this earth with such a variety of colors? Who has formed us to enjoy them? What we learn of God.

This lesson requires no summary. Itself is a summary of the previous lessons.

II. Distinguishing and Naming Tints and Shades.

Minute and accurate perception and power of comparison are cultivated. Vocabulary extended.

1. *Lesson on Tints and Shades of Blue.*

1. Let the children decide on the Color that shall be the subject of this lesson. Suppose them to say blue. Produce varieties of this. Let them recognize each as blue. Let a child select the bluest of the blues, that which comes nearest to the color of the sky in summer. If practicable this selection should be made out of doors, or at the window. When azure is found, compare other blue or bluish objects with it. Children will find nothing bluer than azure. Tell them that because in judging of the blue-

ness of objects we go by this, it is called standard blue. "The bluest blue is called standard blue." (S. R.)

2. Direct attention to the remaining varieties. Children to decide which of these look more like the night, which more like the day. Get the terms *light* and *dark*. Give the terms *tint* and *shade*. (S. R.) "The lighter blues are called tints, and the darker blues are called shades."

3. *Exercises*.

    (*a*) Let the children place the blues in order, from tint to shade and from shade to tint.

    (*b*) Let a child find the darkest shade and the lightest tint.

    (*c*) Let a child find the tint and shade nearest to the standard.

4. Show how convenient it would be if, instead of calling for the darkest shade, or the tint nearest to the standard, we had names for the varieties. Who would like to learn their names? Who can mention something out of doors the color of the standard (the sky)? The name of the standard blue is sky blue, or azure. (S. R.) (W. B.) The name of the lightest tint is hyaline, or water Blue, the color of running water. The name of the tint next to azure is watchet, from an old name which meant weak blue.

The name of the shade next to azure is lazuline, from lazuli, the mineral producing that color.

The name of the darkest blue is indigene, from indigo. (S. R. after each name which is written on the board as given.)

5. The children having learned the names, touch the cards when named, and name them when touched, irregularly, and in order:

Hyaline, Watchet, Azure, Lazuline, Indigene.

2. *Lesson on Tints and Shades of Red.*

1. Let the youngest child select the reddest of the reds, or the standard red. If there be any hesitation, compare with a piece of red coral. The red like this to be the standard. Let another child point out the tints, a third the shades, a fourth arrange them in order.

2. Refer to the object with which the standard was compared, or now make the comparison. The standard, being like coral, is called coraline. Let the children, if they can, name any object like the shade next to coraline. It is like blood. It is sometimes called blood red, sometimes venetian red. We will call it venetia. Let children find an object like the darkest shade; some roses, called black roses, are of this color. It is called morone, which means black red. Children find the tint nearest the standard. They will say it is pink. It is a full pink, the color of a rose. We will call it rosine. There is one tint more. There is something about themselves of the same color. It is flesh color. We will call it carneline.

3. Children name the shades, tints, standard, as called on. Give the meanings, &c., of the names. Say which color they like best; which they would prefer for a dress in winter; which for a dress in summer, &c. Name the colors in order:

Carneline, Rosine, Coraline, Venetia, Morone.

Class draw up sketches on—
Tints and shades of Yellow.
" " Green.
" " Purple and Orange.
" " Citrine, Russet, and Olive.

THIRD STEP.

Distinguishing Colors as Primary, Secondary, and Tertiary. Also Hues of Color.

1. *Lesson on Production of Secondary Colors.*

1. Produce the colors yellow, red, and blue. Desire the children to name other colors, as purple and orange. Show orange, and let children say whether it most resembles yellow, red, or blue. (Yellow.) Show purple. Children will decide whether this most resembles red or blue. Tell the children that all colors bear some resemblance to yellow or red or blue; because all other colors are derived from these. These are the first or primary colors. (S. R.) "Yellow, red, and blue are the primary colors."

2. Mix yellow ochre and indigo blue. Let the children note the operation and the result. (S. R.) "Green is a mixture of yellow and blue." Proceed in the same way with yellow and red (carmine), producing orange; and with blue and red, producing purple. By reference to the term primary, draw from the children the name that will characterize this second set of colors, viz., secondary. (S. R.) "Orange, green, and purple are secondary colors."

3. Write on the board the names of the secondary colors, as dictated by the children.

Yellow + Blue = Green.
Yellow + Red = Orange.
Blue   + Red = Purple.

S. R., till committed to memory.

Class draw up sketch on the Production of Tertiary Colors from Secondary."

2. *Lesson on Hues of Color.*

1. Take yellow and blue pigments. Before mixing, call attention to the proportions of yellow and blue—about half as much yellow as blue. Tell children that were these substances perfectly free from earthy particles, we should take exactly 3 parts of yellow to 8 of blue.

S. R. "Yellow is to blue as 3 is to 8."

2. Let children say how this proportion might be varied: we would take more yellow and less blue. Let them judge of the effect this would have in the product. The green produced would be yellowish green. Perform the experiment, conforming to or correcting their judgments.

Tell them that this green is called, not a tint, nor a shade, but a hue of green.

How else the proportions might be altered: we might take more blue and less yellow than at first. The effect, this would have on the product, inferred, and the experiment tried as before. We have now bluish green, another hue.

Take yellow and red, directing attention to the proportions, which are as 3 to 5. Additional red will produce red orange, and additional yellow pale orange. Children should first see if they can infer the results, and then find them by experiment.

Take red and blue, proportions 5 to 8. Proceed as before.

3. Children led to explain how the "Hues of Secondary Colors are formed by an extra proportion of one of the Primaries, which compose the Secondary." (S. R.)

3. *Lesson on Hues of Red.*

1. Produce varieties of red. Let children select and name those that they know. Standard, tints, and shades.

2. Let them proceed to classify the hues of red, putting them into two groups. They will at once separate the yellowish reds from the bluish reds. Let them try to account for the difference in hue. Should they fail in doing this, produce an orange card. Let them point out the set of reds which come nearest to it, and account for the resemblance. These reds have yellow in them. Children to judge of the color which tinges the remaining set of reds. These reds have blue in them. "Some hues of red are tinged with yellow, and some with blue." (S. R.)

3. Children arrange the yellow reds in order, and learn their names. The deepest scarlet; the next vermilion; something the third is like: the flesh of salmon. It is called salmon color, or salmonine.

Children arrange the blues. The darkest and bluest of the reds is called crimson. The next magenta, from a battle which was fought about the time this particular hue came into fashion. The last peachine. Why? It is the color of a peach blossom.

4. Children find examples of any of the hues; are exercised on the names. They define tint, shade, and hue, thus:

     A tint of Red is Red lighter than the standard.
     A shade   "   "   darker than the standard.
     A hue   "   "   tinctured with some other color.

At the close of the lesson, the colors are thus arranged:

        Salmonine. Vermilion. Scarlet.
  Carneline. Rosine. Coraline. Venetia. Morone.
        Peachine. Magenta. Crimson.

Class draw up lesson on hues of yellow; hues of blue.

Also on hues of green and purple.

Leading the children to see, as a general rule, that a hue of a primary color is produced by a tincture of some other color.

4. *Lesson given on Hues of Black.*

1. Bring before the children several black objects: a piece of jet, a raven's wing, some rooks' feathers, a piece of black silk which has been worn, and some writing fluid.

Let them select the standard black in the piece of jet. Give the term jettine.

Let them examine the other objects, and pronounce what hues of black they exemplify. The wing is bluish black; the rooks' feathers are purplish black; the silk is rusty or brownish black; the writing fluid is greenish black.

Write on the board—

   Jettine or standard Black.
   Hue of greenish Black.
   "   purplish Black.
   "   bluish Black.
   "   brownish Black.

2. Children mention black objects, and define their hue.

Note the difference between jet black hair and raven hair.

Summary.—From the board.

Class draw out sketches on hues of white and gray.

5. *Lesson on White and Black, as representing Light and Darkness.*

1. Ask the children to tell the color of light. "It has no color; light is colorless." (S. R.) What color will best represent it? (S. R.) "White is the representative of light."

2. Present a prism, and direct attention to the yellow, red, and blue rays. Explain, in the simplest language, that this instrument is able to divide the compound colorless rays, and show the primary colored rays that compose them. Children to say what

colored rays each colorless ray must contain. (S. R.) " Light is produced by the blending of red, yellow, and blue rays."

3. Children to judge of the probable result of mixing red, yellow, and blue pigments; to say in what proportion they should be mixed.

Perform the experiment, and let them state the result. Get or give the reason. (S. R.) " The mixture of red, yellow, and blue pigments will not produce white, on account of the opaque and earthy substances all pigments contain."

4. Children to say what is caused by the absence of light —darkness. How they would represent it. (S. R.) " Black represents darkness."

5. Lead the children to see that " as light (or white) is the blending of all colors, so darkness (or black) is the presence of no color." (S. R.)

Summary.—Repetitions of S. R.'s.

Class draw up sketch of lesson on the Rainbow, under the following heads:

I.—Appearance, form, colors; their arrangement. Why the secondary colors alternate with the primary.

II.—Formation of the rainbow.

III.—The rainbow as the sign of a covenant.

FOURTH STEP.

1. *Consideration of Colors as Emblematic.*

The children are exercised in drawing analogies.

I.—Speak of spring. By reference to the cold winter season past, and to the bright long days, the summer flowers, and the harvest we expect, lead the children to look on spring as the time of promise. Refer to the young grass—the budding leaves; contrast the delicate green of these with the sere brown of winter. How we hope to see the trees, the fields look. Tell the children, that because light green is the spring color, people have taken it for an emblem of Hope.

II.—Refer to the sky—its appearance at different times; sometimes cloudy. What the children would see were the clouds dispersed. Always beyond these is the bright, changeless blue. Refer to the pain and sorrow which we all must endure, and to that better place where tears shall be wiped away. When we think of Heaven, at what object do we like to look? Because blue puts us in mind of Heaven, it is taken as an emblem of Faith.

Write on the slate the different colors. Children to give their ideas of the attributes these colors will best represent. Supply deficiencies and correct errors, till the writing on the slate appears thus:

        Green—Hope.
        Blue—Faith.
        White—Innocence and candor.
        Black—Sorrow or mourning.
        Yellow—Desolation, despair.
        Red—Military glory, anger.
        Purple, or } Royal state.
        Crimson

Children to find reasons why the color should be taken as the emblem of the attribute. For white, refer to the snow. How beautiful—how easily soiled, yet how plainly showing the least stain!

For black, when people wear it. Why they prefer black to colors. Of what it puts us in mind.

For yellow, when the landscape looks yellow; with what feelings we view it. Why? So proceed with the other colors.

Children must be told that purple is taken as an emblem of dignity, from its association with the dress of kings. At first it was worn by the Greek magnates only, on account of the rarity of the mollusk that produced the dye. Then it became an emblem of State.

It might also be explained, that in China the royal and noble color is yellow; and why? viz., the sun appears of a yellow color, and the court of Pekin is supposed to be modelled on the plan of the court of Heaven.

III.—*Summary.*—Teacher names the colors; children say what they emblematize. The same thing reversed.

2. *Lesson on White as an Emblem.*

I.—Children to mention objects of the purest whiteness; as snow, a lily, ivory, white marble, swan's down.

Exercise the conceptive faculty. How dazzling the new-fallen snow; how different to the same snow when the thaw commences, and it shows black footsteps! How fair and regal the fresh white lily; how different it looks when it displays faded and yellowish petals! Refer in the same way to the plumage of the swan when wild; to ivory and marble when stained. In which condition are these objects most pleasing to the eye? Thus develop the idea of the beauty of these objects, as consisting in their hue.

II.—Tell the children that there are some things more beautiful than any snow, lilies, or ivory. That these are not outward, but inward things.

Draw the picture of a child always gentle in his manners to the young, and respectful to his elders; kind in his actions, always ready to help and oblige; honest in his dealings with his playfellows, faithful in his duties at school and at home. How lovely a character! To what natural object or quality can we compare this? White. What if the child in question one day commit a manifest fault; what if he be found in a lie, or even in a violent passion? If we compare the former character to whiteness, to what may we compare his fault? To a dark stain, sullying the pure whiteness. (W. B.) "White is the emblem of Innocence."

III.—Children to say at what times people usually like to wear white. At weddings, on holidays, Sundays. How people feel on holidays. How they ought to feel on Sundays. The Lord's day is a festival—not a common, but a sacred one. Refer to Eccles. ix.

8, explaining that in ancient times men as well as women often wore white garments.

Tell them that the ancient Greeks not only dressed for feasts in this way, but were in the habit of marking days of joy or triumph on their almanacs with a white stone, doubtless of the nature of chalk. (Rev. ii. 17.) Children to name the second thing that white is the emblem of—"Festivity." (W. B.)

IV.—Refer to flags of different nations; the use of flags; the colors seen in them. Red, white and blue in the stars and stripes, in the tricolor of France, and the Union jack. The Italians have chosen a tricolor of red, green, and white. Other of the European nations have yellow and black. The Turks hoist a green flag. The standard of each nation floats on its own territory, and in time of war on others' territory; but when, in such a case, armies want to communicate peacefully one with another, they lay the national flag aside, and take a white flag, called a flag of truce. Explain truce. A soldier carrying such a flag as this may go into the centre of the enemy's camp; the flag shows that he comes with a peaceful message; none will harm him. "White is the emblem of Peace." (W. B.)

V.—White emblematizes one thing more. The Bible tells us that the inhabitants of Heaven are clothed in white. It speaks of heavenly armies riding on white horses. (Rev. vii. 9; and xix. 8 and 14.) What kind of place is Heaven? What kind of people its inmates? When these are described as being clothed in white, of what is white the emblem? "Of Purity, or Holiness." (W. B.)

The Bible tell us of the high priest of the Jews, the type of Christ: once a year he went into the most holy place to make intercession for the people; and then he wore white garments only—he represented a holy advocate. The Bible tells of a great white throne, set for the judgment, where the dead, small and great, shall stand before God. The throne is a holy throne. Refer the children to Rev. iii. 4 and 5, as a subject of prayer for the evening. They will repeat what white emblematizes, and give examples in each case.

Summary.—From the board:

    White is the emblem of Innocence.
    White is the emblem of Festivity
    White is the emblem of Peace.
    White is the emblem of Purity and Holiness.

Class exercised in drawing out sketches—

1. On Black, as emblematic of Sorrow.
    "   "   Despair
    "   "   Guilt.
    "   "   Death.

2. On emblematic Mourning:
    The Chinese wear White. Why?
    " Turks wear Blue or Violet. Why?
    " English and Americans wear Black. Why?

3. On Railway Signals:
    White means Safety. Why?
    Green " Caution. Why?
    Red " Danger. Why?

4. On common Flowers as Symbols:
    Rose,
    Lily,
    Violet, } Showing how much their symbolical meaning depends on their color.
    Harebell,
    Forget-me-not.

5. On Color as indicating Flavor. According to Linnæus, red indicates an acid or sour taste. As examples—cranberries, barberries, currants, mulberries; herbs that turn red toward autumn, as sorrel and bloodydock.

Green indicates an alkaline taste. As examples—leaves and unripe fruit.

Yellow a bitter taste; as gentian, aloes, celandine.

White indicates a sweet taste; as white currants, white cherries, apples, sugar, &c.

Black indicates a nauseous, disagreeable taste; as deadly nightshade, sumac.

6. On Colors as Sacred Emblems:
In the tabernacle: In the garments of the high priest.

FORM.

INTRODUCTORY REMARKS.

THAT "the child sees in nature objects, not lines," is a truth which nobody will attempt to deny. On these objects are seen, on closer examination, some common properties belonging to form and outline. That which strikes the eye most, is the *size* and *shape* of the object. Its size is dependent on its length, breadth, and thickness, which properties are treated in the chapter on Size. The shape or form of an object is chiefly visible on its *surface*, which, together with its divisions, or *faces*, will claim most of the child's attention in the First Step.

The principal feature of the First Step is, that it makes the children examine and describe forms on the objects themselves; that it avoids technical names and definitions as much as possible, and makes but very few classifications. In the Second Step, beginning with the directions of the straight line, the child is led to perceive and describe elements of form, that have been *abstracted* from the objects, and are represented by lines and figures. The Third Step describes and classifies solids.

FIRST STEP.

Development of Common Properties belonging to Surface.

1. *Lesson on the Surface and Faces of Solids.*

The teacher presents to the class an object—say a square box. Tell me, which is the outside? Which is the inside? Which is the bottom? Which is the cover, or lid? Where are its sides? We will turn the box over; now, where is the top of the box? Where the bottom? Tell me if you can see any difference between them. Then what can you say of the parts of the outside? They are alike. We will call the outside, *surface*, and the parts of the surface, *faces*. What do we call the outside? What do we call the parts of the outside?

The teacher may then show them a regular solid—a cube, for instance, and ask, What do you call this? A block. Show me its top; its sides; its bottom. I will turn the block over: now show me the top; bottom; sides. How many faces has this block? Let one child point out one of its faces, another a different face, &c., till all are pointed out.

We will now repeat what we have learned. The outside of an object is called its *surface*. The parts of the surface are called *faces*. Show me the faces of the box; of this book; of the bookcase; of your slates, &c.

The teacher may now show the class another object—say a sphere—and call upon one of the children to come and cover the surface with his hands. How many parts has the surface? Do you know the name of this object? (If the children call it a *ball*, the name may for the moment be retained.) Here is another object (a cone). Show me its surface. Move your hand over the whole surface. How many parts are there to this surface? What do we call these parts? Faces. Let us compare the faces of the objects before us. If I move this block, will it roll? Why not? Right; because its faces are flat. Instead of flat, say *plane*. But if I move this object (the sphere), what will it do? Why will it roll? Because its surface is round. Teacher places the cone on its base, and asks, Now will this object roll? Why not? Teacher places the cone on its side, and moving it, asks, And now what can you say it does? It rolls. And why? Now repeat, An object may have a *plane* or a *round* surface. It may also have plane and round faces. Now show me objects in the room that have a plane surface; others which have a round surface; others which have both plane and round faces. (The cylindrical and conical objects belong to this class.)

2. *On the Edges and Corners of Solids; the Idea of Straight and Curved developed.*

The teacher again presents the block, and asks a child to point out two of its faces that meet each other. She bids him further to move his finger along between them. (Presenting the blade of a knife.) Where do the faces of this blade meet? Yes; at the *edge*. Now let us call the meeting of two faces *an edge*. What is an edge? Show me the edges of this block. How many are there? Where do they meet? What do you call this part of a table-top? Yes, a corner; *edges meet in a corner*. Repeat this. How many corners are there in this block? How many edges do you see in this object (a sphere)? How many corners? How many edges in this object (a cone)? How many corners? We might in the latter case call that one corner at the top its *point*. Point out the edges and corners of this table; of this book; of this tumbler, &c.

Now move your finger along one of the edges of the block, and now on the edge of this solid (the cone). Did you move exactly in the same way? Who can tell me the difference?

Although the children may already have both the idea and names of straight and curved, yet we may seize this opportunity of illustrating one of the most important elements, or rather *the* element of form, by means of drawing. For this purpose the teacher draws distinctly and correctly a *straight* line and a circular curve on the blackboard, and gives them the names of *straight* and *curved* lines. She then asks which of these lines represents an edge of the cube, and which of them the edge of the cone.

If any further definition of straight and curved is required, the teacher may say, The straight line never changes its direction, while the curved line is continually changing its direction. The word "direction" may be illustrated by the teacher, in moving from one point in the room to another. By going directly, or the shortest way, from one point to the other, she describes a *straight* line; on the contrary, if she gradually turns to the right or left of this line, and then returns to it again, she has been out of the straight line; and if her motion was traced on the floor, it would be by a *curved* line.

The teacher must make some other curves on the board, beside the circle and the arc, in order that the idea of curve may become somewhat generalized.

She lastly requires the children to name and point out objects, the edges of which describe a straight line; others, of which the edges are curved; others, which have edges both straight and curved.

It may be well for the children, as well as the teacher, to know that in copying objects from nature, we draw what is called their outline; this outline is sometimes analogous to the edges of the solid, which form the boundary of our view. But in some solids, as the sphere, the cone, the cylinder, the outline does not always coincide with the edges, but is visible on the rounded surface.

3. *On Angles and Enclosed Spaces.*

They are classified and named according to the number of their sides. The teacher might here ask the children whether they think they could enclose a space with one straight line, or, to render the case more obvious, with one straight stick? Whether they think it could be done with one *curved line?* The children may suggest a *circle*, or an *ellipse.*

The teacher then may continue the exercise by asking whether a space could be surrounded by two straight lines (to be illustrated by sticks placed in the form of a right angle). On how many sides is this space surrounded? Where is it open? The teacher may make a drawing of this combination, and tell them that this is called *an angle*, and that an angle may be more or less open. (Teacher changes the position of the sticks to illustrate this.)

QUESTIONS.—Show me some angles on the blackboard? Which is the most shut? Which is more open? Which is the most open?

Next require the children to find out whether, with three straight lines, a space can be entirely surrounded or shut in, and to show it by arranging sticks on the floor. This done, a triangle is formed, which the teacher copies, and to which she gives the name, letting the children repeat: A space which is enclosed by three sides is called a three-sided figure, or *triangle*.

(N. B.—The teacher has to tell them, that in speaking of enclosed spaces, we use the word *side*, instead of *line*.)

After this, the children are required to find out how a space can be enclosed by four straight lines, which the teacher copies on the blackboard, representing not only the square, but, if she chooses, the rhomb, rhomboid, trapezoid, trapezium, and oblong, to which the children will easily give the name of *four-sided figures*. The children may now select these from the box of forms.

QUESTION.—What is a four-sided figure?

The same plan is continued, so as to include the five, six, seven, and eight-sided figures.

An excellent plan, still further to impress these forms upon the senses and the minds of the children, will here be suggested, as being within the scope of every teacher. Let her draw the figures described above on pasteboard; after this, the figures are cut out by means of a penknife, so that the holes, as well as the pieces cut out, may serve as illustrations of these forms. It will be well to draw and cut out *several* kinds of four-sided figures, since each of them represents forms of frequent occurrence. It is doubtful whether the proper Greek names ought to be given to these quadrilaterals at this step, such as rhomb, trapezoid, &c. We should propose to take the children's names, such as window-shaped, boat-shaped, etc., which will prove to be more practical, especially for purposes of drawing. "Calkin's Chart of Forms" may be used in connection with these exercises, the children pointing out upon the chart the figures corresponding to the forms cut from pasteboard. The figure on the chart named *parallelogram*, is in this treatise called an *oblong*.

We subjoin here the exercises which this plan suggests, in due order:

1. The children take the pieces which the teacher has cut out, one after the other, and find out to what hole they fit.

2. The teacher herself fits those pieces into the holes from which they have been taken, and asks what figure they represent. Why? Count the sides, and corners, or angles.

FORM.—FIRST STEP. 67

3. She then may tell them to bring her a piece representing a circle, a five-sided figure, a four-sided figure, &c.

4. Finally, she bids them look at the objects in the room, and find out which of them has a triangular surface, or one which is four-sided, circular, five, six-sided, &c.

4. *Application of the last exercise to Drawing.*

The bearing of this last exercise to drawing is so obvious, that we shall bring it in as a part of the lesson.

The teacher proposes to draw a window, and asks them what kind of lines will represent it? What kind of figure? (They will probably refer to the oblong.) Then she herself begins to draw, always asking whether the class knows what part of the window, what edge, corner, &c., she is drawing. After the drawing is completed, she may call the children out, and, pointing to different parts of the window, bid the children point to the analogous parts of the drawing.

N. B.—Although the terms horizontal, vertical, and oblique, have not been developed at this step, the children's meaning will be sufficiently clear in speaking of lines going downward, to the right, left, sloping lines, &c.

DRAWING OF A HOUSE.

It need not be remarked that drawings of this kind apply mostly to the frontispiece of objects, and do not include vanishing surfaces, which represent thickness.

The teacher again may ask what figure they think would represent the front of a house, the door, the windows, &c. What figure do they think would represent the roof? The children may possibly find that the one they have called "boat-shaped"

would best represent it; if not, the teacher may first show some wrong figures, till she hits the right one, which will probably receive the approval of the children.

Other objects that might be drawn by the teacher under the direction of the children, are: a box, a door, a secretary, a chest of drawers, a clock, &c.

Although the children are not, at this step, supposed to draw themselves, the training they receive in regard to form, &c., will be invaluable. The real starting point for children to draw, is by means of the *inventive drawing*.

SECOND STEP.

1. *Directions of the Straight Line.*

For the sake of the recapitulation of one of the previous exercises, the teacher may draw a curved line on the blackboard, and ask what kind of a line it is. Why do you call it a curved line? She then may draw a vertical, horizontal, and oblique line, and ask to what kind of lines they belong. They are straight lines. But can you see any difference in the direction of the lines? The children undoubtedly see some difference, although they may not be able to state it clearly.

In order to develop this subject in a visible and tangible manner, the teacher may place a stick or pointer vertically against the wall or the blackboard, and ask, What do you see? How is the pointer situated? It *stands* against the wall. And now (*letting the stick fall to the ground*)? It *lies* on the floor. And now (*leaning it toward the wall, inclining it to the right*)? It leans against the wall.

The teacher then calls upon one of the class to come forward, and draw, by means of a line, the stick as it looks when standing. Another child is called to draw the stick as it appears when lying on the floor; and a third to represent the stick leaning against the wall. Is this drawing exactly right? Some say, The stick inclines more than the drawing indicates. To which side does the stick incline? Yes; to the right. And now? To the left. Let some of the children come forward, and draw it as it appears now.

After the several lines representing the stick in a standing, lying, and inclined position, are thus made on the blackboard, the teacher may point to one of the lines—for instance to the vertical—asking what name they would give to this line. A standing, upright line, &c. She then gives them the name which is commonly applied to lines of this class in drawing, viz., *vertical*, which she spells, writes on the board, and makes the children repeat. No further definition is necessary, such as are often give in books, and which are mostly beyond the child's experience. Nevertheless, for purposes of drawing, or in mechanics, an accurate standard for measuring the vertical direction becomes very desirable. For this purpose the teacher may attach to the end of a string a weight, and hold it suspended before the class. What line does this string describe? Yes; a vertical line, and in so perfect a manner that we may use it to measure the vertical lines on the blackboard, or elsewhere, as a carpenter or mason measures vertical objects or their edges by means of something very much like this, which he calls a plummet. Let a child come and make some vertical lines on the blackboard. Are they exactly right? Who thinks they are? Let us decide it with the plummet.

The teacher next makes the children examine the horizontal line, and asks whether they have a name for it. She then tells them that instead of *flat*, or *even*, the word *horizontal* is used in speaking of lines. In order to reconcile them to this new name, she may ask them whether they ever stood at the shore of the ocean or some great lake; whether they ever observed a line where the sky and the water seem to meet. She then tells them that this line is called "horizon," and asks which of the lines on the board the horizon seems to resemble most in regard to direction.

Lastly, she inquires for the name they would give the oblique line. If they call it sloping or slanting, she may tell them that these words are sometimes used, but that the name "oblique" is generally preferred when applied to lines. The teacher must take care not to reject unconditionally the names which the children may give to these lines, since they are generally correct when applied to things or objects.

A recapitulation of the lesson may be had as follows:—

1. The teacher points to the lines on the blackboard, and requires their names.

2. She gives the name, and requires the children to draw them, either on the blackboard, or on their own slates. In the latter case she would do well to vary the exercises by saying, Draw four vertical lines of the same length; five horizontal lines, beginning with a short one, and making each successive one a little longer; six oblique lines, inclining to the right; seven oblique lines, inclining to the left, &c.

3. She then requires them to point out objects in the room that have a vertical, horizontal, and oblique direction, either as a whole, or considering their edges only.

2. *Angles.*

We have already considered how angles are formed. We will only remark here, that a pair of scissors or shears are well calculated to illustrate angles; and the fact that their size depends on the width of the opening, and not on the length of the lines, or, in case of the instruments, on the length of the blades.

In order to illustrate the three different kinds of angles, let the teacher present to the class a knife with a straight edge, when questions like the following may be asked:—The teacher (*opening the knife half-way*) asks, How much did I open this knife? Trace the angle which it describes. After shutting it a little, she asks, And what is its opening now? Yes; less than before. And now? More than at first. (*Shutting it entirely*): And now? (*Opening it entirely*): And now? What can you say of the angles in the last two cases? There were no angles.

A scholar is then required to draw the angle which was represented by the knife when it was half open. He can give it, of course, the opening he thinks most appropriate, by guess or otherwise. It will, however, generally be found that the child's practical sense will suggest to him that an angle like the one he is required to draw is most easily made by *erecting a vertical line upon the end of a horizontal one.* In that case, the name and following definition may be given : A right angle is formed by drawing a vertical line from the end of a horizontal one. Let the children repeat this, and try to execute the right angle according to the direction given.

Now draw the angle which is represented by the knife when it is less than half open. What did we call the angle you drew before? What can you say of the one you have just drawn? Yes; it is smaller than the right angle. Now I will tell you: an angle which is smaller or less than a right angle, is called an *acute angle*. Repeat this.

Now draw this angle which is represented by the knife more than half open. How is the angle you have drawn, when compared to the right angle? Greater than the right angle. Now I will give you its name: an angle which is greater than a right angle, is called an *obtuse angle*. Repeat this.

The teacher may finally present to the class a knife with a long blade, together with a smaller one, both half open, and ask, What angles do both of these blades describe? Right angles. Which is the greater of the two right angles? They are alike. Why? Because the blades are both half open, or because they are *equally* open. Then repeat: Angles are alike when their openings are the same. All right angles are equal.

EXERCISES.—1. The teacher draws promiscuously a certain number of angles of different kinds on the board, some of them hardly discernible from right angles, and requires the class to name them.

2. She tells them to draw any kind of angle she describes, as, for instance, an acute angle with a very small opening, another with a wide opening, &c.

3. She asks them to point out right, acute, or obtuse angles, as formed by objects they see about them.

3. *Perpendicular Lines.*

Although the children have hitherto been encouraged to form their right angles by the combination of a vertical line with horizontal ones, it will be necessary to generalize the idea. For this purpose the teacher may hold up horizontally a slate, and ask what angles they perceive on it. Then she may turn the slate so that one corner falls lower than the other, thus:

and ask whether the angle they see there is still a right angle. What kind of lines form it? Yes; slanting lines. Then let them draw an angle in the above position. A child does so on the blackboard, and the teacher appeals to the class to determine whether the angle is right. As there may be a difference of opinion, one of the lines may be prolonged, thus:

What do you see now? Two angles. Where situated? On each side of one of the lines. What can you say of these angles? What about the size of their openings? (This may be ascertained by measuring, at an equal distance from the point of meeting, across the opening of the angle.) If this point is settled, the teacher tells them: *When one line meets another, so that the angles on each side are equal to each other, such angles are right angles.* And again: Any line which forms a right angle with another, is said to be *perpendicular* to the other line.

EXERCISES.—1. The teacher bids one child draw on the board a line in any direction, and then to draw another line perpendicular to the first. If it should be done incorrectly, then the teacher must apply the test suggested above. The questions to be asked in such a case are: What kind of angle is this? Yes; an acute angle. And this? An obtuse angle. Can the line drawn be a perpendicular? Why not?

2. The class is then required to point out edges of objects that are perpendicular to other edges. Pointing to the blackboard, for instance, the teacher may ask, What can you say of these two

edges with reference to each other? Is it also vertically placed on that edge? Then is it both perpendicular and vertical?

REMARK.—As the term perpendicular is frequently used in the place of vertical, it may be well to make the class acquainted with this fact; without, however, recommending it, since it may lead to a confusion of ideas. For instance, pointing to a sloping edge of a desk, the teacher may ask, What kind of edge is that placed under it? A vertical one. Is it perpendicular to the sloping one? It is not.

4. *Triangles.*

The teacher draws a right, an obtuse, and an acute angle on the board, and then shuts the opening of each by a third line. She then asks, What do you call these figures now? Of how many lines or sides are they composed? What can you say as to their resemblance or difference? Point out any difference between them; for instance, between the first and second. In the first there is a right angle, which is not in the second; in the second there is an obtuse angle, which is not in the first. What can you say of the angles in the third of these triangles? They are all acute angles. See if you can find any acute angles in the first and second figures. How many are there? Point them out.

The teacher then may tell them that the names given to these triangles depend on the kind of angles they have. The one which has a right angle in connection with two acute angles, is called a *right-angled triangle*. The other, which has an obtuse and two acute angles, is called an *obtuse-angled triangle*. The third, which has three acute angles, is called an *acute-angled triangle*. Repeat this.

EXERCISES.—1. The teacher may draw any number of triangles of the above kinds, and require the children to give their names.

2. She requires them to draw any of these triangles according to dictation.

3. She bids them to point out triangular faces of one or the other kind on objects they see in the room.

5. *Continuation of Triangles.*

The triangles in the former exercises were classed by comparing their angles. The teacher now proposes to class them by comparing their sides. Who can make a triangle having two of its sides equal, and the other of a different length? Who can make a triangle having all of its sides unequal? Who can make a triangle having its three sides equal? The pupils, in attempting to make these, may possibly fail. In this case the teacher draws the figures for them on the blackboard, and shows them that the angles must have a certain opening, to make the construction possible. The teacher then gives the names:

Fig. 1 is called an *isosceles triangle.*
" 2 " *scalene* "
" 3 " *equilateral* (equal-sided, regular) *triangle.*

After this the children give a definition of each. In the recapitulation the same order of exercises is to be observed as before.

6. *Parallel Lines.*

The teacher, by way of introduction, and with reference to one of the last exercises, may inquire of the class whether they could construct a triangle with *two* right angles in it? In attempting to do it, they would produce a figure similar to

Can you do it? Why not? The perpendicular lines will not meet. Supposing I lengthen them, what then? Why is it necessary they should meet, to make a triangle? Let us now examine those lines which will not meet, however much they may be lengthened. What line measures the distance between them? Supposing I measure the distance higher up, what then? How does this distance compare with that at the bottom? What would be the result should we measure it in other places? Yes; we find that these lines are the same distance apart at every point.

Now I will tell you, that lines which will never meet, however far they may be lengthened, and which always have the same distance between them, are called *parallel lines*. Repeat this. Now draw some *parallel* lines. With what instrument do you think I could make any number of parallel lines with much ease and correctness? Where do you find these lines? On writing paper. Where else? Make on your slates five vertical parallel lines. Now five vertical lines not parallel. Is this possible? It is not. Then say, All vertical lines must be parallel. Draw now six horizontal parallel lines. Draw six horizontal lines *not* parallel. Is this possible? Then say, Horizontal lines must be parallel. Now draw five oblique parallel lines to the left; five oblique parallel lines to the right; five oblique lines not parallel. Is this possible? Then say, Oblique lines may be or may not be parallel. Are there any parallel lines in a triangle? In a four-sided figure? This latter point we propose to consider more particularly in the next lesson.

7. *Four-sided Figures, or Quadrilaterals.*

As the children have, in the preceding exercises, obtained some insight into the principle of classifying geometrical figures, it is proposed that they should, in this exercise, perform the classification themselves, under the direction of the teacher. For this purpose, draw promiscuously on the blackboard the six different kinds of quadrilaterals; as, for instance,* 1, the trapezium; 2, the square; 3, the trapezoid; 4, the rectangle; 5, the rhomboid; 6, the rhomb. It need hardly be stated, that the teacher must refer to these figures by their numbers only, until their names are given.

She now may ask, In which of these figures do you see two pairs of parallel lines—that is, two lines running parallel in one direction, and two running parallel in another? In figs. 2, 4, 5, 6. What can you say of the length of their opposite sides? They are equal.

The teacher then selects the figures just named, and draws

---

* For these figures, see Chart of Forms.

them on another line, and says, *Four-sided figures, having all their opposite sides parallel and equal, are called parallelograms.* Repeat the definition. After this, she asks the children which of these parallelograms bear a strong resemblance to each other? Figs. 2 and 4. In what particular are they alike? They have both four right angles. In what are they different, if you compare their sides? Fig. 2 has all its sides equal, and fig. 4 has two opposite sides shorter than the other two. Is there any resemblance between the other two parallelograms, figs. 5 and 6? Yes. In what are they alike? In what are they different?

The teacher then tells them, that if they will make a full description of each figure she points out, she will give them its proper name. What is this figure? (fig. 2). A parallelogram, of which all the angles are right angles, and the sides equal. The teacher gives the name *square*, and requires the class to repeat the definition, with the name attached to it.

What is this figure? (fig. 1). A parallelogram which has four right angles, and two opposite sides shorter than the other two. The teacher gives the name *oblong*.

What is this figure? (fig. 6). A parallelogram having two opposite angles acute, and the others obtuse, and all the sides equal. The name *rhomb* is then given.

What is this figure? (fig. 5). A parallelogram having two opposite angles acute and two obtuse, and two opposite sides shorter than the other two. The name *rhomboid* is then given.

There remain now only figs. 1 and 3, which are not classed among the parallelograms. The teacher tells the class that in the description of these two figures, neither the angles nor the length or equality of the sides are considered, but simply the fact of their having any sides parallel or not. She then bids them to describe these figures accordingly, after which she will give their names. Pointing to fig. 1, she asks, What do you see? A four-sided figure, which has but one pair of parallel sides. The name *trapezoid* is given.

What do you see here? A four-sided figure having none of its sides parallel. In order to impress these figures in somewhat modified forms, the teacher may ask whether they could make a trapezoid with two right angles, or with two lines, or even three lines equal;—a trapezium with two adjacent sides equal, and having all kinds of angles, right, acute, and obtuse.

Exercises.—1. The teacher draws a number of different four-sided figures on the board, and asks for their names, requiring, if necessary, definitions.

2. She bids the class draw the figures according to her description or classification.

3. She then requires the pupils to point out objects in the room, the faces of which are squares, rectangles, rhombs, rhomboids, &c.

N. B.—There will be no lack of objects presenting rectangular faces, such as panes of glass, boards, walls, tables, steps, boxes, houses, &c. In order to supply to some extent a deficiency in rhombical surfaces, an intelligent teacher may present some minerals, in their crystallized shape, which will moreover give them an idea of some regular solids, not often found amongst the works of man.

8. *Polygons.*

As the children are already acquainted with the meaning of five, six, seven, eight-sided figures, it only remains to give them the names by which they are generally known in geometry, and which have at least the advantage of being shorter. Let the figures be drawn on the blackboard by the teacher.

A five-sided figure is called a pentagon.
A six-sided " " a hexagon.
A seven-sided " " a heptagon.
An eight-sided " " an octagon.

Let the teacher question the children as to the number of sides, angles, and corners in these various figures, and lead them to discover that it is always the same in each.

In order to illustrate the original meaning of *polygon*, the teacher might draw on the board a figure with a great number of sides, and ask the class how many sides it has. If the children are puzzled to tell exactly the number of sides, she may ask whether it has *few* or *many* sides? It has many sides. It might therefore be called a *many-sided* figure. *Polygon* means the same thing. She may further state, that any figure including the triangle is classed among the polygons. The definition is now given: A polygon is a figure enclosed by three, or more than three sides.

In order to develop the idea *regular*, the teacher draws a regular polygon, and asks, What can you say of its different sides and angles? Yes; they are equal. A polygon with its sides and angles equal, is called a regular polygon. Is the square a regular polygon? Is the rhomb? Why not?

In order to develop the idea of *diagonal*, let the teacher draw a line through any of the above figures from one corner to the other, and ask what she has done. The teacher may tell them: *A line drawn from one corner to another is called a diagonal.* Repeat this. Can any diagonals be drawn in a triangle? How many in a four-sided figure? in a pentagon? hexagon? heptagon? octagon? The amount will prove to be respectively, two, five, nine, fourteen, twenty diagonals.

9. *The Circle.*

The circle is mentioned here last amongst the inclosed spaces, although it is in one sense the simplest of all, and the one which is easiest recognized by children. Yet the perfection of its form, and the reflections that are called forth by it, seem to place it on a somewhat higher step.

In order to show the construction of the circle, as well as some of its properties, let the teacher draw, by means of a chalk attached to one end of a string, a circular line. What have I been drawing? A round line, a ring, a circle. Let us call the whole figure a circle, and the surrounding line "the circumference." Can you tell me where the middle of the circle is situated? Where you held the other end of the string. (The teacher makes a dot at the point indicated.) How do you know that this is the middle? What can you say of its distance from the different points in the circumference? It is the same distance from every point. Why must it be so? Let us now call the point in the middle *the centre* of a circle. What is the centre? Give a definition of it. If the centre be equally distant from all points of the circumference, what must the circumference be in regard to the centre? Make a definition of the circumference. But what is the circle itself, as a space? Describe it fully. *A circle is a space surrounded by a line, called its circumference; this line is equally distant at all points from a point called the centre of the circle.*

When the circle was constructed on the blackboard, by what has the distance between the centre and the circumference been measured? By the string. Let us now imagine the string to be a line which, as the thread is moved round, can assume various positions. The teacher draws several of these lines, and calls one of them a radius; several of them, radii. What is a radius? What can you say of the length of the radii? Then say: *All the radii of one circle are equal.*

The teacher then may make two radii going in the same direction, and ask how many lines they form. They form but one line. Describe that line—where it begins, through what point it passes, and where it ends. It is drawn from one point of the circumference, passes through the centre, and terminates in an opposite point of the circumference. Let us call a line of this kind "a diameter." What is a diameter? How many times the length of a radius? Can we draw more than one diameter? How? What can you say of the length of the different diameters?

As it is not proposed here to give a definition of all the parts of divisions of the circle, we limit ourselves to some of the most important ones. As, for instance, *A diameter cuts a circle into two equal parts, each of which is called a semicircle. Two diameters, intersecting at right angles, divide the circumference into four equal parts, called quadrants. Any part of the circle is called an arc.** The teacher may show them by what an easy and graceful movement an arc is produced, by simply swinging the arm. Performing the same movement on the blackboard, with chalk in hand, the children will see the *arc* arise. Does this arc belong to a small or large circle? Where do you think its centre would be?

---

* For these figures, see Chart of Forms.

Is the arc which belongs to a large circle, more or less bent than the one which belongs to a small circle?

THIRD STEP.

1. *Solids.*

It is perhaps premature to suppose that even in these days of educational progress, a box of solids will be considered as necessary an appendage of the school room, as alphabetical cards or a map of the country. If it should not be found there, it is certainly an easy task for the teacher, as well as the pupils, to manufacture the most important solids, such as the cylinder, the cone, and a number of pyramids and prisms, from pasteboard. As the word "solid" will be often used in these exercises, the teacher will do well to remark, at the outset, that every extension in length, breadth, and thickness, is called "a solid," which word must not be confounded with the quality "solid," which would, for instance, never be attributed to water, while nobody will deny that any volume of water has length, breadth, and thickness, and is therefore *a* solid, like all other objects.

2. *The Sphere.*

As the solid which is presented to the class is already known to them under the name of *ball*, the teacher gives the more geometrical name of *sphere;* the object of this lesson being to make them aware of its properties. Where is the surface of the sphere? Mark a point on the surface, and one directly opposite on the other side. Supposing I pass a string or a thread from one point over the other, till it returns to the first point, what line does it describe? Now if I cut through the sphere, along the circular line described by the thread, how would the sphere be divided? (This operation ought to be performed, or, at any rate, illustrated.) These half spheres are called *hemispheres.* How are they called? What can you say of the faces of the hemisphere? Of what shape is it? How can you find the centre of such a circle?

Right; by drawing a diameter, and marking a point in its middle. Suppose we put the two parts together again, so as to form a sphere, what part of the sphere does this point represent? If a great many lines were drawn from one point of the surface to an opposite one, what would they all pass through? What would such lines be called? Yes, diameters. Are these diameters equal? (This might be shown by inserting the sphere in various positions between two vertical sticks, placed at a distance equal to the diameter of the solid.) If diameters are equal, what can you say of the radii? Why? Where is one point of each of the radii situated? On the surface. And the other? In the centre. What can we say in regard to the distance of every point of the surface from the centre? That it is *equally* removed from the centre. Now give a definition of a sphere. A sphere is a solid, bounded by a rounded surface, every point of which is equally distant from a point inside, called the centre of a sphere. If a sphere becomes flattened on two opposite sides, it is called a *spheroid*. This can be illustrated by a ball made of India-rubber. Many objects in nature have the shape of a spheroid. Now name a great many objects which are either spherical or spheroidical. Apples, oranges, peaches, cherries, many berries, raindrops, soap bubbles, &c. Do you know what form the earth has? If the children do not know it, a globe may be produced. Of what shape is the egg? Is it exactly like a sphere or an orange? Then we will call its shape egg-shaped, or, what means the same, *oval*.

3. *The Cylinder.*

Describe the object before you. What do you see on its surface? Two circular plane faces, and a rounded face between them. If you wanted to make this solid stand, how would you place it? On one of its plane faces. Now I will tell you that the face on which it is supposed to stand is called its base. How many bases has the solid? We will compare these bases one with the other. What can you say of them? Yes, they are equal. And what more can you say of them? They are parallel. If the children do not readily give these answers, the teacher may draw them out by putting each end upon the board, and drawing a mark around it. Compare the circles thus made. The idea of a parallel may be brought out by placing objects upon the table parallel to each other. The name of the solid is *cylinder*. Who can describe it? The cylinder is a solid, having two circular bases, which are parallel and equal, and a rounded face between. Now name some objects that have a cylindrical form, as hats, stovepipes, tumblers, rolls, rulers, pillars, &c.

4. *The Cone.*

Describe the surface of this object. It has a circular plane base, and a curved face. Can you tell me the difference between this circular face and the circular face of the cylinder? Yes, it ends in a point. Does it end suddenly in a point, or does it become narrower gradually? Now we will use the word *tapering*, instead of "becoming narrower," and call the sharp point at the top "apex." The name of the solid is *cone*. Who can describe it? A cone is a solid, having a plane circular base, and a curved face tapering toward a point, called its apex. Name some objects which are of a conical shape. The trunks of many trees, carrots, sugar loaves, the peaks of many mountains, &c.

REMARKS.—The teacher may show that by cutting off the top of a cone, the remaining piece, which is called a "truncated cone," presents a form which is common to some objects, as, for instance, coal scuttles, pails, &c.

5. *Pyramids.*

Out of several different solids on the table, including a variety of pyramids, let the children select those already considered, and then ask them if there are any other solids that resemble these. Let some one come forward and select these solids, and place them by the side of the one they most resemble. The children may probably choose those terminating in a point, and place them near the cone. In what do these solids resemble the cone? In what are they different? They have only plane faces, while the cone has a curved one. What can you say of their bases? What is the base of the cylinder? A circle. What is the base of this solid? A triangle. Of this? A square. Of this? A pentagon, &c. Supposing we wished to speak of all their bases together, what could we call them? Polygons. If necessary to bring out this answer, the teacher can refer them to the plane figures they have called polygons. The teacher should always be careful not to answer for children questions which they may be led to answer for themselves. Now look at the faces of these pyramids. What can you say of their number? They do not have the same number. What can you say of their form? They are alike in form. What is their form? Yes; they are all triangles. How does the number of triangles on each compare with the number of sides to the base? Yes; there is the same number of them. Now I will tell you, that all solids of this description are called *pyramids*. Can you describe a pyramid? A pyramid is a solid, having a polygon for its base, and as many triangles tapering toward one point (the apex) as there are sides in the base.

The teacher has to add, that according to the number of sides in the base, these solids are called "triangular," "quadrangular," "pentagonal," "hexagonal," &c., pyramids.

EXERCISES.—1. Select a pentagonal pyramid. Tell how many faces, corners, edges, angles, &c., you find in it.

2. *Think* of a hexagonal pyramid. Tell how many faces, corners, edges, angles, &c., you think it has.

3. Point out as many objects as you can, the shape of which is like a pyramid.

REMARK.—The teacher may make here an allusion to the most ancient of all monuments, the pyramids of Egypt, and demonstrate how difficult it is to overthrow a pyramind resting on a broad base.

6. *Prisms.*

The several kinds of prisms to be considered in the lesson, being placed on the table, the teacher asks, Which of the solids on the table resembles somewhat a cylinder? The children will probably select a many-sided prism, and the teacher can lead them to consider how each of the prisms might become a cylinder, by rolling it over many times, thus wearing away its edges. In what are these solids different from the cylinder? They have only plane faces. If you wished to make them stand, on which faces would you place them? And what do we call the faces on which objects stand? What is the form of their bases? They may be triangles, squares, rectangles, pentagons, &c. If we wished to speak of them all as one class, what should we say? They are polygons. What can you say of the size of the two bases of each? They are equal. What more can you say of them? They are parallel. Of what shape are their surrounding faces? They are all oblongs. But I see some here which are rhomboids. Let one of the children select the rhomboids. To what class do both oblongs and rhomboids belong? To the class of parallelograms. Then what shall we call all the surrounding faces? Parallelograms. How does the number of faces in each compare with the number of sides in each of their bases? It is equal to the number of their sides. Now I will tell you, that solids of this kind are called *prisms*. Who can describe a prism?

It may be necessary to lead the children to this definition at first, by repeating some questions; as, What did you tell me about the bases of these prisms? They are equal. And what more did you say of them? They are parallel. Now tell me in one sentence what you can say of their bases. Their bases are equal and parallel. What did we say of their surrounding faces? Their surrounding faces are parallelograms. Now describe in one sentence a prism. The prism is a solid, having for its bases equal and parallel polygons, whilst the surrounding faces are parallelograms.

The teacher may add that these prisms have particular names, according to the number of sides in their bases. The teacher holds up a triangular prism, and questions the children as to the number of sides in its base. What then may you say of the form of its base? Yes; it is a triangle, or we may say it is *triangular*. Then what kind of a prism may we call this? What did we call the pyramid that had a triangular base? will now call it a triangular prism, and will name the remaining pyramids, as quadrangular, pentagonal, hexagonal, &c. The quadrangular prism is of such importance, that it has been designated by one word, *parallelopipedon*, to which the cube belongs.

EXERCISES.—1. Describe a parallelopipedon; the number and kind of its faces; how many angles, edges, corners, &c.

2. Imagine a heptagonal prism. Describe the number and kind of its faces; how many angles, edges, corners, &c.

3. Name objects in and out of the room, which have the form of a prism.

OBJECTS.

INTRODUCTORY REMARKS.

For many years the sentiment has been gaining ground in this country, that there is something to do in our schools beside simply teaching children to "read, write, and cipher." It is now very generally acknowledged that an acquaintance with Nature, in her varied forms, is also an important educational attainment, and that a knowledge of *things* does in its natural order precede a knowledge of *words*. As a result of this conviction, "Lessons on Objects" have been introduced into very many of the best schools of the country.

These lessons, however, have not always been given in a manner best calculated to awaken and cultivate the early faculties of children, and prepare them for the study of Nature.

These first exercises with children should be of a character calculated to quicken perception, and to cultivate close and accurate observation and expression. For the teacher to tell the child what she knows about objects, is only to burden the memory, discourage investigation, and weaken the perceptive faculties. The effort should rather be to lead the child to *discover for himself,* and then properly to *communicate the result of his observations*. It is with this idea prominently in view that the following sketches and series of lessons have been drawn up.

The truly successful teacher will rather use these as models, as conveying an idea of the general plan and method to be pursued, and will not confine herself either to the subjects or exact method here laid down. Too much importance, however, cannot be attached to the teacher's having a definite plan and aim in each lesson. No teacher should ever go before her class without an exact sketch of the lesson she proposes to give. Without such preparation, the lesson had better never be given.

In the First Step, the Perceptive Faculty is exercised. In the earlier lessons the object is considered as a whole; in the later, as possessing parts—the recognition of these requiring more minute and accurate exercise of perception. In all the early steps, one important aim is the formation of a vocabulary.

In the Second Step, the Perceptive and also the Conceptive Faculties are exercised. In the earlier lessons the object is considered as possessing familiar qualities; in the later lessons, as possessing some important quality which other objects also possess.

In the Third Step, the exercise of the Perceptive Faculties serves as the basis of the lesson, the superstructure of which addresses the Conceptive, and especially the Reasoning Faculties. The object is considered in detail, all its parts noted, and all its qualities, except such as are altogether beyond the range of the children's experience. Especially do children consider the uses of the object, and the adaptation of structure, material, or qualities to these.

In this Step they often consider two objects at a time, comparing and contrasting them. A little information is often given; still it is not the aim of the teacher to tell them what they can learn from books, but rather to form correct and thorough habits of observation, and develop power of thought.

In the Fourth Step, the Faculty of Generalization is exercised, in addition to the other faculties before named. Objects are considered in classes: when a single object is taken, it is with reference to art, manufacture, &c.

FIRST STEP.

I.—Objects Named, Arranged, &c.

1. *Sketch of a Lesson on a Teapot, Milk Pitcher, Cup, and Saucer.*

1. The teacher should first ask the children if they have ever seen such things as these, when they usually see them, and what each of them is called.

2. The teacher calls upon a child to touch the teapot, asking the others if he has rightly done so. The same may be done with each of the objects.

3. The teacher herself touches one of the objects, and desires all the children who know its name to raise their hands; one child is afterward selected to apply the name. The same to be done with each of the objects.

4. The teacher to remove the objects out of sight, and then ask the children what things she has been showing them; this test should be repeated till they can correctly mention all the objects from memory.

5. The teacher may require a child to place the objects in a certain order; as the teapot in the middle, the milk pitcher before it, and the cup in the saucer behind it; the other children saying whether it is correctly done: they may then be desired to place all of them in a row. The teacher may then put the saucer upon the cup, and ask the children if that is its proper place, and then call a child to place it as it ought to be, and also to *say* what are the proper positions of the cup and of the saucer.

6. The teacher, having arranged the objects in a certain order, desiring the children to observe how they are placed, is to remove them, and call upon some child to replace them in the same order; they may then be placed differently, and the same test be applied.

7. The lesson to conclude with a little talk about the objects—their number and names; their uses; what is put into the teapot, what comes out of it; what is put into the milk pitcher; how the cup is used, &c.

Supposing this book to be used by the Educational Teacher,

or Teacher of Method, in the instruction of a class of students, it is of the utmost importance that they should be exercised in drawing up sketches corresponding with the patterns given.

After examination of the above sketch, the students should construct a similar lesson, on plate, knife, fork, spoon, and glass.

2. *Sketch of a Lesson on a Basket, a Book, and a Slate.*

1. See that the children know these objects and their names, and can themselves apply the proper name to each object.

2. Remove the basket, book, and slate, one by one, and after each has been taken away, call upon the children to say which it is; then take all three away, and let them say what the three things which have been taken away are, and how they were placed before they were removed.

3. Call upon some of the children to place the several objects as directed, thus: the basket in the middle, the books nearer to the window, and the slate on the opposite side. Tell them to observe how they are placed, and then, removing them, desire one of the children again to place them as they were.

4. Next talk about the uses of these objects. How are baskets used, and by whom? For what purposes do the children themselves use them? What have they seen their mothers do with them? Place some books in a basket in a neat and orderly manner, and then desire a child to do the same with others; this will teach them to do such things neatly and tidily. Then ask them what people do with books. Read a line or two in a book, and ask what has been done, and if they would like to be able thus to read. Then talk about the slate, by whom they have seen slates used, and for what purposes.

5. Sum up the lesson by asking how many things have been spoken of, their names, and the ordinary use of each of them.

Students construct corresponding lesson on shovel, poker, and tongs.

Their attention should be drawn to the *general* plan of these lessons, thus:

PLAN.

1. Teacher presents the objects; ascertains which the children can name; gives names they do not know, always touching the object named, requiring children to observe it, and causing the names to be *simultaneously repeated*.

2. Teacher exercises the children on the names, by pointing to the objects, and letting the children name them; then by naming the objects, and letting the children touch or bring them.

The last part of the lesson will vary according to the objects selected. If these be plate, knife, fork, &c., the teacher will direct attention especially to the arrangement of the objects—where they would place the plate, if they were going to set the table? where the knife? where the fork? Tongs, poker, &c., candle, candlestick, &c., would be treated similarly; and the arrangement of bonnet, scarf, &c., as parts of dress, show.

In the lesson, "Wood, Hatchet, Hammer, &c.," the use of the tools, rather than any arrangement of them, would be exhibited. Terms for prominent parts, as handle, rim, lid, should be given as the parts are noticed by the children.

LIST OF SUBJECTS FOR SIMILAR LESSONS.

Plate, knife, fork, spoon, glass.
Tongs, poker, shovel, hearth brush.
Candle, candlestick, extinguisher, tray, snuffers.
Bonnet, veil, scarf, gloves, parasol.
Needle, thimble, thread, calico, scissors.
Pen, ink, paper, blotting book, pen wiper.
Penknife, pencil, ruler, India rubber.
Wood, hatchet, hammer, gimlet, nail.
Clay, stone, sponge, wool, string.

II.—Objects for Parts.

Including the consideration of—
1. Names and Number of Parts.
2. Position of Parts.

3. Uses of Parts.
4. Principal, distinguished from Secondary Parts.

Any one or two of these points may be taken up in a lesson, which one or two will generally depend on the subject.

1. *Sketch on a Thimble, for Parts.* (*Pattern Lesson.*)

    Uses of parts.
    Names of parts.

MATTER.	METHOD.
I.—A thimble has a crown, a shield, cells, a border, and a rim.	I.—Teacher presents a thimble. Selects a child to touch a part. Asks the children to name it, and when they fail, gives name, which is simultaneously repeated (S. R.) by the children, and written on the board (W. B.). Teacher selects second child to touch a second part, and proceeds as before, until all the parts are distinguished and named. Children read the names from the board. Teacher erases these, and children give them again in order from the top to the bottom of the thimble.
II.—1. The crown, so called because it is the top part of the thimble.	II.—1. Teacher exercises the children on the appropriateness of the names. Child to touch the crown. Why the upper part is so called. What crowns are. Where they are worn. A part of the head is called a crown. Teacher bids a child touch crown, and then touch some higher part. Why he cannot comply with the latter command. The *top* part of the head is called the crown, and a part of the thimble is called the crown, because it is *the top part.*
2. The shield is so called because it keeps the finger from being hurt.	2. A child to touch the shield. Teacher shows the picture of a soldier with a sword and shield. Children state use of the sword—of the shield, and why this part of the thimble is so called.
3. The cells are so	3. Child to touch the cells; show

called because they resemble the cells of the honeycomb.	honeycomb and its cells. Children say why the holes in the thimble are called cells also.
4. The border is so called because it is an ornament near the edge.	4. A child to touch the border. Its position referred to (near the edge). Children mention any borders they have seen on any objects, as on handkerchiefs, shawls, &c. Where these are placed. Why people have borders. Why this part of the thimble is so called.
	5. A child to touch the only remaining part—the rim—and give examples of rims on other objects.

NOTE.—Nothing is said about the inside, outside, &c., as distinct parts. It is undesirable to mix up the consideration of geometrical with that of material parts; it tends to confuse the children. Students construct sketch on "Penknife," as "Thimble."

The Teacher of Method might next require the class of students to work out exercises on an apple, thus:—

> Find the matter under the heads.
> Parts found and named.
> Position of parts described.

2. *Example of Sketch on an Apple.*

MATTER.—I. Parts of an apple.

The parts of the apple are pulp, core, seeds, peel, eye, dimple, and stem.

II.—Position of parts.

> The peel covers the apple.
> The pulp is inside the peel.
> The core is in the centre of the apple or pulp.
> The seeds are enclosed in the core.
> The dimple is at the base of the apple.
> The stem is at the base, and partly within the dimple.
> The eye is at the top of the apple.

Teacher of Method next requires the class to find the method corresponding.

Exercise.

METHOD.—I. 1. Show an apple. Get the name, and after a little talk about the use, where it grows, &c., desire a child to touch a part (the skin). Give the term *peel.* Children to say what part of the apple they like best. How we are to get at this. Whether, before this is done, they can find any other part by looking at the outside (the speck or bud). Give the term *eye* (the little hole). Tell them there is a better name—*dimple.* The little dent in the apple is also called dimple. What part is near the dimple? (Stem.) Children name all the outside parts of the apple. (W. B. S. R.)

2. Children allowed to name all the inside parts. Apple cut and examined, to prove whether they are right. (W. B. S. R.)

II.—Bring out the position of the peel, by asking why they could not see the pulp of the apple before we cut it open.

Position of pulp, core, and seeds brought out by direct questions. Children led to express themselves properly, and S. R. Idea of base developed by making the children ascertain on what part the apple will stand best. If necessary, remove the stem. Let them find the parts near the base. (The dimple and the stem.) Only one part left—where is it? Not at the base, but at the other end of the apple. Give the expression, *opposite the base.*

Summary.—Teacher names the position by requiring children to fill up the ellipses by naming the parts, thus: Outside the pulp is ———. Under the peel is ———. In the midst of the pulp is ———. Within the core are ———. At the base is the ———. Partly within the dimple, and at the base, is the ———. Opposite the base is the ———.

Students construct the "Penknife" as the "Apple."

3. *Sketch on a Shell.* (*Pattern.*)

 For Names of Parts.
  Principal, distinguished from Secondary Parts.
  Position of Parts.

I.—Parts.

1. *Introductory.*—Object named, where found, and of what use.

2. Parts distinguished and named. Teacher directs the children to find the largest part of the shell. Excites interest by telling them that they can find out the name of this part. What they call the largest part of themselves. (The *body.*) (S. R.): "The largest part of the shell is called the body." The part of shell next in size pointed out. Children told they can find a name for this also; they must not, however, look at themselves for the name, but at the buildings out of doors. Set the shell on its base, and ask, What part of any building goes up like this? The spire of a church. (S. R.): "The next largest part of the shell is called the *spire.*" Terms *body* and *spire* written on the blackboard.

II.—1. Children have next to find the parts of the body—mouth, lips, beak. Teacher gives the names, writes them on the board, and requires the children to say why these names are given.

2. Next, children find the parts of the spire—*whorls, sutures,* and *apex.* Teacher gives the first and second terms. (S. R.) With respect to the third term, if they have had lessons on Form, she bids them select a solid that has a part like this part of the shell, telling them that the same name is given to each. They read what is written on the board, which appears thus:—

Body, { Mouth, Lips, Beak. }   Spire, { Whorls, Sutures, Apex. }

III.—Position of Parts.

Children led to describe the position of principal parts with respect to each other, and the position of secondary parts with respect to principal, or to each other, as may be most convenient, thus:—The spire is at one end of the body; the mouth is in the under part of the body; lips around the mouth; beak proceeds from the mouth, and is at the end of the body opposite the spire. Whorls surround the spire; sutures are between the whorls; apex is at the end of the spire.

If time allow, these questions should be varied, as, Where are the whorls with respect to the apex and the body? or this may be done in recapitulation next day.

Summary.—Parts given from memory. Position given from memory, if children are quite advanced, and about ready to enter the next Step.

Students finally required to construct the "Penknife," as the "Shell."

Students write sketch on "Bunch of Grapes," according to the following heads and directions written on the blackboard:—

4. *A Bunch of Grapes.*

1. Parts found and named. (Lead children to distinguish the principal parts first, then the secondary.)

2. Position of Parts. (Of the principal parts with respect to each other. Next take the secondary parts of the stem; next of the berry.)

While considering the position of the principal parts with respect to each other, develop the idea of "cluster."

PLAN.

Children must discover the parts for themselves, and at first may do so in any order, teacher putting them down in the order of discovery. She rearranges them in proper order, according to direction of children, either at once or at the close of the lesson. See "Sketch on the Thimble."

It is important that children should be accustomed to recognize that there is an order; that "any way" will not do.

When the ideas of principal and secondary parts have been developed, children may be told to find the secondary parts of one principal part first, then the secondary part of another principal part, putting them down as found. This saves time. See "Sketch on Shell."

Children should be encouraged to give any names of parts they know, teacher supplying the rest when arbitrary; but, when the name is suggested by any circumstance or quality not beyond the knowledge of the children, it will be well to help them discover the name. Or she may give the name, and let the children say why given.

EXAMPLES OF NAMES WHICH MAY BE FOUND BY CHILDREN.

Bluebell. Body, spire, and beak (of a shell).
Handle. Dimple (of an apple).
Bowl (of a spoon). Ribs (of an umbrella).

Use of parts should be shown by children whenever possible. Position and uses not usually written on the board.

LIST OF SUBJECTS FOR PARTS.

Watch. Table. Spade.
Wheel. Chair. Fruit.
Shoe. Pail. Articles of jewelry.
Carpenter's tools. Kitchen utensils.

(Refer also to list on page .)

SECOND STEP.

In this Step the children are led to distinguish between the object and its qualities.

I.—An object is distinguished by its most simple and familiar qualities.

II.—The idea of one essential and distinctive quality is systematically developed.

I. Simple and Common Qualities of Objects.

As an example of a lesson on an object distinguished by its most simple and common qualities, take—

1. *Water.* (*Pattern.*)

What is in this cup? Water. (*Teacher pours a little on a piece of paper, or of linen.*) What has the water done to the paper? Made it wet. Now observe me. (*Teacher pours it out in drops.*) Does it hold together, now that I pour it out little by little? No; it forms itself into drops. Tell me, then, how the water is unlike the flint. The flint does not make the paper wet. It does not form itself into drops. Anything you can pour out so as to form it into drops, is called a *liquid*. What, then, can you say of water? Water is a liquid. Tell me some other liquids. Beer, milk, &c. Now look into the cup of water; what do you see? We see a mark at the bottom of the cup. Here is another cup with the same mark at the bottom; look at it. (*The teacher pours in a little milk.*) Look at the mark again. We cannot see it now. Why not? You have covered it with milk. But the mark in this cup is covered by water, and yet you see it; how is this? We can see through the water. What, then, can you say of water? We can see through water. Find some other thing in the room that you can see through. The glass. Look at the water again, and find out something more that you can say of it. It shines. Yes; it is *bright*. All of you repeat, "Water is bright." What color is the flint? Black. What can you say of the water? Look at these colors (*showing a red wafer, green leaf, &c.*). Which of these is the water like in color? None of them, teacher. What, then, must we say of it? Water has no color. (*The teacher calls upon some of the children to taste the water.*) What do you observe? It is cold. What taste do you perceive?—you cannot tell me. Has it any taste? No. What, then, can you say of it? It has no taste. Repeat together, "Water has no taste."

What use have you made of water to-day? We have washed ourselves with it. What quality of water makes it useful for washing? Its being liquid. Beer is also a liquid; why do you not wash in beer? We should smell the beer. Then you prefer water for washing, because it has no smell. What other objection is there against washing in beer? It would not make us clean; it would leave a brown stain. Why, then, is water a proper liquid to use for washing? Because it has neither smell nor color, and it cleanses from dirt. When are you very glad to be able to have water? When we are thirsty. Tell me, then, another use of water. It is useful for drinking. Water, you see, is essential to every one; can you tell me some liquids that we might do without? Yes; beer and gin. But what can we say of water?* What can we most easily procure? Water. Yes; and as every one needs water, God has kindly supplied every country with it in abundance.

Repeat together what you have found out about water. "Water is a liquid; we can see through it; it is bright; it has no color, nor any taste, nor any smell; it is cold; it is used for washing and for drinking; and because water is necessary to man, God has given to every country an abundant supply." †

Students construct lesson on "Milk," as "Water."

2. Lead.

What is this? Lead. Can any of you tell me where lead comes from? Does it come from an animal? Is it part of a plant? Where, then, does it come from? It comes out of the earth. God has not only given us animals and vegetables to be useful to us, but he has stored up in the earth a great many things for our use: tell me one of them. Lead. Now take this lead into your hand; what do you find? It is heavy. Look at it, and tell me what you see. Part of it is very bright, where it has just been cut. And what is it everywhere else? Dull. Repeat, "Lead, when freshly cut, is bright; when it has been some time in the air, it becomes dull." Look at it again. It is gray. Now feel it. It is hard. When you touch it, you find it hard; but look, what am I doing? Cutting it. Lead, to the touch, is hard, but it is easily cut. I put some of it into water; what happened to the lead when I put it into the water? It fell to the bottom. Would the feather have done so? No. Why did the lead sink?

---

* The teacher might remark upon the goodness of God in abundantly supplying every one everywhere with that liquid which is essential to comfort; whilst the noxious spirit is obtained by art and labor, and at great cost.

† It is most desirable that children should be early taught to write, or print; and printing on their slates all they can recollect of their lessons, forms a most improving exercise. In mixed schools this would furnish employment to one set of children while the teacher is engaged with another.

Because it is heavy. Did you know it was heavy before you saw it sink? Yes; we felt it heavy in our hands.

Is there any child here whose father works in lead? Yes;* John's father works in lead. What is he called? A plumber. People who work in lead are called plumbers. Well, John, tell us what your father does with lead. He makes windows. What sort of windows—those like the windows of this school room? No; windows made with little bits of glass. Where do you generally see such windows—in large houses, or in small ones? What is the use of the lead in windows such as these? It fastens the pieces of glass together. What have our windows for this purpose? Wood. And what is used to fasten the glass to the wood? Putty. But in church windows, what is sometimes used? Lead. Yes; lead is used to fasten the glass together. Now, John, what other use does your father make of lead? He makes pipes. All who can tell me what is the use of leaden pipes, hold up their hands. To convey water. Yes; to convey water from one place to another. Who can tell me any other use of lead? It is used for cisterns. What is the use of cisterns? They hold water. What use do fishermen make of lead? They put it on their nets. Why? To make one edge of the net sink in the water. Why does the lead make that part of the net sink? Because it is very heavy.

Well, now repeat all you have said about lead. "Lead comes out of the earth; when it is freshly cut it is very bright; but after it has been in the air for some time, it becomes dull; it is very heavy; its color is gray; it is hard to the touch, but it is easily cut; when put into water, it sinks; people who work in lead are called plumbers; they use it to fasten together the glass of church windows; to make pipes to convey water, and cisterns of lead to hold it. Lead is also used in fishermen's nets."

Students construct lesson on "Wood," as "Lead."

Attention of students should be directed to the general plan

* It may be that the child of a plumber is present at the lesson; it must occasionally happen that some have seen the materials brought before them at school, used by their parents or others. A teacher should always make the most of any information the children may already possess.

of these lessons. The children are led to notice first the qualities, then the uses, and lastly those qualities on which the uses depend.

LIST OF OBJECTS.

This it is unnecessary to give, as any common objects will do.

LIST OF QUALITIES TO BE DEVELOPED AT THIS STEP.

Simple qualities referring to Substance; as, hard, soft, tough, brittle, liquid, &c.
" " Surface; as, rough, smooth, plane, flat.
" " Condition; as, hot, cold, cool, warm, dry, moist, full, empty.
" " Shape; as, tapering, pointed, rounded, jagged, broken, torn, &c.
" " Direction; as, straight, curved, crooked. See "Lessons on Form."
" " Size; as, large, small, thin, thick, deep, shallow, etc.
" " Color; as, red, blue, green. See "Lessons on Color."
" " Number; as, one, two, &c., up to ten.

After a course of these lessons, the children, being made acquainted with common objects and their common qualities, may receive a few recapitulatory lessons on several of these in combination.

EXAMPLE.

3. *Sketch of a Lesson on "Distinguishing Objects by their Qualities."*

I. *Introduction.*—Bring before the children a large, round, ripe apple—a sheet of thin, smooth, pink paper—a slender, pointed cedar pencil—a piece of narrow, blue silk ribbon—an oblong, shallow wooden box—a square, white linen pocket handkerchief. Let the children give the name of each object, teacher writing the initial letter of each on the board as given, and requiring children to say what each letter stands for.

II. *Ideas Developed.*—Teacher requires the children to say something of the apple as to size (large); as to shape (round); as to fitness for food (ripe). How other apples may be unlike this. What we can say of this apple. (It is a large, round, ripe apple.) Children to describe the paper as to texture (thin); as to surface (smooth); as to color (pink). Other papers mentioned unlike this—tissue, brown, &c. How we can describe this sheet of paper. (It is a sheet of thin, smooth, pink paper.) Children to describe the pencil, as to girth (slender). Compare with thicker pencil, as to condition (pointed). Compare with uncut one, as to material (wood and lead). Tell them the wood is called cedar.

Proceed in this way with the remaining objects.

Summary.—Children to name the objects from the board, and describe them from memory.

Students select six objects, upon which they construct a similar sketch.

II. Essential and Distinctive Qualities of Objects.

For the idea of one essential and distinctive quality systematically developed, take—

1. *Sketch on the Development of the Idea of Adhesive Gum, for Adhesive.*

MATTER.	METHOD.
1. Gum will stick.	1. Show this by experiment with postage stamp.
2. Gum is therefore said to be adhesive.	2. Term given. Questioned on. S. R. and W. B.
3. Glue, melted sealing wax, and molasses, are also adhesive.	3. Such examples found by the children.
4. All things that will stick to other objects, are said to be adhesive.	4. Children led to draw this general conclusion, which is committed to memory.

Students construct sketch on "Idea of Inflammable," as "Adhesive."

Toward the close of this Step, two or three qualities connected, or contrasted, may be taken together.

EXAMPLE.

2. *Idea of Transparent, Semi-transparent, and Translucent.*

1. Bring before the children a piece of glass and a key. Hold the key behind a slate, also behind the piece of glass, and require them to notice the difference. What they can say of the glass, that they cannot say of the slate. Give the term that distinguishes things we can see through, and let the children repeat, "Glass, because we can see through it, is said to be *transparent.*" Require them to give examples of things they can see through, as well as through glass; also what such things are said to be.

2. Place a knife with a white handle in some tea, and again behind the glass. What the glass shows about the knife, which the tea does not (the color). Lead them to recognize that they can clearly see through the glass, but only partly through the tea. Refer again to the term which distinguishes things through which we can clearly see, and let them try to find a term for anything through which we can partly see. Give the term, thus: Tea, because we can see partly through it, is said to be *semi-transparent.* Explain the meaning of *semi.* Get examples of both terms, to be written on the board.

3. Place the knife behind a china plate. Children to say how it looks. (They cannot see it at all.) Hold the plate, with the knife behind it, opposite the window; the shape of the knife can be seen. Explain to the children that the light can pass through the plate, except where the knife stops its passage. What they can say of the knife. (It is opaque—idea previously developed.) What they can say of the plate. We can see light through it. Give the term *translucent,* with definition. Get examples, and write on the board as before.

Summary.—Children say how well they can see through anything transparent (clearly). What they cannot see through anything which is semi-transparent (color). What only they can see through anything which is translucent (form). In conclusion, give the general definition of each term.

Students construct sketch on three kinds of Roundness (Globular, Cylindrical, and Circular), as sketch on "Transparent," &c.

As a final exercise, the children may be tested in discovering objects by the mention of their qualities. Teacher says: I have something hidden in my hand (a blade of grass). It is long; it is narrow; it is pointed at one end; it is flexible; fibrous; vegetable; green. Speaking thus, the teacher pauses between each term, allowing the children to judge as she proceeds, and making them name the quality which led to the discovery of the object. Sealing wax:—It is long; it is smooth; it is colored; it is inflammable; fusible; impressible. Drinking glass:—It is bright; it is hard; smooth; sonorous; hollow, and transparent. Judgment must be shown in putting the more general qualities first, and the more special afterward.

LIST FOR DEVELOPING IDEAS AS TO THE QUALITIES OF OBJECTS.

Paper, as being	Inflammable.
Leather	Tough.
Glass	Brittle.
Cotton	Soft.
Cork	Light.
Card or Cane, String	Flexible.
Cloth	Pliable.
Whalebone, India rubber, Sponge	Elastic.
Water	Liquid.
Wood	Solid.
Loaf Sugar	Sparkling.
A Mirror, or Water,	Reflective.
Sponge	Absorbent.
Bread	Porous.
Chalk	Crumbling.
Flax and Hemp	Fibrous.
Gum	Soluble.
Lead	Fusible.

Oil-skin	Water-proof.
Leather	Durable.
Sealing-wax	Impressible.
Glue	Adhesive.
Camphor	Odorous.
Lavender	Fragrant.
Horn or Gum	Semi-transparent.
Cloves	Aromatic.
Water	Tasteless.
Ginger	Pungent.
Salt or Sand	Granular.

LIST OF CONNECTED OR CONTRASTED QUALITIES, FOR RECAPITULATION.

1. Soft, hard, tough.
2. Light, heavy, buoyant.
3. Rough, smooth, polished, adhesive.
4. Stiff, pliable, flexible, elastic.
5. Brittle, rotten, fragile, friable, pulverable.
6. Fibrous, granulous.
7. Inflammable, fusible, soluble.
8. Porous, absorbent, waterproof.

THIRD STEP.

In this Step a more thorough examination of the object is made. We consider

>Parts, Qualities, Uses.
>Adaptation of Qualities to Use.
>Qualities as discovered by the senses, or by *simple* experiment.
>The less obvious Qualities.
>Qualities as depending on one another.
>Adaptation of Material or Structure to Use.

Sometimes two objects are taken for comparison in respect to any of these points.

In this Step, as the subjects of the lessons go beyond the range of the child's immediate experience, some information may be given. Let it be remembered, however, that the mind of the child may be exercised as much on information given him by the teacher, as on anything he can discover for himself. The teacher who tells the child a fact, requires him to state the cause, or the effect, or some other relation. For everything told to the pupil, the latter should be required in return to tell something bearing on what has been told to him. Tell him that a substance cast into the form of a hollow cylinder is stronger than the same quantity of matter in a solid form; let him say why the barrel of a quill is hollow, and not solid. Tell him what places the kingfisher frequents, and let him infer the character of its food. Tell him that the fur of animals thickens at a certain period of the year; let him discover when and why. Tell him that the concentric circles in the trunk of a tree are not equal in diameter; let him find any circumstances likely to account for the fact.

1. *Sketch on an Egg.*

Point.—Parts, qualities, uses, and qualities on which the uses depend.

MATTER.	METHOD.
I. *Parts.*—The parts of an egg are the shell, lining, albumen, envelope, air bag, and yelk.	I. *Parts.*—Show an egg, and let the children name its parts. Break the egg, and show each part, correcting any errors they have made. Let the children observe how these parts are placed with respect to each other: *i. e.*, the shell is outside, the lining is inside the shell, &c. Write the parts, and their position, on the board. Draw the term *lining* from the children. Give the terms *albumen, air bag, envelope.*
II. *Qualities.*—The shell is oval, white,	II. *Qualities.*—Develop *oval*, by comparing the egg with a sphere. Develop

hard, opaque, and brittle. The lining is translucent, white, thin, and tough. The albumen is semi-transparent, adhesive, and liquid. The yelk is yellow, opaque, and semi-fluid.

III. *Uses, and qualities on which uses depend.*—Eggs are used as food for man, and then must be lightly cooked, or we should not readily digest them. As food for young birds, they must be boiled hard like leather.

Eggs are put into cakes and puddings, because adhesive and light. The albumen is used to mend china and glass, because adhesive. The shells are good for fowls to mix with their food.

hardness, by comparing it with an orange. *Brittle*, by referring to the experiment of breaking the egg just performed. Develop *translucent, semi-transparent,* and *opaque* together, by comparing the different parts of the egg one with another, but apply the terms separately to the proper substances. Develop *semi-fluid*, by comparison of a solid and a fluid. Write the qualities on the board.

III.—Draw from the children, by questions, the uses of eggs, and the qualities on which the uses depend. By comparison of eggs as prepared for our food, and for that of little birds, lead them to see that birds must have a much stronger digestion than we. From the use made of the albumen, let them say what quality it must possess. This will prepare them for the next question—why we put eggs into puddings? We need not make a thick, heavy paste of flour: a little flour will do, or even crumbled bread, when we have enough eggs.

Summary.—Read from the board, and repeated from memory. Students construct sketch on "Peach," as the "Egg."

2. *Sketch on Comparison of Orange and Apple.*

Point.—Parts, qualities, uses, and qualities on which uses depend.

MATTER.	METHOD.
I. *Resemblances.*	I. *Resemblances.*
1. Qualities. Both are natural, vegetable, juicy, (nearly) spheri-	1. That these fruits are *natural*, is brought out by reference to the works of God and man, children giving examples.

cal, wholesome, and pleasant to the taste.

2. Parts. Both have seeds in the midst, peel, and pulp.

II. *Differences.*

1. Pulp. The pulp of an orange is yellow, divided, and without a core. The pulp of an apple is white, undivided, and contains a core. It is harder than the pulp of an orange.

2. Peel. Orange peel is thick, somewhat rough, and orange color. Apple peel is thin, smooth, and varies in color.

III. *Uses, and qualities on which uses depend.*

1. Apples are made into sauce, tarts, cider, &c. Are best when cooked.

2. Oranges make candy, marmalade, wine. Are best uncooked. Each eaten because pleasant to the taste, and wholesome.

IV. *Growth, cultivation, &c.*

1. Apples are grown in the Northern and

Vegetable, by referring to the different kingdoms. *Juicy,* by experiment (cutting fruit). *Spherical,* by comparison with a coin or ring. *Wholesome,* by reference to a horse chestnut; distinguished from nourishing, by comparison with an egg. *Pleasant to the taste,* by experiment, or an appeal to memory. (W. B.)

2. Children find out the corresponding parts, and the position of each, by observation.

II. *Differences* in the arrangement, substance, color, and in presence and absence of core, brought out by observation.

III. Appeal to experience and reason of children.

IV.

1. Teacher refers to map, and points out States where apples grow. Children de-

Middle States. They require a moderately warm climate. A plantation of apples is called an orchard.

2. Oranges grow in the Southern States and Cuba. They require a hot climate. A plantation of oranges is called an orangery.

cide as to the kind of climate that is necessary for their growth.

2. Proceed the same for oranges.

Summary.—Write heads on the slate. Children give matter.

Third head left out, because not essential to be committed to memory.

Students construct sketch on "Kid Glove and Kid Slipper," as "Orange and Apple."

3. *Sketch on Comparison of Cork and Sponge.*

Point.—Quality on which uses depend, and dependence of one quality on another.

MATTER.	METHOD.
I.—1. Cork is natural.	I.—1. Brought out by reference to the works of man.
2. Cork is vegetable.	2. Children asked where it comes from. Told that it is the bark of a tree.
3. Cork is foreign.	3. Children told where the tree grows. Map referred to.
4. Cork is light.	4. Children referred to water as the standard weight. The lightness of cork shown by experiment.
5. Cork is brown.	5. Show different specimens, and let children name the color.
6. Cork is compressible and elastic.	6. By experiment.
7. Cork is porous.	7. By direct observation with a magnifying glass, and comparison with dense substances, as minerals.
8. Cork is impervious and buoyant.	8. By experiment.

II. *Qualities dependent one on another.*
1. Cork is buoyant, not merely because it is light, but because it is impervious. Cork is impervious because its pores are small, and but little connected.
2. Sponge is absorbent, because its pores are large and connected.

III. Sponge is a natural animal substance, light, brown, compressible, elastic, and porous.

IV. *Uses, and qualities on which uses depend.*
1. Cork is used for life boats, cork legs and arms, because buoyant and light; for soles of shoes, because impervious; for stoppers of bottles, because impervious, elastic, and compressible.
2. Sponge is useful for washing, because absorbent, compressible, elastic, light, tough, and durable.

II.
1. Children led to discover the buoyancy of cork. They decide whether light or heavy things float on water, and, by experiment, which is the lighter—cork or sponge. Yet, as they perceive, the sponge soon sinks, while the cork still floats. Why this is?
2. Cut the sponge, to show the communication between the external openings and the central channels. Children say what must happen if we put such a structure under water, and why. Try the experiment.

III. For *animal*, children asked where we find sponge? What it is, and a little of the natural history given. Mention the term *marine*. Children give other examples of marine substances, as coral, &c. Children required to mention qualities of sponge, the same as those possessed by cork.

IV.
1. Brought out by referring to previous knowledge (teacher giving any needful information as to uses). In bringing out the qualities on which uses depend, the reason is appealed to.

2. Brought out by getting children to describe the effect of the process of washing, on the sponge. It receives water, because it is absorbent; it discharges the water when used, because it is compressible; it resumes its former shape, and becomes fit for use as before, because it is elastic; it is easily lifted and moved, because it is light; it lasts for a long time in constant use, and is not worn away, because it is tough and durable.

Summary.—Children arrange and classify the "Matter" under "Resemblances and Differences of Cork and Sponge," as:

RESEMBLANCES.	DIFFERENCES.
Both are natural, foreign, light, brown, porous, compressible, and elastic.	Cork is a vegetable substance. Sponge is an animal substance. Cork is impervious. Sponge is absorbent. Cork is buoyant, because light and impervious; impervious on account of the smallness and want of connection of its pores. Sponge, though lighter than cork, is not buoyant, because absorbent; and absorbent, because of the size and open structure of its pores.

Students construct sketch on "Comparison of Salt and Sugar," like "Cork and Sponge."

4. *Sketch on Water.*

Points.—Qualities on which uses depend. Less obvious qualities.

MATTER.	METHOD.
1. Water is tasteless and refreshing; therefore useful to drink.	1. Children say why they like to drink water in summer. Whether there is anything they like better to drink. Whether they would like to drink cider or tea only whenever they were thirsty, and at every meal. (They would get tired of it.) Why they cannot get tired of water. Effect of drinking water when very thirsty.
2. Water is a solvent, without smell or color; therefore useful for washing, for fertilizing the ground, and for dissolving various substances.	2. *Experiment.*—Put a little sugar into water. Children say what the water does. Are told what water is. Find other things of which water is a solvent. Refer to water as nourishing plants, and explain that it does so by dissolving substances in the ground which are their food. Refer to use of water in washing. As beer is a solvent, lead children to find why it would not do to wash in that.
3. Water is reflec-	3. *Experiment.*—Water will serve as a

tive, which makes it a beautiful object in a landscape.

mirror. Children find what does better than water, and why. Refer to the condition of people before mirrors were invented. Objects commonly mirrored in water. Effect of this reflection on the scene.

4. Water takes the shape of the vessel that holds it.

4. *Experiment* with—1, plate; 2, basin; 3, vial. Children describe these as to extent—1, wide and shallow; 2, not so wide, but deeper; 3, narrow across, but deeper. Fill each with water, and measure in different directions, showing how the extent of the water corresponds with that of the vessel. Children called on to say what will happen if the contents of the vessels be exchanged.

5. Water exists in different states—sometimes as a liquid, sometimes as a solid, and sometimes as a vapor.

5. *Experiment.*—Refer to the idea of liquid. Refer to a little girl who went for water on a very cold day. She found only ice. How this differed from liquid water. She put the solid ice into the kettle—put the kettle on the fire. Second change water underwent (vapor). Children to say where they expect to find much ice, and why there is often so little water in very hot countries.

6. Water is found in different places—in the clouds overhead, in the caves of the earth, underneath and on the surface of the ground.

6. By reference to the uses of water, and the sufferings caused by the scarcity of it, show the goodness of God in supplying it abundantly. Children say where it is to be found. Refer to where the vapor went, and tell them the clouds are made of this vapor. Thus some water is always floating in the air, whence it falls in rain. Some in hollow places in the earth; hence it gushes out in springs, and there is generally plenty on the surface of the ground, that we may get it easily.

As each point is worked out, let children form a sentence, which write on the board as found in "Matter."

For summary, read matter from the board, and rewrite from memory.

Students construct sketch on "Mercury," or "Air," as "Water."

5. *Sketch on Loaf Sugar.*

Points.—Qualities as discovered by the senses. Less obvious qualities.

MATTER.	METHOD.
1. Sugar is white, sparkling, opaque.	1. Present a piece of loaf sugar, and ask the children to give the name, and tell what they can discover by looking at it. Compare it with a piece of crystal. Points of difference—one translucent, the other opaque. Points of resemblance—hard, white, bright. Compare the brightness of both objects—one is bright all over, the other full of little bright points. A thing clear, bright all over, is said to be *lucid*. A thing full of little bright points, is said to be *sparkling*. Children name other objects that sparkle, and find by comparison that things that sparkle have usually a rough surface.
2. Sugar is rough and hard.	2. Bring out *rough* and *hard*, by asking children what they can say after feeling of it.
3. Sugar is sweet.	3. By taste.
4. Sugar is fusible, brittle, granulous, and crystallized.	4. Bring out *fusible, soluble, brittle,* and *granulous,* by direct observation and experiment. *Crystallized,* by aid of microscope. (*a*) Children compare the magnified grains with each other, and find that they are all the same shape. (*b*) Children notice that they are solid, by reference to the broken grains. Whether they find anything inside? (*c*) Produce some of the simplest solids, and some amorphous stones, which the grains must resemble. Why? Because some are broken, and others are whole. Show one part of a solid concealing the other part. What children expect to find on the other side—corresponding faces and edges. Will know that crystals re alike. Give term *regular.* Tell children that

OBJECTS. 113

	substances formed in little grains, all of which are regular solids, are said to be crystallized. Refer to sugar as juice of a plant. Children state the origin and original form of sugar (liquid). Produce various specimens of crystals, and after drawing attention to them as such (being regular), tell them that every one of these was once a liquid, and has now become a regular solid. Examples found by children of a liquid that crystallizes (snow). Might be followed by lesson on the forms, into which many objects crystallize.
5. Sugar is vegetable, cultivated, and manufactured.	5. Bring out *vegetable*, by reference to the sugar cane, of which show a specimen. *Cultivated*, by comparison with grass, &c. *Manufactured*, by comparison of the cane with its product (sugar). Some information given as to the processes the article undergoes in the course of manufacture.

Points, as worked out, written on the board.

Summary.—Erase "Matter." Children say which of the qualities they have considered have been discovered by sight; which by feeling; by taste; by experiment; and by reference to previous knowledge. Write the qualities, as the children shall dictate, in separate columns.

Qualities discovered by more than one sense, may be written in separate columns, thus:—

Sense of Sight.	Sense of Feeling.	Sense of Taste.	Experiment.	Previous Knowledge.
White.	Rough(²).	Sweet.	Fusible.	Cultivated.
Sparkling.	Hard.		Soluble.	Manufactured.
Opaque.			Brittle.	
Rough(¹).			Granulous.	
			Crystallized.	

Students construct sketch on "Bread," as "Sugar."

6 *Sketch on a Mould Candle.*

Points.—Material and Structure. Adaptation of each to uses.

I. *Shape and Substance.*—*The candle is long*—length compared with girth. *Slender*—girth compared with length. Term given—*Nearly cylindrical.* Number and kind of sides of a cylinder observed. In what respects the candle differs. Description given—*It is made of tallow and cotton, the tallow outside, the cotton inside, where it forms a loop at one end.* Materials and their position observed. Terms *wick* and *loop* given.

II. *Qualities.*

1. *Tallow is an animal substance*—brought out by reference to whence we get it. *It is white*—by sight. *Adhesive*—a little dropped on some paper. *Impressible*—the candle scratched by a match or pin. *Solid or liquid, according to the temperature*—candle lighted, and the part nearest the flame compared with the rest. What makes the difference?

2. *Cotton wick is white and soft*—by looking and feeling. *Tough*—by reference to breaking a candle; what part remains unbroken. *Fibrous*—compared with chalk, which is formed of little grains. *Is a vegetable substance*—children brought to this conclusion by being told that all vegetable substances are fibrous. What, then, is cotton? How they know this, &c. Told a little about the cotton tree; that it grows in warm climates, &c. Picture shown. *Is absorbent*—lighted wick observed. *Is inflammable, though less so than tallow*—saturated and unsaturated wick lighted. Which takes fire the sooner, and why? *Burns to ashes, and then ceases to absorb.* What we do with the ashes, and why?

III. *Uses, and qualities on which the use depends.*—*Candles are burned to give light. This use depends on the fact that the wick is inflammable and absorbent, and the tallow inflammable and fusible.* Tallow and wick compared—which takes fire soonest? In what respects they are alike. What the wick would do without the tallow—smoulder away without giving much light. The tallow without the wick—flow in all directions while blazing away. What the wick does to the tallow—absorbs it. Then "the wick must be not only inflammable, but absorbent." In what state the tallow is when absorbed—in a liquid state. "Tallow must be not only inflammable, but must be fusible."

Matter put on the board point by point, as worked out. Read by the children. Erased by the teacher, who writes:

I. State the parts of the candle.

II. State on what qualities—1, of the tallow; 2, of the wick—the use of the candle depends.

Children reproduce the lesson on their slates.

Students construct sketch on "Match," as "Candle."

7. *Sketch on a Knife and Fork.*

Points.—Material and Structure.—Adaptation of each to use.

I. *Objects Observed and Compared.*—1. *Resemblance.*—Traced by the children. As to use—both used in taking food. Substance—partly mineral and partly animal. Make—both have handles, shanks, and points.

2. *Difference.*—In use—one to cut up the food, the other to keep it firm and convey it to the mouth. In make—the one has a blade, the other a shank spreading out into three prongs. Why this difference?

II. *Adaptation of Make to Use.*—Children to determine this. Handles and shanks to both. Why? The blade of the knife—why thin at one edge? Why blunt at back?—to allow the pressure of the finger in cutting; also to strengthen the blade. The fork—its shank—why longer than in the knife? Why partly visible, and not, as in the knife, hidden by the handle? Its use. Prongs—their number, and the reason for this number. Why narrowing towards the points? Why edged, and not quite cylindrical?—to give them a firmer hold in the meat. Use of the shoulder.

III. *Adaptation of Material to Make.*—Children to discover this by comparing it with various other substances.

1. *The Blade of the Knife.*—Why not of stone?—a stone blade could not give way when, being used, it might happen to come in contact with any other substance, as gristle, &c. It is

not flexible. Why not of lead?—a leaden blade would bend, lose its shape, and become useless. Not elastic. Why not of tortoise shell?—a tortoise shell blade as likely to break as to yield. Why not of wood?—a blade made of wood, or of any of the other substances, would not take an edge sufficiently fine and sharp. The last two substances not sufficiently hard or tenacious.

Requisites for the blade of a knife determined by the children—*flexibility, elasticity, tenacity, hardness.* Why not of iron, which possesses all these qualities?—the blade must be very smooth, and capable of taking a high polish, to cut thin, smooth slices. Substance possessing all these requisites—steel.

2. *The metallic part of the fork.*—Qualities required—tenacity—hardness—capability of taking polish. Steel required for this also.

3. *Handles.*—Must be light. Why?—the metal is heavy. Smooth. Why?—that the touch may be pleasant to the hand, and that they may be easily cleaned. On these accounts commonly made of bone—the more expensive ones of ivory.

Summary.—The children required to reproduce—first, orally from the board, and afterward in writing on their own slates.

Students construct sketch on "Pen and Pencil," as "Knife and Fork."

8. *Sketch on the Spider's Web.*

Point.—Material and Structure. Adaptation of each to use.

MATTER.	METHOD.
1. The garden spider makes a web in which to take its prey.	1. Draw a diagram of the web on the board, getting the children to notice the kind of lines made—whether vertical or horizontal. Finally, let them say what object the whole represents, and of what use it is.
2. The spider's web is made from a thick glue contained in its body. The creature	2. Question as to material of which web is made. What it is like? How they know it is not cotton, silk, or hair? Having exercised their reason and curiosity,

has five or six holes in its sides, out of which the glue oozes. This substance is very tenacious, and can be drawn into the finest threads.

3. (*a*) To begin her web, the spider presses her side against the wall; then a drop of glue comes out, which sticks.
(*b*) She then jumps to the other side, carrying the thread with her. She goes backward and forward several times, ever adding to the thickness of the thread.
(*c*) She next goes from corner to corner, and then across, until the whole space is filled up with threads regularly arranged.
(*d*) She fastens the sides to the wall by threads projecting from the outer edge.
(*e*) Lastly, she makes a little cell in the middle underneath, in which she can hide while watching for prey.
4. The material of the web is a tenacious

tell them. Show some ravelled silk, and tell them it would take many of the spider's threads to equal one of these—thus giving them an idea of their thinness. Draw threads from some heated sealing-wax, to develop the idea of *tenacious*—give the term. Let them apply it to spiders' threads. Get other examples. If not readily given, refer to melted glass, metal, or even molasses. Then, from experiment with the sealing wax, the children will see that the more the threads are drawn out, the thinner they must become.

3. (*a*) Tell children.

(*b*) Illustrate this on the board. Let the children say how the doubling, trebling, &c., will affect the thread. Whether there would be one thick thread, or several thin ones, and why?

(*c*) Illustrate this by drawing lines in order on the board. Let children notice how closely the threads come together.

(*d*) Draw from the children how this can be fastened to the wall, and what quality enables the threads to fasten themselves.

(*e*) Tell them of the cell; of its situation out of light. Let them say of what use it can be to the spider.

4. Facts, from memory—results, by reason; for instance, let the children discover

glue. Its threads are thin, drawn closely together, and wonderfully strong, first to catch, and then to hold the prey. | what would happen if a fly came to a web, the threads of which were wide apart, or made of a very fragile substance. Refer to an insect in molasses or cream; show that the more it struggles, the more it is stuck fast.

In conclusion, refer to the discomfort of flies in summer, the mischief they do, &c. Let the children say of what use the spider is to man. Refer to the wisdom of God in creating the spider.

Students construct sketch on "Cocoon," as "Spider's Web."

9. *Sketch on the Honeycomb.*

Point.—Material and Structure. Adaptation of the latter to uses—so brought out as to develop the idea of Instinct.

I. *Material.*—Made by bees of a substance obtained from flowers, and called wax. Usually found in a kind of box called a hive. Refer to the condition of bees in wild countries, where no hives are provided for them. What they occupy—cavities in rocks, holes in trees, &c. Refer to the reed baskets used in Africa.

II.. *Structure.*—Why the bees make the comb—to put their honey in. How adapted to *this* purpose—by being full of cells. Give the term *cellular.* Also to keep the young bees in before they are able to fly about, &c. The young of the bee is round in shape. Children say of what shape they would expect their cradles to be. Whether the cells *are* of this shape—they are six-sided. Give the term *hexagonal.* Why hexagonal, and not round? To bring this out, draw two diagrams on the board, one representing round, and the other hexagonal cells. Direct attention to the spaces between the round cells. Suppose this space filled up with wax, as it would be in the honeycomb, of what use would the wax be there? None; it would be a waste of material. But suppose the bee to take away with its pincers all the wax between the cells, except a thin thread; this would save the wax, but what the effect would be—this would be too fragile; the weight of the young bee would crush it. How wonderful to see the little bee meet these difficulties, by making hexagonal cells, which take the least amount of wax consistent with the proper strength of the comb, and are just as good to keep the young bees in.

III. *The faculty of the constructor.*—Refer to themselves, their work, their lessons (as writing). At first they do a thing badly, then better, and at length very well. But the bee makes the first honeycomb as well as the last. If several men had to make each a cradle, and without seeing the work of the rest, their workmanship would be very different; perhaps, too, the material and the design. The work of all bees is just alike in all respects. The bees in the garden of Eden worked as the bees in their gardens to-day. The faculty which enables the bee thus to work, is called *instinct*. Children give examples of instinct as shown by other animals. Children say how they recognize instinct. (*a*) Instinct never improves; its work is as perfect first as last. (*b*) The work is the same as done by all other creatures of the same kind.

Instead of summary, draw from the children a statement of the advantage of hexagonal over round cells, and definition of instinct.

Students construct sketch on "Bird's Nest," as "Honeycomb."

10. *Sketch on the Palm Tree.*

Point.—To exercise the children on information given.

I. *Fruit.*—Show this to the children, and let them say what kind of substance it is. Get or give the name of the fruit. Let them describe it as to *shape, color, parts, flavor*. Let them taste it. Write on the board the following:—The date is a fruit of an oblong shape; it has a tough, smooth skin, a pulpy part, and a very hard stone in the centre.

II. *Tree.*—Tell the children that the dates have been gathered from a tree which grows in a country far away. Describe the country as having large sandy plains, arid and barren. Refer to the heat of the climate, and the intense thirst caused by this.

The condition of travellers after marching many miles. They see a grove of tall trees. Name of these. How travellers feel when they are covered from the hot, burning sun, and can eat the fruit. Draw picture of the tree, and direct attention of the children to the height the trunk of the tree grows without leaves. Tell them it grows from sixty to one hundred feet. To give the idea of the height, compare it with the length of the school room, fence, or yard. (W. B.): "The date palm grows in the desert. It has a trunk which is from sixty to one hundred feet high."

III. *Uses.*—Children to name those parts of the tree likely to be useful to man, and the uses made of them. Correct errors, and supply information. (W. B.): "The fruit is used for food. The stones are bruised for the seeds, which are given to the camels. The leaves are made into fans, baskets, and hats. The wood is used for building houses."

Summary.—Recapitulation of lesson from memory.

Students construct a lesson on the "Cedar," as the "Palm."

LIST OF IDEAS TO BE DEVELOPED AND TERMS TO BE GIVEN, ETC., IN THIS STEP.

1. Terms expressing less obvious qualities; as, buoyant, ductile, malleable, tenacious, sonorous, stimulating, fertilizing, conservative or preservative, aromatic, astringent, medicinal, effervescent, emollient, oily, mixable, irregular shaped, slimy, &c.

2. Terms expressing ideas referring to structure; as, woven, cellular, tubular, netted, serrated, indented, crystallized, concave, convex, spiral, &c.

3. Terms expressing ideas referring to the nature and condition of substances; as, metallic, gaseous, fluid, watery, sweet, saline, vinous, non-conductor, fermented, manufactured, exported, imported, &c.

FOURTH STEP

Includes Classification of Objects, and so leads up to science.

Also, Classification of Qualities. Lessons on the senses themselves should be given at this step.

Where the course of instruction does not contain a course of lessons on Actions, which properly lead to manufactures, arts, &c., some consideration of these subjects may properly be referred to Objects, Fourth Step.

1. *Sketch to Develop the Idea of Distinction between the Essential and Accidental Qualities of an Object.*

I.—Teacher presents a number of various pieces of sealing wax, telling the children to find, state, and classify the differences. They are red, blue, green, &c.; therefore they differ in color.

One is thick, slender, long; therefore they differ in size.

One is flattened, another cylindrical; therefore they differ in form.

By experiment, one is hard, softened, fused, whole, broken, stamped; therefore they differ in condition.

II.—Children required to state the resemblances—vegetable, fusible, impressible, and adhesive. Children led to see that we can have no sealing wax which has not the four qualities; while we often have pieces not red, not cylindrical, or not stamped. Terms and definitions given. "The qualities which a thing must have to be itself, are called essential qualities. Qualities which it may have, but can be itself without having, are called accidental."

2. *Sketch to Develop the Idea of the Distinction between Generic and Specific Qualities.*

I.—The teacher, standing before a large table covered with a variety of objects, including pictures of birds, which can readily be classified, desires first one and then another of the children to group all that should go together. Children group—

Swallow,	Robin,	Kingfisher,	.	.	as Birds.
Silver,	Gold,	Iron,	.	.	as Metals.
Wheat,	Maize,	Oats,	.	.	as Grain.
Water,	Milk,	Ink,	.	.	as Liquids.
Tulip,	Lily,	Rose,	.	.	as Flowers.

II.—1. Children to say how they know a flower when they see it. Definition worked out from their answers, and written on the board, thus: "A flower is the most beautiful part of a plant. It usually has colored leaflets, and contains the seed."

2. Children say how they know a rose when they see it. Definition worked out as before. "The rose is a flower distinguished by a number of stamens, which rise from the top of the seed vessel. Often it is pink in color, round in shape; has many leaves, and a fragrant scent."

III. *Differences in terms distinguished.*—Ask children whether we can call all flowers *roses*? No; for some are violets, some are pinks, &c. Whether there are more flowers or roses in the world, and why? Children thus led to see that *flower* is the name of a large class, while *rose* is the name of a smaller class contained in the large class. Compare this with a school, and its classes.

IV. *Names given and applied.*—Tell the children that words which express the large class are said to be *generic*, and words which express the small class said to be *specific*.

1. Let them apply these terms to flower and rose, respectively.

2. Give jewel as the name of a large class, and let the children give the name of some smaller class belonging to it, as diamond, &c.

3. Then give trout as the name of a small class. Children to find the name of the large class to which it belongs.

Children give as many examples of generic and specific qualities as needful. Put down all the examples in two columns under the proper heads, as the children shall direct.

Examples.

GENERIC.	SPECIFIC.
Picture.	Painting.
Pillar.	Column.
Edifice.	School house.
Temple.	Church.
Furniture.	Chair.
Ornament.	Bracelet.
Servant.	Slave.
Feature.	Nose.

3. Sketch of a Lesson on Shells and their Inmates.

MATTER.

I. *Use.*—Shells are found in the sea; also in rivers, and some on land. They serve both for the homes and armor of certain animals. These have no bones, and cold, white, or colorless blood. These, being soft, are called mollusks.

II. *Of what composed.*—Shells are made by the animals which inhabit them. They are composed of three substances: 1, lime, a sort of chalk, which the creature obtains from the water; 2, a glue given out by it from its own body—this varies in color, and gives color to the shells; 3, part of the skin of the animal,

METHOD.

I.—Bring before the children some shells. Let them say what they are. Where found? Supply information as to shells found inland, and by reference to them as marine objects, lead children to conclude that wherever they are found the sea must once have been. Show an oyster shell containing its inmate. Children state the use of the shell. The last use brought out by reference to its defenceless condition without it. Let a child press the oyster; then press his own chin or forehead. The difference, and its cause. What they can say of the oyster. (S. R.): "The oyster has no bones." Another difference discovered by touch. Its cause. (S. R.): "The blood of the oyster is cold." Refer to the color of our blood. Cut the oyster, to show the watery liquid. (S. R.): "The blood of the oyster is colorless." Children told that all animals living in shells resemble the oyster in all these points, and on account of their soft, boneless structure, are called mollusks. Children dictate the matter of this head. (W. B.)

II.—Refer to storms at sea, the waves dashing the shells against rocks, &c., and lead children to see that shells require to be made very strong. Show a specimen of the lime as one constituent part. Where the animals can find such a substance. Refer to the limestone rocks of coasts, and coating inside teakettle. Whether this substance alone would make a good shell (too brittle). What more required—some substance not brittle, the reverse of brittle, to mix with it. Show glue. Let children recognize it as an animal substance, and show the quality on which its use as a constituent part of the shell depends.

MATTER	METHOD
which lines these. The animals have the power of mending their shells when broken. The new pieces are brighter in color than the old.	Tell children that the glue used to make the shell comes from the animal itself. Note the beauty and color of the various shells. Let the children name the colors, and try to account for their appearance. Give information. Let them give examples of similar variations in other classes of Nature's works (birds, stones, &c.). How the animal obtains the shell—it is part of itself; grows with it. Refer to broken shell. These objects, which are very liable to be broken, can be repaired. Appearance of the new piece on the shell. Refer to a new piece of material put upon an old garment, &c.
III. *Different kinds of Shells.*—Shells are very numerous. There are many thousand different kinds. These are divided into three classes, viz. :— 1, those of one piece ; 2, those of two pieces ; 3, those of three pieces.	III.—Bring the children specimens of each kind. Let them discover how they differ in structure, and classify accordingly. Matter of the lesson dictated by the children, and placed on the board.

4. *Sketch on Plants of the Cruciform Tribe.*

MATTER.	METHOD.
I. *Structure.*—In plants of this tribe the corolla is formed by four petals placed crosswise ; hence the name. There are six stamens, four long and two short. The seed vessel is a pod, differing from that of the pea in having two partitions.	I.—Bring flowers of this kind before the children. Let them observe the distinct parts of these. Direct special attention to position of the petals. Refer to the derivation of the name, the number and length of the stamens, the compartments of the pistil. Let children name all cruciform plants they know. (W. B.)
II. *Qualities.*— These plants bear flowers of different colors. Brown, as the wall	II.—Children, with reference to the list on the board, name the different colors of the flowers. Lead them to see that they have mentioned no blue flower; there is

flower; pink or puce, as the stock; white or yellow, as mustard, turnip, radish. No flower of the tribe is blue, nor can any amount of cultivation produce a blue flower. The flowers have a sweet smell except when decayed, and then the smell is particularly disagreeable, on account of the escape of a gas on which the characteristic qualities of these plants depend. They are all highly pungent, all wholesome, and even medicinal.

not one in the tribe. Let them describe the scent of any of these flowers when fresh. Refer them to the condition of water in which wall flowers have been kept, or in which cabbage has been boiled. Refer to the mustard plant, the chief quality of mustard—pungency, leaving them to infer that all plants of the same kind partake of the same quality.

III. *Uses.*—We cultivate some of these plants for their sweet smell, as the stock and wall flower; some for food, as the cabbage and watercress, for their leaves; the turnip and radish, for their roots; some for what we call a relish, as mustard and horse radish. All this food purifies the blood. Sailors, who take long voyages, and consequently suffer from scurvy, almost always find a plant of this tribe (*Cocheleria*) growing on the shores of uncultivated lands. They eat it, and this cures them.

III.—Refer to the list on the board. Children mention the use of each separately, then classify the uses. Bring out the distinctive use of mustard and horse radish, by asking if these would serve as the only vegetable at a meal. Explain the effect of eating only salted meat, and refer to the goodness of God in providing a cure.

Summary.—Children reproduce the lesson from the heads.

5. *Sketch on Flavors.*

MATTER.	METHOD.
I. *Flavors.*	I.—1. Developed by experiment with sugar. Children give the term. No definition given.
1. Some things are sweet to the taste.	
2. Some things are luscious to the taste.	2. Developed by experiment with molasses. Children describe the flavor. Term and general definition given: "Anything which is extremely sweet, is said to be *luscious.*"
3. Some things are bitter to the taste.	3. Developed by experiment with quinine. Children give term. No definition given.
4. Some things are acid to the taste.	4. Developed by experiment with cream of tartar. Children give the term. No general definition given.
5. Some things are acrid or alkaline to the taste.	5. Developed by experiment with soda. Term and general definition given: "Anything that has a burning, bitter taste, is said to be *acrid.*" Children told that soda is one of the substances called alkalies, whence we sometimes speak of its taste as *alkaline.*
6. Some things are saline to the taste.	6. Developed by experiment with the blue and white papers called Seidlitz powders, after the flavor of each powder has been separately ascertained. Term and general definition given: "Anything having the taste of salt is said to be *saline.*" A saline substance can be obtained by combining an acid and an alkaline substance.
7. Some things are brackish to the taste.	7. Developed by putting a little salt in water. Children describe the taste. Term and general definition given: "Anything that has a slightly salty taste, is said to be *brackish.*" Refer to springs in the desert.
8. Some things are astringent to the taste.	8. Developed by experiment with alum. Children describe the effect on the mouth. Term and general definition given: "Anything which draws up or contracts the mouth is said to be *astringent.*"

9. Some things are pungent to the taste.

9. Developed by experiment with mustard. Children referred to scents of the same character. Give the term. General definition given: "Anything which has a hot, biting taste, is said to be *pungent*."

10. Some things are aromatic to the taste.

10. Developed by experiment with cinnamon. Children being referred to scents of the same character, give the term. General definition given: "Anything which has a hot, strong, pleasant taste, is said to be *aromatic*."

11. Some things are savory to the taste.

11. Developed by reference to gravy, &c. Children describe the flavor. Term and general definition given: "Anything with a rich, saltish, pleasant taste, is said to be *savory*."

II.—The sense by which we discover each of these qualities, we call *taste*; the quality itself we call *flavor*.

II.—Developed by writing two sentences on the board, in each of which the word *taste* is used in a different sense. Children say how used. Are told that there is another word which expresses the quality, and what advantage there would be in using it. Teacher writes the general term *flavor* above the list of specific flavors, which have been written on the board as given.

III.—Things having a flavor are said to be *sapid*. Things having little or no flavor are said to be *insipid*. Things having a highly agreeable flavor, are said to be *delicious*. Things having a disagreeable flavor are said to be *nauseous*.

III.—Terms and definitions given. Examples found by children.

Summary.—1. Children read the list of flavors, and in turn give examples.

2. Teacher gives the definitions in any order, children giving the term which expresses each definition.

3. Teacher erases the list of flavors, children supplying it.

4. Children add each of the definitions given to the corresponding term.

The summary may be omitted until the next day, and used as an exercise on the previous lesson.

6. *Sketch of a Lesson on Qualities, discovered by the Sense of Feeling.*

I. *Introductory.*—Teacher refers the children to a former lesson, in which they have brought qualities of an object to the test of all their senses. Tells them that the subject of this lesson will be all the qualities they can discover by means of one sense— *feeling.* Let them name all the qualities they can think of. (W. B.) Teacher then engages them to try experiments, in order to find out what more can be known.

II.—1. Teacher blindfolds the first child. Presents him with a stone, cotton, water, tube, &c. He says: "By *feeling,* we can discover whether objects are hard, soft, liquid, or hollow."

2. Teacher blindfolds second child, and presents him with a nutmeg grater, an oyster shell, a piece of carved wood, &c., who says: "By *feeling,* we can discover whether things are rough, smooth, level, or uneven."

3. Teacher proceeds as before, by examining the contents of a box of solids, and comparing these with lumps of chalk. The third child says: "By *feeling,* we can discover whether objects are edged, cubical, cylindrical, or (in fact) any regular form, or of an irregular form."

4. Teacher presents measures of different lengths. The fourth child says: "By *feeling,* we can discover whether things are long or short, thick or thin, deep or shallow."

5. Teacher places several similar objects at various distances. Fifth child says: "By *feeling,* we can discover whether things are near or far, and how far." [Exercise on the absolute distance, whether an inch or a foot.]

6. Teacher places the same objects in different positions, and sixth child says: "By *feeling,* we can discover whether things are up or down, without, within, or between."

7. Teacher presents a piece of sealing wax that has just been

used. Seventh child says: "By *feeling*, we can discover whether things are burning, hot, warm, lukewarm, cool, cold, or freezing."

8. Teacher presents a sponge, before dipping it in water, and after wringing it; an eighth child says: "By *feeling*, we can discover whether things are dry, wet, or moist."

III.—Children compare these ideas with those discovered by themselves at the beginning of the lesson. Teacher may do well to refer to the use of *object lessons* in giving accurate and systematic knowledge, instead of the imperfect knowledge that is gathered from a merely superficial observation.

IV.—Children led to find general terms inclusive of each set of the particular terms before used. They dictate what is to be put on the board, thus:

By the sense of *feeling*, we discover,
1. The Character of the Substance.
2. The Character of the Surface.
3. The Form.
4. The Size.
5. The Distance.
6. The Position.
7. The Condition, as to Temperature.
8. The Condition, as to Moisture.

7. *Sketch of Lesson on an Egg.*

I. *Shape.*—An egg is oval, smaller at one end than the other. The word oval is derived from *ovum*, the Latin for egg.

II. *Parts—Order of Position and Formation.*—An egg consists of several distinct parts: 1, the shell; 2, the skin between the shell and albumen, or the *membrane;* 3, the albumen; 4, the skin between the albumen and the yelk, or the envelope; 5, the yelk; 6, the embryo. The order of the original formation of each part is exactly the reverse of the position. To these parts, though not as a distinct part, may be added the follicle.

III. *Use of each Part.*—1. The shell protects the interior parts. 2. The membrane is of use to strengthen the shell and to prevent injury to the young bird; probably also to keep the external air from penetrating, and to keep the albumen from mixing with the shell ere it becomes hardened by exposure. 3. The albumen serves as nourishment for the young bird. 4. The envelope prevents the yelk from mixing with the albumen. 5. The yelk is the substance from which the bird is formed, as the albumen is the nourishment during formation. 6. The embryo is the yelk in process of formation. 7. The follicle contains the air for the use of the young bird.

IV. *Qualities on which Uses depend.*—1. *Shell.*—Advantages of the shape—being oval, it is not so likely to be broken as if it had corners. The shape also renders it more comfortable for the mother bird during the process of hatching, and more convenient to be turned over, that each part may receive equal warmth. This shape, too, suits that of the bird before it is fully developed, and admits of the little creature's free egress.

2. *Obvious Qualities of the Shell.*—Hard, smooth, brittle, thin, porous. *Hard*, that it may keep its shape under pressure; *smooth*, pleasanter to the touch—less liable to be broken when coming in contact with any roughness of the ground; *brittle*, that egress may be afforded to the chick; *thin*, for the same reason, and to prevent waste of material; *porous*, to admit air.

3. *Qualities of the Membrane.*—Tough, smooth. *Tough*, to strengthen the shell; *smooth*, on account of the chick.

4. *Qualities of the Albumen.*—Thick, glutinous, insipid; is soluble in cold water, curdles in hot water. Effect of heat in hatching the bird, &c.

5. *Qualities of the Envelope.*—Strong, thin, impervious.

6. *Qualities of the Yelk.*—Sapid, colored.

8. *Sketch of Lesson on Writing Paper.*

I.—The children are desired to discover the qualities on which the use depends. It is *smooth*, in order that the pen may pass over it; *glossy*, to prevent the ink from penetrating; *flexible*, therefore easily folded into the form of a letter; *thin*, therefore *light;* *portable*, therefore *cheaper.*

II. *Substitutes for Paper.*—Tell the children that paper was unknown in ancient times. Let them say how people could manage when they wanted to send news—they could send messengers. Why this was not so good as writing notes—some trouble, and less certainty. But we have another use for paper. When war breaks out, or some great deed is done, we like to write it in a book, that it may be remembered. How people that had no paper could keep their records. Refer the children to what they have read in the Bible. The commandments were written on tables of stone. Joshua wrote a copy of the law on tables of stone. The high priest had an inscription on a gold mitre. Hezekiah desired that his writing tablets should be brought. Explain to the chidlren that the tablets used in those days were generally of wax.

The rolls mentioned in the Bible were of parchment. Why called rolls? Children dictate the list of substances formerly used in lieu of paper—stone, metal, wax, parchment. Consider the comparative convenience of using each of these. Tell them that the Egyptians used something else. A plant used to grow on the banks of the great river which waters their country. The people took the bark of this, and pressed the edges together till they adhered. Whether the same thing could be done with narrow strips of paper? Children mention things that will adhere, as postage stamps, &c. What quality this bark must have possessed—it contained a sweet gum. Was called *papyrus*. Children say why the pieces of bark were allowed to adhere at the edges only. When a large sheet was formed, it was rubbed with a glass or metal ball. The use of this operation.

III. *Modern Paper.*—Tell them that the first paper, properly so called, was made in Spain, of cotton wool, and afterward of woollen rags. The first mixture of linen rags was accidental; but when it was discovered that paper was improved thereby, more linen rags were added next time, and so on until only linen was used, and the best paper produced as a result. In the reign of Henry III., a ship laden with this paper was wrecked off the coast of England. The booty was considered of so much importance, that several records are still in existence in which the fact is mentioned. In the reign of Queen Elizabeth, the first paper mills were established in England. For a long time, only a little paper was used. Why so much more required now? It was feared that there would not be enough nice white rags to make good paper. An ingenious German—Schaffer—thought he would ascertain of what other substance paper could be made. Some he made of straw, some of vine tendrils, some of fibrous roots. In what these substances were alike. But soon after this another ingenious man found out, that by using a substance called chlorine, he could take the dye out of colored rags, and make them perfectly white.

IV. *Ancient Paper.*—Refer again to the substitutes for paper formerly resorted to. Tell the children there was one nation which in ancient times used paper. Let them enumerate the ancient nations with which they have any acquaintance, as, Jews, Egyptians, Romans. Whether it could be any of those, and why not? Refer to the map, and point out China. Tell them that hundreds of years ago the Chinese were in the practice of making paper, by grinding the bark of a tree, and placing it in water. When steeped to a pulp, it was poured into shallow moulds, placed one on the top of another, with a bulrush mat between each mould, and a reed under each mat. These mats were raised every day, that the paper might dry gradually. Children to say the use of the mats, and the use of the reeds. Produce a specimen of rice paper, and explain how this is obtained. It is the pith of a water weed. In the finest specimens this is found as large as the thumb of a man. This is pared in a circular direction with a knife.

9. *Sketch on Comparison of Wine and Water.*

I. *Qualities compared.*

Wine is
  1. Artificial.
  2. Colored.
  3. Only semi-transparent.
  4. Odorous.
  5. Sapid.
  6. Stimulating. ⎫
  7. Exhilarating. ⎬
  8. Nourishing. ⎭
  9. Astringent.
  10. Heating.

Water is
  1. Natural.
  2. Colorless.
  3. Transparent.
  4. Inodorous.
  5. Tasteless.

  6. Only refreshing.

  7. Relaxing.
  8. Cooling.

II. *How these Qualities in each Liquid render it useful to man.*— Water must of necessity be natural, as such a quantity is needed by man for his use. It must be colorless, transparent, inodorous, and tasteless, otherwise it would not be pure, and consequently of little service, as it would destroy or detract from the taste of substances with which it is mixed. Its cooling and refreshing qualities give it great advantages over any other liquid. The sapid, stimulating, exhilarating, and astringent qualities of wine, render it particularly useful to man.

III. *How these Liquids are obtained.*—Spontaneous evaporation is the origin of any quantity of water. This is continually taking place from off the surface of seas, lakes, &c.: the vapors ascend, and form clouds; these, on attaining a higher region, become condensed; by the power of attraction they descend to the mountains, the particles become separated, and percolate into the earth; then the water, where it finds the least pressure, forces a passage; a fissure is consequently made in the mountains, and a spring is thus originated, which flows onward till obstructed; at such a place the water accumulates, and ultimately gives rise to a river, which in its course is joined by others, and these continue their onward motion till they are lost again in the mighty ocean. Then the same thing again occurs; and therefore we may perceive, as it were, a complete revolution in the formation of water as used by man.

To obtain wine, vines must first be planted. When the fruit is sufficiently ripe, it is gathered, placed in large vessels, and pressed. Perforations in the bottom of the vessel allow the juice to flow out into another, from whence it is taken and casked. Then there is a fourfold repetition of this process: 1. The liquid becomes sweet; this is the *saccharine* fermentation (example, wort). 2. This process evolves another substance, and we have the *alcoholic* fermentation; in proportion to the quantity of alcohol contained in the liquid, the next process is retarded. 3. It becomes sour; this is the *acetous* fermentation. When a fourth change takes place, it is the symptom of decay and corruption, and is called the *putrefactive* fermentation. Wine is fit for use after the second fermentation. The wines of Hungary have been known to form so thick a crust around the inside of the cask, that the wood could be removed without causing the wine to flow out.

IV. *Qualities referred to in Scripture.*

WATER.	WINE, IN MODERATION.
1. Unstable. Gen. xlix. 4.	1. Cheering. Judges ix. 3.
2. A Solvent. Job xiv. 19.	2. Gladdening. Ps. civ. 15.
3. Penetrating. Ps. cxix. 18.	3. Strengthening. Cant. ii. 5.
4. Reflective. Prov. xxvii. 19.	4. Medicinal. 1·Tim. v. 23.
5. Refreshing. Ps. xxiii. 2.	
6. Purifying. Ezek. xxxvi. 25.	IN EXCESS.
	1. Intoxicating. Eph. v. 18.
	2. Infuriating. Prov. xx. 1.

Water is typical of regeneration and sanctification—cleansing and purifying in its nature. It is particularly typical of the work of the Holy Spirit, and is used in baptism.

Wine is *rather typical*—1, of consolation; 2, of the reviving and invigorating graces of the Spirit.

10. *Sketches on the Bible.*

Having drawn from the class, by a few direct and simple questions, that the Bible was not always a printed book—was not first written in English—was not bestowed on mankind at once, complete from Genesis to Revelation, but in detached parts; and having told them to consider the successive portions in which it was given, the languages in which it was first written, and the form in which it then appeared, the children ought to be in possession of most of the facts referred to; therefore, during the greater part of the lessons, the business of the teacher would be to lead them to collect and arrange what they already know.

I.—*Scripture—in what portions given, and at what period.*

1. Possessors of Scripture—the Hebrew nation. Not when we first recognize it in Egypt, but previous to the settlement in Canaan. Date of this event. At that time the Israelites had the writings of Moses, probably including one or two of the Psalms,

and the Book of Job. Thence to the first captivity, they received successively the books of Joshua, Judges, Samuel, Kings, Chronicles, the writings of David, those of his son, a portion of the greater, and most of the lesser prophets. Date of the captivity. During that period, the remainder of the greater prophets, and two of the lesser prophets. After the return, the narratives of Ezra, Nehemiah, and Esther, with the three last prophetical books. Date of the return.

2. Books of the New Testament period. Also considered with respect to writers, titles, and order. Date of conclusion of Scripture. Text learned: Hebrews i. 1—"God, who at sundry times and in divers manners spake in times past unto the fathers by the prophets, hath in these last days spoken unto us by his Son."

II. *Language.—That in which Scripture was first written.—Translations.*—1. Every revelation prior to the date of the first captivity made in Hebrew. This accounted for. Books of Daniel and Ezra written partly in Hebrew and partly in Chaldee. Lead the class to infer the probable reason of this, from consideration as to the subject of the portions written in Chaldee; principally such as include original letters, decrees, &c., of the Babylonish and Persian Governments. Scriptures posterior to the date of the captivity written in Chaldee, and all the earlier books translated into the same tongue. No sooner did the ancient Hebrew become a dead language, than the Scriptures were put into the vernacular tongue by men, such as Ezra, acting under the immediate inspiration of God. Conclusion drawn from this, and text learned, showing the importance of understanding the Word of God: 1 Cor. xiv. 19—"I had rather speak five words with my understanding, that by my voice I might teach others also, than ten thousand words in an unknown tongue."

2. The coming of the time in which the Gentiles were to be led to a knowledge of the truth, marked by the dispersion of the Scriptures among them. Providence of God shown in this. Its design and effect. Give general account of various translations, and particular one on the Septuagint. Refer to, and prove the importance of, the last translation. Refer to prevalence of the

Greek tongue in every part of the civilized world, as connected providentially with the publication of the Gospel in that language.

To connect this period with what follows, touch very briefly on the general professions of Christianity. Division of the Roman Empire, and subsequent spread of the Greek and Roman Catholic Churches. Progress of the latter. Extent of her power. Change with respect to the language of the Bible. Scripture written in Latin throughout all the countries of the Western Empire.

III. *Forms under which the Scriptures have been presented at different periods.*—1. Derivation of the terms *Bible* and *Scripture*. Sacred words of the Jews' writings. Not books. Kind of materials chiefly used, either parchment or vellum. Scroll—when not in use, rolled up on a slender cylinder, like a school map; hence origin of the term *volume*. Refer to the Scribes. Their office. Importance and accuracy of their labors.

2. Describe sacred records of Christians in the Middle Ages. Illuminated MSS. What they were. Why so called. Sometimes rolls; oftener books. Beauty and value of these copies. The copyists—what class of men they were. Their mode of life, position, and character, compared with that of the Jewish Scribes.

3. Sacred records in the modern form. Class observe their own Bibles, and state how they differ externally from those before described. Why composed of many sheets bound together, not of one rolled up? Why made of paper rather than parchment? Why no longer MS.? Give brief account of the invention of printing, and its immediate consequence—the great multiplication of copies. Effect of the distribution of these, all over the world. Specimens of Scriptural translations in one hundred and forty-eight languages, were to be seen at the Great Exhibition. Compare God's present method of making known Himself and His will, to that He adopted in the apostolic age. Then, supernatural gift of tongues, enabling the apostles so to preach that all could understand. Why necessary then? Now, the same object effected without a miracle, by the translation of the Bible into different

languages, so that the nations may still say, "We do hear them speak in our tongues the wonderful works of God." Acts ii. 11.

IV. *Unchangeableness of the Inspired Word—Its Influence.*— Bible to be regarded as a perfect whole. The New Testament not an abrogation, but a development of the principles contained in the Old. Text: Matthew v. 17, 18. This might be proved by reference to the nature of God, but is evidently seen by the invariable influence of the Scriptures on the condition of man in all ages and countries. Compare the mental and moral condition of the Jews prior to their first captivity, with that of the nations surrounding them. Refer to countries in which the Bible is unknown at this day; without exception, utterly barbarous and degraded. Refer to countries in which its doctrines are rejected, and yet, because the people have learned something of the historical events recorded in it, because its precepts (though their origin is not recognized) are interwoven with social laws, they take a far higher rank. Instance, Mohammedans. Refer to countries in which the Scriptures are held to be true, and the people do not read them, because the ecclesiastical power has put a seal on the book; these are better off than those before named, for they hear of the name, and know somewhat of the character of Jesus, and through the thick mists of tradition the light of the Word will sometimes shine.

Conclusion drawn—that the Bible is a great engine of civilization, as well as the source of spiritual knowledge. Effect of its free circulation throughout our own land. Refer to the renovation now commenced in heathen lands, from the spread of the Scriptures and Scriptural teaching. Duty incumbent on us to place the Bible in the households of our own and other countries. We may anticipate the promised blessing, that they who water others shall themselves be watered.

NUMBER.

INTRODUCTORY REMARKS.

LESSONS ON NUMBER introduce the pupil to subjects which afford a higher exercise of mental power than any of those which have hitherto engaged attention.

In the study of the properties of number, Pestalozzi did not aim at the mere acquisition of the science, and of mechanical dexterity in calculation; he considered the subject to be a valuable means of awakening intelligence, of forming the judgment, and of developing the reasoning faculty. His method of presenting the first principles of the science also differs greatly from that ordinarily pursued; he trained the mind to grasp the full perception of the value of numbers, by observation upon them as illustrated in surrounding familiar objects; and when by this process the abstract idea was acquired, he then, but not till then, communicated the symbol by which it is conventionally represented. It was found that pupils trained on these principles were themselves enabled to deduce the practical *rules* of arithmetical calculation from the very examples on which their minds had been previously exercised.

This may be a slow process; but it has been well observed, that " when the true end of intellectual education shall be admitted to be, first, the attainment of mental power, and then the application of it to practical and scientific purposes, that plan of early instruction which dwells long on first principles, and does not haste to make learned, will be acknowledged as the most economical, because the most effectual."

To some persons, the detail, the analysis, the repetition recommended in the following lessons, may seem wearisome; and it is true, a careless or unobservant teacher may make a weariness of such instruction, and, indeed, of any other plan of education. But if those who have long understood the meaning of one, two, and three, were able to remember the mental process by which they themselves acquired their understanding of these numbers, they would find it was by some process not very dissimilar from that here recommended. It may be they were never *taught* on such a plan—truth was never thus clearly presented to the mind in its own natural simplicity, rising step by step into greater complexity; it may be, that instead of learning such truth easily and surely, as those will do who are led through these lessons, they had to gather it here and there, under disadvantages of every kind, so that even still, perhaps, the beautiful properties of numbers, constantly as experience presents them, are but seen through a mist; but it is indisputable, that any amount of clear perception such persons may have attained to, they have attained it by the fact of the mind, itself an observant faculty, having done for itself that which the teacher omitted to do for it, and having done it, also, by some such process as this, with the visible world for its book, and with God's gifts of observation and reflection for its ever willing guides. Remembering these things, the judicious teacher will guard against dwelling too long on these analytical lessons, using them just so long as there may be work to be done by them, while avoiding also the opposite extreme of rapid but unsound progression.

FIRST STEP.

The Numbers One to Ten.

Object.—I. To lead the children to the perception of number, by presenting it as it is exemplified in surrounding objects; and to teach the word by which each number of which an idea has been gained, may be expressed. II. To teach the power and name of each number, when used as an ordinal. III. To exercise the mind on the numbers of which the knowledge has been attained, by exhibiting their gradual increase by ones, and by comparing their general magnitudes.

Plan.—I. Successively develop the distinct perception of the value of numbers, beginning with one, and taking each number separately in its order as far as ten, by the exhibition of the corresponding number of objects. Any convenient appliances,* such as books, balls, pebbles, slate-pencils, or marbles, may serve as illustrations. It is well that these should be diversified, that the child may the more clearly perceive that number is a property of all separate objects—of objects of all qualities, shapes, sizes, and colors alike.

As clear perception is thus successively gained of each of the several numbers, the teacher should tell the *name* of the number. The class must then be practised in associating the number with its name. In carrying out this—

1. The teacher gives the name, the children bring forward the corresponding number of objects.

2. The teacher shows the children a definite number of objects, requiring them to apply the name of the number to them.

3. Lastly, the children enumerate or count from one to the number last attained, ascending; and inversely from it to one, descending, again and again, till perfect in the exercise.

II. The plan of teaching the powers and names of the numbers when used as expressing *order* of *time* or of *position*, is given in II., p. 147, of this Step.

I.—*Examples of Lessons on this Plan.*

To develop the perception of the number expressed by the word ONE, and to communicate the name of the number.

---

* Were the common ball-frame alone depended on for illustration, the children might be led to associate their ideas of number with one species of exclusive objects, and their attainment of the abstract idea of number, as a universal property of *all* objects, might be retarded. The true province of the ball-frame is rather to assist in working out some of the simple processes of calculation, when a notion of number in the abstract has been gained.

NUMBER.—FIRST STEP.

This first lesson is most important, as it involves that which is the foundation of all number—the grand idea of *One*, or UNITY. The teacher must not think the idea so simple as to need no illustration.

The child should be led to appreciate the notion of this number by the means already recommended. One object may be taken from many of its kind, and held before the class, or it may be placed in some unusual place, the teacher telling the children, even though they may already know the fact, that such a number of anything whatsoever is said to be *one* of it. The word should be applied to diverse objects, the children being allowed to describe them. How many do I hold? One. One of what? One marble. And this? One pencil. And this? One book. A child may be told to bring one slate, or one ball, or to give one shout, one clap, &c.; and the attention of each child may be guided to observation on itself as one separate individual, or to those objects in nature which exist in oneness, as one sun, one moon.

A Lesson to Develop the Perception of the Number expressed by the Word "Three," and to Communicate the Name of the Number.

The following sketch of a lesson will show the plan to be pursued with all the numbers as far as ten.

Before commencing a lesson on a number which is new to the children, the teacher should ascertain that they have clear ideas of those on which they have already received instruction. In this instance it is supposed that the number *two* has been the subject of a lesson, and is thoroughly understood, and that the teacher tests this by directing one of the children to bring *two* pencils, or *two* books, &c., while the others look on observantly, and approve or otherwise, as the case may demand. If the requirement be rightly met, the class may simultaneously describe the objects as they are presented, saying, "Two pencils," "Two slates," "Two books," &c. Here also the objects should be diverse.

With this attainment made, the class may be led on to the observation of the number THREE.

1. The teacher should now add one pencil to the two pencils, one slate to the two slates, or one book to the two books, and, as this is done, require the children to say, in each case, "*Three* pencils," "*Three* slates," "*Three* books," &c. As an exercise, groups of *three* of different objects may be placed before the class, and one of the children desired to bring a similar number of the same object, or of some other. When observation has been well exercised by varied examples of this kind, the children may again be told that such a number of any object whatever is called *three* of it, and that the name of that number is THREE.

2. The teacher should then try to discover how far the children are able to connect the word *three* with the corresponding number, by calling upon several of them in rotation to bring three pencils, or three books, or three pins—to bring three of their companions to the teacher, to hold up three fingers, or to clap their hands three times, &c.

3. The object of the next exercise is to ascertain whether the children can promptly apply the proper name to the number, when presented to them in different objects. The teacher may hold up three fingers, and ask how many are held up, and then take up three pencils, and again ask how many there are, or make three strokes upon the slate, and ask how many such a number of anything is said to be.

It may confirm ideas already gained as to the *succession* of numbers, if the children are required to tell in regular succession those they have acquired, while the succession is *enacted*, as it were, by the teacher. Several sets of objects should be at hand, from each of which the teacher takes first one, then a second, then a third; the children saying, as this is done, "One pencil," "Two pencils," "Three pencils;" "One pin," "Two pins," "Three pins," &c.

This should be followed by an exercise in ascending and descending enumeration, thus:—

"Now, all together say with me, *One, two, three;* and again, *Three, two, one.* And now say the same without me, for I shall be silent."

In these exercises, which will need frequent repetition, great care must be taken not to perplex the children; the perception of number should be permitted to grow upon them almost without their being conscious of the attainment. It should be attained by simple observation, rather than by a process of reasoning, although it is true that at a further stage of the child's education it will be found that all the higher calculations of arithmetical reasoning are, in fact, based upon the knowledge for which it is the aim of these initiatory lessons to prepare.

A right method of carrying out this early instruction in number is so important, that it is thought advisable to introduce in this place the following notes of a lesson actually given by an experienced teacher to a class of very young children, on the development of the number *four*. The lesson was given in the presence of strangers, to whom the teacher gave the following introductory explanation of the plan to be pursued:—

1. I shall exercise the children in the number *three*, to ascertain whether they have a correct idea of it. For example, I will call a child to bring me three pointers from among many; then three bottles, &c. To give the idea of *four*, I will add one pointer to the three pointers, one bottle to the three bottles, &c.

2. To ascertain whether they connect the right idea with the name, I will ask them to bring me four pointers, four bottles, &c.

3. To see if they can apply the names themselves, I will hold up four bottles, four pointers, &c., and require them to tell me how many there are.

Lastly, I will make them go over together in succession, the numbers they have learnt, that they may obtain a clear perception of numeration; as, "One bottle, two bottles," &c.; and after this make them say, "One, two, three, four," several times.

THE LESSON.

Teacher. I should like a little child to bring me three bottles. Let Charles bring them.

The child named brought *two*.

T. Is he right? *Several.* No.

T. Who can do it? *Several.* I can.

A little boy rose at the bidding of the teacher, and brought another bottle to her, making up the number three.

T. Now who can bring me three shells? (*pointing to some placed at a little distance.*) *Several.* I can.

T. Let Emma bring them.

The little girl referred to brought the proper number.

T. Now who can bring me three pointers? *A little girl.* I can.

The child rose, and brought the number of pointers required.

T. Has she brought the right number? *All.* Yes.

T. Now some child bring me three stones.

A little girl brought three stones.

The teacher, finding that the children had a correct idea of three, placed before them the same objects in groups of four, and called upon them to repeat after her, "Four pointers."

All. Four pointers.

The words were repeated three or four times.

T. Now say, "Four stones." *All.* Four stones.

The same repetition took place as in the case of the bottles and shells.

The teacher's next point was to ascertain whether, when she used the name FOUR, the children connected the right idea with the name.

T. Who can bring me four pointers? *A little girl.* I can.

The child rose, and brought them to the teacher.

T. How many pointers are there here? *All.* Four.

T. Then did Lizzy bring the right number? *Three or four voices.* Yes.

T. Now I should like to have four bottles.

A little boy rose, and brought *three* to the teacher.

T. Is he right? *Several voices.* No.

T. Who can make the number to be four? *A little boy.* I can.

He then rose, and brought one bottle more.

T. Now, how many bottles are there? *Several voices.* Four.

T. Who can bring me four shells? *A little boy.* I can.

He brought them to the teacher.

T. Is he right? *Many voices.* Yes.

The same thing was repeated in the case of four stones: "One stone, two stones, three stones, four stones;" "One bottle, two bottles, three bottles, four bottles," &c.

The teacher's third point was to find if the children could themselves correctly apply the name. To do this, he called upon them to pick up four shells, four stones, &c., which they did correctly. They then practised numeration up to the point they had reached, to obtain an accurate perception of the *increase* of numbers, saying after the teacher: "One stone, two stones, three stones, four stones;" "One bottle, two bottles, three bottles, four bottles;" "One, two, three, four."

T. Now, Thomas (*addressing one of the children*), can you bring me four children? four who are sitting up nicely.

The little boy spoken to, rose, selected *three*, and led them to the teacher.

T. Well, Thomas, have you brought four? *Thomas.* Yes.

T. (*to all*). Thomas says he has brought four children; are there four here? *Nearly all.* No.

T. Let us count them: one child, two children, three children. Let me have four, Thomas.

He brought another boy, who walked before the rest to take his place by their side.

T. (*to all*). Should he have gone in front of the other children? *Two or three voices.* No.

T. Certainly not; he should have come round behind them.

The child was then led round, and placed by the side of the three children.

T. Now say, "One child, two children, three children, four children." This was done.

T. Now let three children go to their seats. Now one child.

The children then went to their seats.

T. Who can show me four fingers?

A little boy held up all the fingers and the thumb of both hands.

T. (*to all*). Are there only four there? *Several voices.* No.

T. See what a number of fingers! How many did I ask for? *Several voices.* Four.

The teacher then counted four on her own fingers.

T. Now, Emily, show me four.

The little girl addressed held up that number of fingers.

T. How many does she hold up? Four.

It is unnecessary to pursue these detailed lessons further. In working out the idea of the higher numbers, it is necessary simply to adhere to the plan here recommended, adding one additional marble, pebble, or book, to the group last considered, recognized, and named, the teacher then calling on the class to form successive groups of objects, to the numbers of which the names *four, five, six, seven, eight, nine,* and *ten* are applicable; and then requiring the children themselves to give the proper name, as groups of objects containing such numbers are successively presented to them, concluding the lesson by ascending and descending enumeration.

It must be left to the discretion of the teacher where to put a limit to lessons such as these. "The degree of power in children, and the time of development, are so various, that nothing but careful observation can make the teacher aware what time or labor each step will require, before it is thoroughly understood by the pupil." One child will be embarrassed when required to tell the number of ten or twenty objects which lie before him, while another will determine it at a glance. In one of these cases the power of perception needs to be developed by a patiently conducted gradual process; in the other it will steadily acquire increased scope as larger numbers are presented to the child's observation. As a general rule, the number *ten* should be the limit of these initiatory lessons on number for some considerable time.

II.—*The Order of Numbers.*

The object of this lesson is to bring out the relation in which numbers stand to each other when used as ordinals, and when the perception has been awakened, to communicate the name applied to each number when so used. It is manifest that, though closely allied to the abstract value of a number, its power as an ordinal is a *relative* quality. The number three is *always* three, under all possible circumstances; but an object is *third*, only when some other is *second;* and that object again is *second*, because some other separate object is *first* in order. The idea of *three* is quite unchangeable, but the notion of *third* is mutable, as regards the object which for the time is qualified by the word; for the object which is third may be made the second, or the first; and the object which is first, may be made second, third, fiftieth, &c., infinitely. These facts deserve a distinct lesson for their elucidation, lest the mind should indulge an ill-defined perception of a well-defined truth. When, also, each new property of numbers is thus made the subject of concentrated attention, the mind gradually gains power to think with vigor, to rely on its own attainments, and to apply the knowledge gained with accuracy and precision. If, however, the teacher should not consider the children sufficiently advanced for these lessons, the Exercises, No. III., page 149, may precede them; and even addition may be commenced upon before they are given.

A Lesson to Develop the Idea of the Order of Succession in Numbers, as First, Second, Third, &c., to Tenth.

In giving this lesson, as is suggested in "First Ideas on Number," a small ladder containing but ten "rounds" may be used for illustration. This, being a new object, will arrest attention. It is also an extremely appropriate object for such a purpose.

The children should first count the rounds or steps; they should then be led to observe their order. If a boy wished to mount this ladder, what would he first do? He would put his foot on the step. On which? Would you say on the *one* step? No, teacher; on the *first* step. And then on the *two* step? No; on the *second*. And so on, to the tenth. When would you say, "One step, two steps, three steps," &c.? When simply counting how many there are. And when would you say, "First step, second step," &c.? When using the steps in going up or down, or when thinking of them as coming before or after each other.

If these ordinal names are already known to the children, as some of them will probably be, the teacher will merely have to superintend the correct application of them. If, however, they are not known, as may be the case with very young children, one child may be called out and placed in front of the class, ready, when directed by the teacher, to place his hand on each round, beginning with the lowest, as he supposes himself climbing to the top. As each round is touched, the teacher may give its ordinal name of *first, second, third, fourth,* &c., to *tenth,* the whole class pronouncing it after her. After several repetitions of this ascending process, the descending enumeration may begin, and be followed out in the same way. The teacher may then vary the exercise by enumerating from first to tenth, and from tenth to first, immediately. After this the teacher should require the children to give the ordinal name of each step when pointed out by another.

The attainments of the children may be tested, by their being required to lay the hand upon any round named by another, and again to give the name of any round on which the teacher places the hand. They may be asked to say what is the name of that step which is above the second, and of that below it; and then to give the name of each *alternate* step, beginning with the first, so as to elicit the series—*first, third, fifth, seventh, ninth;* and then starting from the second, so as to produce the series—*second, fourth, sixth, eighth, tenth.* This may be done also in descending order, beginning consecutively with tenth, and ninth.

In applying the ordinals to other groups of objects, an attractive illustration might be afforded by placing a class of ten children in front of the gallery, in which the relative position of each individual might be ascertained and described. Small objects, which may be easily moved from place to place, and put in a variety of relative positions, are most useful in lessons such as these. The number of the objects presented should be first determined, and then their relative position. One of them may then be moved into a new place. The effect upon the whole series, as

NUMBER.—FIRST STEP. 149

well as upon the single object moved, will attract attention, and deepen impressions already made.

A few original miscellaneous questions may now be asked, as tests of acquirement.

What is the first meal of every day? What the second? What the third?

In what place does this child stand in this class? &c.

III.—Exercises.

This First Step may conclude with the following series of exercises, which are valuable as affording practice on the numbers which the children have learnt to distinguish and to express by name.

The Gradual Increase of Numbers from One to Ten.

To lead the children to form an accurate idea of the increase of numbers, the teacher should draw lines on the slate in the following order, and afterward call on the children to name the numbers as they are successively pointed to, and to say how two is formed by adding one to one, three by adding one to two, &c. :—

```
I
I I
I I I
I I I I
I I I I I
I I I I I I
I I I I I I I
I I I I I I I I
I I I I I I I I I
I I I I I I I I I I
```

The teacher may then point to any number, asking the children to name it, and then to tell what is the number next above it, and what the next below it.

Again, a number may be mentioned, and the children required to say what numbers are next to it, above and below.

The children may then be called on to state, first by means of strokes, and then in words, what number is between any two numbers named; as, what numbers there are between seven and nine; four and six; eight and ten, &c.

Lastly, the teacher should lead the children to see that numbers naturally increase by unity, and that each number above unity is greater *by one* than that preceding it. This will prepare the way for the process of addition: thus, one and one are two, two and one are three, three and one are four, four and one are five, &c., to ten. Again: two is one and one, three is two and one, four is three and one, &c., to ten; or, two is one more than one, three is one more than two, four is one more than three, &c.; or, in inverse order, ten are nine more one, nine are eight more one, eight are seven more one, seven are six more one, &c., to two.

Comparison of Numbers with each other as to their General Magnitude.

EXERCISES.—It is not here intended to measure the actual amount of difference between numbers, but only to compare them with each other as to their general magnitude.

In three and four, which is the greater?

And in two and six; in three and five; in four and eight; in eight and nine? &c.—which is in each case the greater number?

Tell me a number which is more than three.

Now name a number that is more than six; another greater than eight, &c.

Tell me a number that is less than eight.

Another that is less than six, five, and three, respectively.

Tell me all the numbers you know that are less than five, four, six, eight, one, &c.

Now tell me all the numbers you know that are more than five, four, six, eight, one, &c.

Four, two, six—which is the least of the numbers I have named? Which is the largest? Then two is the smallest, or least of the three, and six is the largest of the three. Now what can I say about the four? That it is larger than the least of the three, and smaller than the largest of the three; for these reasons it is called the *mean*, or middle number.

Tell me a *mean* number between three and five; between four and eight, five and seven, two and eight, eight and ten, seven and nine, &c., respectively.

ILLUSTRATIONS.—I had eight apples, and my brother six; which of us had the greater number?

That child is five years old, and the one next him is seven; which is the elder?

If one child sleep eight hours, and another ten hours, which of them sleeps the longer?

It is four miles from Oswego to Scriba, and ten miles from Oswego to New Haven; which of these two places is the greater distance from Oswego?

The teacher should ask a variety of questions such as these. They may be invented as they are needed.

Addition and Subtraction.

Object.—To teach the addition and subtraction of numbers under ten.

Plan.—This is exemplified in detail in the exercises which follow.

It is clear that the simple enumeration of a series of numbers gradually increasing by one, call the process by what *name* we please, is in fact an exercise in the *addition* of ONE, and that the simple enumeration of a similar series in descending order, is in fact the *subtraction* of ONE. Hitherto, however, the gradual increase or decrease of numbers has been presented as a matter of sensible perception, rather than as an appeal to the reasoning faculty of the mind. While, however, it is almost impossible, and perhaps equally undesirable, to separate these two processes, it is important that the child should now be taught to *use* those numbers of which he has gained a clear perception, in a manner more allied to an act of reasoning. Neither will it do for him to enumerate by *ones* all his life; he must learn to bound over the minute intervals which separate one number from another, and still to be sure of his ground. He must learn to be as ready in enumerating, ascending and descending, by *nine*, as he is in enumerating by *one*. This facility is to be attained by a graduated series of exercises, with the aid of objects, which shall make each step sure before a further step is ventured upon.

ADDITION.

1. *The Addition of the Number One.*

The children are supposed to have become familiar with the increase of numbers from one to ten, as carried out practically by the exhibition of objects. Lines should now be drawn on the slate in the order indicated by the following table, the children observing and describing each line as it is constructed:

| and | are?
| | and | are?
| | | and | are?
| | | | and | are?
to
| | | | | | | | | and | are?

The teacher, drawing two lines, says: "One line and one line are?" The children take up her words, and complete the sentence: "One line and one line are two lines." Again: "Two and one are?" "Three;" and so on, to "Nine and one are ten." Their answers may be written in strokes as they are given, each opposite its component numbers.

The teacher should now exercise the children in the addition of the number one to other numbers without the use of objects or strokes; bringing these forward, however, when necessary to prove the correctness of calculations, or to detect errors.

The subject may now be illustrated by some miscellaneous questions, such as the mind of an apt teacher will at once be able to propose. A few examples are given:

James has one orange. If I give him one more, how many will he then have?

Jane has eight walnuts. If her father give her one more, how many will she have?

A boy had two rabbits given to him. His father bought him one more; how many had he?

A baby had nine teeth. One day, another came; how many teeth had the baby in all?

2. *The Addition of Two.*

The mind of the child, having acquired the power of adding ONE *once*, will now be prepared to add it *twice;* for into this the addition of *two* resolves itself.

The teacher should arrange objects, or draw lines on the slate, in the following order:

The children being required to repeat together, first with the use of the lines, and then without:

"One line and two lines are three lines;
Two lines and two lines are four lines;
Three lines and two lines are five lines;"
to
"Eight lines and two lines are ten lines."

The teacher should then question the children individually upon the lesson, without any reference to order of numbers, avoiding any result exceeding the number ten.

Here, also, a few practical questions should be put to the class, as in the addition of one:

Three boys were going to school. Two others joined them; how many boys were there then?

Two little girls went to buy bread. One of them carried home four loaves, the other two loaves; how many loaves had they in all?

In a working-man's cottage there are three rooms on the ground floor, and two rooms up stairs; how many rooms does the cottage contain?

The apt teacher will invent many other simple illustrative questions of this kind, until the class has had sufficient practice.

3. *Addition of Three.*

This is to be taught on the same plan.

The teacher arranges objects, or draws lines on the blackboard, in the following order:

The children then say together, as each line is pointed to.

"One line and three lines are four lines;
Two lines and three lines are five lines;
Three lines and three lines are six lines;"

and so on, to ten lines.

The children should then, as before, recapitulate the lesson, without reference to the objects or lines on the board. In doing this, the word *lines*, &c., may be omitted, saying only, "One and three are four; two and three are five; three and three are six," &c.; only do not suggest the answer to the children, nor lead on too rapidly.

After this repetition, as in every other lesson of this kind, the teacher should energetically question the children individually upon it, introducing also questions bearing upon the instruction given in preceding lessons on the same subject. The necessity of this cannot be too strongly impressed upon the minds of teachers. A few practical illustrations are given by way of example:

A boy has two cents. His uncle gives him three cents; how much has he then?

There are five apples in a basket; how many will there be, if I put in three apples more?

I gave a boy six cents yesterday, and I have given him three cents to-day; how many cents have I given him in all?

A boy, fond of playing at marbles, has a hole in the pocket in which he keeps them. He lost seven marbles last night, and three this morning; how many has he lost?

4. *Addition of Four, Five, Six, Seven, Eight, and Nine.*

These operations need no further illustration; the plan adopted is the same as with the previous numbers. The teacher must carefully avoid advancing too rapidly, and must not be weary under the frequent repetition of previous instruction. It must be constantly borne in mind, that as the children are supposed to know little or nothing, as yet, of any number more than ten, all operations are to be so adapted as to involve no higher number.

ILLUSTRATIONS OF THE FOREGOING EXERCISES.

The scope afforded by the preceding lessons is so narrow, that it is found difficult in actual practice to extend the instruction upon them to that point which nevertheless must be reached, if they are to be fully comprehended and indelibly fixed on the mind.

The following exercises have been devised in order to meet this difficulty. They will be found useful, as presenting the numbers to the observation of the children in new aspects, and as exercising their faculties upon them in a manner less formal and methodical than the lessons already given, whilst at the same time the operation of addition is adhered to.

1. To FIND WHAT NUMBER MUST BE ADDED TO A GIVEN NUMBER IN ORDER TO PRODUCE A THIRD NUMBER.

In some of the above lessons on this Step, *two* numbers have been given, and the children required to find a *third* number which should be the sum of both.

In the following exercise two numbers are given, the one being always larger than the other, and the children are required to find what number must be added to the smaller number to make it equal to the larger number.

The use of objects or lines must be continued. Suppose the

given numbers to be two and three, the teacher arranges objects or strokes thus:

| | | | |

and asks, "How many strokes must I add to the first of these groups, in order to make it equal to the second of them?" The teacher may proceed: "What must I add to *two* lines, in order to make *three* lines?" or, "What must I add to *two*, if I wish to make it *three?*"

This method must be pursued with all the numbers up to ten, those numbers being commenced with which present the *difference of one*. After this, those exhibiting a difference of two; this progression being maintained till ten is reached. As the lessons proceed, the objects or lines may to some extent be laid aside, and referred to chiefly for correction of error, or for proof of accuracy.

EXAMPLES.

To find what must be added to a number to produce another number larger than the first by one:

To FIVE to produce SIX?
" SIX " SEVEN?
" SEVEN " EIGHT?
" THREE " FOUR? &c.

To find what must be added to a number to produce another number larger than the first by two:

To TWO to make it FOUR?
" FOUR " SIX?
" FIVE " SEVEN?
" EIGHT " TEN? &c.

To produce another number larger than the first by three:

To THREE to form SIX?
" FOUR " SEVEN?
" FIVE " EIGHT?
" SEVEN " TEN? &c.

NUMBER.—FIRST STEP. 157

Larger than the first by four:

  To two to form six?
  " four " eight?
  " five " nine?
  " six " ten? &c.

2. THE PRODUCING A NEW NUMBER BY COMBINING TWO OTHER NUMBERS.

EXAMPLES.

To produce the number FOUR *in every possible mode:*

In the first place, the teacher questions the children in such a manner as to lead them to dispose objects, or to draw lines on the board, according to the following arrangement:

   I I I   I
   I I   I I
   I   I I I

The class, with their attention closely directed to this arrangement, is then to be required to repeat aloud:

"Four lines are formed by
  "Three lines and one line.
  Two lines and two lines.
  One line and three lines."

The children should then be required to describe from memory the various modes of producing the number four, after which they may be called upon singly to come forward and construct the number four in every practicable manner, with objects or by lines.

To produce FIVE *in the same manner:*

Here also the children should first be led to the construction of the lesson with something they can handle, or examine by the eye. In the present case the arrangement will be this:

To be read as before. Suppose the construction to be of books:

"Five books are formed by
"Four books and one book.
Three books and two books.
Two books and three books.
One book and four books."

This to be followed by the repetition from memory: "Four and one are five; three and two are five; two and three are five; one and four are five."

To produce the number SIX *on the same plan:*

"One and five are six.
Two and four are six.
Three and three are six.
Four and two are six.
Five and one are six."

To produce the number SEVEN:

"Six and one are seven.
Five and two are seven.
Four and three are seven.
Three and four are seven.
Two and five are seven.
One and six are seven."

These lessons should be extended to the number ten, each of them to be followed by a variety of illustrative examples for practice; such, for example, as the following:

I buy a book for eight cents. If I cannot pay for it in one payment, in how many ways can I pay for it in two payments?

A boy has to visit his aunt, who lives at a town nine miles from his home. His mother tells him he may rest for an hour once on the way. If he rest at the fourth milestone, how many miles will he have to walk when he sets off again? How many if he rest at the fifth? At the sixth? At the seventh?

3. THE SIMPLE ADDITION OF THREE OR FOUR NUMBERS, OR MORE.

The use of objects or lines should at first be adhered to in this exercise also, and the children should repeat aloud the given numbers, as well as each successive step of the process. Thus, supposing the numbers given to be two, three, and four, they should say:

"Two and three more are five; five and three more are eight;" or, "Three and three are six; six and four are ten."

When the class has had some practice in this kind of addition, the teacher may slowly pronounce the given numbers, and the class be required to give the final sum only, the intermediate results being omitted.

The addition of other numbers is to be carried out on the same plan. The exercises on this head will of necessity be limited, as no result exceeding ten should be attempted; but they may be varied, and many examples given of the same nature as those before introduced.

4. THE PRODUCING A FIXED NUMBER BY COMBINING THREE OTHER NUMBERS.

These exercises are to be illustrated in the same manner as those on the combination of *two* numbers. Where objects are used, the teacher may put them together as the children audibly perform the addition. Two examples of this exercise may suffice.

To produce the number SEVEN *by every possible combination of three numbers:*

The arrangement of lines or of objects will be this:

```
  I         I       I I I I I    =    I I I I I I I
  I         I I     I I I I      =    I I I I I I I
  I         I I I   I I I        =    I I I I I I I
  I I       I I     I I I        =    I I I I I I I
```

To produce the number TEN:

One	and	two	and	seven	are	ten.
One	"	three	"	six	"	ten.
One ·	"	four	"	five	"	ten.
Two	"	three	"	five	"	ten.
Three	"	three	"	four	"	ten.
Four	"	four	"	two	"	ten.
Six	"	two	"	two	"	ten.

When the lines have been gone over in this order, it may be useful, without changing the position of the strokes on the board, to calculate each line backward, reading the top line of the second table, for instance, thus: "Seven and two and one are ten," &c.

The producing a number by the combination of *four* numbers, will suggest itself to the teacher, as a simple extension of the method recommended above.

Each separate exercise should be illustrated by examples having an application to visible objects and the events of every-day life.

SUBTRACTION.

The children, having acquired facility in increasing numbers, by combining them in the process of addition, must now be led on to the equally important operation of separating them in the process of subtraction. The use of objects must still be continued. The lessons in addition having been entered into at so much length, that which follows will be given more briefly. The teacher must not, however, suppose that the same patient repetitions, the same varied examples, are not necessary. Very young children cannot be *well* taught in any other way.

NUMBER.—FIRST STEP.

1. TO TAKE ONE GIVEN NUMBER FROM ANOTHER.

   The Subtraction of the Number One:

Objects are to be arranged, or strokes to be made on the board, in the order indicated by the column on the left. The teacher should then remove one object to a little distance, or rub out one stroke from each line of strokes successively, the children repeating aloud, as this is done, "Two less one is one; three less one are two," &c., through the whole series of subtractions, and leaving the objects as represented in the right column; or, if lines are used, leaving the column on the right everywhere diminished by one.

It is important, as an exercise, that the operations of addition should be constantly returned to, and it is found in practice desirable to combine them with those of subtraction, as helping to a clearer comprehension of both processes. To effect this, after the above lesson on subtraction has been given, it may be recapitulated, or a second lesson may be given, with the additional exercise of recombining the numbers which have been separated by subtraction; thus:

Two less one is one.   One and one are two.
Three less one are two.   Two and one are three.
Four less one are three.   Three and one are four,
                           to
Ten less one are nine.   Nine and one are ten.

After this lesson the children should be separately questioned on it, and exercised in its application to objects of daily use.

The subtraction of TWO should now be taught by objects or strokes, as in the case of the subtraction of one, and, after that, *the subtraction and addition of two in one operation,* thus :

Ten less two are eight.	Eight and two are ten.
Nine less two are seven.	Seven and two are nine.
Eight less two are six.	Six and two are eight,
to	
Three less two are one.	One and two are three.

The subtraction of THREE, followed by the addition and subtraction of three in one operation :

Ten less three are seven.	Seven and three are ten.
Nine less three are six.	Six and three are nine,
to	
Four less three are one.	One and three are four.

Every successive number must be treated in the same manner till the number *nine* is reached, each lesson being frequently repeated, and each being illustrated by questions involving the practical application of the number under consideration.

2. SUBTRACTION AND RECOMBINATION OF SEVERAL NUMBERS IN SUCCESSION.

To subtract in succession the numbers one, two, three, and four, from the number five, recombining each by addition :

Five less one are four.	Four and one are five.
Five less two are three.	Three and two are five, &c.

To subtract the numbers one to five from six :

Six less one are five.	Five and one are six.
Six less two are four.	Four and two are six, &c.

The intermediate numbers to be similarly treated, as far as the subtraction of the numbers one to nine from ten :

Ten less one are nine.	Nine and one are ten.
Ten less two are eight.	Eight and two are ten,
to	
Ten less nine are one.	One and nine are ten.

This exercise should be followed by a series of miscellaneous questions.

3. To FIND WHAT NUMBER MUST BE TAKEN FROM A GIVEN NUMBER IN ORDER TO REDUCE IT TO ANOTHER GIVEN NUMBER.

It will be seen that this lesson is the inversion of one of the exercises in addition. The teacher should draw two groups of lines on the slate, or arrange two sets of objects in unequal number, and require the children to decide how many must be taken from the larger number to make it equal the smaller number. The subtraction should also be practically carried out, that the result may be *seen* to be accurate. Begin with numbers having the difference ONE, increasing the difference progressively.

EXAMPLES.

What number must be taken from the number *ten*, to make it nine? eight? seven?—to one, successively.

What number must be taken from the number *nine*, to reduce it to seven? five? &c.

What from *eight*, to reduce it to five? three? two? &c.

The teacher must be careful that a sufficient number of examples are given and well understood before proceeding to a new lesson.

4. THE COMPARING TWO NUMBERS IN ORDER TO FIND THEIR DIFFERENCE.

This idea may be developed by simple questions. A few examples are given:

You have four apples, your brother has five apples; which of you has the more apples?

But if you have five marbles, and your brother four marbles, how many more have you than he?

If you have six peaches, and he four peaches, how many more peaches have you than he?

Objects may then be arranged on the table, or lines drawn on the slate in two groups, one containing five, the other four. The class may repeat, "Five is one more than four; four is one less than five." One by one the number may be diminished, the class in each instance explaining the result; thus:

Comparison of *five* with all numbers below it:

   Five is two more than three.
   Three is two less than five.
   Five is three more than two.
   Two is three less than five, &c.

Comparison of *seven* with all numbers below it:

   Seven is one more than six.
   Six is one less than seven.
   Seven is two more than five.
   Five is two less than seven.
   Seven is three more than four.
   Four is three less than seven.

The word "difference" may be used as these exercises become familiar:—"The difference between seven and six is one; the difference between seven and five is two," &c.

5. THE SUBTRACTION OF A GIVEN NUMBER FROM THE UNEXPRESSED SUM OF TWO OTHER GIVEN NUMBERS.

  Take six from the sum of five and five.
  " nine " three and seven.
  " three " six and six.
  " five " eight and two.
  " eight " six and four.
  " six " four and four.
  " four " seven and three, &c.

These examples may be varied to a great extent, at the discretion of the teacher. They should be followed by a series of well-adapted miscellaneous practical questions.

NUMBER.—FIRST STEP. 165

6. THE SUBTRACTION OF A GIVEN NUMBER FROM THE UNEXPRESSED SUM OF THREE OTHER GIVEN NUMBERS.

Take six from the sum of three, three, and three.
" five " three, four, and three.
" four " seven, two, and one.
" seven " six, two, and three, &c.

7. THE SUBTRACTION OF THE SUM OF TWO LOW NUMBERS FROM THE SUM OF TWO NUMBERS OF HIGHER VALUE.

From the sum of six and four take that of five and three.
" six and three " four and two.
" five and five " four and four, &c.

8. THE SUBTRACTION OF THE SUM OF THREE LOW NUMBERS FROM THE SUM OF TWO NUMBERS OF HIGHER VALUE.

From four and five take two, two, and two.
" six and three " three, two, and one.
" four and four " two, three, and two.
" three and five " one, four, and two, &c.

9. PROMISCUOUS ADDITIONS AND SUBTRACTIONS.

Add seven to two, and take away five.
" six to three, " four, &c.

From the sum of seven and two take away six.
" five and three " four, &c.

At first, these exercises should, as far as possible, be carried out with the use of objects or lines, and the teacher should be careful not to discontinue the use of these too soon. A variety of miscellaneous questions, bearing upon all the lessons hitherto given under the heads of addition and subtraction, should be introduced before the next Step is commenced upon.

MULTIPLICATION AND DIVISION.—ONE TO TEN.

Multiplication.

Object.—To lead the children to the comprehension of the operation of multiplying numbers into each other, to prove to them that this is but a simplification and abbreviation of the process of addition which they have already acquired, and to make them familiar with the arrangement of numbers called the Multiplication Table.

Plan.—Illustrate the subject by means of objects or lines, as indicated in the following outline :

In the process of addition the children have learnt to find a new number, which is the sum of two, three, or four numbers, which may be of differing value. They are now to be taught to find the result of taking one and the same number a given number of times. Make one stroke on the large slate, and ask, What have I done? You have made one stroke. How many times have I made it? You have made one stroke once. What number do I get when I make one stroke once? You get one. If I put my hand into a basket once, and take out one apple, how many apples do I get? You get one. How much is one taken one time? It is one.

Make one stroke more on the slate beside the other. What have I done? You have put one stroke to one stroke, and now there are two strokes. Yes; one and one are?—Two. How many times have I made one stroke? Two times. Then two times one are?—Two. Pursue this exercise till one has been taken *ten* times; in each case, as one is added, first calling out observation on the process, as being one of addition, and then as being one of multiplication.

Place two cubes of wood on the table. How many cubes are there here? There are two. How many times have I now put two cubes on the table? Once. How many are two taken one time? Once two are two. Add two cubes to these. What have I done? You have added two cubes to the two which were there before. How many cubes are there on the table now?

There are four. Yes; two and two are?—Four. How many times have I put two on the table? You have done so twice. How many are two taken twice? Twice two are four. Let two more cubes be added. What have I done? You have put two more cubes on the table. How many were there before I added them? There were two and two—four. How many are there now? There are two and two and two—six. How many times have I put two cubes on the table? Three times. Then two taken three times are?—Six. Repeat: Three times two are? Six. This lesson on the multiplication of two should be carried to " Five times two are ten."

Let the same plan be carried out with the number *three*, as far as " Three times three are nine ;" with the number *four*, as far as " Two times four are eight ;" and with *five*, as far as " Two times five are ten." These lessons should not be carried beyond this point as yet, because the children are not supposed to be familiar with numbers more than ten, the higher numbers being gradually introduced. Little is gained by pressing forward quick children to the higher numbers; it is far safer to proceed gradually and systematically.

It will be seen, that although the range of these exercises is necessarily limited, they are important, as awakening perception of a new mode of using numbers. When the children have gone through them, they should recapitulate the facts, thus:

Once two is two.   Once three is three.
Twice two are four.   Twice three are six.
Three times two are six. Three times three are nine.
Four times two are eight.
Five times two are ten.
Once four is four.   Once five is five.
Twice four are eight.   Twice five are ten.

Miscellaneous practical examples should follow each exercise.

DIVISION.—ONE TO TEN.

Object.—To lead the children to the comprehension of the

operation of dividing one number by another, and to teach them to divide other numbers by one, two, three, four, &c.

Plan.—This is illustrated in the following exercises:

1. Make two lines on the slate, and say, Rub out two lines from the slate. How many times can you take away two from two? Once. How many times is two contained in two? One time.

Make four lines on the slate, and say, Rub out two lines. What remain? Two lines remain. Rub them out. What remain now? There are none left. How many lines were there at first? There were four. How often can you take away two from four? Twice. How often is two contained in four? Twice.

Now I make six, eight, ten lines on the slate. Try how often you can take away two from each of these numbers.

Now I place three cubes on the table. How often can you take three cubes away from them? Once only. But if I put three cubes on the table, twice over, how many will there be? There will be two times three, or six cubes. How many times can I take three away from six? You can take three cubes away twice. How often are three contained in six? Two times.

Now I make three, six, and nine strokes on the slate. Tell me how often each of these numbers contains the number three, and how often you can take three away from each of them.

2. *The Division by Two of Numbers under Ten.*

The teacher may construct the following table upon the school slate, in order to illustrate the subject. It will be seen that it includes to some extent the exercises on multiplication, as assisting to the comprehension of the process of division.

How much is twice 1? 2.   How many ones in 2? 2.
How much is twice 2? 4.   How many twos in 4? 2.
How much is twice 3? 6.   How many twos in 6? 3.
How much is twice 4? 8.   How many twos in 8? 4.

The questions should then be put in another form; as, How often is two contained in two? in four? in six? in eight? How much is two, four, six, and eight, divided by two?

A few miscellaneous questions might be introduced, even at this early stage of the subject, to make the nature of the operation clear.

If I measure four yards of cloth by a yard measure, how many times shall 1 have to apply it to the cloth?

If I measure four yards of cloth by a measure two yards long, how often will the length of the measure be contained in the length of the cloth?

Into how many sets of two can I divide eight marbles?

To how many boys can I give four pens, if I give one pen to each of them?

To how many, if I give two pens to each of them?

A farmer and his son are going to market; they wish to take four baskets of apples with them; how many baskets must each of them carry?

At the market they buy eight new spades; how many must each of them carry?

SECOND STEP.

NOTATION.

Hitherto the several numbers have been represented to the eye solely by objects or strokes; the expression of the higher numbers by these means will already have become inconvenient. The pupil must now be introduced to the more simple and practical method afforded by the Arabic* numerals.

Object.—1. To make evident the need of some brief and ready method of expressing the value of numbers in writing; to teach the form and power of the ten numeric signs, 1, 2, 3, 4, 5, 6, 7, 8, 9, 0.

2. To make the children familiar with the meaning of the words *more* and *less*,† and with the algebraic signs + and —, as

---

* They are, in fact, Indian in their origin, though we have received them through the Arabians.

† If the children are advanced, they may be also taught that the Latin words *plus*, for more, and *minus*, for less, are often used, particularly in books of Arithmetic.

respectively expressive of the operations of addition and subtraction; and also with the sign = as expressive of equality or result.

Plan.—This, as it regards carrying out the first object, will be gathered from the following suggestions to the teacher:

1. In order to illustrate the need for the use of figures in expressing to the eye the value of numbers, let the children suppose a case in which it is required to state some high number in writing; as, for instance, the age of an old man. They will at once see that the doing this by means of strokes would occupy so much time and space as to be most inconvenient, and that to avoid this must be most desirable. Various illustrations will suggest themselves.

When the perception of the want has been awakened, the teacher may communicate the numeric value of the several numeral characters by means of groups of strokes, each group having written over it the figure which has been adopted as its unvarying symbol; thus:

  1 2 3 4
  I I I I I I I I I I

This should be carried as far as the number *nine*.

When these groups of strokes and their representative figures have been thoroughly scrutinized, the children should be led on to apply them for themselves. The teacher may write any one of the figures on the slate, and require a child to place against it the number of strokes or units it represents, while the other children of the class determine whether this is correctly done. To vary the exercise, the teacher may make any definite number of strokes, not exceeding *nine*, upon the slate, and require the children to apply the right numeric sign; or, for variety, the teacher may present a definite number of objects, requiring the children to express the number, both by the utterance of the name of the number, and by the formation of the corresponding figure on the slate. They ought to acquire familiarity with the nine numerals in two lessons.*

---

* It would be a useful lesson for the children themselves to make the figures, indicating opposite to each of them, by the proper number of strokes, the number of units it expresses.

2. The children, having acquired the knowledge of nine figures by which the nine lowest numbers are briefly expressed for convenience of calculation, may now be led to see that the word *two* and the sign 2, the word *three* and the sign 3, &c., have an unchangeable, or *absolute* value, which may be used to qualify any objects whatever; so that we may say, two elephants or three elephants, two flies or three flies, two ones or three ones; the number being always the same number, however different the objects to which it is applied.

3. The teacher may now introduce the words *more* and *less*, and the algebraic signs of addition, subtraction, and equality or result. First, let the teacher write a column of numbers to be added, on the school slate. This may be done in different modes:

1 and 1 are 2	1 more 1 are 2
2 and 1 are 3	2 more 1 are 3
3 and 1 are 4	3 more 1 are 4
&c.	&c.

Then let the teacher write on the slate the same numbers as before, connecting them by the signs of addition and equality, as in the margin; or the words may be erased, and the signs substituted. The sign $+$ should not be made in a careless manner, and attention should be called to the fact that the one line is exactly vertical, the other exactly horizontal, in order that this sign may be the better distinguished when that which indicates multiplication is hereafter presented.

$$1 + 1 = 2$$
$$2 + 1 = 3$$
$$3 + 1 = 4$$
$$4 + 1 = 5$$

The process is the same with the sign of subtraction, columns of some length being first constructed, with the use of words, afterward exhibiting the superior simplicity and utility of the signs:

2 less 1 is 1	$2 - 1 = 1$
3 less 1 are 2	$3 - 1 = 2$
4 less 1 are 3	$4 - 1 = 3$
5 less 1 are 4	$5 - 1 = 4$

THE DEVELOPMENT OF THE NUMBERS ELEVEN TO ONE HUNDRED, AND THE EXTENSION OF NOTATION.

Object.—This Step is but an extension to higher numbers of the principles already laid down, and the extension of the power of numeric notation to the expression of such numbers.

To explain the nature of the *local* value of figures, as distinguished from their *absolute* value.

Plan.—I. Develop the perception of the numbers eleven to one hundred, on the plan proposed in the development of the numbers one to nine, tangible or visible objects being still used with the lower numbers. The number ten should be much employed as a means of classification, and as a help both to the eye and to the mind in the comprehension of the higher numbers.

Teach the children to enumerate simply by combinations of tens and units before using the common contractions; for example, saying after 10, one ten and one, one ten and two, &c., up to one ten and nine; then two tens and one, two tens and two, &c., up to nine tens and nine; thus learning the meaning of the terms *fourteen, twenty-one,* and being enabled to see more clearly the plan of numbering by ten, and that the highest number is merely a repetition of ten units.

II. Communicate the names of each of these numbers, and test the children's attainments as already recommended and illustrated, concluding with simple ascending and descending enumeration.

III. Illustrate the powers and names of these numbers when used as ordinals.

IV. When a clear perception of such numbers has been attained, the children may be introduced to the effort of expressing them in numerals. To do this, they must be led to see the necessity for changing the numerals in the second, or tens' place of figures from 1 and 2, as hitherto used in the numbers 11, 12, and in 21, 22, &c.; to 3, in 31, 32, 33, &c.; to 4, in 41, 42, 43, &c., up to 99.

This subject is important, not at this stage of instruction only, but throughout the whole range of number. It introduces the mind to the perception of a new feature in numerical *notation—*

NUMBER.—SECOND STEP.

that of the *local value* of the ten figures (inclusive of 0, which indicates the absence of number); for it is to these *figures* or signs alone, and not to the *names* of numbers, that this property of local value belongs.

In the first place, lead the children to feel the need of some brief mode of expressing the value of numbers more than 9.

To do this, the teacher may once more form groups of strokes on the slate, from one to ten, requiring a child to place over each stroke or group of strokes its representative numeral. This will be easy as far as 9. When the child has reached the group containing ten strokes, and is at a loss for a numeral by which to express it, the teacher may communicate the fact that only nine numeral characters (exclusive of 0) have been invented for the written expression of all numbers, how large soever they may be.

Having reached this point, the mind of the children should be led to think out this fact of local value. With a view to this, the teacher may draw two columns on the school slate, and write at the top of each of them the name of some familiar object, as in the margin; telling the children to call the column on the right the *first* column,* that on the left the *second*. Any numeral, say 4, may then be written in the first column.
What does it mean? It means *four* of boys. What would it mean if written in the *second* column? It would then mean four of *men*. Write 3 in the first column, 8 in the second. How will you read these figures? *Eight* of men and *three* of boys. Transpose them, and how will you read them now? Three of *men* and eight of *boys*. Diversify both names and numbers for further exercise.

Again, draw two columns on the slate, and at the top of the first column, write "ones," at the top of the second, "tens," as in the margin. Place the numeral 1 in the first column. What does it mean? It means one *one*, or one unit. Remove it to the next column. What does it mean now? Now it means one ten. Write the same numeral in both columns.

---

* This order is important as a right beginning, the "place of figures" being always enumerated from right to left.

What is it now? Now it is one *ten* and one *one*. Have you learnt any name for one ten and one one, or for ten more one? Yes; ten more one is called "*Eleven*." The teacher may then successively change the figure in the *first* column to two. What is it now? One ten and *two*. Its name? *Twelve*. To three. What is it now? One ten and three. Its name? *Thirteen*. And so on to nine. What is it now? One ten and nine. Its name? *Nineteen*.

The teacher may now rub out the vertical lines, leaving the words "tens" and "ones" still standing as before, with the figures under them, and may ask if the value of the figures is altered at all by removing the lines? Not at all. Why? The *words* still remain to tell the respective value of the figures to be one ten and nine ones, or nine and ten, or nineteen.

TENS.	ONES.
1	9

The words may now be removed also, and the teacher may ask if the children can themselves remember the respective values of the figures? Yes; their relative position indicates this: that figure in the *first* place of figures means nine units, or ones; that in the second place of figures means one ten, the whole sum being one ten and nine ones, or nineteen.

The children may now be told that whenever two figures stand side by side thus, that they always bear this relation to each other, and they may be led to see that the value of a figure is increased tenfold by being moved one place to the left.

The children should now be exercised in reading and putting down numbers to ninety-nine.

THIRD STEP.

Exercises with Numbers, the Sum or Product of which does not exceed 100.

INTRODUCTION.

Since the decimal system in its principal features, together with its notation, has to some extent been presented to the children in the preceding chapters, it becomes the duty of the teacher to show the children its advantages, even in mental arithmetic, and not to leave it entirely to chance, or to an appeal to memory alone; remembering that in every school a large proportion of the children do not belong to that privileged class who seize everything by the force of native talent, or of genius. The teacher may make use of the hints given in these introductory remarks whenever the opportunity, or rather the necessity, presents itself. For instance, if there should be some difficulty in the addition of $26 + 3$, $56 + 3$, &c., the teacher has but to ask what $6 + 3$ would make, showing that the above questions are related, or rather based upon this fact, and that, whilst the sum of the units is 9 in every one of these examples, the number of tens remains unchanged.

The same advantage is taken, when the subtraction of such examples as $37 - 4$, $57 - 4$, $97 - 4$, &c., is to be performed, since they are all based upon the fact that $7 - 4$ leaves 3, and that the number of tens is not affected.

In such examples as $57 + 5$, $67 + 5$, $87 + 5$, the number of tens becomes affected—that is, increased by one ten; but as the sum of the units $7 + 5$ make 12, it is easy to perceive that the number of units in the answer to any of the above questions must be 2, whilst the number of tens becomes increased by one.

A little more thought is required in solving such questions as $72 - 5$, &c., where the number of units to be subtracted exceeds the number of units in the number from which they are to be taken. In such a case, the teacher would do well to ask, into what parts they could divide 5? Answer, $1 + 4$, $2 + 3$. Ask them further, whether to take $1 + 4$, or $2 + 3$ away, would be the same as taking away 5? Then let them take off 2, leaving 70, and then 3 from 70, leaving 67 for the answer. Ask, then, whether it would not have been as convenient to have taken first one away, and then 4 afterward. Why not? What arrangement would they make in taking away 7 from 54? What would be the most convenient division of 7 in this example?

Another advantage presented by the decimal system, and often used for the rapid solution of questions, is found in the addition and subtraction of numbers near ten; as, for instance, of 8 and 9. To see this fully, the teacher may ask them to add 10 to any number she gives, which is the operation of a moment. She may then ask how much less 9 is than 10? If they would add 10 to any number, instead of 9, whether the result would not be too great? By how much? What must be done, to conform to the question?

Similar questions may be asked in regard to the subtraction of 9 or 8, and it will be found that the common sense of the children will never be slow to seize this legitimate advantage, which the more talented children will have found out for themselves. An intelligent teacher, who acts in this spirit, need not be afraid of having many slow or stupid children in the class.

Addition and Subtraction of a Number not exceeding 10 *successively.*

We consider it of the utmost importance, that pupils should not merely receive a few isolated questions of an exercise, but should be led to answer questions arranged in a series where no link has been omitted. There is, however, a danger, that many teachers may commit mistakes in the presentation of such a series, which will render it useless. For instance, let us suppose that a class is required to answer the following questions:—What does $1+2$ make? $2+2$? $3+2$? $4+2$? $5+2$? $6+2$? The respective answers to these questions are, 3, 4, 5, 6, 7, 8, &c. Now it is evident that every child, in giving his answers, has but to add *one* to the answer given by his predecessor, which can be done without thought, mechanically; since, as far as the work is concerned, it requires but the addition of *one*. To avoid this mistake, the questions given below have been arranged upon a different plan.

First Series of Addition.—Add 2 to 1, and to the successive results. The teacher asks: $1+2$, how many? $3+2$? $5+2$? $7+2$? $9+2$? $11+2$? $13+2$? $15+2$? $17+2$?

To what extent these exercises are to be carried, depends on the discretion of the teacher, and on the number of the scholars,

NUMBER.—THIRD STEP.

since every one of them should take a part in the formation of a series. As a general thing, it is sufficient to add the number about nine times.

First Series of Subtraction.—Subtract 2 from 19, and from successive remainders. 19 — 2? 17 — 2? 15 — 2? 13 — 2? 11 — 2? 9 — 2? 7 — 2? 5 — 2? 3 — 2?

REMARK.—After constructing a series, the teacher must not forget to ask questions promiscuously.

Second Series of Addition.—Add 2 to 2, and to successive results. 2 + 2? 4 + 2? 6 + 2? 8 + 2? 10 + 2? 12 + 2? 14 + 2? 16 + 2? 18 + 2?

Second Series of Subtraction.—Subtract 2 from 20, and from successive remainders. 20 — 2? 18 — 2? 16 — 2? 14 — 2? 12 — 2? 10 — 2? 8 — 2? 6 — 2? 4 — 2? 2 — 2?

In order to allow the teacher to superintend and conduct several classes at the same time, she may call upon those who have gone through one or more of the preceding exercises, to commit them to writing on their slates, giving them the signs of + for addition, — for subtraction, = for equality.

The work, as seen on their slates, would then stand thus:

1 + 2 = 3	19 — 2 = 17	2 + 2 = 4	20 — 2 = 18
3 + 2 = 5	17 — 2 = 15	4 + 2 = 6	18 — 2 = 16
5 + 2 = 7	15 — 2 = 13	6 + 2 = 8	16 — 2 = 14
7 + 2 = 9	13 — 2 = 11	8 + 2 = 10	14 — 2 = 12
9 + 2 = 11	11 — 2 = 9	10 + 2 = 12	12 — 2 = 10
&c.	&c.	&c.	&c.

It is of little consequence whether the series of addition are presented in close succession, or alternate with subtraction. We follow the former method in presenting the series, which can be made in the addition and subtraction of 3.

First Series.—Addition of 3 to 1, and its successive results. 1 + 3? 4 + 3? 7 + 3? 10 + 3? 13 + 3? &c., to 25 + 3?

Second Series.—Addition of 3 to 2, &c. 2 + 3? 5 + 3? 8 + 3? 11 + 3? 14 + 3? 17 + 3? &c., to 26 + 3?

Third Series.—Addition of 3 to 3, &c. 3 + 3? 6 + 3? 9 + 3? 12 + 3? 15 + 3? 18 + 3? &c., to 27 + 3?

SUBTRACTION.

First Series.—Subtraction of 3 from 28, and from successive remainders. 28 — 3 ? 25 — 3 ? 22 — 3 ? 19 — 3 ? &c.

Second Series.—Subtraction of 3 from 29, &c. 29 — 3 ? 26 — 3 ? 23 — 3 ? 20 — 3 ? &c.

Third Series.—Subtraction of 3 from 30, &c. 30 — 3 ? 27 — 3 ? 24 — 3 ? 21 — 3 ? 18 — 3 ? &c.

MISCELLANEOUS QUESTIONS.

28 + 3 ? 17 + 3 ? 22 + 3 ?
31 — 3 ? 16 — 3 ? 25 — 3 ?
16 + 2 + 3 + 2 + 1 + 3 ?
31 — 3 — 2 — 1 — 2 ?
15 + 2 — 3 + 1 — 2 + 3 ?

The above merely indicate the kind of questions that should be put to the children after having gone through with the several series. Many similar examples should be given by the teacher.

The addition and subtraction of 4 presents 4 series for each:

First Series.—1 + 4 ? 5 + 4 ? 9 + 4 ? &c., to 33 + 4 ?
Second " 2 + 4 ? 6 + 4 ? 10 + 4 ? " 34 + 4 ?
Third " 3 + 4 ? 7 + 4 ? 11 + 4 ? " 35 + 4 ?
Fourth " 4 + 4 ? 8 + 4 ? 12 + 4 ? " 36 + 4 ?

SUBTRACTION.

First Series.—37 — 4 ? 33 — 4 ? 29 — 4 ? &c.
Second " 38 — 4 ? 34 — 4 ? 30 — 4 ? "
Third " 39 — 4 ? 35 — 4 ? 31 — 4 ? "
Fourth " 40 — 4 ? 36 — 4 ? 32 — 4 ? "

Similar tables should be made out with 5, 6, 7, 8, and 9. If the teacher does not deem it necessary to include all the *series* in each table, the first and last may be taken, and the intermediate series omitted; as,

First Series.—1 + 5 ? 6 + 5 ? 11 + 5 ? 16 + 5 ? &c., up to 41 + 5 ?

Fifth Series.—5 + 5 ? 10 + 5 ? 15 + 5 ? 20 + 5 ? &c., up to ten additions.

The Second, Third, and Fourth Series being omitted. If there is sufficient time, however, it is better to include all. It is quite important that the last series with each number, in which the number itself is repeated, should always be included, as this has an important bearing on multiplication.

MULTIPLICATION.

There are people who do not consider either Multiplication or Division as a distinct operation, or as one involving a new principle, since, philosophically considered, these two operations of arithmetic can but do one of two things—either *increase* or *diminish*—which was done equally by the two processes already described. Moreover, multiplication, as everybody knows, is undoubtedly the result of the *addition* of equal numbers. When these results have been committed to memory, so that they can be immediately reproduced, we give to this act the name of *multiplication*. All being agreed that the instantaneous production of the facts of multiplication are of the utmost importance, in the arithmetical transactions of practical life, the question remains whether they have simply to be committed to memory, without thought or reflection, or whether they ought to be found or produced by the efforts of the pupils themselves. The first view led to the mechanical learning by rote of the so-called table of multiplication; the second view arose from the conviction, that it is unworthy of the most logical of all sciences, to give distinct and easily ascertained truths merely as a matter of belief, for parrot-like repetition, and that memory itself has no stronger ally than the full conception and understanding of a fact. The plan of the following exercises, as will be seen, advocates the latter of these views.

In the original treatise, which contains Pestalozzi's plan of teaching arithmetic, was seen the so-called table of "units," consisting of groups of strokes, intended, by their combination and repetition, to establish the facts of multiplication. Since, however, the counting by units (for which the lines are designed) is altogether discarded at the step at which the pupils are supposed to be, it is proposed to use a less cumbersome method of illustration, by making use of the figures representing numbers, and by arranging them thus:

Table of Addition to Illustrate Multiplication.

$$1+1+1+1+1+1+1+1+1+1$$
$$2+2^a+2^b+2^c+2+2+2+2+2+2$$
$$3+3+3+3+3+3+3+3+3+3$$
$$4+4+4+4+4+4+4+4+4+4$$
$$5+5+5+5+5+5+5+5+5+5$$
$$6+6+6+6+6+6+6+6+6+6$$
$$7+7+7+7+7+7+7+7+7+7$$
$$8+8+8+8+8+8+8+8+8+8$$
$$9+9+9+9+9+9+9+9+9+9$$

REMARK.—Each number, as will be seen, is represented 10 times. The table of *ones* is the first, although it reproduces but the results of counting; as, 1 time $1=1$; 2 times $1=2$. The table of *tens* is omitted, since it is supposed to have been already treated in establishing the laws of numeration and notation up to 100. The tables of 11 and 12 are here omitted, as involving compound numbers, although they may be profitably learnt by rote on some other occasion.

FIRST EXERCISE.—*Multiplication of Twos.*—The first operation to be performed on this table is obviously this, to have the sums produced by the addition of twos, threes, fours, &c., distinctly expressed. The power to do this has already been established in the previous exercises; for instance, the teacher asking, How many are $2+2$? $2+2+2$? $2+2+2+2$? &c., will undoubtedly obtain the correct answer. It becomes necessary, however, at this step, to obtain the answers quickly, without delay or hesitation. For this purpose, the teacher may point to the right of a number (for instance to *a*), and ask, What is the sum of units to the left of my pointer? *Ans.* 4. And now? (*pointing to b.*) *Ans.* 6. And now? (at *c.*) *Ans.* 8. She then moves the pointer to the numbers farther to the right, always requiring the children to tell the number of units.

This is done forward and backward (in which case it becomes subtraction), with always increasing rapidity, till the children, or at least the greater part of them, give their answers almost instantaneously. When this is accomplished, the teacher may go back to the first method of questioning, and ask, without pointing to the table, Can you tell me once more how many units $2 + 2 + 2 + 2 + 2$ make? *Ans.* 10. Then say, "Two and two and two and two and two are ten." Is there not a shorter way to express this same fact? How many twos did I give? Five twos. And how many units do they contain? Ten. Then say, "Five twos are ten units, or five times two are ten."

The teacher then tells them, that the taking of a number a certain number of times, and expressing the result in units, is called *multiplication;* and the act of doing it, to multiply. She then requires a child to take two 1, 2, 3, 4, 5, 6, 7, 8, 9, ten times, in the way already indicated: "One time two is two; two times two are four," &c. She then asks others, and finally bids the class repeat it in concert. She then tells them to write the facts they have just expressed, which can be done thus:

1 times 2 = 2	6 times 2 = 12
2 " 2 = 4	7 " 2 = 14
3 " 2 = 6	8 " 2 = 16
4 " 2 = 8	9 " 2 = 18
5 " 2 = 10	10 " 2 = 20

Or, by giving them the sign of multiplication, together with its meaning, the same facts would be rendered thus:

$2 \times 1 = 2$ $2 \times 4 = 8$
$2 \times 2 = 4$ $2 \times 5 = 10$
$2 \times 3 = 6$ $2 \times 6 = 12$, &c.

NOTE TO THE TEACHER.—It is generally the custom to read this table in a reversed order, and to call the above facts, 2 times $2 = 4$; 2 times $3 = 6$; 2 times $4 = 8$; but this cannot be defended on any philosophical principle. In the first place, it is not what the children have learned; for in practising, for instance, the table of twos, they have not learned that twice *three* are six, but that three times *two* are six. Secondly, it gives a wrong view about the meaning of the sign of multiplication, ×, which cannot be translated by the word "times," but signifies "multiplied by." The expression 2 × 3 means, therefore, 2 multiplied by 3; or, in other words, 2 taken 3 times, which is equivalent to 3 times 2.

Those who wish to test the accuracy of the children's conception, in any school where arithmetic is taught on sound principles, have but to ask whether they think 3 times 4 and 4 times 3 are exactly alike, and to illustrate each fact by means of lines or objects. They will probably be told, that whilst the product or result in both questions is the same, *the arrangement or grouping of the objects is different.*

After the children have written the table of twos, they should proceed in the same way with the tables of 3, 4, 5, 6, 7, 8, 9, and commit them to memory.

MISCELLANEOUS QUESTIONS ON MULTIPLICATION.

$7 \times 5?$ $4 \times 8?$ $9 \times 7?$ $7 \times 7?$
$3 \times 2 + 7 + 9?$ $7 \times 4 + 5 + 8 + 3?$
$9 \times 9 - 4 - 8 - 3?$ $7 \times 8 - 5 - 3 - 9?$
$8 \times 6 + 4 + 7 - 8 - 3 + 6?$
$7 \times 2 + 3 \times 2?$ $4 \times 3 + 5 \times 3?$ $7 \times 4 + 2 \times 4 + 8 + 6 - 7?$ &c.

The teacher should give many more examples of this character.

DIVISION.

INTRODUCTION.—It has already been hinted, that Division is an operation which implies Subtraction. This can be shown in the following manner: Let us take the example, $12 \div 3$, which asks how many times 3 is contained in 12? Now if we ascertain how many times 3 can be subtracted from 12, the question is solved. But $12 - 3 - 3 - 3 - 3 = 0$. Thus we see, that 3 could be subtracted 4 times from 12; consequently 3 is four times contained in 12, or $12 \div 3 = 4$.

It is obvious, however, that at the present step it is easier and shorter to consider Division the inverse operation of Multiplication, or as one which analyzes the result of multiplication into its factors. Thus, since 3, *four* times taken, makes 12, it is evident that 3 is, for this reason, contained in 12 four times.

Division of a Number by 2, 3, 4, 5, 6, 7, 8, 9, *provided the Number does not exceed Ten Times its Divisor.*

Division by 2.—Who can tell how many times 2 is contained in 12? *Ans.* Six times. Why? Because 6 times 2 = 12. This answer, as well as the argument, may be expected to be given at once by many of the class. In order, however, to bring the matter within the comprehension of even the dullest scholar, the teacher may draw 12 strokes on the blackboard, | | | | | | | | | | | |, and bid a child to show how it might be proved that 2 (or a group of two strokes) is contained six times in 12.

The practical analysis of this question is found in the adjoined diagram:

$$\underset{\text{| |}}{\overset{1}{\frown}}\ \underset{\text{| |}}{\overset{2}{\frown}}\ \underset{\text{| |}}{\overset{3}{\frown}}\ \underset{\text{| |}}{\overset{4}{\frown}}\ \underset{\text{| |}}{\overset{5}{\frown}}\ \underset{\text{| |}}{\overset{6}{\frown}}$$

She may also ask, how the same fact can be shown on the multiplication table, on the series representing twos:

$$\overbrace{2+\underset{1}{2}+\underset{2}{2}+\underset{3}{2}+\underset{4}{2}+\underset{5}{2}+\underset{6}{2}}+2+2+2+2$$

The child has first to point out the sum of 12 units (at the right end of the arc), and then count the number of twos situated under the whole arc. One or two examples of this kind will probably establish the facts of division, in so far as they are related to the table of multiplication.

The further questions must, of course, be put in a systematic and progressive manner, taking care that all the units below 10 are brought into play as divisors of a given number.

The second and third series of additions in the preceding table, for illustrating multiplication, contain the answers to the following questions:

How many times is 2 contained in 2, 4, 6, 8, 10, 12, 14, 16, 18, 20? Why?

How many times is 3 contained in 3, 6, 9, 12, 15, 18, 21, 24, 27, 30? Why? &c., &c., &c.

If the teacher finds it necessary to make the children write out the table of division, she may give them the sign of division, $\div$, and tell them that $12 \div 4$ is generally expressed as 12 *divided by* 4.

MISCELLANEOUS QUESTIONS.

$18 \div 2?$ $27 \div 3?$ $16 \div 4?$ &c.
To $21 \div 3$ add $7 + 9 + 4?$ To $56 \div 7$ add $4 + 2 + 5?$
To $64 \div 8$ add $3 + 5 - 9 - 7?$
$(27 \div 3) 9?$ &c. This must be read, $27 \div 3$ multiplied by 9.
To $(18 \div 9) 2$ add $7 + 9 - 4 - 8?$ &c.

Division of Numbers leaving a Remainder.

How many times is 2 contained in 15? *Ans.* 7 times and 1 over. Why? Show it by lines. ⌒⌒⌒⌒⌒⌒⌒|. The teacher now may tell the scholars, that in future examples of this kind they would do well to arrange the given number into two unequal parts, the first or larger one containing a number a certain number of times, and the latter forming a remainder.

In this operation she appeals to the memory of the children in regard to the products of the table of multiplication. For instance, in the question $29 \div 3$, she may ask whether they think that 3 is contained in 29 a certain number of times without a remainder? Whether this is the case with 28? With 27? Yes; 3 is contained in 27, 9 times. Then how many units are over, to make up 29? Two units. Express now the whole question: $29 \div 3 = 7$ and 2 remaining.

All the following examples, which the teacher may give promiscuously, are to be solved in a similar manner; for instance, $39 \div 5?$

Solution: $39 \div 5 = 7$, with a remainder of 4.

Some Suggestions on the Application of the foregoing Exercises to so-called Concrete* Numbers.

The purpose of these lessons being principally to develop a clear insight of numbers, their relations and properties, and the operations performed with them, the subject of their application does not seem to belong within the compass of this book; and the less so, as the examples to which we refer may be found in every treatise on Arithmetic. On the other hand, it may not be inappropriate, in connection with the principles advocated here, to render the teacher, to some extent, even independent of the examples supplied by a book.

In regard to one kind of examples which suggest the addition, subtraction, &c., of given objects, some of them of commercial interest, such as cents, dollars, pounds, &c., it need not be stated how easily these can be supplied at every step; nor should they be neglected, since they form an absorbing subject of consideration to every clerk, accountant, shopkeeper, and to other persons. As mental exercises, they must, however, be limited to numbers that can be easily remembered.

There is, however, one set of questions in which the terms usually adopted in the operations with abstract numbers, such as "adding," "subtracting," "multiplying," &c., are discarded, and other verbs supplied which imply the above named operations. For instance, there is addition implied in the actions to receive, to find, to earn, to borrow, to gain, to collect, &c. On the contrary, the idea of "getting less," or of subtraction, suggests itself to the mind by the actions of "leaving," "losing," "throwing away," "dying," &c. In the transactions of *buying*, we have an increase of articles, and a diminution of money; whilst in those of *selling* the case is reversed.

Now it would seem no difficult task to any thinking teacher to do what she is supposed to do in the preparation of all her other lessons, namely, to prepare for herself some examples of a concrete and practical character; as, for instance, "I had 28 cents;

---

* We protest against the word "concrete," as applied to numbers. Objects must be concrete, but numbers are always abstract.

of these I spent 6, and lost 2. On the other hand, I earned 12 cents one day, 18 cents the other; how many cents have I now?"

In regard to multiplication, the teacher's examples must be applied to objects which present some uniform repetition. For instance, in the example, "7 square tables have how many legs?" we find a repetition of 4 legs in each, and therefore 7 times 4 legs in all. The same is the case with the question, What is the price of 7 articles, at 4 cents each?

In regard to division, the first practical view which suggests itself is that of dividing a certain number of objects among some persons, or arranging them within some spaces; as, for instance: If I divide 20 apples among 4 persons, how many will each receive? If 28 chairs are equally distributed in seven rooms, how many are there in each room?

In these examples it would be simply absurd to say, Divide 20 apples *by* 4 persons, or 28 chairs by 8 rooms. This is another proof that the operations of arithmetic are performed mainly with abstract numbers, since the substitution of pears, cherries, marbles, and other objects, would not have affected the numerical operation.

There are a great many practical examples where division is not suggested by name, but simply by the circumstances attending the transaction. For instance, "I bought 5 articles with 35 cents; how much did I give for each?"

FOURTH STEP.

Addition, Subtraction, Multiplication, and Division, extended to Higher Numbers. Also a Short Course in Fractions.

This Step, which is thoroughly connected with the preceding one, is often neglected in common arithmetical works, and its solutions merely left to chance. Although at this step the visible illustrations may be to a great extent discarded, yet it becomes the more necessary to appeal to those sound principles which oblige the pupil to give to number a *real* value, and not, as is sometimes the case in cyphering, a mere *nominal* one.

Where cyphering begins too early, the child will often operate in a mechanical manner, even when he is required to perform a mental example. In order to illustrate this, we will assume that 25 and 47 have to be added. A child taught by rules will probably imagine the 47 placed under the 25; then adding 7 and 5 together, he will probably put two and carry one, which he adds to the sum of the two figures to the left, 4 and 2. The sum he will thus obtain he calls 72. Now it need not be said that this method is very cumbersome for mental arithmetic, and becomes nearly impracticable when applied to an example of subtraction. On the other hand, a child taught by natural principles will mark out a true path for himself, after having started in the right direction. We state here some of the most obvious features of this Step:

1. In performing operations of *mental arithmetic* with numbers composed of tens and units, it is safer to consider first the tens, and then the units.

2. The tens have to be treated as if they were units, as far as the operations are concerned.

3. The exercises have to be so arranged, that each one explains the following.

4. The solutions must not be *given* to the children, but *drawn out* by questions.

ADDITION AND SUBTRACTION.

EXERCISE I.—*Addition of Tens to Tens, and Subtraction of Tens from Tens.*

Example in Addition: How many are $20 + 20$? How many are 2 and 2? How many tens do 2 tens and 2 tens make? How many units?

The solution then stands as follows: 2 and 2 are 4; 2 tens and 2 tens are 4 tens, or 40; therefore $20 + 20 = 40$.

Example in Subtraction: How many are $50 - 20$? How many are $5 - 2$? 5 tens less 2 tens are how many tens? How many units?

Solution: $5 - 2 = 3$; 5 tens less 2 tens leave 3 tens, or 30; therefore $50 - 20 = 30$.

A great many questions of this kind must be given, and their solutions required.

EXERCISE II.—*Addition of Tens and Units to Tens, and Subtraction of Tens from Tens and Units, or of Tens and Units from Tens.*

Example in Addition: How many are $35 + 20$? How many are $30 + 20$? And 5 more?
Solution: $30 + 20 = 50$; $50 + 5 = 55$.

Example in Subtraction: How many are $59 - 20$? What is $50 - 20$? $59 - 20$? Why do you add 9 to the former result? Are the units changed in this example? Are the tens?

REMARK.—The child will see at once that the diminution only takes place in the tens, and that the units are left unchanged. The children will now be able to solve similar examples, which should be abundantly supplied by the teacher.

Example in Subtraction: How many are $50 - 37$? How many are $50 - 30$? $20 - 7$?
Solution: $50 - 30 = 20$; $20 - 7 = 13$.

EXERCISE III.—*Addition of Tens and Units to Tens and Units, and Subtraction of Tens and Units from Tens and Units.*

Example in Addition: How many are $43 + 29$? $43 + 20$? $63 + 9$?
Solution: $43 + 20 = 63$; $63 + 9 = 72$.

REMARK.—If some of the children should make the solution thus: $40 + 20 = 60$; $9 + 3 = 12$; therefore $60 + 12 = 72$, it should be accepted, although the former method will be more expeditious.

Example in Subtraction: How many are $73 - 28$? $73 - 20$? $53 - 8$?
Solution: $73 - 20 = 53$; $53 - 8 = 45$.

The teacher must use her own judgment as to the number of examples that should be given under each exercise. Before proceeding to the next exercise, the children should be able readily to solve any examples given them.

MULTIPLICATION.

The exercises in this step comprise examples in which one of the factors may go as high as 100, whilst the other must at present be limited to numbers not exceeding 10.

EXERCISE I.—*Multiplication of Tens by Units.*

REMARK.—This exercise will prove extremely easy, but not the less important. Since, however, the results obtained will soon exceed 100, and will reach as high as 1,000, it will be necessary for the teacher to extend the pupil's knowledge of notation and numeration, so as to enable him to write down correctly all the numbers from 100 to 1,000. This she can do on the plan suggested in a previous Step, under the head of "Notation."

In order to do full justice to this fundamental exercise, the children should compose several series by multiplying 10 successively by all units; after this 20, next 30, next 40, &c., up to 100.

The questions composing these series should first be given orally, and analyzed, after which they may be written on their slates.

The series will stand thus, when written:

$10 \times 1 = 10$	$20 \times 1 = 20$	$30 \times 1 = 30$
$10 \times 2 = 20$	$20 \times 2 = 40$	$30 \times 2 = 60$
$10 \times 3 = 30$	$20 \times 3 = 60$	$30 \times 3 = 90$
$10 \times 4 = 40$	$20 \times 4 = 80$	$30 \times 4 = 120$
&c., to	&c., to	&c., to
$10 \times 10 = 100$	$20 \times 10 = 200$	$30 \times 10 = 300$

This table should be read, "One time ten, two times ten," &c., and not "Ten times one," &c.

REMARK.—The first of these series needs no comment, since it was discussed in a previous Step, on Notation. In order to prove, in the second series, that 2 times 20 = 40, the teacher may ask, Of how many tens is 20 composed? 2 times 2 are how many units? 2 times 2 tens are how many tens? How many units?

The succeeding examples may be treated in the same way, till the children readily see the analogy between the multiplication of tens and that of units.

Many miscellaneous questions should be given, and their solutions required; as, for instance, 5 times 80?

Solution: 5 times 8 = 40; 5 times 8 tens = 40 tens = 400.

EXERCISE II.—*Tens and Units Multiplied by Units.*

Example: 53 × 4? The teacher must first show that this question requires that 4 times 50 and 4 times 3 should be added together.

Solution: 4 times 50 = 200; 4 times 3 = 12; 200 + 12 = 212.

Example: 97 × 9?
Solution: 9 times 90 = 810; 9 times 7 = 63; 810 + 63 = 873.

Let many questions be added, until the children can readily solve any question given.

DIVISION.

EXERCISE.—*Division of Numbers not falling below Ten Times, and not exceeding Twenty Times their Divisor, which must not exceed* 10.

Example: 37 ÷ 2?

As examples of this kind are in their analysis somewhat different from those in multiplication, they require a fuller development. The teacher may ask first, into what parts they would divide the given number, before operating upon it? The probable answer would be, Into 30 and 7. The teacher then must proceed to show, that however convenient such an arrangement would have been for any of the preceding operations, it might not prove to be so in this case. Let us take another example: How many times is 2 contained in 30? If the children hesitate in their answer, the teacher proceeds: How many times is 2 contained in 20? 10 times. By how many more is 37 than 20? Seventeen. Then we may arrange 37 into 20 and 17. How many times is 2 contained in 20? Ten times. And in 17? Eight times and 1 over. How many times in 20 + 17; or in 37? 10 + 8 times and 1 over, or 18 times and 1 over.

Example: 49 ÷ 3. Into what parts would you separate 49 to be divided by 3? Into 30 and 19. Why would you do so? Because we know that 3 is contained in 30 10 times. And in 19? 6 times and 1 over. Therefore it is contained in 49 how many times? 16 times and 1 over.

The children are thus led to separate all the numbers which they are required to divide in this Step, into two numbers, one of which is equal to ten times its divisor, and the other the difference between this and the given number. Both these numbers are then divided, and their quotients added together.

The teacher should not, however, be satisfied with giving a few isolated examples, but should occupy the class during several lessons by examples arranged like those below, the children giving a solution for each example:

27 ÷ 2? 37 ÷ 2? &c.
33 ÷ 3? 42 ÷ 3? 56 ÷ 3? &c.
46 ÷ 4? 53 ÷ 4? 61 ÷ 4? 73 ÷ 4? &c.

And so on, using 5, 6, 7, 8, and 9 as divisors of any number which does not give a quotient greater than twenty.

The teacher should continue similar examples, until the children can readily solve any question conforming to the conditions laid down.

The preceding questions, and their solutions, will prepare the children to solve on their slates questions written on the blackboard by the teacher, not by a mechanical process, but by a true analysis of the numbers which compose them. The following example will suggest the manner in which it may be written by the children:

Example: 167 ÷ 9?

Solution : 90 ÷ 9 = 10
77 ÷ 9 = 8 and 5 over.
―――――――――――――――
167 ÷ 9 = 18 and 5 over.

FRACTIONS.

Summary of the Exercises.

I.—Exercises on the names and values of Fractions.
II.—To convert whole numbers into Fractions.
III.—To convert Fractions into whole numbers.
IV.—Conversion of Fractions from one denomination to another.
V.—Addition of Fractional numbers.
VI.—To find how much must be added to a Fractional number, in order to produce a given number.
VII.—Various applications.

I.— On the Names and Values of Fractions.

Divide this apple into two equal pieces or parts. What is one of these parts called? What the other? And the two parts taken together? What, then, is a half?

A half is one of two equal parts of a whole.

How many half apples are there in one apple?

Then one whole apple is the same as ―――.

How did I obtain the half of this apple?

By dividing it into 2 equal parts, and taking one of these parts.

If, instead of 2 parts, I divide the apple into 3, what should I have? 3 equal parts. Say 3 thirds. And each of these parts? 1 third.

What, then, is the third part of a thing?
The two thirds?

To make one apple, how many thirds of an apple are necessary? Then one whole apple is the same as ―――.

How did I obtain the third of the apple? How two thirds?

The idea of the *fourth* may be developed as the half and third, or as follows :—

If, after having divided an apple into halves, I divide each half into two other equal parts, how many parts shall I have?
Ans. 4.
Each part is called a *quarter,* or a *fourth.*
To make one apple, how many quarters or fourths of an apple are required?

OBSERVATION.—It is necessary to familiarize the child with these words, *half, third, fourth,* and to endeavor to give him a precise idea of them, by making him take a certain part of some whole; for example, of a roll of paper, of a piece of wood, &c. The different kinds of unity should be varied as much as possible, in order that the pupil may not regard fractions absolutely, but merely as they relate to the unity employed.

Having taken 3 different objects as units, divide one of them into 2 equal parts, another into 3, and the third into 4; form them into 3 groups, and desire the child to point out *a half, a third, two thirds, a quarter, two quarters, three quarters.* . These objects may be apples, small wands, or cubes. Let him also compare these different fractions with reference to size, by asking him which is the larger, a half or a third? a third or a quarter? two thirds or three quarters? &c. The object here is not to teach him to find the difference with great exactness; it is sufficient for him to know that *a half* is more than *a third,* a third more than *a quarter;* for the greater number of parts there are in a unit, the smaller they are; that three quarters are more than *two thirds,* &c., &c.

II.—*Conversion of Whole Numbers into Fractions.*

How many half apples are there in 2 apples?
The same question upon 3, 4, 5, 6 apples, &c.
How many half feet are there in 2, 3, 4, 5, 6 feet?
How many thirds are there in 2, 3, 4, 5, 6 apples?
How many thirds are contained in 2, 3, 4, 5, 6 yards?
The same questions may be asked respecting quarters.

How many parts would there be, if each half were divided into 3?

Ask the same question, if they were divided into 4, 5 parts.

How many parts would there be, if each third were divided into 2, 3, 4, 5, 6 equal parts?

Ask the same questions, if each quarter be divided.

OBSERVATION.—The pupils should perform these operations themselves, either upon apples or some other objects. As a great quantity of apples would be necessary for such operations as these, cards may be used, divided into as many parts as are requisite; but it is better not to cut them entirely through, in order that the child may preserve the idea of unity formed by the reunion of the several parts. Lines may now be used; they are more convenient than objects.

Repeat all together.

1 whole is equal to 2 halves.
2 wholes make   4   "
3   "   6   "
4   "   8   "
5   "   10   "   &c., &c.
1 whole is equal to 3 thirds.
2 wholes make   6   "
3   "   9   "
4   "   12   "
5   "   15   "   &c., &c.
1 whole is equal to 4 quarters.
2 wholes make   8   "
3   "   12   "
4   "   16   "
5   "   20   "   &c., &c.
1 whole is equal to 5 fifths.
2 wholes make   10   "
3   "   15   "
4   "   20   "
5   "   25   "
6   "   30   "   &c., &c.

III.—*Conversion of Fractions into Whole Numbers.*

How many apples are there in 3 half apples?
Ans. 1 apple and a half.
Let the same question be asked respecting 4, 5, 6, 7, 8, 9, 10 halves, &c.

The children will easily perceive that they must find how many times 2 halves are contained in the number of halves of which the wholes are to be formed. This may be done first by allowing them to put two halves together to make a whole, then two more, and so on, until all have been counted. But they must not be told.

They should also be required to find how many wholes there are in a certain number of thirds, of fourths, and of fifths.

Simultaneous repetition.

Halves.				Halves.
2 make	1 whole.	1 whole is equal to	2
3 "	1 " and a half.	1 " and a half make	3
4 "	2 wholes.	2 wholes make	4
5 "	2 " and a half.	2 " and a half make	5
6 "	3 wholes.	3 " make	6
7 "	3 " and a half.	3 " and a half make	7
8 "	4 wholes.	4 " make	8
9 "	4 " and a half.	4 " and a half make	9
10 "	5 wholes.	5 " make	10

Thirds.				Thirds.
3 make	1 whole.	1 whole is equal to	3
4 "	1 " and 1 third.	1 " and 1 third make	4
5 "	1 " and 2 thirds.	1 " and 2 thirds make	5
6 "	2 wholes.	2 wholes make	6
7 "	2 " and 1 third.	2 " and 1 third make	7
8 "	2 " and 2 thirds.	2 " and 2 thirds make	8
9 "	3 wholes.	3 " make	9
10 "	3 " and 1 third.	3 " and 1 third make	10

Quarters.
```
4  make 1 whole.
5   "   1   "   and 1 qr.
6   "   1   "   and 2 qrs.
7   "   1   "   and 3 qrs.
8   "   2 wholes.
9   "   2   "   and 1 qr.
10  "   2   "   and 2 qrs.
```

Quarters.
```
1 whole is equal to       4
1   "    and 1 qr. make   5
1   "    and 2 qrs.  "    6
1   "    and 3 qrs.  "    7.
2 wholes are equal to     8
2   "    and 1 qr. make   9
2   "    and 2 qrs.  "   10
```

Fifths.
```
5 make 1 whole.
6   "   1   "   and 1 fifth.
7   "   1   "   and 2 fifths.
8   "   1   "   and 3   "
9   "   1   "   and 4   "
10  "   2 wholes.
```

Fifths.
```
1 whole is equal to           5
1   "    and 1 fifth make     6
1   "    and 2 fifths  "      7
1   "    and 3 fifths  "      8
1   "    and 4 fifths  "      9
2 wholes are equal to        10
```

IV.—*Conversion of Fractions from one Denomination to another.*

OBSERVATION.—The analysis in the following exercises must be made slowly, by the children themselves, upon objects, under the guidance of the teacher

How many quarters are there in 3 thirds?
Ans. 3 thirds make 1 whole; 1 whole is equal to 4 quarters.
How many thirds are there in 4 halves?
Ans. 4 halves make 2 wholes; 2 wholes make 6 thirds.
How many quarters are there in 6 halves?
Ans. 6 halves make 3 wholes; 3 wholes make 12 quarters.
How many halves are there in 6 thirds?
Ans. 6 thirds make 2 wholes; 2 wholes make 4 halves.
How many halves are there in 6 quarters?
Ans. 6 quarters make 1 whole and a half, or 3 halves.

V.—*Addition of Fractional Numbers.*

One apple and a half, and one apple and a half, make how many apples?

2 apples and a half, and 2 apples and a half ——?

3 wholes and a half, more 3 wholes ——?
4 wholes and a half, more 3 wholes and a half ——?
1 whole and a half, more 1 whole and a half, more 1 whole and a half ——?
2 wholes and a half, more 4 wholes and a half ——?
2 wholes and a half, more 2 wholes and a half, more 2 wholes and a half ——?
3 wholes and 2 thirds, more 2 wholes and 1 third ——?
3 wholes and 1 third, more 2 wholes and 2 thirds, more 2 wholes and 1 third ——?
5 wholes and 2 thirds, more 5 wholes and 2 thirds, more 1 third?
3 wholes and 1 third, more 2 wholes and 2 thirds, more 3 wholes and 1 third?
3 quarters, more 3 quarters?
2 quarters, more 1 whole and 2 quarters?
3 quarters, more 3 quarters, more 3 quarters?
1 whole and 3 quarters, more 1 whole and 1 quarter?
1 whole and 1 quarter, more 1 whole and 3 quarters?
3 wholes and 3 quarters, more 3 wholes and 3 quarters?
5 wholes and 1 quarter, more 3 wholes and 3 quarters, more 1 whole and a half?
3 fifths, more 3 fifths?
2 fifths, more 4 fifths, more 3 fifths?
4 fifths, more 4 fifths?
3 wholes and 2 fifths, more 3 wholes and 3 fifths? &c., &c., &c.

VI.—*To Find how much must be Added to a Fractional Number in order to Produce a Given Number.*

How much must be added to
1 half to produce   2 wholes?
3 halves   "   2   "
3   "   "   3   "
2 wholes   "   3   "   and 1 half?
3   "   "   4   "   "
2   "   and 1 half to produce 4   "   "

3 wholes and 1 half to produce 5 wholes?
5 " to produce 7 " and 1 half?
4 " and 1 half to produce 8 "
3 halves to produce 6 "
5 " " 5 "

What must be added to
  1 third to produce 1 whole?
  2 thirds " 1 " and 1 third?
  1 whole " 2 wholes and 1 third?
  1 " " 2 " and 2 thirds?
  1 " " 3 " and 1 third?
  1 whole and 2 thirds to produce 3 "
  1 " 2 " 4 "
  1 " 2 " 3 " and 2 thirds?
  2 wholes and 1 third " 3 "
  2 " 1 " 3 " and 2 thirds?
  3 " to produce 5 " and 1 third?
  5 " " 7 " and 2 thirds?
  10 " and 1 third to produce 12 "

How much must be added to
  1 quarter to produce 1 whole?
  2, 3 quarters to produce 1, 2, 3 wholes?
  1 whole " 2 wholes and 2 quarters?
  1 " and 3 quarters to produce 2 " and 1 half?

How much must be added to
  2 wholes and 3 quarters to produce 5 wholes?
  2 " " 1 half " 4 "
  2 " " 1 quarter " 6 "
  3 " " 3 quarters " 7 " and 1 half?
  4 " to produce 8 " " 1 quarter?
  5 " " 10 " " 3 quarters?
  3 quarters " 10 "
  1 whole and 3 quarters to produce 10 " &c.

OBSERVATION.—Other fractions require less attention than halves, thirds, and fourths. It is, however, necessary that the pupil should be slightly exercised upon them, in order that he may have an idea of them—more or less development being given to the subject, according to his age and information. Some exercises, similar to the preceding, should therefore be given upon fifths, sixths, and sevenths.

VII.— *Various Applications.*

If a person gives to two children 1 apple and 3 quarters for each, how many apples will he have given?

He gives to one child 1 pear and 1 third; how many will he give to 6 children?

He gives 2 apples to 4 children, dividing them equally; how much will each have? *Ans.* 1 half.

Two apples are given to 3 children; they divide them equally; how much will each have? *Ans.* 2 thirds.

The same question may be asked, if 3 apples be given to 6 children, 3 to 4 children, 4 to 5 children, 4 to 8 children, &c.

A child has been desired to write 1 page and 3 quarters; he has done the half of 1 page; how much has he still to write? *Ans.* 1 page and 1 quarter.

Ask the same question, if he had 3 pages and a half to write, and if he has written one and a half. If he had 2 pages and 3 quarters, and has done one and a half, &c.

A child had bought 3 pounds of cherries; he has eaten 1 pound and a half of them; how much has he left?

I work every morning 1 hour and a half; how many hours will that make in 2, 3, 4, 5, 6 days?

I work 3 hours and 3 quarters every day; how many hours will that make in 2, 3, or 4 days?

What do 2 hours and a quarter, 2 hours and 3 quarters, and 1 hour and a half, make?

The teacher may continue questions of this character in her discretion.

SIZE.

INTRODUCTORY REMARKS.

Size, as existing in all objects, is, as well as form and color, taken cognizance of by the eye, and soon attracts the attention of children. It forms also an interesting subject for lessons, from its blending amusement with instruction, when the children are permitted to test the correctness of their judgment of the size of any object, by actual measurement of it. It is important they should receive correct first impressions on a point so essential to future usefulness.

In accordance with our plan in all elementary instruction, we begin by appealing to the intuitive perception of the quality under consideration, leading the children to perceive the existence of such a property as *size;* and this is effected by drawing their attention to various groups of objects, the components of each of which differ only in their dimensions. Observation being thus concentrated on this one property, the idea of it will be realized without an effort of reasoning. This may seem like giving undue prominence to an unimportant process, inasmuch as the knowledge to which it leads will be necessarily acquired by after experience; but the results of an education which commences thus, laying its foundation in clear, distinct, and vivid ideas of all that falls within the legitimate range of a child's observation, will fully justify the principle here advocated; materials of the highest value will be treasured up for the future superstructure; habits will be encouraged unwilling to be satisfied with vague, indefinite knowledge;

and the organs of the senses also, stimulated to healthy exercise, will learn the better to perform their appointed tasks.

When the children have gained a clear notion of size in the abstract, they will be prepared to observe its *extension* in different directions, and to gain an idea of *relative* size, exercising comparison, calculation, and accuracy of thought and expression; while, by referring to examples not present, the conceptive faculty is called out. In the Second Step they are led to see the necessity of a standard of measurement, and opportunity is afforded them for the practical application of those measures of length and capacity which are in ordinary daily use.

FIRST STEP.

Object.*—1. To develop the general idea of size. 2. To distinguish size, as it is exemplified in the different dimensions of familiar objects. 3. To exercise the faculty of *cómparison*, in deciding upon relative size and proportion, as also that of *conception*, by applying ideas gained by actual observation to objects not in sight.

I.—*The Development of the General Idea.*

Plan.—The children may be led to this, by having placed before them sets of objects, such as cubes of wood, balls, books, &c., differing only in size. They should be directed to separate from the rest those cubes, balls, &c., that are quite alike. When the general idea of size has been in some measure developed by such exercises, the teacher, pointing to each series of objects in its order, may require the children to describe them, by saying together several times, "These are small balls," "These are large cubes," &c. They may then be exercised on a wider variety of objects, such as small and large books, or small and large boxes. They may then be desired to touch or bring whatever the teacher may ask for, as the small books, or the large balls; and lastly, to say whether the objects on which the teacher places her hand are large or small.

---

* Unless the children are quite young, the first two points may be passed over quite rapidly, or be entirely omitted.

II. *Development of the Idea of Size, as Extension in Different Directions.*

The attention of the class must first be directed to extension in *length*. The teacher may place before it laths or strings of different lengths, arranging them in sets of uniform size; and also draw lines on the board, grouping them according to their length; these illustrations will give the first idea of the extension of size in one direction. After some questions as to what difference they see in the laths, strings, &c., the children should repeat, "The laths, strings, &c., are of different lengths." They may then obtain some idea of *relative* length, by the teacher holding up the longest and shortest lath or string, and leading them by questions to the idea of *longest* and *shortest*. They may next be called on themselves to select the longest and the shortest of each class of objects, and having thus given practice to the eye, they may simultaneously express the result of the exercise, saying, "This is a long lath," "This is the shortest," "This is the longest," "This is a long string," "This is the longest," &c. Their observation of length may now be extended to other objects in the room; as, Who has long hair? Who has short hair? Point out the longest form—the longest board—the longest side of the room, &c. After this, a variety of objects may be placed before the class, and the children will be required to describe the length of each by its suitable term.

In the same way the children should be led to acquire the idea of *breadth* or *width*, and *narrowness*. Ribbons of differing breadths afford convenient illustrations. They may be told to select the widest, the narrowest, &c., of these, and to arrange them according to their respective widths.

The idea of *thickness* and *thinness* may be illustrated by the use of blocks of wood, wafers, buttons, &c., or by familiar conversation about thick and thin slices of bread and butter, or of cake.

The kindred idea of *depth* may be elicited in the same manner, as it is exemplified in a well, a hole, a jug, or bucket; and that of *height*, by observing the room, a tree, or the spire of a church. The teacher might show the real identity of depth and height, by asking how the elevation of a cliff would be spoken of, under differing positions of an observer. If he stood at the top, and looked *down*, he might say, "It is *deep;*" if he stood at its base and looked *up*, he would say, "It is *high*."

The several steps of the lessons on color, form, and size, should be carried on simultaneously; but after a while, objects may be produced, in each of which the children will recognize several diverse qualities. For instance, they may be told to select a small white round object; a long narrow piece of blue ribbon; or a shallow white plate. They will thus, in the same object, find an example of form, of color, and of size.

III. *Relative Size and Proportion of Objects.*

Plan.—Laths of different lengths may be placed before the children, from which they may first select all those which are of the same length, and then arrange these according to their relative lengths, from the shortest to the longest. The teacher may then require them to select two short laths, which together are equal to the long one she herself holds; and afterward three or four others which together form the same length: this may be done also with tape or string. Similar exercises may be carried out with *curved* forms. Several sets of concentric circles, of varying size, cut out of thick pasteboard, may be placed before the children: they may first select all the circles of one size, and then arrange them according to their relative size, beginning with the largest; finally, they may prove how far their arrangement of them is correct, by fitting them one into another till the dissected circle is complete.

The following series of exercises will be found suitable at this step:

Let the children determine the relative lengths of lines drawn in differing directions, as to which is the shortest, and which the longest; and let them decide the relative distances between dots placed in different positions on the board; or the distance between various parallel lines; or the relative size of angles, &c. They may also determine which of a number of lines slope the most, and which the least—first, by comparing them with a vertical line drawn on another part of the board, and afterward without this help. The same exercise may be carried out with horizontal lines. The children may also determine the proportion which one line bears to another—whether it is half its length, or double its length, &c., without at present attaining actual precision. The children should pursue these exercises till they are enabled to judge of the relative size of an object by the eye, with tolerable accuracy.

They may next be called upon to divide straight lines drawn in different directions, into two, three, four, &c., equal or given parts; their companions being required to give an opinion as to the correctness with which the direction is executed. This exercise may be carried out also upon curved lines, and may be applied to the lengths of different parts of the room and of its furniture.

The power of conception may be called out, by referring to things not present; for example, the children may be required to say what animals have long or short tails—long or short ears; what streets or roads are broad, narrow, or long. A variety of similar illustrations will at once suggest themselves to the mind of the intelligent teacher.

SECOND STEP.

Object.—To lead the children to perceive the necessity for the adoption of standard measures of length, &c., and to make them familiar with those established by law or usage.

Plan.—The teacher holds up a long and a short lath, or a long and a short piece of string, and asks the children what they can say of them; thus awakening the consciousness of their having already acquired ideas of general and relative size. They should then be led to feel that this is not enough. The teacher might suppose herself wanting some ribbon for her bonnet, and might ask whether it is probable, if she sent to the shop for a *long piece*, that they would know exactly how much to send? Having, by a few such illustrations, convinced the children that something more definite than the general and relative measures, long, short, broad, narrow, &c., is absolutely necessary, the teacher may show them a yard measure, and tell them that this is a standard of length, which has been universally adopted in this country, and that it is called a *yard*. She may then send to another room, and ask some one to cut a yard of string, and send it to her. The children should be told to measure this; they will find it exactly the same length as the standard yard she had produced. It is desirable that some such act as this should fix the idea on the mind. The children may then be told that the yard-measure is this length in every store in the country, as well as in the next room.

The standard measures of length might be marked horizontally on the floor, or perpendicularly on the walls of the school-room, in order to accustom the children to the use of them in measuring lines and objects.

A Lesson on Measuring by the Standard Measures of Length.

No opportunity should be lost of giving practice to the eye in determining the length of objects by these measurements. Children are greatly interested in themselves endeavoring to determine the size of things, and in having their judgment tested by actual trial. The children should carefully observe the length of the yard, as it is held by the teacher in various positions, and at various distances from the eye: they should notice the apparent change which takes place in its length under each change of position, that they may be prepared to take this fact into consideration when calculating the size of objects in different positions and at various distances. They may also be required to find *two* objects, as two pieces of string, or two laths, which are together equal to the yard; thus introducing the idea of the half-yard, as being the length of one of these. Again, they may produce *four* similar objects, which, when united, also form a complete yard; and thus gain the idea of a quarter of a yard, as being the length of one of these.

In a further lesson, the idea of a *foot* may be communicated in the same manner, showing that it is the third of a yard; and also the idea of the *inch* and of the *nail*. The children should be exercised in determining the relative size of these measures, *i. e.*, the proportion each of them bears to the yard; and also their positive size, as unvarying standard measures.

These exercises may be continued, until the eye can decide on particular lengths with tolerable accuracy; after which the children may be called on to *determine* the length of lines combined in various figures; the circumference or girth of various objects; they may then proceed to dimensions of greater extent—those, for instance, of the floor and walls of the schoolroom, or of the playground.

Dry Measure.

Bring before the children the peck, the half-peck, and the quarter-peck measures, and ask if they know what things are bought and sold by this measure? Then select the largest of the measures, and having told a child to fill it with bran, turn out its contents upon a cloth, and tell the class that the measure is called "a peck measure," and that the quantity of bran it contained is called "a peck" of bran. Then require a child to fill the next smaller measure, and to empty its contents into the peck measure. How much of the peck does it fill? Half of it. By what name, then, may this smaller measure be called? If this is half a peck, how many of them will make one peck? Prove this by measurement. Then let the children repeat, "Two half pecks, equal to one peck." The same plan may be pursued with the quarter-peck; and when these measures have become familiar, the children may be questioned upon them, thus:

If one person buy four quarters of a peck of bran, and another buy half a peck, how much has the one more than the other? How many half pecks in four quarter pecks? How many whole pecks? If I pay five cents for half a peck of peas, what must I pay for one peck? Require the children to go through the process thus: One half peck costs five cents; two half pecks, which are equal to one peck, will cost two times five cents, or ten cents. If the teacher cannot produce a bushel measure, the children may be told that four pecks are equal to a measure called a *bushel.* They may then be questioned on that measure also.

The following table of these measures of capacity may now be written on the blackboard, thus:

Quarter.	Half Peck.	Peck.	Bushel.
2 =	1		
	2 =	1	
		4 =	1

The children should then read out the table once or twice simultaneously, that the teacher may ascertain that it is understood. They should then learn it thoroughly by silent repetition. They may afterward be required to write it out from memory.

The first four denominations in wine measure may be treated in a similar way, viz., gill, pint, quart, and gallon. Beyond this it is perhaps hardly profitable to go until the children come to learn the tables.

Actual measures, both those of linear and superficial extension, and those of solid and liquid capacity, should be set before the children, until both sight and touch are perfectly familiar with them. Practice in these, and in the use of the scales and weights used in lessons on weight, should precede the learning by heart of formal tables of weights and measures. Such practice affords most useful mental exercise, and secures a thorough understanding of the importance and value of standard measures. When this has been attained, the children may commit the tables to memory with advantage, and then, with a thorough comprehension of their several gradations, proceed to the acquirement of facility in the practical application of them.

WEIGHT.

INTRODUCTORY REMARKS.

MANY important scientific truths are involved in this subject, but it is obvious that scientific details are inexpedient in lessons such as these, which are intended to help those whose minds are just opening to the perception of truth as it meets them in daily experience. Still, while *the whole* of truth cannot just yet be told, because the mind of the little listener cannot properly receive it, it is essential that whatever *is* told should be *part* of that great whole, on the further steps of which the more matured mind may exercise itself without having to retrace the path.

In the subject now before us it is important that the *teacher* should remember that the WEIGHT of any object is *the force with which it is drawn toward the centre of the earth.* Any one who would raise a heavy stone from the ground must exert an amount of force in lifting it up, somewhat exceeding that by which the earth's attraction drags it down. It is chiefly in this aspect of *resistance* that the property of weight is an object of infantile perception.

Through what medium does a child attain to this perception? Possibly through several bodily powers. It is not by means of the sense of *touch* alone that the idea is attained; for this sense may be *perfect*, where a child is too weak to lift a pencil. It is in truth through the exercise of *muscular power* that a weight is raised or moved; and therefore it is by this capability, aided and directed by sight and touch, that the idea of weight in the abstract is acquired, and different degrees of it compared.

FIRST STEP.

Object.—To lead the children to the perception of WEIGHT in the abstract, and to the difference in the relative weight of various substances, both solids and liquids, as compared with their relative bulk.

Plan for Developing the General Idea of Weight.—The children should be told to lift various objects presented to them, or to poise them in their hands, and to mention any differences they perceive. They will notice that the things they have lifted differ in weight, some possessing much weight, others comparatively little. They should then learn that those things of which the weight is considerable, are said to be *heavy*, and that those of which the weight is little, are called *light*. They should then be taught, by the comparison of objects of various weight, properly to apply the terms *heavy* and *light, heavier* and *lighter, heaviest* and *lightest;* and lastly, let the children arrange them in order according to their weight. The teacher may then lead the children to analyze their perception of weight. When you lift a very heavy stone, by what means do you raise it? By putting out all our strength. And when you lift a feather? We do so with great ease.

Plan for Developing the Idea of Relative Weight, and of Weight as Compared with Relative Bulk.—Bring before the children a miscellaneous collection of objects, differing in both weight and bulk, as also objects of the same bulk, but differing in weight; as, lead, iron, coal, wood, cork, bags of shavings, sand, feathers, shot, peas, pebbles, beans, &c.; a phial of quicksilver; also various liquids, as water, milk, spirits, oil, &c.

1. Develop idea of *bulk*. Exercise the children in finding objects great in bulk, small in bulk, same in bulk; lastly arranging them in order according to their bulk.

2. Compare objects as to weight and bulk; as, This cork has much bulk, but little weight; This lead has little bulk, but much weight, &c.

3. Children find objects same in bulk, but differing in weight; same in weight, but differing in bulk.

4. Compare solid objects as to weight, at first making simply individual comparisons; as, This lead is the heaviest, this stone is next heaviest, this wood is next heaviest, &c.

5. Let the children now make a general classification of objects as to their weight; as, Metals are heaviest, minerals next heaviest, wood next, textile fabrics next, &c.

6. In a similar way compare liquids, giving water as the standard.

A small quantity of oil may be poured into a phial, and upon it some water; the water will displace the oil, and sink below it. Why? It is the heavier liquid. Then some quicksilver may be added; it again sinks below the water. Why? Because quicksilver is heavier than either water or oil. In a similar way compare the other liquids.

The children should be encouraged to describe the facts they observe in their own language; as, The feathers are light, the shot is heavy; oil is light, quicksilver is heavy. They should also be led to perceive that there may be large quantities of some substances, as of bran or feathers, which, though of great bulk, possess but little weight; whilst but a small portion of other substances, as, for instance, of metals, is heavy. They will thus arrive at the conclusion that the bulk of an object is no reliable indication of its specific weight.

SECOND STEP.

Object.—To lead the children to perceive the necessity for adopting standard measures of weight, and to make them practically acquainted with those in most common use.

Plan.—The children have already been led to see that *heavy* and *light* are *relative* terms—the thing which, when compared with one object, is called light, being said to be heavy when compared with another. Hence arises the necessity for an unchanging standard of weight, with which the weights of substances may be determined.*

---

* Exercises with scales and weights may be used at this step with much

In developing this idea, the same plan may be pursued as in illustrating the necessity of standard measures of size. The children should also here be taught the use of scales and weights, and the necessity of standard weights, in the same manner as the measures of size were learned (page 201.) They should be much practised in judging of the weight of miscellaneous objects, always testing the correctness of their judgments by varying the objects before the class. As a last exercise, the children may learn the table of avoirdupois weight. This may be formed after the example given in the lesson on dry measure.

In all the exercises on weight, the pound is taken as the standard.

In exercising the children to judge of weight, begin by passing around the class weights, or objects, that weigh just a pound. Tell the children their weight, and request them to hold them in their right hands, and think just how heavy they are, as they will soon have some other objects, to decide whether they are heavier or lighter than this weight, and how much. Next pass around half-pound or two-pound weights, requesting the children to hold them in their right hands, just as they did the pound weights, and *think* how much they weigh. When the weights have gone round, call for the judgments of the class, and let one of those who come the nearest to the correct weight, test the correctness of the guessing by weighing. These exercises should be frequently repeated with miscellaneous objects, until they can judge with tolerable accuracy of the weight of various objects. Request them to bring in objects of a given weight, always testing, or rather allowing them to test, the correctness of the selection by weighing. These exercises never fail to interest the children, and it is astonishing how accurate they will soon become in judging of weight, and thus will have cultivated a sense of great practical utility, but which is ordinarily neglected.

advantage. It is better to begin at first with the larger weights, as, the pound, half-pound, and quarter-pound, these being most readily distinguished.

SOUND.

INTRODUCTORY REMARKS.

FEW things are more useful, in all positions of life, than a delicate and discriminating perception of the varied qualities of SOUND, with facilities of reproducing known sounds at will. It is on these attainments that the effectiveness of the good reader and speaker, as well as that of the skilled musician, chiefly depends. These faculties are in constant activity in all the familiar scenes of daily life and social intercourse; unitedly they form one noble distinctive feature, by which man is exalted far above all other animate beings of God's creation, and, in their exercise, may be found at all times a fruitful source of innocent, profitable, and exalting pleasure.

Under judicious exercise, the organ of hearing is susceptible of a high degree of perceptive cultivation. The organs of voice also are equally capable of practical improvement; and the earlier in life the education of these organs is commenced, the more certain and satisfactory will be the results attained.

FIRST STEP.

Object.—To develop the general idea of sound, and also to show that it possesses great variety.

Plan.—The teacher to utter some sounds with her own voice, and also to produce others by means of sonorous objects; thus leading the children to perceive the existence of the quality of sound, and to observe that it is made known to us by the organ of hearing. They may then be exercised in distinguishing common and familiar sounds, and in determining by the ear by what means they are produced; and in endeavoring to imitate some of them by the voice. The teacher may then sing some simple tune, to awaken the perception of *melody*, and to encourage the dawnings of musical taste.

Subjects for Lessons at this Step.

1. Objects for producing different tones to be sounded, and the children to be exercised in deciding by the sense of hearing only, from what kind of substance the sound was produced; as, a bell, a drum, a glass full of water, another half full, another empty, china, different metals, &c.

2. Sounds made by men and animals to be imitated; the children to say what the sound is intended to represent.

3. Simultaneous movements to be carried out, especially those involving sound in measured time; such as clapping hands, marching in time, stamping with the feet, simultaneous counting, &c.

4. The children to be called on to decide which of their companions is speaking, having first been directed to close their eyes.

5. The teacher to sing some very simple melodies, some of them quick and lively, others slow and solemn; the children to say which of them they prefer.

Sketch of a Lesson on Sounds.

I.—*Sounds distinguished.*	I.—Children to say with what they hear. Teacher tells them she wants to find out who can hear best. She goes behind a screen, or asks the children to close their eyes, rings a bell, asks what the noise was, and how made; rings a quarter dollar on the table, blows a whistle, sounds a tuning-fork, strikes an empty glass, also a glass full of water, knocks with a hammer, with a ruler, &c., the children always deciding how each sound is made. Should they be at a loss, the teacher produces the

noise in their presence, desiring them to listen in order that they may discover how it was produced.

II.—*Sounds compared.*

II.—1. Children told they are going to hear four of the sounds they heard before, in order that they may decide which are most alike. The teacher, still behind the screen, touches the bell so as to produce one tone, rings the quarter on the table, sounds the tuning-fork, rings the bell sharply. Children decide by ear that the first and third sounds resemble each other; also the second and fourth.

2. Teacher again sounds the tuning-fork, blows the whistle, touches the bell so as to produce one sound; children to describe whether the third sound resembles more the first or the second.

3. Teacher strikes a small hammer on the table, strikes an empty glass, knocks with her heel, knocks a full glass. Children compare sounds, and decide which resemble each other.

III.— *Sounds arranged.*

III.—Children hear the sounds once more, to decide which they like best, and then arrange them in the order of sweetness or melody, going from the least to the most musical. When they disagree, compare the sounds, and train the ear in deciding.

The sounds will probably stand as follows, written on the board:

1. Sound of ruler on wood.
2. Hammer on wood.
3. Full glass.
4. Empty glass.
5. Coin.
6. Bell.
7. Whistle.
8. Tuning-fork.

SECOND STEP.

Sketch of Lesson for this Step.

Point.—To exercise the children in distinguishing sounds, and also tune, in order to cultivate an ear for music.

I.—*Voices distinguished.*

I.—Bring a girl and a boy before the children. Require them to give their names, and let the rest call them by their names. Tell the children in their seats that these are going to say something, and that they must listen to their voices so as to distinguish them. Let the boy and girl repeat individually, "The clock strikes." Require the rest to notice the difference in their voices. Bring another boy. Let each of the boys repeat the same sentence, the rest to decide as before. Bring another girl, and repeat the same exercise, the rest deciding.

Tell the children that they must now decide on the voice without seeing the speaker. Put the two boys out of sight; touch the boy who is to speak, and let the children decide who it was that spoke. Proceed in the same manner with the girls. Put all four out of sight, letting one of them repeat the same sentence, or sing a verse, exercising the rest in deciding whether it was a boy or girl who spoke, and which boy or girl.

II.—*Sounds distinguished as to Times.*

II.—Require them to clap hands as the teacher counts one, two, three; children to count as the teacher claps hands. Repeat these exercises four, five, and six times, instead of three, and call on individual children to perform them. Strike the pointer against the frame of the board, making the beats regular and irregular, till they can distinguish the difference.

III.—*Sounds distin-*

III.—Sing some very simple melodies,

guished as to Time and Tune.

without words. Let the children decide which they like the best. Sing these melodies twice over, with or without the words, first slowly and then quickly. Try and get them to see that some airs are naturally plaintive, and some lively.

LIST OF LESSONS ON SOUNDS, FOR THIS STEP.

Hammer, Bell, Whistle.
Glasses full and empty.
China, Delft, Glass.
Coins of different metals; as, gold, silver, copper, selecting those of as nearly the same size as may be.
Voices.

Further exercises should also be had to lead the children to discover that musical sounds have the three distinct properties of length or duration, pitch or tone, and force or volume. At first these qualities should be taught separately, and the idea of *time*, as being the most easy of apprehension, should be that commenced with. The children should also be led to observe that there may be either a prolongation of the sound of the notes themselves, or of the interval or pause between them.

Plan.—To give the children the idea of the quality of *time* as applied to sound, some notes should be uttered, at first very slowly, and afterward rapidly, making them observe and state the difference in these two methods. Next the teacher may sing some simple air, requiring the children to listen and beat time, first under guidance, and then unaided. They should then practise singing an air in unison with the teacher, she taking the lead and beating time. After this they should sing the exercises by themselves, she beating time; and lastly, they may be exercised in both singing and beating time themselves. Practice in simultaneous movements, actions, and utterances, helps to the cultivation of a correct perception of time; and children derive great pleasure from such measured simultaneous exercises, for they appeal to the powerful agent of sympathy. Children may easily be taught to appreciate the difference in the intervals between notes, by counting whilst the sounds are being uttered—at first the time between the notes being considerable, and therefore obvious.

The next quality to be brought under observation is that of *pitch* or *tone*. The teacher should run up the common scale, through a whole octave, to give the children an idea that there are different notes; and then by selecting a deep note, and afterward sounding its octave, point out their agreement. The class may then be practised in imitating these sounds. At this point various exercises may be introduced which will greatly interest the class, and they may now be taught that each sound is represented by its particular symbol; and by a comparison of the letters as used as representatives of sounds in music, with the use of them as symbols of sound in language, they may be taught the mode in which one thing may represent another, and to what end standard symbols have been established for general convenience. If the children cannot grasp the idea at this step, though in most cases it may be impressed upon the mind, it should not be lost sight of by the teacher.

The third quality of musical sounds which the children should learn to distinguish, is that of *force* or *volume*. This depends upon the power by which tones are produced, and may be increased or diminished indefinitely. It may be exemplified by comparing the deep sound of the ocean in a storm, or the roar of the majestic lion, with the faint cry of the infant. To give the idea, the teacher should sing a note in a soft but steady tone, following it up by another in a loud and full tone, calling upon the children first to state the difference between the two, and then themselves to join in the exercise. This should afterward be frequently repeated by the children alone, loud or soft, at the discretion of the teacher. They may then be exercised on different notes in the same way. The next practice should be to commence a note softly, and increase it gradually, till it become loud, and then to begin loud and to end soft. This is a most important exercise in aid of a right management of the voice.

These three qualities may be illustrated by school songs, and thus the style of singing in a primary school much improved.

10

Learning pieces of poetry, not only as an exercise of memory, but also of intonation, would be very suitably introduced among lessons on sound.

For a course of lessons and exercises in the Third Step, as leading to music, we cannot do better than recommend to teachers the use of the "Primary School Song Book," by Lowell Mason and Geo. Jas. Webb, and published by Mason Brothers, New York.

LANGUAGE.

INTRODUCTORY REMARKS.

ALTHOUGH direct and systematic lessons on language are, for the most part, unsuited to a primary school, much may still be done by the teacher to cultivate the habit of correct speaking. To this end care must be taken that ideas communicated to the children are conveyed to them in appropriate terms, and that, when giving expression to their own thoughts, they do so in correct and appropriate language.

In carrying out these objects, the following points deserve special attention:

1. All erroneous expressions made use of by the children should be immediately corrected, and the proper words fixed upon the mind by repetition. This incidental mode of teaching is the most natural and simple method of correcting those errors in language which the children of the poor acquire at their homes, and of supplying those deficiencies which belong to their as yet limited vocabulary.

2. In the daily work of the school room, all definitions of the meaning of words, and all descriptions of places, objects, or events, whether given by the teacher to the children, or elicited from them, should be clothed in simple and definite language, and fixed in the memory by repetition. A double object is thus attained; the mind is stored with knowledge for its own benefit, and furnished with appropriate language in which to convey it to others.

3. The children should be trained to give *complete* answers to

all questions which are put to them. Teachers too often content themselves with such answers as merely indicate that the child is in possession of the idea they wish to convey, without caring for the clearness or otherwise with which that idea is expressed; whereas experience teaches that nothing more tends to make an idea clear to the mind, and to render it a permanent possession, than the act of clothing it in accurate language. Monosyllabic answers, as "Yes" and "No," should be rejected, except when they express all that can be said on the subject.

Besides the above incidental mode of teaching language, which should be adopted in all the classes of a primary school, the following exercises are given for the special use of children from six to eight years of age.

The following exercises in Language are designed as Third Step lessons:

Exercise I.

To form sentences from given words—(1) the name of an object, (2) a word expressing quality, and (3) some part of the verb "to be."

Plan.—The children to name a number of objects, beginning, for example, with those of the various articles of furniture, &c., in the room; the teacher to write these names under each other on the slate, requiring the children to spell each word as it is written, assisting or correcting when necessary.

The children to be then required to say something regarding each object, the teacher helping them to determine how far the terms they apply are appropriate. The teacher to add these descriptions to the names already on the slate, and thus lead the children on to the formation of simple sentences, in their shortest form. A few examples follow:

>The ink is black.
>The slate is smooth.
>The form is long.
>That window is large.
>This pencil is sharp, &c.

The children should then read over the sentences, and be led to observe that each begins with a capital letter, and ends with a full stop. The slate may then be turned away, and the class required to reproduce the lesson on their own slates, without its aid. When this has been done, the slate should be again referred to, that they may correct their exercises.

The children may be supplied with little books, in which to write out these lessons at home. For some time they should not be required to originate anything for themselves, but merely to reproduce that which has been taught in school. They will find pleasure in doing that which they can do well.

When all the objects in the room have formed the subjects of such lessons, those in the playground, the street, or in the fields, may be resorted to, gradually extending the circle to more remote objects. At the least a dozen lessons of this description should be given.

Exercise II.

The forming of contracted sentences. Of these there are two varieties: 1. That in which different qualities are ascribed to one and the same object. 2. That in which the same quality is ascribed to various objects.

First kind: The describing an object by various qualities.

Plan.—The teacher writes the name of some familiar object upon the school slate, and calls upon the children to apply it to its various qualities, writing them down as they give them. The teacher should assist the children in determining the suitability or otherwise of the qualities suggested, and also in spelling the more difficult words.

We may suppose a lesson in which the given name is "paper." It would present itself in some such form as this:

> The paper is white.
> The paper is thin.
> The paper is smooth.
> The paper is pliable, &c.

The teacher should next lead the children to notice that the word "paper" need only be written once, and that the four sentences may be contracted into one. Then the teacher, directed by the children, writes:

"Paper is white, thin, smooth, and pliable."

The children then read this over, and are led to perceive the necessity for commas in those places where the words "the paper is" are omitted, and also the use of the word "and" between the two last words of the sentence. Lastly, the slate is turned away, and the children reproduce and correct the lesson, as in the case of the former exercise.

The words, chalk, iron, clay, coal, salt, water, air, snow, ice, sugar, glass, leather, thread, a pen, a needle, fire, wood, &c., &c., are suitable for lessons of this kind. The children may be encouraged to reproduce such lessons at home, forming, in the first place, the several simple sentences, and then contracting them as above suggested. Two or three such exercises will generally suffice for one lesson.

Second kind: The same quality attributed to several objects.

Plan.—A quality selected, sentences made, contracted, reproduced, and corrected, as above.

> Glass is brittle.
> Chalk is brittle.
> Coal is brittle.
> Glass, coal, and chalk are brittle.
> Iron is hard.
> Flint is hard.
> Glass is hard, &c.
> Iron, flint, and glass are hard.

The children to be led to notice the stops, as before, and the change of the word "is" for "are."

Subjects for sentences of this kind: Black, white, light, heavy, bright, sweet, sour or acid, cold, tough, porous, inflammable, soluble, fusible, pliable, &c., &c.

Exercise III.

An exercise on discrimination in the use of words.

Select an object, say a tree, and let the children apply to it every descriptive term that they can think of as applicable to any tree, thus: A tree may be young, old, tall, short, graceful, stunted, withered, green, bare, branching, large, small, smooth, gnarled, fruit-bearing, barren, upright, drooping, &c.

Then let them select all the terms that might possibly be applied to any one tree, and thus draw out a description of two or more trees from the above list of attributes, thus:

The tree is young, small, graceful, green, and smooth; or,
The tree is old, tall, large, branching, and fruit-bearing; or,
The tree is old, short, stunted, withered, gnarled, and barren.

Subjects for these exercises: Flower, man, monkey, house, sky, river, horse, mountain, book, water, an apple, &c.

Exercise IV.

Following the order in which a lesson on an object is usually given, we now take the verb "Have;" and the children are required to form sentences, naming the parts of objects, and the number of those parts introducing that verb.

1. To form sentences, describing the parts of objects, without reference to their number:

>The tree has leaves.   A bird has wings.
>The cow has feet.   The cube has faces.

2. Contracted sentences of this character:

>The tree has branches.
>The tree has leaves.
>The tree has roots, &c.

Contracted—The tree has leaves, roots, and branches. The contracted form may be at once adopted, as its nature is understood from previous exercises.

3. Sentences in which the several parts of an object may be distinguished by a word expressive of quality:

> The cat has soft feet.
> The knife has a sharp point.
> The cow has a long tail.

4. Sentences in which the several parts of an object may be described by their number:

> The cow has four feet.
> The cow has a tail.
> The cow has two horns.

Contracted—The cow has four feet, two horns, and a tail.

The preceding exercises are confined to objects described as to their *qualities* and their *parts*, and only one example of each is given; but the teacher will, of course, take care that the children have as many as are necessary. We now proceed to sentences which include words expressing action or condition. As the vocabulary of the children at this stage is usually very limited, it is desirable to increase the stock of words at their command. This may be done by writing out lists of the names of objects, and of words expressive of actions. Each list should be formed of words which may be arranged under some general head, itself familiar to the children, and thus the principle of *association* will be brought to the help of the memory. Rigid classification should be avoided, as well as the introduction of terms difficult of explanation.

The children may be assisted in drawing up lists of words expressive of domestic and social relationship, of trades, occupations, and professions, or of the names of quadrupeds, birds, fishes, and insects; trees, garden vegetables, fruits, grain; minerals, metals, and liquids; articles of clothing, household furniture, &c. By way of variety, the children may be required to name the objects they have seen in the sky, in the field, or on the river; the various goods sold in a grocer's shop; the tools used by the carpenter, the shoemaker, or the smith.

Similar lists of words descriptive of actions should be made, beginning with those describing the powers and capabilities of the several organs of the human frame:

The hand—open, shut, hold, catch, grasp, &c.
The foot—stand, walk, run, stamp, dance, &c.
The mouth and voice—eat, drink, sip, speak, sing, &c.
The eye and ear—look, stare, gaze, listen, hearken, &c.

This may also be extended to acts of the mind; as, think, study, consider, invent, love, hate.

Actions peculiar to specific trades and occupations—cut, stitch, sow, plough, reap, mow, bore, saw, &c.

Actions characteristic of certain animals—walk, trot, gallop, fly, swim, crawl, climb, &c.

Sounds made by animals—sing, bark, neigh, low, bray, croak, hum, hiss, &c.

The children should also be required to write out words expressing some of those less evident actions effected in plants; as, grow, increase, spread, shelter, fade, wither, &c.; or those applied to liquids; as, pour, drop, flow, overflow, &c., &c.

The following remarks point out how such lists of words may be made so as to give them interest:

Suppose the children required to make a list of insects. Each of the children in turn gives the name of an insect, which is written on the board. When they can remember no others, the teacher may supply the names of any familiar insects they may have overlooked. The board may then be covered, and the children required to reproduce them. This done, the list may again be showed them, that they may correct errors in spelling, and supply any words they may have omitted.

These lists may also form very useful lessons for home work. In correcting them, the teacher asks the first child in the class to read out his list, writing it upon the board as he does so. Another child is then desired to mention any words his list may contain which are *not already on the board*. The same plan to be adopted with the other children, until a complete copy of all the names the children have noted will be formed upon the board.

10*

From this the children are then permitted to correct their errors in spelling, and to complete their several lists of words.*

Much varied information may be given to the children in connection with the new words they learn as these lessons proceed; but great care should be taken that the lesson on language is not lost sight of in the communication of this general information.

Exercise V.

Sentences containing words expressing action. I. The subject and the action complete the sense. II. An additional word is required to complete the sense. III. Exercises on sentences of both these classes.

I. Sentences containing a word expressive of an act which, with its subject, makes a complete and significant sentence.

Plan.—The teacher writes in column on the board a list of words expressing actions; as, stand, walk, run, &c.; and the children, with the assistance of the teacher, form these into sentences, by the addition of the name of an object, animal, &c. They are then erased, and the children reproduce the exercise without help.

1. Sentences where the subject and the action complete the sense:

> The horse stands.
> The child sleeps.
> The scholar sits.

These exercises to be repeated, putting both the object and the act in the plural form:

> The horses stand.
> The children sleep.
> The scholars sit, &c.

The actions characteristic of animals, and the sounds they utter, will afford great variety in these exercises:

---

* It is not necessary that any large number of lists of words should be made before proceeding to the following exercises. The object is to furnish with words, and the teacher may resort to the lists whenever the introduction of new words is found desirable.

The fish swims.
The bird flies.
The serpent crawls.
The bee hums.
The frog croaks.
The dog barks, &c.

II.—Sentences in which, beside the subject and the object, an additional word is required to complete the sense:

I hold—the pencil.
He opens—the book.
The monkey climbed—the tree, &c.*

The children should be led to see the necessity for each additional word.

Actions peculiar to trades or employments:

The gardener digs—the ground.
The tailor cuts—the cloth.
The carpenter planes—the wood, &c.

As a more extended exercise, the name of the instrument by which an act is performed may be introduced into the sentence:

The gardener digs the ground with a spade.
The tailor cuts the cloth with scissors.
The grocer weighs sugar with a pair of scales, &c.

Words expressing quality may now be added to the subject or object; as,

The *little* boys play.
The *bright* sun is shining.
The *strong old* horse drew the *heavy* wagon.

Great variety may be given to these lessons, and the attention and interest of the children well sustained, by leading them to try

---

* The teacher need not object to the use of the past or future tense of the verb, provided the children use it correctly.

to find out how many qualifying words may be added to a sentence, and the peculiar force of each.

Exercise VI.

In the exercises which follow, the children are led to observe and describe some of those circumstances which are connected with various actions, and so identified with them that the mention of one is often suggestive of another. For example, such sentences as, The fish swims, The worm crawls, The bird flies, which call up simultaneously in the mind the ideas, In the water, On the ground, In the air.

Combinations such as these are simple, and readily understood; those of a more abstract nature should be avoided. There should be no attempt to lead where the children cannot follow.

Sentences.

 The children sit on the forms.
 Lions live in forests.
 Ships sail on the ocean.
 The leaves fall on the ground, &c.

Sentences with phrases expressive of time:
 The sun rises in the morning.
 We prepared our lessons last night.
 The birds sing in the morning.
 Dogs bark during the night, &c.

Sentences with words expressing the manner of performing an act:
 The child walks slowly.
 The dog barks loudly.
 The lion growls fiercely.
 Jane writes neatly.

As an example of the manner in which these lessons may be varied, we give the following sentences, in which two or more of the preceding circumstances are expressed:

Place and Manner.—The children sit quietly at the desks, &c.
Time and Manner.—The rain fell violently during the night.
Time and Place.—The rooks rest all night on the trees.

This is, perhaps, as far as it is desirable to lead the children of an infant school in such lessons as these. The subject may close with an example showing the mode in which two or more of the preceding sets of exercises may be combined in the simple description of an object. The teacher need not, however, wait till the foregoing exercises have been finished before such examples are introduced.

An Apple, described as to its qualities, its several component parts, its mode of growth, and its uses, or as to any other simple fact connected with it.

Exercises 1 and 2. An apple may be round, russet, smooth, juicy, odorous, wholesome, acid, and refreshing.

Exercise 3. It has a stem, a rind, or outer covering, a pulp inside the peel, a core, and seeds.

Exercise 4. It grows in orchards and gardens; it is sold at stalls in the streets, in fruit markets, at greengrocers' shops, and is used for making cider, as a table fruit, and for making apple pies.

In working out such descriptions, the children should be required to point out the value of each word, and to state what it adds to the description.

Thus, in the preceding lesson, the word *round* describes the shape of the apple; the word *russet*, the color of it; the word *smooth*, the nature of its surface; the word *sweet*, its taste; the word *wholesome*, the effects of it when eaten as food, &c.

Treated in this way, the lesson becomes truly a lesson on language. The children learn to distinguish between the idea and the word representing it.

Such a course of instruction on language, given in connection with objects, *insensibly* develops the perception of the nature of the principal words or parts of speech, probably better than could be done by lessons specially directed to that object. It only remains now that the teacher bring the subject of classification *directly* before the children. This may be best done by leading them to *analyze* a few of their own lessons, arranging the words into *names, words expressing actions, qualities, relations,* &c. When this has been done, the teacher may communicate the grammatical names of nouns, verbs, adjectives, as introductory to more methodical lessons on grammar.

Such a course of teaching also prepares the mind for grammatical analysis.

READING.

INTRODUCTORY REMARKS.

THERE is perhaps no subject of school study that has presented more difficulties to the minds of the little learners, than Reading. This has been owing very much to the manner in which it has been usually presented. The English language is full of difficulties; and if we introduce the child to them all at once, we shall most certainly confuse and discourage him.

The principles of Pestalozzi so prominently insisted upon, that but one difficulty should be presented at a time—that the business of the teacher is analysis—that all difficulties should be divided and subdivided, until reduced to their simple elements—and that the work of the infant learner is *synthetical*, are peculiarly applicable in the prosecution of this subject.

It has been our aim, in the following lessons, to treat the subject in conformity to these principles. We claim for the plan here presented the following advantages:

1. It puts the child in possession of a key by which he is able to *help himself*—a very important principle in education.

2. It is an excellent disciplinary exercise, cultivating accuracy of observation and expression.

3. It presents but one difficulty at a time, and thus avoids that confusion, and consequent discouragement, that so often attend the early efforts in learning to read.

4. It is thorough. By means of a progressive arrangement and classification, it puts the child in possession of a knowledge

of important elements in the English language that are often entirely neglected.

5. The plan is calculated to cultivate clearness of articulation, and lead the children, by easy and progressive steps, to a knowledge of the orthography of words.

We believe it to be an easy, thorough, and rapid method of learning to read and spell.

A set of cards and a little reading book have been prepared with special reference to accompanying these lessons, which we think the teacher will find of great assistance.

PHONIC READING.

FIRST STEP.

While in this Step, the children learn to distinguish and imitate forms, and to distinguish and imitate sounds. To each character is attached but one sound. We first begin by teaching the children to recognize the forms of the small letters, and their appropriate sounds. For this purpose we use both the large and small cards, and the blackboard.

Hold before the class a small card with the small letter *a* on it. Ask one member of the class to select another like it from the table, calling upon the class to decide as to the correctness of the selection. Ask another to point to a form like it on the large card. Let other members of the class select other forms like it on the card and on the table. Teacher makes several letters on the board; the children decide when she makes this letter. The teacher now tells the children that this is *a*, repeating the short sound of *a*.* Children repeat the sound several times, until they can all give it correctly. Different members of the class are called upon to select as many letters of this kind from the table and card as they can find, always repeating the sound as they select them.

---

* The short sounds of the vowels, as heard in hat, pen, pin, hot, hut, the hard sound of *c* and *g*, the sound of *x* as heard in wax, are used in every case in this Step; and *s* has the sound of *c* soft, as heard in sent. The letter *k* is omitted. The *names* of the letters are not given to the children at present.

The letter *t* is next presented, and treated in the same manner. The children are then shown card No. 5. Teacher points to the letter *a* on this card, and the children give the sound. Teacher repeatedly points to these letters, and the children give the sounds, each time pronouncing them in more rapid succession, until they get the syllable "at," which they pronounce repeatedly. This is as much as can be accomplished with one lesson.

Either at this point, or before giving the above lesson, which perhaps would be the better course, let the children learn at sight to recognize the following words, as an aid in forming short, easy sentences, as we proceed: *the, is, his, this*. These words are found on both the large and small cards, and may be treated very much in the same way as in learning the letters *a* and *t*, selecting cards with the required word from the table and from the large card. In all these exercises, the class should be called upon in every case to decide upon the correctness of the selection, or work done by any member.

In case the Reading Cards are not used, the work may be placed on the blackboard in these and the following exercises. The teacher who can print readily will be likely to interest her class more thoroughly by taking this course, than by confining herself closely to the cards. The cards, however, will be found a great aid to the teacher in indicating the exact course of the lessons, and in supplying a collection of easy sentences adapted to the progress of each lesson.

In the next lesson the children learn to recognize and sound the letters *m* and *c* (*hard*). These letters are treated in the same manner as *a* and *t*, combining them with the syllable *at*. Place this syllable upon the board, and let the children analyze and pronounce it. At a little distance from it, at the left, place the letter *m*, and let the children sound it as pointed to; also pronounce the syllable *at*. Below, and a little nearer each other, place the same letter and syllable, and let the children sound them as pointed to, more rapidly than before; and so proceed until they are brought into close proximity, and they pronounce the word *mat*. This may be repeated several times, and a little conversation may be had with the children about a *mat*; as, How many ever saw a mat? Where they have seen it? What it is used for? &c. In all these early lessons with the children, the meaning of each new word should be made clear to them. Proceed in the same way with *c*, and so with all the succeeding lessons.

Should there be any difficulty in getting the children to repeat the desired sound distinctly, the teacher may make use of the key word used in forming the combinations at the head of each lesson, pronouncing it very distinctly several times, making the children repeat it after her. Next pronounce the same word, emphasizing the desired sound, requiring the children to listen, to observe her lips, and then to imitate her. Next separate the sound from the remainder of the word, and pronounce the two parts distinctly, requiring the children to do the same. Thus they will be led to associate the power of the letter with the word, and may make use of it when they wish to recall it.

It is well, when the power of a consonant has been learned as an initial letter, for the children to have a lesson upon the same letter when it is a terminal. The following will serve as a plan that may be continued in teaching the powers of all the consonants:

The teacher makes the children repeat after her a word ending with a consonant, the power of which she wishes them to learn. Supposing it to be the power of *m*, the teacher repeats such a word as *jam*, emphasizing the letter *m*. Calls upon the children to listen, to observe her lips as she finishes the word, and to imitate her. In this way, if possible, lead them to discover for themselves what the sound is that they hear at the end of the word; and if they fail to give it correctly alone, repeat it for them, telling them that it is the power of the letter *m*; and when they wish to remember the sound, they may think of the word *jam*.

By way of exercise, and an occasional review of what they have learned, the teacher points to or prints a letter, and the children give the sound; or the teacher gives the sound of a letter, and the children either print, or point out the letter which has that sound.

The letters may be taken up in the following order: *a, t, m, c, b, r, h, v, f, s, d, l, p, g, n, j, w, e, i, o, x, u, y, q,* and *z*; and the combinations *ow*, *oy*, and *th*, may be added. For the full exemplification of the methods of working out these lessons, as also for the practice in reading, see "Phonic Reading Cards."

During the progress of these lessons, if the teacher finds the children have difficulty in distinguishing the letters *b*, *p*, *q*, and *d*, it will be well to give them a separate lesson on these letters.* The following may serve as a specimen of the way of treating them:

1. Select these letters, and lead the children to observe and describe them as to resemblance and difference. They are alike, in that each is formed of one straight and one curved line. They are unlike in the position of these lines. The first is formed of two lines—one straight and vertical, and the other curved. The curved line lies to the right of the vertical line, and touches it at the middle and base.

2. The second is formed of two lines, as the first, but the curved line touches the straight line at the top and middle on the right side.

3. The third has the curve at the left of the straight line, and touches it at the top and middle.

4. The fourth has the curve at the left of the straight line, and touches it at the middle and base.

5. EXERCISE.—Let the children say how they know each letter from the other three. Bid them put the letters into two groups—those which have curves at the top, and those that have curves at the base. What letters have curves at the top, and what at the base? Let them divide again into those that have curves at the right, and those that have curves at the left. Which letters curve to the right, and which to the left? &c. How *p* is distinguished from *q*, and *d* from *b*.

After the children have learned to recognize all the small letters, and to attach to each its appropriate sound, they should be taught the capital letters, which they will be able to describe and

---

* Before giving this lesson, the ideas of *straight, curved, vertical,* and *base,* should be developed with the children, for the method of which, see "Lessons on Form." The terms *long* and *short, longer* and *shorter, upward* and *downward, right, left, upper, lower,* and *between,* if not already familiar to the children, should be developed.

draw upon their slates. Before commencing these lessons, however, it will be well to have the following

INTRODUCTORY EXERCISES.

Alphabetical Forms of Capital Letters.

I.—*Comparison of Large with the Small Letters.*—Let the children select from the capital letters all that resemble the small letters that they have already learned. This will dispose of *C, K, O, P, S, U, V, W, X, Y,* and *Z.*

II.—Next take some letters not included in these, which, with reference to their simplicity in making and describing, may be presented in the following order:

1. *I, L, T, F, E, H, A, N, M,* straight lined letters.
2. *Q, G,* curved lined letters.
3. *D, B, R, J,* straight and curved lined letters.
4. Interest the children, by asking whether they would not like to find out to what capitals the remaining small letters belong?
5. Select the capital *I*; place the small *i* beside it. Give the sound of short *i,* or let the children give the sound of the small *i,* and then tell them that the capital has the same sound, and let them repeat it, and describe the letter.
6. Proceed in the same way with *L,* which the children distinguish as being formed of a vertical and a horizontal line. Proceed thus with *T.*
7.—*Sketch on the Letter E.*—The following sketch may serve as a pattern of the way in which each of the capitals may be learned and described:

Teacher places the capital *E* beside the small *e,* and calls upon the children to give the sound of small *e.* Tells them that the large letter has the same sound. Children repeat it. Calls upon the children to select *E* on the large card; also from the table; to find as many large *E*'s as they can. The teacher now provides the children with strips of wood or pasteboard, and says, "Make this letter."* The teacher asks, "How many lines in

---

* A small box containing both curved and straight strips, for this purpose, can be obtained of the Publisher.

your *E*?" (remembering to use the short sound of *E*, and not the name). Point out the longest line. Tell the number and direction of all the lines. Let us describe *E*: "It is formed of three straight lines; the longest is a vertical line, and the two shorter are horizontal; the two horizontal lines touch the vertical line at the top and base. It has also a little mark in the middle of the vertical line, on the right side."

Description of the Letter D.—It is formed of two lines, one straight and vertical, and the other curved. The curved line lies to the right of the vertical line, and touches it at the top and bottom.*

III.—1. EXERCISES.—Hold up the small letters, and let the children select the capitals that belong to them, and then reverse this.

2. Let the children give the sounds of the large letters when pointed to, and point to them when sounded.

Imitating Sounds of Letters.†

During the progress of the preceding exercises on the forms and sounds of the letters, the teacher may have a daily drill with the children in imitating the sounds of the letters, without any reference to their forms, taking them in the following order (see Card No. 4). By varying the key on which these sounds are given, sometimes high, and again low, sometimes at a shouting pitch, and again in a whisper, the exercise may be made a very interesting and pleasing one.

In the general classification of sounds, the terms *vowel* and *consonant* sounds are used.

---

* For this purpose letters without ornament should be used.

† The teacher will observe, that in these exercises no reference is to be made to the *forms of the letters*, the children simply imitating the *sounds* as made by the teacher.

I.—Vowel Sounds, or Tonic Elements.

Sketch on Long Vowel Sounds.

1. Pronounce *E, A, A* in *air, A* in *far,* and *A* in *aw, ŏ, oo.* Children repeat each sound in concert, and then call on individual children to give them.
2. Proceed as before with *bē, bā, bare, far, fall, bō, boo.* Children repeat as before.
3. Lead the children to notice the position of the organs of speech in making these sounds.

II.—Double Vowel Sounds.

Sketch on Double Vowel Sounds.

1. Pronounce *i* in *pine, u* in *tube, oi, ou.* Let the children repeat the sounds in concert, till they can say them in order, and then individual children called upon to go over them.
2. Pronounce, and exercise the children in pronouncing, *cy, dry, try, fly, sky; boy, hoy, joy, cloy, Troy; bow, cow, now, plow; new, dew, lieu, stew.*

III.—Short Vowel Sounds.

1. Children sound these after the teacher, as before. The sounds may be made more audible by repetition, thus: *It, it, it; et, et, et; at, at, at; ot, ot, ot; ut, ut, ut,* as in *put; ut, ut, ut,* as in *nut.*
2. Exercise the children on other words containing the same sounds.

IV.—Consonant Sounds.

1. *Subtonic Elements.*

1. Pronounce *mat, mat, mat,* emphasizing *m.* Children repeat, &c. So proceed with *net, lamb, rat, ding.* In the last word let the last sound *ng* be emphatic. Continue to exercise the chil-

dren on these elements, as directed with the vowel sounds. Proceed in the same manner with the remaining subtonic elements, *b, d, g, j, v, w, z* in *zeal* and *z* in *azure,* and *th* in *thine.*

2. Atonic Elements.

Sketch on the Aspirate h.—(*a*) Sound the long vowels first without and then with the aspirate; as, *c̄, ā, a* in *air, a* in *far,* and *a* in *aw, ō, oo, hē, hā, hair, hah, haw, ho, how.*

Lead the children to notice what they do in pronouncing the second line; viz., breathe forcibly at the commencement of each word.

(*b*) Exercise the children in the same way on the double vowel sounds; as, *i, u* (sound as heard in *tune*), *oi, ou, hi, hu, hoi, hou.* In the same way, if necessary, proceed with the short vowel sounds.

(*c*) Utter the vowel sounds, requiring them to give them aspirated; then pronounce the vowel aspirated, requiring the children to drop the aspirate.

Proceed with the remaining atonic elements as with the subtonic, viz.: *p, t, k, f, c* in *nice, tch* in *fetch, th* in *youth, ci* in *vicious.*

Pronounce such words as *pull, tin, kill, fan, celery,* &c., repeating each word several times, making the first letter emphatic. Let the children repeat the words after the teacher, and then the sounds. Lead the children to discover the difference between the subtonic and the atonic elements, not using, however, these terms. They will discover that in making one, there is a tone, and in the other there is not. To lead them to this, sound them in connection; as, *bale, b, pale, p.* Repeat them one after the other. So take *d* and *t, g* and *c* hard, *f* and *v, th* in *thin* and *th* in *thine, s* in *seal* and *z* in *zeal, ch* in *chest* or *tch* in *fetch,* and *j* in *jest, sh* in *shall,* and *z* in *azure.* (These are sometimes classed as *sharp* and *flat;* the sharps being the atonic elements, as *p, f, t,* &c., and the flats being the subtonic elements, as, *b, v, d,* &c.)

Give them these sounds, both subtonic and atonic, indiscriminately, and let the children classify them as those having a tone, and those having no tone.

Let the children give sounds of the class called for, as "those having a tone," and "those having no tone."

V.—EXERCISES ON THE SUBTONIC AND ATONIC ELEMENTS, WITH REFERENCE TO THE ORGANS OF SPEECH.

When the children can perfectly imitate the sounds, direct attention to the organs of speech used in forming them. Let the children discover which are formed by the lips almost entirely; which by the tongue with or near the teeth; which by the palate and throat.

VI.—ORDER OF SOUNDS.

Any word which contains a certain sound chosen by the teacher, to be distinctly pronounced by her. Children to decide whether the sound comes first, middle, or last.

VII.—RHYMES.

1. Exercise the children in repeating lists of words or syllables that rhyme, after the teacher; as,

Long vowels: *me, be, te, we, he,* &c.; *ha, ma, ra, sa, pa,* &c.; *lone, cone, tone, known,* &c.

List of rhymes containing double vowels; as, *fine, tune, coy,* &c. Also short vowels, as, *lip, nop,* &c., should be repeated slowly, loudly, softly, &c., according to direction.

SECOND STEP.

In this Step the children will be introduced—

1. To words containing the long sounds of the vowels, together with a few words which are to be learned at sight, containing different sounds of the vowels; to words containing silent letters; also the sound of *k*, and the two sounds of *c* and *s*.

2. To words formed with more than one consonant initial or terminal.

3. In this Step, also, the teacher will see that the children learn the names of the letters.

In writing out this Step, the teacher must at first be prepared to furnish most of the examples; but soon, and often surprisingly soon, the children will relieve her.

At first the children will perhaps be inclined to give non-significant words; but they must be encouraged to give significant words.

Accompanying the Reading Cards is a little book, which may in this Step be put into the hands of the children.

Over these lessons, both on the cards and in the books, printed in different type, are words containing different sounds of the vowels, and other combinations than those to which their attention has been called, which may be taught in the same way as the words at the beginning of the First Step. To aid in this, both large and small cards have been prepared, containing these words. Before the children are introduced to a new lesson, they should be made familiar with these words, so that they can readily pronounce them at sight. These may be treated in the same way as the words at the commencement of the First Step.

PLAN TO BE USED IN READING FROM BOOKS.

FIRST LESSON.—*Object to secure Fluency and Accuracy.*

I.—Word by word.

1. The teacher first pronounces a word, the children the next, and so on. Then reverse the order.

2. Any words that have any peculiarity in spelling selected, and put upon the board; sounds distinguished; silent letters noticed.

II.—Clause by clause.

1. Read each clause, as word by word.
2. Attention paid to pronunciation.

III.—Simultaneous reading.

1. Word by word.
2. Clause by clause.
3. Sentence by sentence.

IV.—Individual children selected to read the paragraph. The

teacher should select the poorest reader, except sometimes when she takes the best as an example to the class.

SECOND LESSON.—*Object to secure Intelligent Reading.*

I.—1. Teacher and children read, as before, sentence by sentence.

2. Children questioned on the meaning of difficult words; the board used.

II.—When two or three paragraphs have been read, the substance of each is drawn from the children, and an abstract put upon the board.

III.—General questions. Object of the lesson; moral, if any. What they have gained from the lesson? &c., &c.

SILENT LETTERS.

At this point in the Step we may call the attention of the children to the fact that some words have letters that are not sounded. At present, however, these words are not presented systematically in classes, but the attention of the children is called to the fact of these silent letters, and a few miscellaneous examples given, such as will occur, or have already occurred in their reading lessons.

The following will answer as a sketch, to show the way in which these may be treated, both at this point and in the latter part of the Step, when they are more fully discussed.

1. Write on the board, *well, ill, bill, fill, will, dell, mill, have, copse, live, cock, lock, dock, Dick, stick, trick, lick, mess, dress, press, less,* &c.

2. Let the children sound separately every letter in *bill;* then give the number of sounds, and point out the letter to which no sound is attached. Give the term *silent.* Proceed thus with at least one of each of the class put on the board. Let the children cross out, but not rub out, the silent letters in each.

3. Exercise the children in other words containing silent letters as they occur in their reading lessons, observing this suggestion, however, to have these exercises previous to reading the les-

son. Many examples of this kind will occur after they are introduced to words containing the

LONG VOWEL SOUNDS.

The following sketches will illustrate the method of treating these sounds:

1. Write *mad* upon the board. Children analyze it, and give the vowel sound. To the right of it write *made*, and treat it in the same way.

2. Develop the idea of *short* and *long*, by reference to the time it takes to pronounce *mad* and *made*. Get examples of each sound.

3. Give examples, and let the children distinguish the vowel sounds, and decide which are long, and which are short.

4. *E, I, O*, and *W*, may be treated in a similar way.

K, the Hard and Soft Sounds of C, and the Two Sounds of S.

1. Place the letter *k* upon the board. Give the sound, and ask the children whether they have ever heard this sound before? Ask them to select a letter which has this sound. If they fail to find it from the card, place several letters on the board, and among them the letter *c*, and ask them to select the letter that has this sound. Now place upon the board, in opposite or parallel columns, lists of words having *k*, and the hard sound of *c*; as,

    cat can cup
    kill kind kid, &c.

Let them pronounce the two lists, and give the sounds in each. Give a further list of words having the letter *k*, and let the children give the sounds; such as, *hark, bark, bank, sank, kind*, &c.

2. *Hard and Soft Sounds of C.*

Sketch.—Develop the idea by comparing such words as *cat, cut, copse, cold, can,* with *cedar, cell, cinder, cider.* Give the terms *hard* and *soft.* The children see that the hard sound is like *k*, and the soft is like *s*.

3. Let the class, in training, give a sketch of the two sounds of *s*, as of *c* hard and soft, as it may be treated in the same general way.

It would be well, at this point, to have some exercises with the children on the card, on which are arranged words such as actually occur in their reading lessons, having the long and short sounds of the vowels, silent letters, the hard sound of *c* as expressed by *c* and *k*, the soft sound of *c*, and *s* subtonic and atonic; the children analyzing the words, indicating the silent letters, the different sounds of *c* and *s* by the terms suggested.

In the following lessons the teacher may make use of the names of the letters in speaking of the various consonants. This will probably be sufficient to familiarize the children with their names. If the teacher, however, should find this not effective, methods similar to those used in teaching the words at the heads of the reading lessons may be adopted.

DOUBLE INITIAL CONSONANTS.

As an illustration of the method of treating these lessons, we subjoin a report of a lesson actually given:

Bl Initial.

1. The teacher wrote these letters on the board, and exercised the children in sounding them.

2. The teacher desired the children to find words beginning with *bl*. As they hesitated, she wrote on the board, *blot, bless, black*.

3. Children gave other examples, viz.: *bland, blank, blind, blink, blab, bladder, blose, blister, block, blanket, bloss, blood, blote, blick*.

4. The children not being able to think of any more words with these combinations, the teacher rubbed out all those that had no meaning. She also rubbed out other words which she had not time to explain, leaving about ten words on the board.

5. She required the children to give the meaning of these,

supplying the meaning of those they did not know. In the afternoon, the children copied this list of words on their own slates.

Sketch on the Initials Sc.

1. *Sc* written on the board. Children name and sound it.
2. Exercised in finding words with this commencement; as, *scan, scot, scum, scatter,* &c. They will probably give words with other than short and long vowels; as, *scar, scald,* &c. These should be added to the list; but should they give words having the sound of *sc*, but spelled differently, as *skip, skin,* the teacher should put them in another column, and direct their attention to the difference in spelling. Children questioned on the meaning as before.
3. Children print on their own slates all the words they can remember beginning with *sc*; also with *sk*.

Sketch on Ld and Lt.

The teacher writes *told* on the board, and directs the attention of the children to the last two sounds. Children exercised as before, and list made out; as,

   ld—held, gild, weld, hold, told, scold.
   lt—hilt, gilt, melt, felt, salt.

Should the children give such words as *heal'd, seal'd, smil'd,* these should be written in another column, and the children led to notice the apostrophe, and shown that such words are usually spelled with *e*, and thus end with *ed*. If we leave out the *e*, we must put the little mark in its place.

The above sketches will answer as models after which future lessons in this Step may be given.

The teacher will observe that in all the following exercises only a few words are given under each head as examples. The children will, of course, produce many more words of each class.

Subject-matter of lessons to be given in this Step:

I.—*Terminal Diphthongs.*

aw	*ow*	*ew*	*ay*	*oy*
caw	bow	few	day	boy
raw	cow	mew	may	coy
taw	vow	new	pay	joy
paw	now	dew	hay	toy

II.—1. *Two Initial Consonants.*

bl	*br*	*cl*	*cr*	*dr*
block	brick	clod	crab	drag
bliss	brink	clinch	crib	drip
black	bran	cliff	crock	drop

dw	*fl*	*fr*	*pl*	*pr*
dwell	flock	frog	plug	prop
dwindle	flint	frock	plum	press
dwarf	flag	frisk	plant	print

sc	*sk*	*sl*	*sm*	*sn*
scum	skim	slip	smell	snap
scant	skull	slop	smack	snag
scud	skip	sled	smut	snug

sp	*st*	*sw*	*tr*	*tw*	*qu*
spill	stand	swing	tramp	twang	quit
split	step	swell	trip	twill	quill
spent	stick	swam	trot	twist	quilt

2. *Two Terminal Consonants.*

lb	*ld*	*nd*	*ff*	*lf*	*ck*
elb	gild	wind	cliff	pelf	brick
bulb	weld	band	puff	self	crick
	sold	rend	scoff	gulf	track

lk	*nk*	*sk*	*ll*	*lm*	*sm*
elk	ink	task	drill	elm	prism
silk	think	frisk	dill	helm	chasm
sulk	sink	mask	till	realm	ism

lp	*mp*	*sp*	*ct*	*st*	*ft*
help	cramp	lisp	act	most	draft
yelp	stamp	wisp	fact	post	drift
pulp	romp	crisp	sect	rust	loft

lt	*nt*	*st*	*ss*
hilt	went	west	fuss
melt	sent	rest	muss
felt	bent	best	loss

NOTE.—The words are still to be spelled by sound, but as the children become familiar with the names of the letters, they may be spelled by names of the letters also.

III.—1. *Three Initial Consonants.*

scr	*spr*	*str*	*spl*	*squ*
scrap	spring	string	split	squib
screw	spry	strong	splint	squint
scratch	spread	strung	splash	squills

2. *Miscellaneous Terminals.*

ar	*or*	*ur*	*arl*	*oil*	*url*
star	for	fur	snarl	broil	curl
far	nor	bur	marl	toil	furl

arm	*orm*	*ume*	*am*	*own*	*one*
farm	worm	fume	cram	crown	tone
warm	storm	exhume	ham	drown	lone

urn	*rb*	*rd*	*rf*	*rk*	*rl*
turn	herb	hard	serf	lurk	girl
burn	curb	card	turf	bark	pearl

rp	*rt*	*ng*	*ly*	*sion*	*tion*
harp	part	song	fly	mission	motion
carp	cart	wrong	ply	session	notion

IV.—*Recapitulation of Initials.*

sc, scr, sk, bl, cl, fl, gl, pl, sl, spl, sm, sn, sp, cr, scr, dr, fr, gr, pr, spr, str, tr, st, qu, squ, dw, tw, sw, wh.

V.—*Recapitulation of Terminals.*

ck, ct, ff, ft, lb, ld, lf, lk, ll, lm, lp, lt, mp, nd, ng, nk, nt, rb, rd, rf, rk, rl, rm, rn, rp, rt, sk, sm, sp, ss, st, ly, sion, tion, ar, or, ur, oil, ume, am, one.

In conclusion, give a few lessons on the same combinations used both as initial and terminal; as, *sk, sm, sp, st,* &c.

Let the children give any words containing one or more of these combinations. Place them on the board, and let the children classify them.

INITIAL.	TERMINAL.
skip	ask
skin	musk
skate	risk,
sketch	task, &c.

Silent Characters.

The following lists of words containing silent letters may be treated as per sketch given on page 242, illustrating a method of teaching words having silent letters:

1. *Initial Silent Consonants.*

g	*h*	*k*	*p*	*w*	*w*
gnat	herb	knife	psalm	whole	wrong
gnaw	heir	knob	ptarmigan	who	write
gnash	hour	knot	psalter	whoop	wring

2. *Central Silent Consonants.*

b	*c*	*c*	*d*	*d*	*g*
debt	fickle	victuals	pledge	handsome	sign
doubt	scent	indict	lodge	handkerchief	reign
subtle	muscle	pickaxe	judge	Wednesday	deign

h	*h*	*h*	*h*	*gh*	*l*
ghost	rhomb	Thames	scheme	light	talk
ghast	rhubarb	Thomas	school	height	stalk
ghaut	rhyme	asthma	schooner	naughty	folk

READING.—SECOND STEP.

l	*p*	*t*	*t*	*w*	*s*
calm	tempt	castle	pitch	answer	isle
palm	receipt	often	hitch	sword	aisle
balm	symptom	chestnut	match	toward	viscount

3. *Terminal Silent Consonants.*

b	*k*	*gh*	*h*
lamb	wick	plough	Sarah
comb	dock	though	verandah
plumb	lock	sigh	burgh

4. *Central Silent Vowels.*

e	*i*	*u*
open	marriage	build
listen	carriage	gauge
risen	tarried	guilt

5. *Terminal Silent E.*

ce	*ble*	*cle*	*dle*	*fle*
nice	able	uncle	handle	baffle
rice	fable	treacle	saddle	snuffle
peace	warble	circle	riddle	ruffle

gle	*kle*	*ple*	*tle*	*te*
eagle	freckle	ripple	tattle	etiquette
wriggle	sprinkle	cripple	rattle	brunette
struggle	tickle	supple	battle	coquette

6. *Terminal Silent ue.*

ue	*ue*
league	grotesque
plague	opaque
tongue	picturesque

11*

THIRD STEP.

Ambiguities.

The children, while in this Step, learn to distinguish the consonants, subtonic and atonic, and to consider the various and anomalous sounds of vowels and diphthongs; also *g* hard and soft.

At this Step children may be introduced to reading books, such as are ordinarily used in schools of this grade, having no reference to a classification of sounds.

Consonants.

We have already considered the different sounds of *c* and *s*. The remaining consonants to be considered are *g, th, ph, gh, ch, z*, and *x*.

1. *G; also Th, Hard and Soft.*—Treat this in the same way as *c* hard and soft, giving lists of words; as,

Hard:	Gilbert	getting	unguent
Soft:	gipsy	George	pungent, &c.
Hard:	thin	think	truth
Soft:	thou	thine	thus, &c.

2. *Ph. Sketch.*—Words containing this combination written and sounded.

Children recognize the sound as expressed by *f*. Words are given, which the children classify; as,

physic	sphere	tough
phonic	camphor	triumph
photograph	orphan	seraph

As a second lesson, the children may be employed in finding proper names containing this sound. Names spelled with *f* should be put in a separate column.

INITIAL.	CENTRAL.	TERMINAL.
Phebe	Humphrey	Joseph
Philip	Alphonso	Ralph
Phillis	Sophia	Adolph
Phipps	Euphemia	Guelph

3. *Gh.*—Proceed in a similar way with words having this combination; as, *cough, laugh.* Compare these with words having *gh* silent, as, *plough, bough,* &c.

4. *Sounds of Ch.*—Children give words containing the sound of *ch* called for by the teacher, which will stand on the board thus:

English.	*French.*	*Hard.*	*English Ch Classified.*	
			INITIAL.	TERMINAL.
child	chaise	Christmas	child	watch
china	chivalry	chord	chip	match
church	chandelier	chaldron		

French Ch Classified.		*Ch Hard Classified.*	
INITIAL.	TERMINAL.	INITIAL.	CENTRAL.
chagrin	blanche	character	ache
chamois	barouche	chasm	echo
champagne	mustache	chaos	scholar

5. *Z.*—In teaching the sound of this letter, proceed as in teaching the sound of *k*, with this exception, that the children will now select their own words as examples. If they hesitate in doing this, it is only necessary to get from them a variety of words containing this sound, some of which will be likely to contain the desired examples, which may be arranged in columns, and compared; as,

is	his	arise	risen
zeal	zinc	zounds	zany

Let the children add as many words as they can in which *s* has the sound of *z*.

It will be well also to compare such words as

azure	glazier
assure	sugar

They will discover that both *z* and *s* have here different sounds than in the former list. Let them decide which has a tone, and which has not. They will give many examples in which this sound is represented by *s*; as, *osier, crosier, treasure, usual, vision,* &c. Observe, in fact, that it is more frequently represented by *s* than *z*. Practice them in interchanging these elements, pronouncing *azure* as *asure* (*ashure*), *sure* as *zure*, &c.

I.—*Sketch on the Letter X.*

1. Various examples of words containing *x* given. Children examine these, and discover that *x* has the sound of *ks*.

2. Teacher gives other examples; as, *anxious, complexion, luxury*. Children discover that the sound here is *ksh*. Classify, putting in separate columns the words having these two sounds; as,

ks	ksh
mixture	luxury
exhaust	fluxions

It may be well, at this point, to review some exercises that have been slightly passed over.

II.—*Sketch on D as T.*

1. Let the children sound *d* repeatedly. Ask them, with the organs in position for sounding *d*, to utter it without a tone. They will discover that it is the sound of *t*. Let them give examples of both, and classify them; as,

INITIAL.		CENTRAL.		TERMINAL.	
din	tin	udder	utter	nod	not
den	ten	madder	matter	shod	shot
dinner	tinner	ladder	latter	trod	trot

The teacher may use the terms *subtonic* and *atonic;* or, if preferred, *sharp* and *flat*.

2. In the same manner take *b* and *p*, *g* and *k*, *v* and *f*, *th* in *thine* and *th* in *thin*, *z* in *zeal* and *s* in *seal*, *j* in *jest* and *ch* in *chest*, *z* in *azure* and *sh* in *shall*, *g* in *go* and *k* in *kid*.

The subtonics are *d, b, g, v, th* in *thine, z* in *zeal, z* in *azure, g* in *go*.

The atonics are *t, p, k, f, th* in *thin, s* in *seal, ch* in *chest, sh,* and *k*.

III.—1. In reviewing *c* hard and soft, introduce examples of *c* before *e, i,* and *y*.

2. Soft sound of *g*, as expressed by *j* in *jelly, just, Joseph*. In seeking for examples of this sound, the children may possibly give

such words as *obedient, individual, obdurate.* There is a tendency in such words to pronounce *d* as *j*. This should be guarded against.

IV.—*Sketch on Ch.*

The children may be employed in making a list of Scripture names containing *ch*, and in learning how to pronouce them. *Ch* is hard in all except *Rachel* and *cherubim*. In seeking for examples containing English *ch*, they may give such words as *creature*, and will require a lesson on the sounds of *t* before *u*. Let them make a list; as, *scripture, culture, lecture, fortune, virtue, rapture*. A double list may also be made out; as,

fracture	tincture	rupture
child	cheese	church

The children will discover that these sounds, represented by *tu* and *ch*, somewhat resemble each other, but that the sound represented by *tu*, properly spoken, is not quite like *ch*.

V.—*S, C, and Z.*

Lessons might be given on all the sounds expressed by *s*, *c*, and *z*.

The sound of *s*, in *sure*, is expressed by *s*, *ss*, *sh*, *ce*, *ci*, *cy*, and *ti*.

Direct attention to the common change of *s* atonic to the subtonic, in pronouncing plurals; as,

> birds, pronounced *birdz*.
> days,   "   *dayz*.
> dogs,   "   *dogz*, &c.

ANOMALIES.—FIRST DIVISION.

One Sign representing Various Sounds.

1. Sounds represented by the letter *a*:

Short.	Long.	Broad.	Italian.	Long a before r.	Short o.	Short e.
bag	baby	fall	far	fare	watch	any
nap	cape	warm	father	pair	warrant	many
parrot	natal	walk	calm	care	wallow	Thames

In the above, and in succeeding exercises, the title at the head of the column is put upon the board, the sound given by the teacher, and, if necessary, an example added, and the children dictate the words. For lists of classified words, see "Worcester's Spelling Book."

2. Sounds expressed by the letter *e*:

Short.	*Long.*	*Long* a *before* r.	*Short* i.	*Short Obtuse* u.
met	mete	there	England	her
men	complete	where	English	fern
ferry	secrete	ere		term

Show that sounds in the first and third columns are identical with the sounds in the seventh and fifth, under *a*.

3. Sounds expressed by the letter *o*:

Short.	*Long.*	*Broad.*	*Long and Close.*	*Short* u.
dock	note	storm	move	glove
stock	close	horn	lose	color
lock	rose	adorn	prove	sponge

4. Sounds expressed by the character *u*:

Short.	*Long.*	*Middle or Obtuse.*	*Short and Obtuse.*	*Short* e.	*Sound of* w.
tuck	tune	pull	fur	bury	queen
run	mute	full	turn	busy	languid
sun	pure	push	hurt		lingual

Lead the children to see that the *u* in *tune* is really a compound sound. That the sound in *bury* is really the sound of short *e* expressed by *u*. Lastly, that *u* has the sound of *w* after *q* and after *g*, when sounded at all. (It is often silent, as *guest*.)

5. Sounds expressed by the letter *i*:

Short.	*Long.*	*Long* e.	*Long and Obtuse* i.
kin	mite	marine	bird
nit	write	machine	fir
sit	fire	fatigue	stir

Lead the children to see that *i* in *mite* is a compound sound, or diphthong; that *i* in *marine* is identical with *e* in *mete;* and that *i* in *bird* is like *u* in *Turk* and *purse.*

6. Sounds expressed by *y*:

Short i.	*Long* i.	*Consonantal Sound.*	*Short and Obtuse* u.
mystery	tyrant	yet	myrrh
sylvan	style	year	myrmidon
symbol	type	your	myrtle

7. Sounds expressed by *ou*:

Proper.	*Long* o.	*Broad* a.	*Long & Close* o.	*Short* u.	*Short and Obtuse* u.
flour	soul	wrought	group	country	scourge
hour	mould	brought	soup	cousin	courteous
sound	shoulder	bought	through	touch	courtesy

SECOND DIVISION.

Single Sounds represented by Various Signs.

1. The long sound of *a* is expressed by *a*, and by

ai	*ay*	*ea*	*ei*	*ey*	*au*	*ao*
slain	stay	break	eight	they	gauge	gaol
pain	play	steak	skein	obey		
rain	day	great	weigh	prey		

2. The Italian sound of *a* is expressed by *a*, and by

al	*ea*	*au*
calm	heart	haunt
balm	hearth	daunt
psalm	hearken	taunt

3. The broad sound of *a* is expressed by *a*, and by

aw	*au*	*o*	*ou*	*oa*	*or*
fawn	daub	snort	fought	broad	lord
straw	haul	north	brought	groat	horn
raw	vault	lord	thought		storm

4. The long sound of *a* before *r* is expressed by *a*, and by

ai	*ea*	*ay*	*e*	*ei*
air	bear	prayer	ere	heir
chair	pear		there	their
fair	wear		where	

READING.—THIRD STEP.

5. The long sound of *e* is expressed by *e*, and by

ee	*ea*	*ei*	*eo*	*ey*	*ay*	*i*	*ie*
feet	reap	receive	people	key	quay	machine	grief
queen	heap	perceive				police	piece
green	neat	conceive				marine	priest

6. The short sound of *e* is expressed by *e*, and by

ai	*ay*	*ea*	*ei*	*eo*	*ie*	*u*	*ue*
again	says	leather	heifer	leopard	friend	bury	guest
against		feather		jeopardy			guess
said		endeavor		feoff			quench

7. The long sound of *i* is expressed by *i*, and by

ie	*ei*	*ye*	*ui* or *uy*	*y*	*ai*	*eye*
die	height	lye	buy	style	aisle	eye
lie	sleight	eye	guy	my		
pie		dye	disguise	deny		

8. The short sound of *i* is expressed by *i*, and by

e	*y*	*ey*	*o*	*u*	*ui*
England	sympathy	money	women	busy	biscuit
English	symptom	journey		lettuce	circuit
	paroxysm	coney		minute	guitar

9. The short sound of *o* is expressed by *o*, and by

a	*ow*
wast	knowledge
wash	
watch	

10. The long sound of *o* is expressed by *o*, and by

oo	*oa*	*oe*	*ou*	*ow*
door	coal	foe	four	own
floor	board	hoe	pour	flow
brooch	loaf	toe	soul	sow

ew	*eau*	*au*	*eo*
sew	beau	hautboy	yeoman
shew	bureau	hauteur	
strew	plateau	hautgout	

11. The long sound of *u* is expressed by *u*, and by

ue	*ui*	*ew*	*eu*	*ieu*	*iew*	*eau*	*ewe*
blue	suits	blew	feudal	adieu	view	beauty	ewe
glue	juice	mew	neutral	lieu			
sue	sluice	Jew	feud	purlieu			

12. The short sound of *u* is expressed by *u*, and by

o	*ou*	*oo*	*oe*
come	rough	blood	does
done	touch	flood	
dove	young		

13. The middle or obtuse sound of *u* is expressed by *u*, and by

oo	*ou*	*o*
book	could	wolf
good	should	woman
took	would	bosom

14. The short and obtuse sound of *u* is expressed by *u*, and by

e	*i*	*ea*	*o*	*ou*	*y*
her	girl	dearth	word	adjourn	myrrh
defer	twirl	hearse	worm	scourge	myrtle
prefer	mirth	yearn	worth	journey	myrmidon

15. The sound of *ou* is represented also by *ow*, as *howl, vow, allow.*

16. The diphthong *oi* is otherwise represented by *oy*, as *boy, coy, toy.*

hw is represented by *wh*; as, *when, whip, whim*, &c.

DICTATION.

INTRODUCTORY REMARKS.

IMPORTANT as it is that every one attempting to write in English should be able to spell correctly, it is but too manifest that the painful exercises to which children in former years were subjected failed to give them the power of doing this. The learning by heart of column after column of spelling lessons, in which many words not in common use would constantly occur, as well as many others in which the combination of letters is quite arbitrary, exercising only memory, has proved, to a great extent, a wearisome waste of time. This plan of instruction is now happily superseded by dictation lessons, which, when rightly given, call out close observation, and thus tend to fix the correct spelling of words in the mind.

FIRST STEP.

Object.—At this step dictation may be considered an exercise in writing. The children first learn how to print letters which are simple in form, as *i*, *t*, *n*, and to join them together, so as to make words of two letters.

Plan.—1. The teacher to print a letter—the letter *L*, for instance—on the board, the children being required to observe carefully how it is done, to say what kind of lines are made, and also their direction, a simple definition being sufficient. The children to observe, further, where the teacher begins the formation of the letter, and where the formation of it ends. The teacher then makes a second letter, *O*, and joins it to the first, directing the children's attention also to the mode of its formation. The children to say what word is made.

2. The teacher to print the same word very slowly two or three times over; to require the children to observe closely, and to imitate the act by moving a finger as if writing in the air.

3. The teacher to require two or three children to print the same word on the board, to compare the word they have printed with the copy, and to say in what they are alike, and in what they differ, and how they could be improved.

4. The children may then print the same word three or four times over on their own slates, the teacher seeing that the copy is constantly referred to, and also carefully and frequently examining the slate. As improvement in writing mainly depends upon the children attentively observing the copy, and comparing their own work with it, the teacher should occasionally print on the board an imitation of one of the children's productions—either a very good or a very bad one; the rest of the children to say in what the letters are rightly or wrongly formed; then to look at their own slates, and see to which their own copy bears most resemblance.

SECOND STEP.

Object.—There are three points in which this Step is in advance upon the First Step: 1. The children are led to observe the proportion between the different parts of letters; and 2. The position of the words printed on the slate. 3. They are taught to hold the pencil properly.

Plan.—The teacher gives a word, the children spell it; then this word is printed on the board, as in the First Step. The children are then led to observe the relative position of the letters, their size, and the proportion of their parts. They are directed to begin to print the words at the top of the left-hand corner of their slates, and to continue them successively in a straight line toward the right. They are usually led to print such words as occur on the boards from which they read. After the children have printed two or three words, and these have been carefully examined, these words, as well as those from which they were copied, are rubbed out, and they are required to print the same words from dictation. They are then instructed in the proper mode of holding a pencil, practising this before they commence writing.

THIRD STEP.

Object.—To teach the children to substitute *written* for printed characters. The daily practice of the children in reading the summaries of lessons written on the board, during their object lesson, will assist in preparing them to pass from *printed* to *written* characters. The latter are introduced at this Step, together with the use of the comma and period.

Plan.—1. The two different alphabets are written on the blackboard, and the children exercised in writing the two forms of the same letter on their slates. The teacher next gives out the first word of a sentence, the children spell it, and one of them writes it on the board, being directed to begin with a capital letter; the rest examine the word, saying whether the letters are of the proper height and inclination; any points not noticed by the children to be taken up by the teacher. All the words in the sentence are in succession similarly dealt with.

2. The teacher supplies the stops, and directs the children's attention to their use and their position. The children are required to look at the sentence carefully for two or three minutes, and to notice the spelling of each word.

3. The whole is then rubbed out, and the children write the sentence on their own slates, at the dictation of the teacher. The slates are constantly and carefully examined by the teacher, and faults or excellences pointed out.

FOURTH STEP.

Object.—To lead the children to a more close observation of the spelling of words, especially that of some of the peculiar words of our language. They are also exercised in the use of capital letters, and of the notes of interrogation and exclamation, and taught the rules which regulate the use of all these. Any dictation spelling book may be used as a text book.

Plan.—This is exemplified in the following suggestions:

1. Words are given, similar in sound, but differing in spelling and signification; as, for example, *all, awl; piece, peace,* &c.

2. Words similarly spelt, but differently pronounced or applied; such as, *close*—shut fast; *close*—to join, to shut; *conduct*—behavior; *conduct*—to lead, to manage, &c., treated in the same way as the former class of words.

3. Words spelt and pronounced alike, but differing in signification; as, *hail*—drops of rain frozen while falling; *hail*—to call out.

4. The children learn the distinction between vowels and consonants, and are made acquainted with a few simple rules of spelling; as, for example, under what circumstances a consonant is doubled, as in *beg, begging, run, running,* &c.; when one *l* is to be omitted, as in *almost,* made up of *all* and *most; skilful,* made up of *skill* and *full.* During these lessons, the capital letters and different stops are used.

The following plan may be adopted when the lesson is on words similar in sound, but differing in spelling and signification:

1. Suppose the words to be *see* and *sea.* The teacher writes *see* upon the board, directs the children's attention to the spelling and meaning (the latter to be written opposite the word); and the teacher asks whether they have heard a word of the same sound used in any other sense? If not, to tell them that a portion of the ocean is called *sea.* This word, *sea,* to be then written under the other, the children to compare the two, to say in what they are alike and in what they differ, and to give the meaning of each:

See—to look.
Sea—part of the ocean.

2. The teacher to dictate the sentence, "I can see the sea;" to require a child to write it upon the board; the rest of the chil-

dren to examine the sentence, and especially the spelling of the two words, *see* and *sea*, and to say whether each is spelt correctly; why, in that particular sentence, the last word is spelt *sea*, and not *see*.

3. The teacher to dictate two or three sentences containing both these words; the children to write them on their own slates. After each sentence is written, all the slates to be examined by the teacher. If the teacher meets with a sentence in which the two words are not spelt correctly, to copy it on the board, and submit it to the inspection of the class. When they have decided where and what the error is, they are to examine what they have written on their own slates, and, comparing it with that on the board, make the necessary corrections.

ELEMENTARY LESSONS, PREPARATORY TO GEOGRAPHY.

INTRODUCTORY REMARKS.

The elementary principles of geography are those which relate to *position or place*, including both the relative position of places with respect to each other, and also their position as determined by the points of the compass. Under this head may also be arranged the idea of *distance*, as leading to the necessity of a standard of measurement by which such distance may be estimated and described.

The second principle is that of *form*, which introduces the consideration of the outline or boundaries of countries.

The third is that of *physical geography*, which affords most interesting materials for instruction; for by the help of models, and by observation on the physical features of their own immediate neighborhood, even very young children may be led to appreciate the grander and more developed features of other countries. The study of topographical geography should commence with the accurate observation of the locality in which the instruction is given, thus carrying out the Pestalozzian principle of *proceeding from the known to the unknown*. The following remarks by Mr. Moseley, one of the inspectors of Government Schools in England, are so very valuable, and so much in harmony with the principles upon which all Pestalozzian instruction is based, that it is thought well to repeat them here:

"In proposing that a course of instruction, addressed to an elementary school in geography, should commence with the topography of the school district; that, aiming at the description of nature under remote and inaccessible forms, it should begin with the description of those under which it is familiar, and which are at hand; that, in speaking of the social and political relations of distant regions, it should begin by instructing the child in those of its own, I take into my view the eminently *educative* character of this course, and that natural process of the development of the faculties of the child which is implied in it. In the first place, that faculty of observation will have been practised which admits of so vast an enlargement of its sphere of operation by *habit*. The child will first have been led to *observe* the directions of lanes and footpaths, the irregular figures traced out by the boundaries of fields and farms, the varieties of surface level, the lines of direction of elevated grounds, and valleys, and streams, the plants and trees, the crops of the neighboring lands, the mines and manufactories; and the questions addressed to him at school on these matters will have led him to observe these with *precision* and *accuracy;* for above all, and as a necessary condition to every other valuable result, his *attention* will have been gained, because it is directed to matters which he can *understand*, and which *interest* him. Next, his faculty of *memory* will have been constantly exercised under that form in which it ministers most readily to the uses of life, *i. e.*, concerning *things* rather than *words*. Then his *imagination* will have been educated and directed, in its operation, to legitimate objects. To abstract—to separate the idea from the object on which it has formed itself; to enlarge and to generalize that idea; to compare it with others, and to combine ideas under new forms, giving order and proportion, and beauty of arrangement and disposition to the parts so assembled together in the mind, and correspondence to some proposed model, or adaptation to some result; this is the process of invention, and the work of imagination. And what but this is done, when, from ideas collected from present objects, a picture is formed in the mind wholly different in the arrangement of its parts and their distribution, and vastly increased in its dimensions? It is in leaving this picture on the mind of the child, vivid in its colors, and complete in all its characteristic features, that consists the art of the teacher.

"No single step in this process can be taken without some

exercise of the *intelligence*. It is, in fact, from one end to the other, a process of induction, every element of which is linked to another by an obvious causation. Independently of this relation in everything made the subject of observation, there will moreover be some *adaptation* of that particular thing—whether it be a sensible object, or a social or political relation, or a process of art or manufacture—to an end or a result; an adaptation which, if it be not obvious, will form a legitimate subject of instruction, and a means of educating the reasoning faculty in the child.

"It is this *educative* character which gives to the course its highest value; and it is, in point of fact, with a simple reference to that character, that I have thought it worth while to record here the exposition of it.

"Geography acquires its full value as a branch of education only when it loses the character of an accumulation of facts, undigested by the child's mind, but heaped up in his memory, linked by no association with the world of thought and of action which immediately surrounds it, or with that which is within it. Tell the child to observe the lines of the map which hangs perpetually before his eyes, and talk to him only of the *names* of the places indicated upon it, and you will soon weary his attention; but speak to him of the living men who inhabit it; tell him of their stature, and aspect, and dress, and ways of life, and of their forms of worship; speak of the climate of that country; of the forms of vegetable and animal life with which his eye would be conversant if he dwelt there; of the trees and flowers that grow there, and of the birds and beasts, and you will carry his interest with you. That relation to external things which characterizes their mode of being and condition of life, he will understand by a reference to his own; and he will have acquired a knowledge of some of those things, in reference to *them*, the like of which are of interest to himself."

FIRST STEP.

Object.—1. To prepare the children to enter with intelligence upon the study of geography, by first drawing their observation to *relative position* or *place*, beginning with the situation of the things which they see around them, and the distance of these from each other. 2. To give the children a knowledge of the cardinal points of the compass, and their use in geographical descriptions. 3. To bring before them the mode of representing distances, and to teach them a scale of measurement of distance, and the nature and use of a map.

These points are carried out in the following

LESSONS ON PLACE.

Lesson 1.

I. Position of Objects.—Bring before the children three objects, say two ink wells and a book. Place the book in the middle, with an ink well on each side of it. Let a child do the same with two other ink wells and another book, the rest to say if rightly done. Alter the position of the objects, putting the ink wells in line, and the book in front of them. A second child to imitate, &c. Produce four objects, and arrange them, say the ink wells in the middle, and the books on each side. Then the books in the middle, &c. Then ink wells and books alternately. Then ink wells and books, one at each of the four corners of the table, children always engaged in imitating, or deciding on the correctness of another's imitation.

II. Having arranged the objects as before, disarrange them, and let the children rearrange them from memory. After going through the exercises before performed in this way, introduce one or two new exercises; as, for instance, two ink wells behind, and two books before.

Lesson 2.

Relative Position of the Parts of the Room.

I. Let the children name the place in which they are sitting. See if they can distinguish, by name, the parts of the room; as, floor, wall, ceiling, pointing to each as directed. To bring out the position of these, let them point to that part of the room which is nearest to their feet. Name that part (floor). S. R.: "The floor is below our feet." Teacher ascends a chair in the middle of the room, desiring the child to point to that part of the room nearest her head. S. R.: "The ceiling is above our heads." Require the children to put their slates above their heads, also below their feet. Lead them to observe where the ceiling is, with reference to the floor; and the floor, with reference to the ceiling. Next desire them to point to the walls. A child to go round the room, touching the wall as he goes. S. R.: "The walls go round the room." In the same way develop the ideas of *between, before, behind.*

II. Exercise the children in pointing out the position of various parts of the room, with respect to other parts of the room, or to themselves, or articles of furniture, exercising them in applying the terms learned.

Lesson 3.

Representation of Position.

Place upon the table five objects; as, book, pen, slate, ink well, india rubber. Require them to notice and describe the relative position of each of the objects on the table. Then draw an outline of the table on the board, or on the floor, marking within, the objects as they stand, according to the direction of the children; *e. g.*, the slate in the middle; the books in the farthest corner, on the side nearest the wall, on the left hand; the india rubber in the opposite corner, on the right hand; the pen and the ink well in the remaining corners respectively. Exercise the children in touching first the objects, and then their representations, on the board or floor. Then alter the positions of the objects, putting them in line, from the right-hand corner on one side, to the left-hand corner on the other side. Again mark them on the board or floor, as directed. Lastly, rearrange the objects in any other way, and let a child mark the position on the board. Several exercises to be had in this way.

Lesson 4.

East and West.

When the children have been accustomed to determine the relative position of *objects*, they must be led to consider *places* in the same point of view, and to this end they should be made acquainted with the use of the several points of the compass. Begin by collecting from them anything they may have observed with respect to the apparent course of the sun; where they have seen it rise in the morning, and where set in the evening; and tell them that the place in the heavens where it rises, is called the *East;* that in which it sets, the *West.* Then question them in different ways, to see that they have understood the information given, and that it is well fixed in their minds. Call out some of the children, and tell them to place themselves with their right hands to the east, and their left hands to the west. Bid them look toward the east. Ask them what they might expect to see there early in the morning? Desire them to look to the west, and say when they would see the sun in that direction. Ask which is the western, and which the eastern side of the room, and the same of the playground. Through which windows will the sun shine in the morning, and through which in the afternoon? The other afternoon, as I was walking, I saw the sun before me like a great ball of fire, and then it gradually sunk, till I lost sight of it; in what direction must I have been walking? My bedroom window is very nicely placed, for the sun shines into my room the first thing in the morning, to tell me it is time to get up; to what part of the heavens is my window opposite? By similar questions fix well in the children's minds which are the eastern and western points. Excite them to observe, both at home and at school, where the sun may be seen at different parts of the day, and close the lesson by a simultaneous repetition: "That direction in which the sun rises, is called the *East;* and that in which it sets, the *West.*"

Lesson 5.

North and South.

This lesson should commence with a repetition of the preceding one. Some children may then be called out, and bid to place themselves with their right hands to the east, and their left to the west, and then be told that the point directly before them is the *North*, and that directly behind them the *South*. Make them repeat together: "If we stand with our right hands to the east, and our left hands to the west, the point directly before us is the *North*, and that directly behind us is the *South*." What must you observe, in order to find out where the east and west are? If you know the east and west, how can you find out the north and south? Ask the direction in which the children who have been called out must walk, if they wish to go to the north side of the room, and in which if they wish to go toward the south? Let them determine the north, south, east, and west sides of their school-room and playground. Call out one child, and bid him walk from north to south, another from south to east, and another to walk in whatever direction he pleases, the children in the room determining which way he goes. Let the children place a stick or draw a line with chalk upon the floor in the direction of north and south, east and west. Hold up two pieces of wood or card, crossing each other at right angles, one of them pointing directly north and south, and let the children say which end points north, and which east.

In such exercises, the object is to occupy only so much time upon each new idea as may suffice to fix it on the mind. The manner in which it is presented should be varied, that the lesson may be interesting. To effect this, the children should themselves be actors as far as is consistent with tolerable order. A teacher should recollect that it is both unnecessary and unwise to expect little children to be always in precise order; this would be unnatural to the joyous and active habits of infancy. The teacher should know when the strictness of discipline may be safely relaxed, while, on the other hand, the *power* of maintaining order should never be relinquished.

Lesson 6.

Repetition of Preceding Lessons.

It may be desirable that this lesson should consist of exercises on the points of the compass. Let the children determine the position of the different articles in the room. Call upon some of them to say in what direction they must move to go to these; in what direction they must walk in order to reach their homes, and in what direction on coming from home to school. The teacher's own judgment must determine as to whether or not she bring a new subject before the children in this lesson. This will depend much upon the aptitude with which past lessons have been acquired. She must see to it that her children are firm on one step of the ladder of knowledge, before they proceed to another; and she must be careful not to weary and disgust them, by keeping them too long on one idea.

Lesson 7.

Semi-cardinal Points.

In order to test the clearness of the children's apprehension, the following questions might be put:

Suppose you wished to describe the particular direction of some place, how would you do it? Yes; you would tell me it was either to the north, or south, or east, or west. And how should I be able to find out which is the north, south, east, or west? By observing where the sun sets or rises.

When we wish to represent the situations of different places on paper or on a slate, we call the top the north; where, then, will the south be represented? At the bottom of the blackboard. Where the east? and where the west? The teacher writes the four cardinal points on the blackboard. How many points have you learned? But are things or places always *exactly* at the north, the south, the east, or the west? Where may they be? They may be between any two of these points, and you should know how to describe their position in this case. Now attend, and I will teach you this. A point halfway between the north and east is said to be northeast. What do you think halfway between north and west is called? Yes; northwest. And what between south and east? Yes; southeast. And what between south and west? Yes; southwest. The teacher writes these names on the board. How many points do you now know? Repeat them together. Where is the northwest? where the southwest? &c. Call a child to point to these on the board, the other children say what is pointed to. Then call upon the children to determine the place of these eight different points in the room. Then call out a child, and tell him to take a position at the northeast, another at the northwest, &c. Then desire a child to go to any point he may please, and another to point out upon the board the direction in which he stands. Such exercises will show whether the children understand the direction of the cardinal points, and those positions in a map which usually represent them. The lesson should conclude with a simultaneous repetition of the names of all the cardinal points of the compass.

SECOND STEP.

Lesson 1.

The Necessity for Standard Points of Direction.—The Relative Position of Objects.

Of how many points of the compass do you know the names? Repeat them. Show me where you would look for each point, and where each point would be represented on the board. When we know where these points are, we can easily direct each other here and there, which is very convenient. Can you tell me any other way of directing a person except by these points? Yes; by telling him to go to the right, or to the left. Let us try this. Now direct me in which direction to walk; I wish to go to the door. You must go to the right. The teacher turning half round: Must I go to the right now? No. Is the door in all cases to my right? No. What must you know before you can direct a person to go to the right or left? We must know in what position he stands. If, then, a person in the next room, or at a distance, were to send and ask you how to find some place, would it do to say, It is to your right, or left? No. Why not? But if you tell him that the place he wishes to find is to the north or south of the place in which he then is, will this help him to know the situation of the place he seeks? Yes. Why? Could his moving alter the place of the north or south? Your right hand or your left hand may change their position, but the points of the compass are always fixed, and this is the reason they are so useful in describing the position of different places. You can direct people how to travel, by telling them that the places to which they go are toward the north or south, &c. Now you shall say where the different objects in this room are situated. Where is the table? the stove? the windows? the door? the cabinet? any particular picture? &c. Now we will represent the position of all these upon a slate.

Name something in this room. The cabinet. On what side of this room is the cabinet? It is on the north side. Which part of the slate represents the north side? I will put a mark there to represent the cabinet. Now tell me what object is on the west side of the room. Which side of the slate represents the west? I will put marks at this side of the slate for those things which you describe as being to the west.* In this manner the situation of the principal parts of the room and its various contents may be represented on the slate. What have I done? You have put marks on the slate which show where the different things in the room are situated. Yes; whether they are toward the north, south, &c.

Lesson 2.

Boundaries of the Schoolroom.†

Repeat the names of those points of the compass which you have learned. One of you come and show me where each point

* The slate should be first placed horizontally, this being the natural position of the earth's surface; afterward it should be placed in a vertical position, opposite the class.

† It has been suggested that lessons on Physical Geography might be well

would be represented on the blackboard. We will now draw on the board the shape or plan of this room. How many sides has the room? Four. Which is the north side? Where must I place the line representing it? At the top of the board. Where is the south side of the room? Where must I represent it on the board? At the bottom. What length must this line be? The same length as that which represents the north. Why? Because the north and south of the room are of the same length. In what side of this room is the door? It is in the west side. Where must I draw a line, that it may represent the west side of this room? On the left side of the slate. What length must the line be? It must be longer than the other lines. What side remains to be represented? The east side. Where must I draw the line representing it? To the right of the other lines. What length must I make it? The same in length as the west side. What sides of the room are alike? What figure have I drawn? An oblong. What do the lines represent? The walls of the room. How far does the room extend? As far as the walls. How many walls has the room? These four walls are the boundaries of the schoolroom; they bound it. What are the walls to the rooms? They are its boundaries. How are these boundaries represented on the blackboard? By lines. And what figure do these four lines make? An oblong. And what does this oblong that I have drawn on the board represent? The shape of the room. I have drawn lines representing the boundaries of the room, and these show its shape. If, then, I wish to draw the plan of any room or place, what must I do? You must draw its boundaries. The children should repeat together: "The walls are the boundaries of the room. They are represented on the board by lines, which describe its shape."

introduced at this stage of instruction, before the consideration of the nature of a map. On this point teachers should be guided by their own judgment and experience.

12*

Lesson 3.

Boundaries Continued.—The Playground.

What was the subject of the last lesson? It was on the boundaries of the room. And what did the boundaries show? The shape of the room. By how many walls is it bounded? By four walls. The teacher calls a child to point out which line represents the northern, which the southern, which the eastern, and which the western boundary. Now we will draw the boundaries of the playground. This may be done in the same way as those of the schoolroom.

Lesson 4.

The Relative Distances of the Various Parts of the Schoolroom and its Furniture.

The plan of the schoolroom is presented, and the children asked what it represents. The form of the schoolroom. What determines its form? The boundaries of it. By how many lines are these boundaries represented? By four lines. What more do you learn from this representation of the schoolroom? We find out where its different parts are situated. How would you describe the situation of any one part of it? I would say, It is to the north, the south, the east, or the west. Now that you have learned how the parts of the room and the things it contains are situated with respect to *the cardinal points* of the compass, tell me the two things you have learned from this representation of the schoolroom? We have learned the shape of the room as marked by its boundaries, and the situation of the things it contains with respect to the points of the compass. Repeat this together.

You may call this representation of the schoolroom a *plan* or *map* of it. And now we will talk about the distances things are from each other; as to which are near each other, and which are far from each other. Point out to me two things which are near each other. And now two things which are far from each other. What object is near the table? What halfway between the table and the cabinet? Where is the middle of the room? Which parts of the room are farthest from the middle of it? One of you go and stand halfway between the middle of the room and the end. By how much are the ends of the room further from the middle of it than the sides are? See, I will measure the distance of each of these by my feet. In this manner the teacher must endeavor to make the children determine the relative distances from each other of the several parts of the room and its contents, and also their relative positions.

Lesson 5.

The Relative Distance from each other of the Parts of the Schoolroom and its Furniture as Marked on a Map.

What was the subject of your last lesson? The distance from each other of the things in the room. We will now mark their several positions upon our map. Which is the northern boundary of the room? Where on the map is this recess to be drawn? What things are placed along the northern wall? Now show me which line represents the northern boundary of the room, and tell me where to put marks so as to show the place of each of the things which stand near that wall of the room. Having marked the relative position of the windows, doors, and school furniture, and thus produced a map of the room, the children will begin to understand its use, and what it is intended to represent. What have we been doing in this lesson? Representing the situation of the things in the room. Did you not learn in a former lesson how things are represented on a map? What did you learn in that lesson? We learned how to determine whether they were north, or south, or east, or west. And what have you now learned? We have learned to notice the distance one thing is from another. You learned in the former lesson how things are situated with respect to the cardinal points of the compass, and now you have learned to observe their situation as it respects each other.

Lesson 6.

The Scale to which a Map is Drawn.

A map of the schoolroom on a large scale is shown to the children, and then another, drawn to a scale much smaller. What difference do you observe in these two maps? Yes; one of them is much smaller than the other, yet they both represent the same room. Then a map may equally represent a place, whether it be large or small. This idea may be further worked out by drawing a large picture of some familiar object, say of a pair of scissors, and also a small picture of the same. What are both these? They are the representations of a pair of scissors. Does each of these represent the same pair of scissors equally well? The teacher draws another picture in which the bows are disproportionately large. Does this picture also properly represent the scissors? Why not? The bows are not in proportion to the other parts. The children repeat: "We may have a large or small picture of a thing, but the several parts must be in proportion to each other." So we may have a large or small map, but each part must have its true proportion, and we will now draw such a map of the schoolroom. What does this map of the schoolroom represent? Its boundaries. Now we will measure the length of the schoolroom by a foot measure. One of the children should measure it, and another see that this is correctly done. How many feet of length, then, are represented on this map? Let us measure how many inches the map is in length. How many inches of length on the map will represent the number of feet of length in the schoolroom? How many feet will half the length of the room be? By how many inches will they be represented on the map? Now we will draw a line across the middle of the room, and also across the middle of the map. How many feet will there be in a quarter of the length of the room? We will draw lines at the quarters. This may go on until a complete scale of the map is made; and the exact position of each object may be determined, and a mark made on the map for each, the number of feet being represented by a corresponding number of inches. The children may be asked a variety of questions as to the distances of the different parts of the room and the objects it contains, and where the points or figures representing them are to be placed on the map.

THIRD STEP.

Lesson 1.

Measurement by Miles.

When we drew the plan or map of the schoolroom, what size did we find it? What was the length of the map or plan in inches? How much, then, of the room, did each inch of the map represent? But when we come in from a walk or ride, do we talk of how many *feet* or *inches* we have walked? No; such distance is too great to be reckoned by inches or feet, so we estimate it by the mile. Can any of you tell me the name of a place which is a mile or half a mile from this place? How many miles can you walk in an hour? It is very important that the children should first form a definite idea of a mile. If they know any two places a mile distant from each other, they can compare other distances with this, thus following the plan taken from "Geography for Young Children:"

"If practicable, a mile, or an aliquot part of it, as a quarter or a half, should be actually measured by the pupil, which he may do with ease by means of a string ten yards long, 44 of which are a quarter of a mile, and 176 are a mile. Boys are found to take great pleasure in such measurements. As mistakes are apt to arise with large numbers, one of the pupils who is measuring, and who goes first, should be provided with eleven bits of stick and four pebbles. This first boy lays down one stick for each space of ten yards, measured by the string, which the second boy picks up. When the eleven sticks have been picked up by the second boy, they must be given back for one pebble; and when the second boy has got all the pebbles, the measurement of the quarter of a mile is completed. This may be repeated until a mile has been measured. They may afterward try how long they take in walking a quarter of a mile or a mile, and then from this calculate how long it would take them to walk greater distances.

"Either boys or girls may also easily measure a mile with tolerable correctness, by pacing it. They should learn to take two paces to the yard, when 880 such paces are a quarter of a mile, and 3,520 a mile. Those who step two feet more conveniently, make 2,640 paces to the mile."

LESSON 2.

A Map of the Neighborhood, with a Scale of Miles.

When the children have been well exercised in determining the distances of places in their own neighborhood by the standard measure of a mile and its aliquot parts, they should learn how an idea of such distance is given by a scale. Having first determined how many miles she will represent by an inch, let the teacher draw the principal road of the locality, and, knowing the distances of different houses or other points of interest, mark them down according to her scale of distance, and thus work out before her class a map of the immediate locality. The children may be exercised on this for two or three lessons, as the calculations such a subject involves, and the fact of its drawing out the knowledge they have acquired by their own observation, will be sure to interest them, and prepare them to understand the construction of maps embracing an area of many miles.

In larger towns and cities an outline map of the locality should be presented to the class, containing the streets, the streams, bridges, canal or railroad, the depot, the principal places of business, all public buildings and prominent points of interest. Preparatory to this, however, the children should draw a map of the block or ward in which their school is situated, locating the homes of the children. If practicable, then take them to some high hill or eminence overlooking the town, and either make a rough map of it on the spot, or, with an outline map before them, point out on the map the objects seen in the landscape. This map should be drawn to a scale, so that the children can calculate by measurement the distance of one point from another. Question them as to their relative position. How long it would take them to go from one locality to another, knowing the distance. Describe various localities by the streets, and direction from other points; the uses of the race, the canal, the railroad, the light-house, the harbor; the object of the mill, the machine shop, the factory, the various things manufactured in them; the uses of the public buildings, the parks, &c. In short, make them quite familiar with everything connected with their own locality.

The following lessons are designed to introduce the study of Physical Geography, by careful observation of the natural features of the immediate neighborhood, or, in the absence of any local exemplification, by the exhibition of models or pictures, or by the construction of examples of the ordinary irregularities of the earth's surface, in a box of moist sand. The usual verbal geographical definitions should be taught the children when they have acquired a clear perception of the objects they describe. The following valuable suggestions on this subject are quoted from Mr. Moseley's report:

"Violence is done to the intelligence of a child, hitherto limited to the narrow range of objects of which it is itself the centre, and bound up with associations so purely local, when, by a rude attempt, its mind is made to expatiate over half the globe, and pass to the conception of a region, placed, perhaps, under a wholly different relation of external circumstances. These things are not to be approached by any such abrupt or compendious process, or otherwise than by the steps of a slow and gradual progression. Not, for instance, by teaching the child geographical definitions,*

---

* Taking into account, not only the entire ignorance of everything connected with geography which the elementary teacher must suppose in the outset of her task, but the poverty of the vocabulary of the children as to all forms of speech which are not strictly colloquial, I cannot but think *that* a strange idea of the world which a child would derive from a definition such as the following, which forms the first paragraph of many books on geography: "Geography is a description of the earth. The figure of the earth is that of a sphere or globe, slightly flattened at the top and bottom, like an orange. A straight line passing through its centre from the north to the south is called its *axis*, and the points in which this line meets the surface of the earth are called respectively its *north* and *south poles*. The earth turns round upon this *axis* once in the course of twenty-four

or by accustoming it to recognize by their names places pointed out to it on the map.

"To understand the distinction, we have only to consider how many things go to our own conception of a distant region. The map serves, indeed, to define the idea we have of it, to give it vividness and completeness, but it does not originate it.

"We already know what a country is, which the poor child does not. When a *country* is pointed out by name to him upon the map, and he has learned to tell how, in respect to the four cardinal points, it is bounded by other countries, and what are the names of its rivers, and mountains, and chief towns, his memory may have been largely taxed, and yet his principal idea of the country may, nevertheless, remain, in a great degree, identified with an irregular figure upon a piece of paper. A vast chasm is interposed in the child's mind between the objects with which he is himself familiar, and those of which, in such instruction, he is required to conceive the existence—a chasm which his imagination is not strong enough to bear him over.

."In truth, he has never accustomed himself to observe with any precision or accuracy that part of the world which is close around him. The whole scene has painted itself daily before him, but has left no well-defined traces in his memory. His perceptions are too vague and too incoherent to be separated from the material things on which they have been formed, or to be presented to the imagination, and made the subject of comparison, of analogy, of accumulation, and of invention.

"The first step in his education is to teach him to *observe*. Under the direction of a skilful instructor, many qualities of the things around him, which had before altogether escaped his notice, will, by more careful observation, be added to his knowledge, and all his former impressions will acquire an unaccustomed distinctness and precision. This accomplished, and the child knowing at

hours, from which revolution follow the appearances of *day* and *night*." Notwithstanding that the acquaintance of the children who have learned geography with the words of this or some similar definition, is almost universal, I never yet was fortunate enough to meet with one who knew what the earth's *axis* really is, or the earth's *poles*.

length adequately, for the purpose in hand, the characteristic features of that portion of the earth's surface which is within his own country, its varieties of elevation and aspect, its hills, valleys, and streams, his attention may be directed to the divisions into towns; also into fields, and the fences which bound them. The boundaries of these, with which his memory is familiar, being represented on the blackboard by chalk lines, will convey to him his first idea of a map and its uses; that idea will, moreover, be precise and truthful. The next step might make him acquainted with the general features of the watershed of the district; and then the teacher would bring under his view the useful productions which it is made to yield by labor, whether pastoral, or agricultural, or mineral, associated as these are with the characteristic features of its surface-level, its climate, drainage, aspect, and soil. Then the pursuits of its inhabitants, whether agricultural, or manufacturing, or commercial, in alliance with these, and dependent upon them. Next, the domain of natural history may be made to yield much for his instruction, in respect to the infinite variety of animal and vegetable forms which are assembled within the reach of his immediate observation; the birds which frequent that region, the domestic and wild animals, some of the tribes of insects, the commoner plants which grow around him, and the different kinds of trees. It is not proposed to burden the child's mind, in respect to any of these matters, with scientific distinctions or a hard nomenclature; all that is sought is a knowledge of them in their *ordinary relations;* such a knowledge as the child acquires in respect to those other things with which he is most familiar."

Plan.—First, to call attention to the immediate locality, the schoolroom, playground, street, &c., gradually extending the sphere of observation by embracing the physical features of adjacent places, noticing each point of variety, either in inequality of the surface of the ground, or in the form of any natural collections of water which may be accessible. This close observation of home and its neighborhood will give distinctness and vividness to the perceptions of the children, and enable them easily to conceive the analogous natural features of other countries as similar in kind, though on a larger scale. The children should learn to describe the different appearances of land and water, and their variety in form and general character. They should also be made acquainted with the various means of travelling, as on railroads, turnpike roads, canals, rivers, and seas. Much attention should be paid to accuracy of language in describing the different appearances of land and water. The terms used should be thoroughly explained, and repeated, till they become impressed upon the memory. Too much importance cannot be attached to this idea of thoroughness in all these exercises.*

Lesson 1.

The Earth on which we Live.

The teacher may first lead the children to see that the surface of the earth on which we live may be divided into land and water, the one solid and immovable, the other liquid and flowing.

They may then be led to consider the adaptations of land and water to our necessities, convenience, and habits of life.

They will readily discover that we need the solid earth that we may walk upon it, and build our dwellings on it, and also for the production of food for men and animals.

Water is necessary to the life of man, and also to that of animals and vegetables. It supplies us with drink, and affords an easy mode of conveyance.

The lesson may be summed up. God has covered our earth with land and water, both of which are necessary to us; thus proving to us His goodness, and His care for our happiness and well-being.

Lesson 2.

The Division of Land into Mountains and Plains.

The teacher refers to the last lesson, proposing to find out something more respecting the land. Ask the children whether,

---

* The teacher may derive considerable assistance in these exercises from a little work called "First Ideas of Geography," published by J. W. Parker, Strand, London.

when they walk across the schoolroom or the playground, they can do so easily, and if they have ever, in other places, found it more difficult to walk than it is there? Then ask if they have ever seen horses drawing a cart with ease along a road, and then coming to a place where they could with difficulty drag it? thus leading them to the recollection of some rising ground or hill.

What kind of land is that upon which it is easy to move along? That which is flat and level. And what kind of land is that on which it is more difficult to move? What difference may we then say there is in the land? Some ground is quite flat and even, and some rises up.* Sometimes a large extent of land is flat. We call such land a *plain*. If I talk to you about a plain, what will you understand the word to mean? Repeat together: "A large piece of land, that is quite flat and even, is called a *plain*." And what name do you give to those places at which the land rises up? We call them *hills*. Can you tell me the names of any hills you may have seen? When do you call the land a hill? But sometimes the land rises a great deal higher than the hills you have seen, so high that the top of it is in the clouds; it is then called a mountain. In what are hills and mountains alike? They both are rising ground. In what do they differ? Mountains rise higher than hills. Repeat together: "A mountain is land that rises a great deal higher than a hill."

Lesson 3.

Mountains.

The teacher calls upon the children to say how the earth is divided, and what differences they have already noticed in the form of the land. They may then be allowed to see a model or picture of some country, and to determine which elevations represent the hills, and which the mountains.

The teacher should then call upon them to find out the parts into which a mountain may be divided.

What part of a mountain do we first come to as we walk

* Here reference may be made to some adjacent hill or rising ground.

toward it? The bottom of it. This is called the *base*. Look at this model of a mountain, and run your finger round the base. Repeat together: "The lowest part of a mountain is called the *base.*" When you go up a hill, where do you begin to ascend? At the base. You may call that part of the base at which you begin to ascend, the *foot* of the hill. What part of anything do we call its foot? The lowest part. Now point to the foot of the mountain or hill on this model. Where do you begin to go up the hill? At the foot.

Now point out to me some other part of a mountain. The top. This is called the *summit*. What part of a mountain would you call its summit? The highest part. Now tell me some other part that you observe. Those between the summit and the base. These are called the *sides* of the mountain. When you look downward from the summit of a mountain, what appearance have the sides? They seem to slope downward. And when you look at them from the base, what appearance have they? They seem to slope upward.* The children should then repeat together the names of the several parts of a mountain, and describe each of them.

The teacher may now propose that the children should help to describe a walk up a mountain, supplying whatever they may omit to notice. We came first to the—*foot*—of the *mountain;* we then began—*to go up the side*—with some—*difficulty;* at last we arrived at the—*summit,*—where the wind blew fresh, and we could see the country on every side to a great distance. When we had rested, we—*came down the side*—of the mountain, which we did much more—*easily*—and—*quickly*—than we went up, and at last came again to the—*base.*

Lesson 4.

A Chain of Mountains—Valleys.

What do we call elevated portions of land? *Hills* and *mountains.* A mountain seldom stands alone. Look at this chart.

* These questions may seem tedious and unnecessary, but it is by such teaching that children are led to realize that which is brought before them.

What do you notice as to the mountains? Many of them are joined together. Try to find out a word to express the idea of a set of mountains of which one joins another, and that another, and so on. What do you call a number of rings of metal, when thus joined together? A *chain*. What, then, do you think would be a proper name for a set of mountains which are joined together in a somewhat similar manner? A *chain* of mountains.

Now look at this representation of a chain of mountains, and tell me anything you notice.

The children will observe that smaller mountains run from the sides of the principal chain, and that deep hollows are left between the several elevations.

You know what the land is called when it is flat or even for a considerable distance? A *plain*. And you know what it is called when it rises up, but not very high? A *hill*. And what is it called when it rises higher than a hill? A *mountain*. I think there are some parts of the picture you have just examined which you can neither call a mountain, hill, or plain. The land that lies between the mountains. What can you say of it? It is deep and hollow. These deeps are called *valleys*. Now repeat together: "The hollow land that lies between hills or mountains is called a *valley*." If I were to tell you that I was going into a valley, what would you know there must be on each side of it? Hills or mountains. Sometimes such mountains are very near each other. Of what form will the valley be in such a case? It will be narrow. And what if the mountains be far apart? It will then be a broad valley.

Lesson 5.

Mountains, Plains, and Valleys—(*Continued.*)

You now can tell me three different forms of the land on the earth's surface. It may be a plain, a mountain, or a valley. In which of these do you think it would be most pleasant to live? Supposing the wind were high, and it were piercingly cold, what would be the feelings of people living on a flat open plain? They would be very cold. Why? Because there would be nothing to shelter them from the cold blowing wind or driving storm. A large open plain is a very cold place in winter, but what will it be in summer? What are you glad to find when the sun shines very powerfully? Yes; something to shelter and shade you. But would you expect to find this in the open plain? There is no rising ground in such places, nor will you find trees, for they do not grow well in such exposed places.

Repeat together: "A plain is cold in winter, and hot in summer, because it is open to the cold winds and hot sun. It has no mountains or trees to afford shelter."

In what other place might you live? In a valley. Of what kind of valleys have we spoken? Of narrow valleys and broad valleys. When is a valley narrow? When the hills or mountains between which it lies are near each other. When a valley is very narrow, and its direction north and south, what sunlight will it have? The sun can shine fully upon it only when it is in the south. Where is the sun in the morning? In the east. By what will it be prevented from shining upon such a valley in the morning? By the mountains on the eastern side of it. And what will prevent the setting sun from being seen? The mountains on the western side. When, then, will the inhabitants have any sun? Only for a short time in the middle of each day. When do you think it is very cold in such a valley? When the wind blows from the cold north. Yes; the wind blows down such valleys in strong gusts, and the air does not circulate freely; and on these accounts such narrow valleys are not healthful. In what does a broad valley differ from these? The mountains bounding it are widely separated. What of the air in such valleys? It can freely circulate. What advantages have such valleys over the wide open plain? The mountains afford a shelter. Yes; in such plains you find the air pleasantly blowing, the sun cheerfully shining, and still you may find shelter and shade. Now tell me where you would like to live, and for what reasons?*

---

* These lessons are not intended to complete the subjects treated of, but only to suggest the mode in which they should be handled. A residence on a mountain might be considered.

Lesson 6.

Benefits Derived from Mountains.

We have still much to learn about mountains, for, like everything that God has made, they exist for great purposes. I will try and help you to find out some of these. When you are at the summit of a mountain, what appearance have its sides? ˙They slope downward. When the several summits of a chain of mountains are joined together, they form a ridge. Do you know any part of a house which is like the ridge of a chain of mountains? The roof. And why are roofs made to slope on each side? That the rain may flow off from them. Into what is it received? Into gutters. Something very like this happens upon mountains and hills. What do you suppose becomes of the rain which falls upon them? It runs down the sides. There is always a great deal of rain in mountainous countries, for the mountains attract the clouds, and these often hang so heavily about them, that they hide their summits from our view. As the water runs down, it wears away the softer parts of the earth, and forms grooves or channels. Look for these on the chart, and tell me what you observe in them. Several of them seem to unite. And what will they then form? At first small streams, and then rivers. And what will occur when these come to a hollow? The streams will fill it with water. Yes; this constantly happens on mountains; these little streams form little stores of water to supply our springs and rivers.

But it is not the rain that flows down the mountains which alone affords us water; the tops of very high mountains are covered with snow. Do you know the manner in which this does its part in supplying our springs and rivers? What happens to snow in summer? It dissolves, and becomes water. And what then takes place on the mountains? The water from the dissolving snow flows down their sides. Yes; and in the countries where there are snowy mountains there are always rivers. It is a beautiful sight to see the little streams rushing down the hills and feeding the rivers that run along the valleys, and to think they are all performing their appointed work. What is one great use of mountains? To supply our springs and rivers with water. Yes; we may call them river-feeders.

Lesson 7.

Further Benefits Derived from Mountains.

The teacher recalls the ideas of last lesson by asking the children what benefits we derive from mountains.

We derive many other benefits from mountains besides those we have noticed. They contain many treasures. Do you know of what hills and mountains are formed? You know what this is. It is a piece of chalk, and it is part of a hill.* We do not find chalk in high mountains, but in hills. What happens to chalk when it is rubbed? It crumbles. And what do you think happens to chalk hills when the water rushes down their sides? Some of the chalk is carried down by the water. If water is constantly acting upon a substance not very hard, what form does it give the substance? A smooth form. For this reason chalk hills are never of sharp and pointed outline, but are rounded and gradually sloping. Here is a piece of a mountain. What is this? It is a piece of slate. Large portions of some mountains are formed of slate, which is so useful for roofing our houses, and many other purposes. Here is another substance, of which many mountains are composed; it is called limestone, and is most useful in building.

The children should not at present be detained on the geological structure of mountains longer than they may gain an idea of their formation, and of the benefit we may derive from them.

The children may repeat together: "Mountains are useful to us as being river-feeders, and as containing abundant mineral treasures."

Lesson 8.

Lakes.

Into what did we say the surface of the earth is divided? Into land and water. Have you anywhere seen a quantity of

---

* Whilst these lessons are being given, the children's object lessons should be on mineral substances.

water? You have seen a pond; tell me what it is. It is a piece of water. What must there be in the land to hold the water? A hollow. There must be a hollow place in the land to contain the water; and what will there be round the edge of the water? The ground, or land. What differences have you noticed in ponds? They differ in size. But in what are they alike? They all consist of a hollow in the ground, which is full of water. The water is bordered by the land. Yes; you can walk round a pond. Sometimes such pieces of water are very large—so large that you cannot see how far they reach; and it would require many hours for you to go from one end to the other. These large ponds are called *lakes*. In what are lakes like ponds? They consist of water in deep hollows, with the land round them.

Repeat together: "A large piece of water surrounded by land is called a *lake*."

Lesson 9.

Rivers.

What is a lake? In what is it like a pond? Have you ever seen any water that is not surrounded by land, and round which you could not walk? The children will in all probability have seen a stream or a river; if not, the picture must be used to give them an idea of it. They should endeavor to find out the difference between a lake and a river. Tell me all you observe in a river. A river is long. What do you observe of the land at the bottom of the river? It is hollow. Is it like the hollow place that holds the water of the lake? In what does it differ? It is narrow, like a groove. It is called the *channel*, or the *bed* of the river. Find some other parts of a river. The sides. Of what are the sides of a river formed? Of the earth or land. These are called the *banks* of the river. The banks of rivers are often very green, producing beautiful flowers; do you know what occasions this? The water of the river gently moistens the soil, and makes it fertile.

Look at this picture, and tell me where the rivers begin? They begin near mountains. What did we call mountains? River-feeders. Now tell me where the rivers end? Some end

13

in lakes, and others in the sea. The spot at which they begin is called the *source*, and that at which they empty themselves into some large collection of water, as a lake or sea, is called the *mouth*. What more can you say of the water of the river; is it *still* water? No; it is flowing water. The little streams rush down the mountains, and open into the rivers; what must they do to the rivers? They supply them with water. Through what kind of land does the river flow? Often through valleys and low grounds, receiving supplies from all the little streams as it flows along. And what good does a river do in its course? It waters the country through which it passes, and supplies animals and vegetables with that which they need for the support of life. And what more? It supplies the inhabitants of the country with water. Is it of any other use? Have you ever seen anything borne on the water? Boats and barges. Why were they floating on the water? They were going on the water from one place to another. Yes; and there were people living on those vessels, and travelling easily with their goods from place to place.

Now tell me the parts of a river. The bed or channel, the banks, the source, and the mouth. Now tell me the uses of rivers. To sustain the life of animals and vegetables, to supply us with water for many useful purposes, to float us along from one place to another.

Lesson 10.

The Sea.

Where is water found? In ponds, lakes, and rivers. Yes; but there are places where you will find much more water than in these. Do you remember into what we said that the earth's surface is divided? Into land and water. There is more water than land. Do you know what that very large body of water is called, upon which so many ships sail? The *sea*. Can any of you tell me anything about the sea? Do you know the taste of sea water? It is salt. What can you say of the surface of the sea? It is often rough. What makes it rough? The waves. What are these? They are the water of the sea disturbed by the wind.

In giving lessons upon the sea, much depends upon the locality in which the children reside. If there is an opportunity of looking at the sea, some very useful lessons may be given, calling observation into activity; but if the children have not seen the ocean, it may be well to leave the subject, till, at a later period, they take up a fuller course of physical geography, when their conceptive faculties can be more fully brought to bear on the subject. At this early stage, it will be enough that they understand that a large portion of our globe is covered with salt water, ever heaving and flowing, and that in size and depth the sea is greater than anything they can imagine; that the ocean, as well as every other work of God, is formed for some wise purpose; that it also has an office to fulfil, in which it obeys the laws of infinite wisdom, goodness, and power.

The children may now take an outline map of the county, which may be treated in the same general way as the city map. In the next step or grade they may take the outline map of the State, and then of the United States, before going to the map of the world.

THE HUMAN BODY.

INTRODUCTORY REMARKS.

LESSONS on the human body are a good introduction to the study of the natural history of the animal creation. They form a commencement quite in accordance with the Pestalozzian principle of starting from the *known*. Children should be somewhat familiar with their own frame; they ought to have correct ideas on that which so nearly concerns themselves. The subject is also ever present, requiring nothing for its illustration other than that which is common to all. Such lessons will furnish opportunity for correcting any vague and imperfect notion the children may have acquired, for supplying them with a vocabulary of expressive terms, and for giving them such an acquaintance with their own organization, as may make it a standard for comparison with that of other animals, thus preparing them to understand many wonderful details in the modification and adaptation of the organs of animals to their peculiar habits, propensities, and localities.

The following exercises are designed as First Step lessons:

First Object.—To lead the children to a consideration of their own organs, and to teach them a proper nomenclature.

Plan.—The children to touch any part of their body, when the teacher gives the name; as, *the eye, ear, shoulder, leg, foot; the right hand, the left hand; the arm, hand, fist,* &c.

The teacher next to touch these different parts, the children giving the names; as, You are touching your head, your eyes, your chin, cheeks, legs, &c.; being required to express the idea in a short sentence, instead of merely naming the part.

Sketch of a Lesson on the Parts of the Principal Parts of the Body.

The teacher to touch one of the arms of a child, asking the other children to say what part of the person she is touching; and then lead them to notice that the arm also has parts. Another child to point to some part of the arm—the shoulder, for instance—the others being asked its name. If they do not know, they are to be told it is the shoulder; and so on with the other parts.

The teacher next to desire the children to point to any part of the body she may name, as the shoulder, the elbow, the upper arm, forearm, wrist, or hand. If any mistake is made, the others to correct it.

The children next to name the parts to which the teacher points; as, the elbow, shoulder, arm, forearm, wrist, and hand. Require them to give the name of each part.

The teacher next to question the children on the different parts, as to their number. How many joints have the arms? also the number of fingers on one hand, and the number of joints in each finger? If they make a mistake in the number, they should correct themselves by examining their own arms and hands.

The teacher to question the children on the use of each part of the arm, commencing with the shoulder joint. To call upon them to say what they could not do if they had not that joint; asking them to try and lift their hand to their head without bending that joint, &c. In the same way, to ask them to tell the use of each of the other parts of the arm, and lead them to discover the action and utility of the joints of the arm and fingers.

Second Object.—To make the children well acquainted with the principal parts of the body, and to lead them to compare them with the different forms of the corresponding organs in other animals.

Plan.—Shown in the following hints for lessons:
1. What is the upper part of the body called?* The *head.*

* In order that these lessons may be brought within a moderate compass, the answers are not given where they are quite obvious. Teachers should remember that those which are put down are not to be told to the children, but rather to be drawn from them.

What is the largest part of it called? The *trunk*. What have you besides a head and a trunk? Arms and legs. What are these called? *Limbs*. Now tell me the three principal parts of your body. The head, the trunk, and the limbs.

2. *The Limbs*.

How many limbs have you? What are the upper limbs called? What are the lower limbs called? How many legs have we? How many legs has the dog, the cat, the horse? Tell me some other animals that have four legs. How many more legs have these animals than we have? What is the consequent difference in their way of standing? In what does the position of our body differ from theirs? How is this suited to our different manner of eating and habits of life? What limbs have we? Two legs and two arms. How many limbs have the animals we have been talking about? What are their limbs? What difference is there then between these animals and ourselves? Yes; they have two legs, where we have two arms. What do you call those legs which they have in the place of our arms? *Fore legs*. What do you call the other pair? *Hind legs*. Tell me some other animals besides man that have only two legs.* What have birds in place of arms? What can birds do with their wings, which they could not do if they had only legs? Where are the legs of birds placed? Where are ours placed? How is the body of birds placed? Compare its position with the position of our body. What animals move without either arms, legs, or wings? How do worms move? What other animals besides worms and serpents have no limbs? Where do fish live? How do they move? What have they where we have limbs? Now you have told me of some animals that have two legs, of some that have four, and of some that have none; can you mention some little animals that differ from any of these? How many legs has a fly or bee? Tell me some other animals that have six legs. A but-

---

* Children might here describe the actions performed by the leg in man, and compare them with the different actions of other animals.

terfly, a wasp, a beetle, a lady-bird, &c. What do you call all these animals? Insects. How many legs have insects? Insects have six legs. How do insects move on the ground? How do they move in the air?

As a summary of this lesson, the children should state how animals differ as to the number of their legs, and as to their movements, giving examples of each variety.

3. *The Joints.*

What can we do with our legs? In how many places can we bend them? Try and find out. In three places. The place where we bend a limb is called a *joint*. What can we do at a joint? Where is the lowest joint of the leg? Move your leg, and find out. At the ankle. That is called the *ankle joint*. How many ankle joints have you? Which is the highest place at which we move the leg? At the hip. That is called the *hip* joint. How many hip joints have we? Where is the middle joint of the leg? How many knee joints have we? Now tell me all the joints of the legs? Two ankle joints, *t*wo knee joints, two hip joints. How many joints have we altogether in the legs? When do we make use of our legs without bending any joint in them? When do we bend the knee joint only? When do we bend both the hip and knee joint? When do we bend all three joints of the leg? Describe our joints when we sit down. When we sit down, we bend the joint at the hip, and that at the knee also.

Summary.—The different joints; what they are; their use; how many in each leg; whether the same in other animals.

4. *The Lower Limbs.*

What do you call that part of the lower limb between the hip and the knee? The *thigh*. And what the part between the knee and ankle? The *leg*. What kind of substance is that which is at the hinder part of the leg? What do you call that fleshy part? The bone in front of the leg is called the *shin bone.* What part is called the *calf* of the leg? That between the knee and ankle, at the back of the leg. Where are the shin bones? In front of the leg. Now tell me where the thigh is. Between the hip and knee. Into how many parts may the lower limb be divided?

5. *The Feet.*

Upon what do we stand? Where are our feet? How are we able to stand upon our feet? They are wide and flat, and so placed on our legs as to rest on the ground. How many feet have we? Think of all the different kinds of feet which animals have. What kind of feet have birds? How do birds move with their feet? What more do birds do with their feet? How have you seen hens use their feet? Yes; scratching up the earth, which they easily do with their long claws. And how do they use their claws when they sleep? The claws of birds are so formed that they cling more tightly when the bird is asleep, so that it does not lose its hold. What differences have you observed in the feet of birds? In what respect do the feet of ducks differ from those of hens? They have a skin stretched between the claws. Yes; this kind of foot is called a *web-foot*. Of what use is a foot of this kind to ducks? Why, then, have hens and ducks such different feet? What kind of feet have cats and dogs? What kind of feet have horses and cows? Tell me some animals having hoofs. What is the difference between the hoof of a cow and that of a horse or an ass? The hoof of the cow is a cloven hoof. Tell me some animals that have cloven hoofs. Upon what do animals which have hoofs feed? What do cows, horses, &c., eat? In what way do they eat? They put their heads down to the grass, and bite it off. Why have they no need of claws to lay hold of their food? What kind of feet have cats? Tell me some other animals having paws. What do lions, tigers, and wolves feed upon? What are cats fond of catching?

Try and find out why God has wisely given claws to those animals that have to catch the prey they feed upon, and hoofs to those which feed on grass? How does God show his care for animals in the different kind of feet which He has given them? You see that God takes care that every animal has that which is necessary for it. If He takes such care of animals, what may we feel sure He will do for us? And as we can speak, what should we do when He gives us so much?

Now tell me a part of the foot. The toe. How many toes have we on one foot? How many on both? What can we do with our toes? What do you call the places where we can bend our toes? What have our toes besides joints? What difference do you observe when you hit or cut your nails, and when you do the same to any part of your flesh? What can you then say of the nails? The nails have no sensation. Why are they placed at the end of our toes? To guard that part which is most sensitive, and most exposed to injury.

Tell me some other part of the foot. The lowest part is called the *sole*. Where is the sole of the foot? There are some other parts of the foot which you have not mentioned. Yes; the part that rises up in front; it is called the *instep*. What causes it to rise up? Where is the instep? The instep is in front of the foot, and rises up between the toes and the ankle bones. What is there at the back of the foot? Where is the heel? Repeat the different parts of the leg and foot.

And now tell me what it is that makes the legs stiff and strong, and able to support us. What covers the bones? What covers the flesh? What makes the flesh look pinkish?

How do we use our feet? What is the difference between running and walking? How do we use our feet when we jump? How when we hop? What do naughty children sometimes do with their feet? What makes them kick? They give way to anger and passion. Whom does this always displease? Why does it displease God? All such misuse of useful members displeases the great God whose eye is ever upon us, and who sees when we are angry or in a passion. Tell me some texts that teach us how we ought to feel and act toward each other.

Summary.—The use, position, and number of the feet in man; the parts described; the differing feet of animals; and what we learn in these things of the wisdom and goodness of the Creator.

6. *The Arms.*

What are the upper limbs called? How many arms have we? Where are our arms placed? At the upper part of the body, on either side of the trunk. In what direction are they placed? What advantage is it that they come forward? How many joints are there in one arm? Try where you can bend your arm. Which is the lowest joint of the arm? It is called the *wrist*. Which is the uppermost joint? The shoulder joint. Which is the middle joint? The elbow. That part between the shoulder and elbow is called the *arm;* the part between the elbow and wrist is called the *fore arm*. Point to the fore arm; to the arm. Tell me where the fore arm is; where the arm is. What is below the wrist?

7. *The Hands.*

Tell me the different parts of the hand. The inside of the hand is called the *palm* of the hand. Show me the palm of the hand. What do you call those bones on the back of the hand which project? The *knuckle bones*. What use do we make of the knuckles? What, then, are the knuckles? How many fingers have we? Tell me the different parts of a finger. How many joints are there on each finger? How many on all the fingers of one hand? What is the use of the nails? Where are they placed? Why are they so placed? What kind of substance is the nail? Horny. Find out some uses in its being horny. It guards the tender part of the fingers, making them most useful in various delicate operations. What other part of the body is without feeling? What are those parts of animals which have no feeling? What are the names of the several fingers? *The thumb, fore finger, middle finger, ring finger, little finger.* What do you call this hand (*holding up the right hand*)? What this? Now tell me, as I hold up a finger, what particular finger it is, and of which hand. Middle finger of left hand; fore finger of right hand, &c. What is the shape of the fingers? How do the fingers differ? What can we do with our hands? In what manner do we pick up anything? How do we hold a needle? Why cannot we use our toes in the same manner as our fingers? Because the toes are all placed in a row; but the thumb can be brought opposite to the fingers, and thus the hand is fitted to lay hold of things.* How can women fully employ their hands? How can men use their hands in earning their daily bread? What animals have hands? Monkeys. How many hands have monkeys? Where do monkeys live? In trees. What is the use of their hands? To lay hold of the branches. How, then, are they well fitted to live in trees? They have four hands to lay hold of the branches of the trees. Can the monkey point at anything with the first finger, as you can? No; man only can do this; he has on this account been called "the pointing animal."

Summary.—To repeat all the different parts of the arm and hand; and the adaptation of hand and foot to their respective offices.

8. *The Head.*

You have now told me about the arms and legs. By what other name may we call our arms and legs? To what are the limbs joined? Where is each placed? The arms at the upper part of the trunk move forward ready to lay hold of things; the legs at the lower part, and in a line with the body, to keep it erect. What is at the top of the trunk? What do you feel when you touch your head? The bone of the head is called the *skull.* Within the skull is the brain—a very tender organ; how is it guarded? What is the front of the head called? Tell me the different parts of the face; begin at the top. The forehead. What are on the sides of the forehead? The temples. Where is the forehead? At the top of the face, above the eyes; between the temples. What is next to the forehead?

9. *The Eyes, and Sense of Sight.*

How many eyes have we? What do you call this eye? The

---

* It should be made obvious to the children, that as the foot is well formed to support the body, so is the hand for an organ of prehension, that they may be led to see how beautifully the Creator has adapted everything to its appointed work.

right eye. And this? The *left* eye. Look at the eye of the child next to you, and tell me the different parts of it. Look at the middle of the eye. The dark spot is called the *pupil*. Look and see if it is the same in every eye. What is it called? What do you observe round it? That colored ring round the pupil is called the *iris*. Look and see if the iris is the same in every eye. In some it is blue, in some brown, &c. In what are the pupil and iris placed? That part of the eye which is round like a ball is called the *eyeball*. How many eyeballs have we? What have we in the eyeball? In what part of the eyeball is the pupil of the eye? In the front of it. Tell me exactly where the pupil of the eye is? The pupil is in the middle of the front of the eyeball, and has the iris around it. Where is the eye placed? In a sort of cup in the skull. This is called the *socket* or *orbit* of the eye. By what is the eye covered? How many eyelids have we to each eye? What do you call the eyelid nearest the forehead? What the other? What eyelid am I touching?* The upper eyelid of the right eye. What is at the edge of the eyelids? What do you call the hairs at the edge of the eyelids? Are there any other hairs near the eye? What are these called? What is the form of the eyebrows? Where are they placed?

Now try and tell me what you think is the great use of the eye? What do you call those who cannot see? When is it that we who have sight, cannot see? When it is dark. What, then, is necessary to enable us to see? Where does light come from? When do we lose the light of the sun? From what other natural object have we light? When does the moon give us light? What happens when we have neither moon nor sun? We have no natural light, and cannot see, when neither the sun nor moon shines.

Now listen seriously to me, and I will tell you a truth like this about our souls. God must send the light of his Holy Spirit into our souls, or we shall not know what to do to please Him, or how to walk in the way of his commandments. What, then, must we

---

* It is desirable to vary the lessons by a change in the kind of questions. The hints here given may be followed out and extended as far as they may interest the class.

pray for? David, in Psalm xliii. 3, prays that God would lead him by His light.

Now tell me all that we can do with our eyes, besides seeing with them. What happens when we weep? Tears fall. Why do people weep? Sometimes because they are hurt; sometimes because they are sorry; sometimes from passion. Is it ever right to weep? Try and find out the pleasures which we enjoy through our sight. What are the uses of sight?

You see now that for many reasons the eye is very valuable to us; and our kind Heavenly Father has taken great care to guard it from accident, as you will discover, if you attend to me. Where is the eye placed? It is lodged in a hollow socket, surrounded by bone, just as if it were in a box. Now tell me the bones that project around it. What is above it? The forehead. What on the sides? The temples and the nose. What below it? The cheek-bones. These cheek-bones, like walls, guard the eyes from being hurt.* Now tell me exactly how the eye is placed. How does the eye act when anything comes near it? Observe when I put my hand quickly near this child's eye. Yes; the eyelids close before there is time to think that the eye is in danger of being hurt. There is always dust floating in the air; how is it that we are so seldom inconvenienced by it? The fringe of the eyelashes preserves the eye from dust; but if any should fall in, what immediately happens? Yes; the tears at once begin to flow, and carry it out of the eye. The tears also keep the eye constantly moist and clean.† If you wished to have something that would roll about easily, of what shape would you have it? And what shape is the ball of the eye? How, then, is the eye fitted to move easily? It is round in form.

---

* In giving this lesson, the teacher can enter into more details as to the beautiful protection provided for the eye, and draw out other facts *from the children* themselves.

† Should the party consist of very intelligent children, the teacher might lead them to see that the overhanging eyebrow protects the eye like the roof of a cottage; that the iris always dilates, making the pupil smaller, when a sudden or strong light comes near the eye, so that less light enters; and that the superfluous moisture of the eye is carried into the nose, where it moistens the lining membrane, and makes the sense of smell more delicate than it could otherwise be.

Summary.—Repetition of the parts of the eye, and their relative position; the manner in which it is protected from injury; the wisdom and goodness of the Creator; the advantages and pleasures connected with the sense of sight.

10. *The Nose, and Sense of Smell.*

What is there in the middle of your face? What is above the nose? what below it? what on each side of it? How does the nose help in guarding the eyes from injury? Tell me the parts of the nose. The holes are called *nostrils*. How many nostrils have we? How are they divided? By gristle. The end of the nose is called the *tip*; the high part of it, the *bridge*; the outside of the nostrils, the *wings*. To what do the nostrils lead? There is a passage through them to the back of the mouth, through which we breathe; and there is also a passage from the eye to each of them, through which the fluid which cleanses and moistens the eye flows. Of what use is the nose? Do we use the nose in smelling only? How do we feel when we close the nostrils? We cannot breathe freely. Tell me some animals to which the sense of smell is very useful. What animals are guided in their search for others by the sense of smell? Dogs are very remarkable for their good scent. A dog, having lost his master, has been known to follow his steps, street after street, through a crowded city, by his scent. What use does man make of dogs in consequence of their fine scent? Not only dogs, but many other animals are directed in finding their food by this faculty. Some birds have wonderful scent, and can discover putrid flesh at a great distance, even when they are high in the air; such birds are very useful in clearing away that which would make the air very unhealthy. What animal has a *long* nose called a *snout?* How does the pig use its snout? Many animals besides the pig use the snout in grubbing up the earth to get at roots or worms, and some use it for making in the earth the holes in which they live. Can you mention any of these? The hedgehog and mole; both these animals have pointed snouts full of muscles, which make them very strong. What has the pig at the end of its snout? This ring of gristle helps it in grubbing up the earth. What animal has a much longer snout than a pig? What is it called? How can the elephant use its trunk? It can twist it about in every direction. The elephant's trunk is most useful to it. Upon what does the elephant feed? It feeds on vegetables, on the grass and herbs that grow on the ground, and also on boughs of trees. Now look at this picture of an elephant. Do you think it could put its *mouth* down to the ground? or could it raise it so as to bite off branches? No; it could not. You can tell, then, the use of its long flexible trunk. With its trunk it uproots the grass and herbs on the ground, and snaps off the young twigs from the trees above, and then carries them to its mouth. And how does it drink? It draws water into its trunk, and conveys it to its mouth. Tell me what use we make of the nose. Tell me the different uses animals make of it. What do you find, when the nose has to be used for other purposes than smelling? That God fits it for its special use by changing its form.

Summary.—Position of the nose; its parts and uses; the diversity of its form in different animals.

11. *The Mouth, and the Faculty of Speech.*

What is under the nose? What do you call the edges of the mouth? How many lips have you? What do you call the lip nearest the nose? What the other? What is the color of the lips? What can we do with our lips? Say what we do when we smile? How do we use our lips to show that we love a person? How do we use our lips in eating? Tell me the different parts of the mouth. What is there within the lips? What color are the teeth? Of what are they made? What use is there in their being so hard? What are the parts of a tooth? The naked part of a tooth is called the *crown;* the part fixed in the jaw is called the *fang* or *root.* What differences do you observe in the teeth? How many kinds of teeth have we? Those nearest the lips are called the *front* or *cutting* teeth. What sort of an edge have they? A sharp edge like that of a knife or scissors. What use is there in their having such an edge? How many cutting teeth have we? What sort of teeth come next to the cutting teeth? Pointed teeth. These are called the *eyeteeth*. How many have we? And what other teeth have we? Those at the back of the jaw are called *double* teeth, or *grinders*, because we grind our food between them. In what are our teeth set? How many jaws have we? What are the two jaws called? Which jaw do we move when we eat? How do we move it? What covers the jaws? The two cheeks. What animals have large teeth projecting out of their mouths? Which of the teeth are very large in some animals? They are called *tusks;* such animals generally use them either in defending themselves, or in destroying their prey. What sort of teeth have dogs or cats?* Lions, tigers, and wolves have the same kind of sharp-pointed teeth. Now call to mind what we said about the *feet* of these animals. They are fitted to catch their prey. What, then, is the use of their having sharp-pointed teeth? To tear the flesh of their prey. What kind of feet have cows, horses, &c.? What do these animals feed upon? Did you ever see a cow lying down and chewing? How did it move its lower jaw? From side to side. What kind of teeth has it? And by thus moving its jaw from side to side it bruises its vegetable food between its great flat grinders, till it becomes a soft pulp. What part of an animal should we examine in order to find out what kind of food it eats? God, who gives to every animal the desire for the particular food that is suitable for it, gives it also the means of procuring that food, and proper teeth wherewith to masticate or chew it. When have we no teeth? What food has God provided for infants? Why, then, do infants not need teeth? What is there in the middle of the mouth, within the teeth? —In what do we use the tongue? In talking and eating. We not only use the tongue in talking; but when we eat, we use it in bringing the food between the teeth, and in helping us to swallow. What use do some animals make of their tongue? † What do you call that which the dog does

* If the children cannot answer such questions from their own knowledge, they should not be told; but a cat or dog should be brought in for the next lesson, or they should be directed to observe the animal at home.

† Some animals use their tongues as an organ of prehension. The cow gathers the grass into its mouth with its tongue, and the cameleopard twists the tongue round the boughs of trees.

when he drinks? What other animals use their tongues in lapping? What kind of tongue has the cat? What can we do with the mouth? For what purposes do we open the mouth? To eat, drink, speak, laugh, gape, scream, sing, whistle, &c. What parts of the mouth do we use in speaking? Utter some words, and observe. We open and shut the mouth. And how do we use the tongue and lips? Observe what we do in sounding each of the five vowels, and tell me. Observe what we do in sounding the different consonants, and tell me.* Can we utter a sound by merely opening the mouth, and putting it in different positions? Try and find out what more we need to do. To whom has God given the power of speaking? Tell me the best mode of using this power. When do we make a bad use of this gift of God? What do we call those who cannot speak? Tell me the different sounds that animals make with their mouths. What sound do we make when we are happy? What when we are in pain? What sound is a sign of mirth?

Summary.—Repeating the names of all the parts of the mouth, and their position; the diversity in the teeth of animals, as well as in their food, to suit their habits; how we use our mouths in speaking, eating, &c.

12. *The Chin, and Cheeks.*

Where is the chin? What is the shape of the chin? Tell me where the cheeks are? What is the general color of the cheeks? When is the color of the cheeks lost? What is the substance of the cheeks?

13. *The Ears, and Sense of Hearing.*

Where are the ears placed? How many ears have we? Tell me the parts of the ear.† The lower part is called the

---

* This may be made a very interesting lesson, and lead the children to the habit of observing the details of the process by which they produce certain sounds, thus cultivating perception of the relation between cause and effect.

† The teacher must here, as in all such lessons, let the children point to the part before its name is told them.

flap; the edge that curls over it is called the *hem.* Whither does the inner canal lead? It is a passage which leads to the drum of the ear, so called because it has a skin or membrane stretched tightly over it, as the parchment is over a drum. What do you observe in the ears of animals? What is their most common shape? Like that of a trumpet. This is the best shape for collecting sound and conducting it to the passage of the ear. Did you ever see a poor hare or rabbit, when the dogs were chasing it? What was then the direction of its ears? They were turned backward. What was it trying to hear? Those animals that are liable to be pursued by others have their ears turning backward, that they may hear whatever may be coming after them. What kind of ear would best suit those animals that have to pursue their prey? And so we find that lions, tigers, cats, &c., have their ears pointing forward, that they may hear anything before them. What does all this teach us of God? Who made all animals? And if God has taken such care for the comfort of animals, how much must He be displeased with those who hurt and tease dumb creatures.* What is the use of the ear? What sounds do we hear easily? what with difficulty? What do you call people who cannot hear? Why is it a misfortune to be deaf? When do we make a good use of the sense of hearing?

Summary.—The parts of the ear, and its position; how fitted for receiving sound; peculiarities in the ears of different animals; the uses of the ear.

14. *The Hair and Head.*

What covers the back and the top of the head? What is there beneath the hair? What under the skin? Have any animals besides man hair on their bodies? Where is the hair of other animals? What is the use of hair to animals? What can man do to supply the place of a covering of hair? Is the hair of all animals alike? What difference, then, do you find in the hair of animals? What do you call the hairy covering of sheep? What

---

* A teacher of infants, while improving every opportunity of conveying moral lessons, should take care to avoid introducing either these, or passages of Scripture, when they do not naturally arise out of the subject.

kind of hair has the pig? what kind the cat? &c. Name the various kinds of these coverings. Hair, wool, bristles, fur. What is the shape of the head? Are the heads of animals of the same shape as ours? What difference do you see? Look at this picture of a dog, a pig, &c. What makes the heads of these animals less round than ours? The nose and mouth stand out more.

15. *The Neck.*

Upon what are our heads placed? What is the form of our neck? The neck is like a pillar to support the head; but what is it in front? It is a passage. There are two passages in the neck. You know very well the use of one of these. But, in addition to the throat, which is the passage for conveying the food to the stomach, there is another called the *windpipe*, through which we breathe, and which conveys air to the lungs.

16. *The Bones.*

Now feel the bones below the throat. That in front is called the *breastbone*. Feel the bones that stretch from the throat to the shoulders. These are called the *collar bones*. Now feel the bones on each side of the body in front. These are called the *ribs*. Where are the ribs? What is the shape of the ribs? They curve, and form a hollow for the lungs by which we breathe, and for the heart, and for the stomach into which the food is received. Feel the bone that goes down the middle of the back. It is called the *spine*, or *backbone*. Where is the backbone? Can we bend the backbone? How is the backbone formed? It is formed of a great number of small bones, most beautifully joined together. If our back were formed of one single bone, and were solid like this stick, could we bend it? Can we now bend the back as we may require? What advantage is there in the backbone being formed of many small bones? What is the use of the backbone? What is the direction of the backbone? In what position is it when we lie down? In what direction is the backbone of most animals?

Tell me now the names of the chief bones of the body as you

have mentioned them. To what part of the body do they belong? What have we besides a trunk? How many limbs have we? What do our bones form altogether? The skeleton, or bony framework which sustains all the rest of our person.

17. *The Blood.*

What is the liquid that flows through the body? What is the color of our blood? What is our condition when the blood no longer flows through our bodies? In what does the blood flow? Listen to me, and I will tell you about the blood, and the journey it makes. It comes from the heart, and travels to all parts of the body, nourishing every part; it then returns to the heart, but on its way it has become weakened by giving off strength to every part of the frame. As it returns to the heart, just before it enters it, it receives the nutriment taken up from the food, which restores much of the vigor it had lost. It is then sent from the right side of the heart into the lungs, where, by breathing, it is further purified, and returning to the left side of the heart, bright and pure, it is again sent on its wonderful course, visiting every part of the body, to give nourishment and strength. As long as we live, it regularly flows on, without our thinking of it or troubling ourselves about it; and when it ceases to flow, we die. The food we take supplies nourishment to the blood. (The children should be questioned upon all this information.) Now, which of you can tell me about the blood, and its journey through the body? Do you know what liquid flows through plants in somewhat the same manner, giving them life and nourishment? It is called the *sap*.

Now you have learned something about your body; tell me who formed it. Yes; and David truly says, in the 139th Psalm, 14th verse, "I will praise Thee, for I am fearfully and wonderfully made." Repeat these words. What does David declare about God? What does he say he himself will do? What does he mean by *praise?* God made us, and not we ourselves, and therefore we ought to praise Him. But He also takes care of us. If He should cease to care for us, what would become of us? Do you wish Him to take care of you? If you wished some one to do anything for you, what should you on your part do? May we ask God for that we want? But how do we know that He will hear us if we pray to Him? Give me some text from the Bible, the Word of God, to show that He has promised to hear us when we pray to Him.

Summary.—The color, action, and office of the blood; the changes it undergoes; its importance; how its waste is supplied; what feelings the consideration of our bodies ought to produce..

SKETCH FOR A LESSON.

On the Difference between the Hand and the Foot.

1. Draw the attention of the children to the difference in the *position* of these two organs; the hand being placed at the upper part of the body at the end of the arm, and in a line with it; the foot at the lower part of the body, at an angle with the leg. Again, the difference as to *form;* the hand thin, the palm capable of being formed into a hollow cup; and termiating in four long, flexible, slender fingers, ranged in a row, with an opposing thumb which can be brought to meet any one of them, so as to pick up or grasp objects. The sense of touch, also, as being so exquisitely delicate in the fingers, enabling women to do the finest needle-work, and men to carry on the most delicate operations. The foot thick and stiff; the instep arched for strength; the sole of the foot broad and flat; the toes short and thick, the whole five being arranged in one plane.

2. The use of the hand, to lay hold of things; that of the foot, to support the body when in an upright position, or when moving or standing.

3. How both these organs are fitted by their position and form for their different offices. The hand, by its thinness and flexibility, being capable of being formed into a hollow; its long, delicate fingers opposed to the thumb, forming a complete organ for grasping and touching; the foot, by its thinness, flatness, and the breadth of the sole, by the muscular power of the instep, and by its position, fitted for its office of supporting the body in an erect posture.

COURSE OF LESSONS ON ANIMALS.

INTRODUCTORY REMARKS.

THE natural history of the animal creation furnishes abundant materials for instruction. First, that of a religious character; for the wisdom and goodness of the Creator are manifestly proclaimed in the wonderful construction and beautiful adaptation of animals to circumstances, evidencing design in a manner which no one can gainsay. Secondly, that of a moral character; for, by awakening interest in animals, kind and humane feelings are promoted, which those who have witnessed the pleasure even very young children take in tormenting creatures over which they have any power will acknowledge to be an object of no small importance. Thirdly, that of an intellectual character; for the faculties of observation, of comparison, and of conception, are brought into exercise, whilst reason takes its part in tracing cause and effect, and drawing inferences and conclusions from facts.

In the First Step, the perceptive faculty is exercised on the general appearance and external parts of animals. The teacher must not seek either to promote precocious development, or to store the memory with information, but simply to direct aright the activity that exists; to form, and not to fill the mind.

In the Second Step, not only the perceptive, but also the conceptive faculty is exercised. The teacher directs attention to the actions of animals and their mode of life, as well as to their forms, parts, &c. Subjects of lessons are no longer limited to native and domestic animals, but include such as are foreign; at least the more prominent of these.

In the Third Step, the reasoning faculty is exercised. The teacher leads her class, already somewhat acquainted with the structure and habits of animals, to see the wonderful adaptation of one to the other. Sometimes this is best shown by comparison of individual animals.

In the Fourth Step, the faculty of generalization is exercised. The work of the last Step, which is consideration of adaptation, is extended to classes of animals. More general comparisons are made.

Moral lessons should constantly be drawn from these subjects, not with cold, dry formalism, but in such a manner as to interest and to improve. In the lower steps, the object of the teacher will be chiefly to excite feelings of humanity and sympathy for the lower animals. In the higher steps, the thoughtful teacher cannot help referring to the wisdom and goodness of the great Creator and Adapter.

All that can be done to help teachers in carrying out this subject, is to furnish them with principles, give a few patterns of model sketches and exercises, and to suggest hints. But if the mind of the teacher be barren and uninventive, the instruction will be dull and wearisome.

FIRST STEP.

I.—General conversation about an animal. Observation of its most prominent parts, as the children advance.

II.—More accurate observation; referring to,

    1. Parts, names, and number and uses of these.
    2. Distinction of parts, as principal and secondary.
    3. Position of parts.
    4. Characteristic parts, or those which especially distinguish the animal.

Any one or two of these points may be taken up in a lesson, as the subject may be best adapted to work them out. But as a general rule, the teacher will commence the Step by working out Point 1, and conclude it by working out Point 2.

312 LESSONS ON ANIMALS.—FIRST STEP.

In preparing students to teach this subject, the teacher of Method may begin by directing their attention to the pattern lesson on the "Hen and Chickens."

Let them examine the sketch, note what ideas are taken up, in what order, and form a corresponding lesson on the "Cat and Kittens."

1. *Hen and Chickens.* (*Conversational Lesson.*)

1. Present a picture. Let the children examine it, and determine what the animals are; what doing; what the hen is to the chickens; the chickens to the hen; what the hen does for the chickens (scratches up food for them all day, watches over them, defends them from any dog or hawk that threatens them). This gives her trouble, and exposes her to danger. Why she does it? She loves her chickens. Children to say what their mothers do for them, and why? Refer to the goodness of God, which inspires mothers with so much affection.

2. Children compare the hen and chickens as to their ways, &c. The hen is active, industrious, intent on supplying the wants of the chickens. The chickens are weak, helpless, and can do nothing for themselves. How they act on the approach of danger. How the hen behaves under the same circumstances. How loving she is; how brave; how unselfish. How we should feel and behave toward the hen.

2. *The Horse.* (*For Parts, their Names, and Number.*)

MATTER.	METHOD.
1. A horse has legs, body, head, eyes, ears, mane, tail, and hoofs.	1. Children name the parts when pointed to, and point to them when named. (S. R.)
2. A horse has a long round body, long thin legs, a handsome flowing tail, flowing mane, and upright pointed ears.	2. Children led to talk about the parts; their number and kind. Teacher gives terms required to express ideas; as, *handsome; flowing*, by comparing the tail and mane of the horse with the tail and mane of the lion. *Pointed*, brought out by comparing the two ends of a cut pencil.

3. The horse has one head, one body, one tail, two eyes, two ears, four legs, and four feet.	Which end most resembles the ears of a horse? *Upright,* by holding the pencil in different directions. 3. Children referred to the parts they have before noticed. Teacher bids them to name some part of which the horse has but one; some part of which it has two; whether they can find any part of which it has exactly three? If not, let them find parts of which it has four.
4. We should never treat the horse unkindly, but always be good and gentle to it.	4. Children say who made the horse. How He would like to have us treat it? To name any ways in which they can show it kindness.

Summary.—Teacher asks each child individually to name a part of the horse. Goes around the class a second time, asking each the number of part he names; *i. e.,* the child who says, "The horse has an eye," should say how many eyes. Third time each child is required to describe any part named by the teacher.

Students in training to construct a sketch on "The Mouse," as "The Horse."

3. *The Sparrow.* (*Parts.*)

I.—Principal and secondary parts. II.—Position of parts.

I.—1. *Principal Parts.*—These are, *head, body, wings,* and *legs.* (S. R.) Call on a child to touch a large part of the bird. When body and wings have been found, cover them up, that the remaining parts may be ditstinguished.

2. *Secondary Parts.*—(*a*) Of the head—*eyes* and *beak.* (*b*) Of the body—*feathers, back, breast,* and *tail.* (*c*) Of the legs—*feet* and *claws.* (S. R.) A child to find a part of the head; as, the *eye.* How many eyes? What the bird does with them? The *beak.* How many parts? Its use? What children have, instead of a beak? What, instead of the feathers? Why the bird wants feathers? &c.

II.—*Position.*—1, Principal. The *head* is at *one end* of the *body;* the tail at the *other end.* The wings *are on either side,* and the legs underneath. (S. R.)

2. *Secondary.* The *eyes* are on *either side* of the *head*. The beak is in front of the head, and below the eyes. The back is the *upper part of the body*, the breast *the under part*. The feet are *below the legs*. The toes are at the *end of each foot*—three before, and one behind. The feathers are all over the bird, except the legs, beak, and eyes. (S. R.) Children to notice where the head is. Teacher give the proper expression, if needed. Question thus : What is at one end of the body ? What at the other ? Then reverse the questions ; as, Where is the head ? Where are the legs ? the feathers ? Children distinguish the unfeathered parts.

Students construct sketch on "The House-fly," as "The Sparrow."

The teacher, having led the class in training to decide on the characteristic parts which are written on the board, requires them to supply the method.

4. *The Duck.* (*For Characteristic Parts.*)

MATTER.—1. The duck has feathers of many colors—green, blue, brown, white, and black.

2. The duck has thick, glossy plumage.
3. The duck has a flat, boat-shaped body.
4. The duck has strong yellow legs, placed far back.
5. The duck has broad, webbed, yellow feet.
6. The duck has a broad, flat-toothed, yellow bill, rounded at the end.

METHOD.—1. Let children select colored cards to match the feathers of the duck, and name the colors.

2. Unless there is a stuffed specimen, and not merely a picture, omit this. With a specimen, bring out *thick*, by observation, and *glossy*, by comparison with the feathers of an owl.

3. Present a card-board cylinder. Children bend it so as to represent the general shape of the body. Give term *flat*. Draw an oblong to represent shape, and ask what object they see on the water nearly of the same shape ?

LESSONS ON ANIMALS.—FIRST STEP.

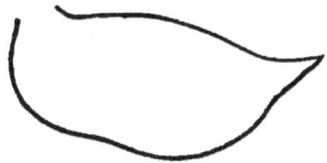

4. Measure the diagram from end to end. Mark it in the middle.

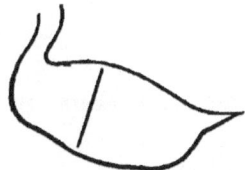

Children to mark where the legs are placed.

5. Compare with feet of a hen. Give the term *webbed*.
6. Compare with the beak of a hen. Give the term *toothed*.

Summary.—Teacher names the parts. Each child in turn gives a term which describes the part named.

Students may construct a sketch on "The Hen," as "The Duck."

Subjects for Lessons at this Step.

A Dog.	A Cat and Kittens.
A Cat.	A Cow and Calf.
A Cow.	A Sheep and Lambs.
A Sheep.	A Donkey in Draught.
A Horse.	A Pig.
A Goat.	A Duck.
A Hen.	A Hen and Chickens.

A Cock.	A Mare and Foal.
A Rabbit.	A Goose.
A Mouse.	A Rat.
A Newfoundland Dog.	A Guinea Pig.

SECOND STEP.

I.—Characteristic Parts continued.
II.—Mode of Life.
    1. Habitation.
    2. Food.
    3. Actions; especially characteristic actions, including Sounds.

III.—Disposition; involving special traits of character or intelligence. Lessons of this kind are best worked out by anecdotes. Moral lessons should be derived from them.

IV.—Uses of the animal, living or dead; our duties with respect to it. The uses to be considered are those which have direct reference to man. The uses of animals in the economy of Nature is a subject in advance of the Step. When the lesson is on a domestic animal, it should not close without asking the children what they can do for the comfort and pleasure of the creature.

V.—Comparative size.

As was the case in the First Step, any of these points may e taken as the subject of a lesson. Thus: In the first exercises, we have Characteristic Parts and Actions, with Uses; in the second, Sounds; in the third, Characteristic Parts and Traits; in the fourth, Form, and Use as depending on the food of the animal; in the fifth, Mode of Life. The same, or other animals, would be chosen to bring out the remaining points.

The teacher of method, in commencing the Step, may begin with a pattern sketch on

1. *The Cow.*

I. *Parts.*—Bring a picture of a cow before the children, who, after describing its general appearance, according to the picture, point out what distinguishes the cow from other animals: A square bulky body, thin legs, broad head, curved horns, straight back, rounded sides, dewlap, covering of short hair, long slender tail with a tuft at the end, and cloven hoofs. (W. B.)

II. *Actions.*—Let the children mention *anything* a cow can do; then leave them to make out a list of actions proper to a cow. Gathering the grass together with the tongue when feeding; chewing the cud, lying down meanwhile; tossing with the horns; kicking; lashing its sides with the tail; whisking off flies wth its tail; lowing; bending the fore legs first in lying down; standing in the water. Children to say under what circumstances each of these actions is performed.

III. *Uses.*—Children find out all the uses of the cow. She gives milk; we eat her flesh; in some countries used for the plough and for the draught; her hair is used in making mortar; her hoofs make glue; her horns to make cups and knife handles; her fat to make tallow. Children say in what ways the cow is useful while living, and when dead. Who gave us this useful creature? How we ought to treat His gift? What the cow likes? What she ought to have? &c.

Students may construct a sketch on "The Dog," as "The Cow."

Exercises on this pattern should be continued until the students can readily select and arrange the points each involves. "The Pig," "The Elephant," "The Cat," "The Lion," "The Robin," and "The Ostrich," are good subjects.

2. The following general directions, involving the heads of an exercise on the Sounds of Animals, are given, to which the students may supply the Matter and the Method:

HEADS.—I. Enumerate sounds made by different kinds of Birds. Draw a general conclusion from a consideration of these.

II.—Enumerate sounds made by different kinds of Beasts. Draw general conclusion.

III.—Enumerate sounds made by Reptiles. Confine your attention to the sounds made by vertebrated animals.

Students construct sketch on "Sounds of Insects."

3. *The Parrot.* (*Characteristic Parts. Characteristic Traits.*)

1. Children determine how they know a parrot. By its green or gray plumage, with a mixture of red; its curved and curious beak, the upper part loose; its strong legs; the arrangement of its toes—two before, and two behind; also by its power of learning to talk.

2. Children name the birds that can be taught to speak: Raven, magpie, daw, jay, starling. (W. B.) How birds learn to speak. Whether any one in the list speaks as well as the parrot? How much of what it says does the parrot understand? How children can talk, and learn their lessons, just like parrots? Whether it is right to do so?

Lead children to see that, as God has given us a power of reflection, not possessed by birds, we ought not to speak without thinking.

Students construct a sketch on "The Pheasant," as "The Parrot."

4. *Lesson on the Sheep.* (*For Uses.*)

1. Form of the animal's body. Large trunk compared with slender neck, and small head. Thick covering noticed.

2. Uses of the animal to man for food and clothing.

3. Food of the animal—grass, that grows plentifully everywhere, even on the tops of high hills, where corn will not grow.

4. The blessing this animal is to man. The goodness of God in giving it to him.

5. What the sheep likes. What we can do for it.

Students may construct a sketch on "The Ass," as "The Sheep."

After a sufficient number of individual lessons, a more general lesson may be given. In the one that follows, the Matter is given, that the students may write out the Method:

5. Animals. (*Mode of Life.*)

1. Where living?
2. How moving?

MATTER.—1. God made animals and plants. He made the animals to move about, and the plants to keep in one place.

2. God made some animals to live and move in the air, some on the earth, and some in the water.

3. To those animals that live in the air, God gave wings, and they fly; to those that live in the water, He gave fins, and they swim; to those that live on the earth, He gave feet, and they walk.

Comparative Sizes of Animals.

As the Natural History prints are not constructed at all with reference to their comparative sizes, to guard against any wrong impression that may be formed by the children, it is well to call their attention to this point.

For this purpose, it is desirable to have a chart to show this, such as those sold by the Home and Colonial Institution.

The teachers of the children may exercise them in finding:

1. Ten of the largest animals.
2. Ten of the smallest animals.
3. Six not so large as the first ten, nor so small as the second ten.
4. Ten animals of various sizes, to be arranged in order, beginning with the largest.
5. The same, beginning with the smallest.
6. Animals nearly the size of a horse; as, cow, bear, &c.
7. " " a sheep; as, goat, &c.
8. " " a cat; as, rabbit.
9. " " a rat; as, guinea pig.
10. " " an elephant; as, the rhinoceros.

It were better, perhaps, that the lessons on size should not come in series. They will make an agreeable variety if interspersed with other lessons on animals. In each lesson, as the animals are chosen, their names should be placed on the board.

When the children can readily give examples from the chart, they may be required to do so from memory.

Subjects for Further Lessons.

All native animals that are familiar, and a few of the more prominent foreign animals, as lion, elephant, &c., may be taken. Lessons from Scripture Natural History may be included.

EXAMPLES.

Raven,
Serpent,
Camel,
Fish,
Dove,   } See Religious Instruction,
Lion,   Part 2.
Ass,
Sheep,
Bee,
Eagle.

THIRD STEP.

In this Step the instruction is more systematic than in the former ones. The teacher selects her subjects from Class Mammalia, with a view to classification in the succeeding Step. Although the attention of the children is not directed to the animals as forming different groups, they are led to trace the gradual change that takes place in their organization; fitting them for different habits, propensities, and localities. The faculty of comparison, as well as that of simple observation, is exercised.

In considering structure and habits with special reference to the adaptation of the first to the last, it is often well to begin with the mode of life, leaving the children to judge as to the kind of structure this renders necessary.

LESSONS ON ANIMALS.—THIRD STEP.

1. *Lesson on the Bat.* (*Point—To Show the Structure of the Wings.*)

1. Bid a child touch different parts of his own body, to lead the rest to distinguish the head, trunk, and limbs. Children state the number of limbs in a man. How terminating? Other animals that have four limbs. How terminating? Generally in feet only. Give the term *quadrupeds*. Whether man is a quadruped? Why not? By comparison with different animals, show that only man has two hands and two feet.

2. Refer to a creature having four limbs, the hinder terminating with feet, the fore formed into wings. Children will think of a bird. May be told that there is such a creature amongst beasts. Produce a specimen. Direct attention to the wing, and explain that an equal number of bones form the arm of man and the wing of a bat. Children to find out the bones in their own arms. (W. B.)

    1. From the shoulder to the elbow.
    2. From the elbow to the wrist.
    3. The hand bones.
    4. The thumb bones.
    5. The finger bones.

Draw a diagram of the arm, numbering the parts; then a diagram of the bat's wing, numbering corresponding parts, which children observe and compare.

1. Longest bone in man; shortest in the bat.
2. Shorter in man; *very* long in the bat.
3. Scarcely appear in the bat.
4. In the bat terminating as a nail, serving as a hook.
5. In the bat thin, and extremely elongated, with extended skin between. (W. B., in opposite columns.)

Lead children to observe, that they find no new part in the wing, but an accommodation of common parts to special circumstances. Children to say why the bat has wings at all—(it lives in the air). What its food is. What it can find in the air. Children may examine the beak, and observe how it is adapted for catching insects. Tell them that at one time of the year the bat seeks the hollow of a tree, or goes into the steeple of a church, because torpid; remains motionless; folds its wings around it, and hangs to some projection by its hook. Children to say *when* this would happen? And why then? Who gave the bat its wings? Whether any one can suggest any improvement? Let children notice the *size* of the wing, extending down the side to the feet. Why a smaller one would not do? Skin—why thin? Why tough? Color—corresponding with the body; appears black at dusk. Why? Let us praise His wisdom, who gave the bat its wings, and of whom we can say, "He hath done all things well."

2. *The Hedgehog.*

MATTER.	METHOD.
I.—1. We will speak of a little animal called a hedgehog. It lives in this country, under hedges or in gardens; sleeps during the day; takes its food at night, and becomes torpid in the winter.	I.—1. Information given, where the children fail to supply it.
2. It eats insects, worms, and the soft parts of the roots of trees.	2. From the places which it frequents, children to infer what its food would be.
3. It burrows under ground.	3. Children to say what parts it must have in order to burrow—(snout and claws).
II.—1. The snout is hard and bony; claws very sharp; legs very short.	II.—1. Facts discovered by observation of the specimen now produced. Children judge whether a creature employed in scraping away earth with its claws could act better with long or with short legs. In order to this, let the children imitate the action of scraping, first with the arms stretched out, and then with the elbows bent. They will decide in which way they could work the longer.

LESSONS ON ANIMALS.—THIRD STEP. 323

2. Its back is covered with spines.	2. Children to say whether the legs are suited for running. How the hedgehog is to be defended from its enemies.
3. When in danger, it presents the spines, and conceals the unprotected parts.	3. Children discover why the spines need not cover the whole body.
4. The tail is very short.	4. Children observe the fact, and, from what they know, find out the advantage.
III.—Summary.	III.—Children give from memory, first, the habits; secondly, parts; thirdly, state how adapted.

3. *Comparison of Cat with Dog.*

I. *Resemblance.*—Both are quadrupeds; have paws and claws; three kinds of teeth; eat flesh.

II. *Differences.*

Structure.

DOG.	CAT.
1. The dog's head is pointed.	1. The cat's head is round.
2. The dog's teeth are large, flat, and rounded.	2. The cat's teeth are small, sharp, and pointed.
3. The dog's claws not retractile.	3. The cat's claws retractile.
4. The dog's hairy covering.	4. The cat's furry covering.
5. The dog's skin with few pores.	5. The cat's skin porous.
6. The dog's legs usually long.	6. The cat's legs short.

Habits.

1. The dog prefers meat in a putrid state.	1. The cat likes fresh meat.
2. The dog eats any flesh he finds.	2. The cat, in a state of nature, eats only what it kills for itself.
3. The dog runs down its prey.	3. The cat watches for and springs on its prey.
4. The dog secures it by teeth.	4. The cat secures it by claws.
5. The dog runs.	5. The cat leaps and climbs.
6. The dog has good scent.	6. The cat has good sight.
7. The dog howls, and, when domesticated, barks.	7. The cat mews.

8. The dog bites when angry.	8. The cat scratches when angry.
9. The dog wags the tail when pleased.	9. The cat purrs when pleased.
10. The dog licks the hand to show affection.	10. The cat rubs the head *against* you.

Children might also distinguish between habits natural to the animal, and habits acquired by domestication, rearranging the matter accordingly.

The three previous sketches on "The Bat," "The Hedgehog," and the "Comparison of Cat with Dog," are given as examples of the manner in which the succeeding lessons may be treated in practice.

MAMMALS.

The Monkey.

First lead the children to describe the monkey, helping them by showing stuffed specimens and pictures, and by bringing to their recollection the living animals they may have seen.

Points to which their attention should be directed: The head approaching in form nearer to that of man than the head of any other animal, in consequence of the mouth projecting but little. The slender, slight figure, adapted to agile motion; the long flexible limbs, terminated by hands fitted for grasping—that is, having four fingers, with a thumb which can be brought opposite to each of them. They are called *four-handed* animals.*

Then their habits. They live in the woods and forests of warm countries; they feed on nuts and fruits; they spring from bough to bough, and from tree to tree, with surprising agility.

Next lead the children to consider how their form and organization fit them for this arboreal life. That they derive the power of springing and rapid motion from their slender, flexible limbs; and their facility in grasping from the form of their limbs and teeth, aided often by the tail.

Consider next their disposition: cunning, intelligent, ridiculously imitative, lively, restless, chattering, and quarrelsome.

* Quadrumana.

In conclusion, lead the children to infer from the facts brought out in the lesson, viz., that the monkey dwells among trees; is peculiarly fitted for springing and grasping, and for feeding on hard vegetable food, that the Being who made it, and fixed its habitation, is as benevolent and kind as He is powerful and wise; that *He* is *our* God, and we are His creatures.

The Orang-outang.

First, its general appearance and form. It approaches nearer to a human being, in form and attitude, than any other animal, and can maintain an erect posture, though, owing to the different position of its hinder limbs, and the fact of its extremities being better fitted for prehension than support, it walks with difficulty.* The fore limbs are of a great length, the hinder limbs shorter, all slender and flexible, and, from the peculiar construction of the joints, possessing great freedom of motion. The skin, except that of the face and palms of the hands, is covered with long, coarse hair. They are less noisy and tricky than monkeys, but equally intelligent and sagacious.

The monkeys of America might form the subject of a separate lesson. They are remarkable, as possessing in their cheek-pouches a most singular provision for enabling them to keep a store of food; and in their long, prehensive tails, by which they can maintain the firmest grasp. With these they also link themselves together in a chain, and when they wish to pass to trees at a distance, they swing this chain with a sudden jerk, so that the last of them catches hold of the tree they wish to reach. Their throats also are curiously formed, enabling them to utter a most terrific yell. They often assemble together in great numbers, and join in a tremendous howling.

In conclusion, the children should give a description of the monkey; pointing out in what it resembles man, and in what points he is altogether its superior.

* In such short sketches as these the *subject* only of the lesson can be suggested. The teacher must get up the information required, and collect illustrative anecdotes from books, such as "The Class Mammalia," published by the London Tract Society, and "the Menageries" of the Library of Entertaining Knowledge; also Smellie's "Philosophy of Natural History."

The Mole.

After a few questions to arouse the children's recollection of the characteristics of the animals already examined, they may be told, if they do not know the fact, that the abode of the mole is under ground. What, then, should we expect as to its conformation? That it is fitted to burrow in the earth, and to live under ground. What organ fits the monkey for its life amid trees? What limb of the bat did we find accommodated to flying? What enables the hedgehog to burrow in the earth? In what very different places have we found animals living? In trees, in the air, under ground. Which organ is changed to fit each animal for its peculiar mode of life?

If, then, we would see that the mole is fitted to make its way under ground, what ought we especially to examine? Let the children examine the animal, and describe anything they see. Let them observe the beautiful adaptation of the fore limbs to the work of digging and boring, and lead them to admire this. This extremity is broad, strong, and spade-like in shape, being scarcely divided into distinct fingers. It is placed obliquely, so that the inner edge is the lowest, thus forming a complete instrument for throwing the soil behind the animal as it proceeds in its excavations. The arm on which this hand is placed is thick, strong, and muscular. How beautifully is all this contrived for a little mining animal! Continuing the examination, we see other adaptations no less admirable than these. The head is pointed; the end of the snout is bone rather than gristle; the body is of a conical form, and the chief strength lies in the fore part. The animal is covered with a close, soft, velvety fur, which does not impede its progress while burrowing, and which does not retain the wet and mud. As the mole works in darkness, it therefore needs but little sight; and we find its eyes are small, and are protected from injury by the fur which surrounds them. It is directed in the pursuit of its prey, and in escaping from its enemies, by the senses of smelling and hearing, both of which are very acute. Thus, by an adaptation of the same organ which in the monkey is a perfect hand for grasping, and in the bat a wing for flight, the mole is fitted by its Creator to live under ground. But why should its habitation be under the earth? It finds there the food on which it subsists, viz., worms, and the grubs of various insects. It belongs to the class called *insect-feeders*,* and, whilst satisfying its own cravings, it also renders essential service to the farmer, by clearing the soil of creatures that might injure his crops.

Under the mole-hills, which are often so abundant in fields, are the nests of the mole. These are of a conical form, and, being carefully lined with vegetable fibre, are made most comfortable for its young, which are reared with great care and tenderness. There are always several galleries leading to the nests, which furnish roads of egress and ingress.

How beautiful an instance does this animal afford of the wonderful instinct implanted in animals, to guide them in the preservation of life! Remark to the children that God has given to every animal just the particular organ that it needs. The bird has wings, and flies; the monkey has four hands, and grasps the trees. Animals do that which God intends them to do. What lesson does this teach us? To use aright that which God gives us. Animals know not who gave them the organs which are so necessary to them, but we do know who made us. What, then, is our duty? To praise and bless God.

The Bear.

First call upon the children to state what organs undergo a change to adapt each animal to its peculiar locality and varied propensities, and then let them describe the changes they have already traced. Present them with a picture of a bear. Call upon them to describe its general appearance—it is thick, clumsy, and shaggy, with short limbs and a lazy gait. Now in these respects it is very different from the animals upon which they have had instruction. Draw from them all they know as to the habits of the bear. Let them examine especially the organs connected with the procuring of food, and consequent preservation of life. They should observe the manner in which the bear places the

---

* Insectivora.

entire sole of the foot on the ground, in which it differs so much from the cat tribe, and by which it is enabled to maintain an upright position. Such animals are called, from their mode of walking, *plantigrade*. Do we use our feet thus when we run? No. When we run, we move on our toes. At what pace do we proceed when we place the entire foot on the ground? Of what character, then, must be the motion of the bear? Might we expect a slow-moving animal to feed on vegetables, or on animals? The bear feeds by preference on vegetables, such as roots, leaves, and berries; it is also very fond of honey; and only when these fail, has it recourse to animal food. Its claws are strong, blunt, and well fitted for climbing trees, or for digging. It is found in northern countries, chiefly in forests or inaccessible rocks, and in solitary places. While the double teeth of animals feeding on insects are pointed, those of the bear are obtuse. During the winter season, the food on which it subsists entirely fails. What usually happens under such circumstances?

But when that all-wise and gracious Being who rules over all creation, fixed the bounds of this animal's habitation, He made provision to meet this periodic failure of his food.

What occurs to the bat under similar circumstances? In the same manner the bear also falls into a deep sleep, during the continuance of which it is insensibly nourished by the fat in which it is incased. When in the spring it rouses from its slumber, it issues forth from its cave thin and gaunt, and so ravenous that it will face whatever falls in its way.

Recapitulate the peculiarities that distinguish the bear and adapt its structure to its special propensities, and to the situation it occupies.

The Bear—(continued.)

The polar bear may be the subject of a second lesson, and the children may be led to see in what it differs from the brown bear, especially in its color, which is white, with a tinge of yellow; and also in the form of its body, which is much elongated; and in what manner its immense paws, covered underneath by coarse hair, give it security in walking over the slippery ice; and that the layer of fat in which it is incased is the best covering for preserving it from the injurious effects of the cold of a polar region. It feeds of necessity almost entirely on animal food, such as the whale, the seal, the walrus, and fish. It is an excellent swimmer.

Bears are very remarkable for maternal affection. The following history, related in one of the polar voyages, develops this trait in their character, and may be made use of by the teacher to illustrate the affection bestowed on the children themselves by their own mothers; the trouble, anxiety, and pain they undergo, and the return of obedience and love which such affection claims:

Early one morning the man at the masthead gave notice that three bears were fast making their way across the ice to the ship. They had no doubt been invited by the scent of the blubber of a walrus, which had been set on fire, and was burning on the ice. They proved to be a she bear and her two cubs. They ran eagerly to the fire, and drew out from the flames part of the flesh yet unconsumed, and devoured it voraciously. The crew from the ship threw out great pieces of the flesh of the walrus. These the old bear carried away singly, laid each piece before her cubs, and dividing them, gave to each a share, reserving a very small portion for herself. As she was fetching the last piece, the sailors levelled their muskets at the cubs, shot them both dead, and wounded the dam in her retreat, but not mortally. It would have drawn tears of pity from any but savage hearts, to have witnessed the affectionate concern manifested by the poor beast, in the last moments of her expiring young. Though she was sorely wounded, and could scarcely crawl to the place where they lay, she carried the lump of flesh which she had fetched, as she had done others before, tore it in pieces, and laid it before them; and when she saw that they refused to eat it, she placed her paws first upon one, then upon the other, and attempted to raise them up: all the while it was piteous to hear their moan. Finding that she could not stir them, she went off, and when she had got to some distance, she looked back and moaned; and that not availing to entice them away, she returned, and smelling around them, began to lick their wounds. She went off a third time as before, and having crawled a few paces, looked again behind her, and for some time stood moaning. Finding at last that they were cold and lifeless, she raised her head toward the ship, and growled her resentment to their murderers, which they returned by shooting her dead. She fell between her cubs, and died licking their wounds."

The attachment of the bear to her cubs, and her wrath when deprived of them, is often alluded to in the Scriptures. In Hosea xiii. 8, the Lord threatens to meet his people who had forsaken him, "as a bear bereaved of her whelps." There is a similar allusion in 2 Samuel xvii. 8: "For, said Hushai, thou knowest thy father and his men, that they be mighty men, and they be chafed in their minds, as a bear robbed of her whelps in the field."

A Weasel.

The recapitulatory questions may be put in the following manner, with a view to variety in the mode of presenting the subject to the children. This is very important, as a means of keeping up interest, and giving more exercise to the mind.

What animals have you found fitted to live amidst trees? What kind of animal is suited to chasing its prey in the air? What change in the formation of another animal renders it a good miner, and suited to feed on insects? What kind of feet are best adapted to a heavy, slow-moving animal? Would such an animal be able to pursue its prey? Of what nature, then, may we expect to find its food? But we now come to a bloodthirsty, flesh-eating race, of which the first family live upon vermin and poultry; they must therefore be able to creep through very small holes, to thrust themselves into crevices, to crawl under fences, and sometimes to climb heights. The children should endeavor to conceive what description of body and what organs would adapt these creatures for such habits and propensities. Who ordained their food to be of such a kind, and gave them the desire for it? What, then, may we be sure of, as to their particular formation?

By such questions as these, the children may be led to see that animals with propensities such as are implanted in the weasel, need a slender, light, flexible, yet powerful body, with a small tapering head, and short limbs armed with claws. Let them observe that such is the form of the weasel tribe, by the actual examination of a stuffed specimen or a picture. Prompt them to call to mind any creatures they may know that force their way through the earth, or wind about through the grass, and under stumps and fences. What is the form of worms, and what their peculiar motion?

The weasel, and other animals of this tribe, are called *worm-shaped*,* from their resemblance to worms in shape and movement. Their limbs are short and strong; and instead of placing the entire sole of the foot on the ground like the bear, they walk on their toes.† This fact having been told them, the children should themselves draw the inference, that their step is consequently free, light, and active. Their bodies are so tapering and flexible, that they move with grace and rapidity. Their teeth, being pointed, are fitted for seizing and tearing their prey. They all emit a very unpleasant odor. We find that their disposition is bloodthirsty, and that their form and organs are adapted to the gratification of these propensities. Then, by similar instances of the form and organization of animals being suited to their several habits and propensities, of which the children themselves may remember several, lead them to the conclusion, that in God's works all is harmony.

There is another point to which attention should be drawn, viz., the providence of God in the creation of a race of animals, which, while satisfying their own appetite, prove useful to man by preventing the excessive increase of vermin that by feeding upon grain do farmers so much injury.

The Stoat.

The children should compare this animal with the preceding one, and point out any features in which they are alike, or in which they differ. The stoat is larger than the weasel, and is especially distinguished by the changes that take place in its fur as winter approaches. In summer this is of a reddish brown; but in those animals which inhabit northern countries it becomes of a pure white in winter, except the tip of the tail, which is always

---

* Vermiform.
† They are called *digitigrade*, or *movers on the toes*.

black. Why this change? One reason is, that the gracious Creator thus enables this creature to escape observation when the ground is covered with snow. The change has also another advantage; for its white coat enables it better to resist the intense cold of Siberia, as the heat of its body does not pass off so rapidly as it would if its color were dark. (The children may not understand the reason of this, but the fact is very interesting.) Another provision for its comfort is, that the fur becomes thicker in winter. Man, being possessed of reason, is able to provide for the changes of seasons; but God administers more immediately to the necessities of the brute creation.* The fur of the stoat is called *ermine*. It is considered very valuable, and forms the robes of kings and nobles. The hunter seeks it in the winter season. Why? The facts on which the answer to such a question depends have been already told the children.

The Ferret.

The children should describe the animal, its slender, worm-like body, short legs, sharp claws, pointed teeth, and piercing eyes, and then determine to which of the animals already examined it bears the most resemblance. They should state any differences they perceive, and be led to infer, from the similarity of the organs and form of this animal to those of the weasel and stoat, that its habits and propensties must be similar to theirs. The sanguinary disposition of this creature is turned to account, in using it to clear our premises from vermin; but though employed and domesticated by man, it seems quite incapable of attachment to its owner.

The Sable.

This digitigrade, vermiform, carnivorous creature, is interesting from the high value at which its fur is estimated.

The sable is found in the forests and mountains of Siberia; and owing to the extreme cold of this icy region, and the fact of the

---

* The children may be led themselves to notice such facts. They know that man has reason, and animals instinct, and they will be able to see the reason for this different provision.

chase being generally pursued in winter, the fur of the animal being most thick and rich at that season, the poor hunter is exposed to extreme peril, and often perishes amidst the pathless wilds. The chase of this animal is a punishment imposed on the exiles of the Russian Government, who are required to furnish a certain number of skins annually.

Points of interest to which the children's attention may be directed: The beautiful provision made for the necessities of this animal by a beneficent Creator, in the thickening of its fur in the winter season, and in the continuation of this covering to the extremities of the toes; and also the fact of man being able to appropriate such animals to himself so as to derive advantage from them.

As a summary, the children should describe whatever is common in the habits and organs of this race of animals. They should also remark upon the office they perform in nature.

DOMESTIC DOGS.

Spaniels.

The children should again examine the picture of the varieties of dogs, and then endeavor to make out what peculiarity distinguishes the spaniel from others of its race. It has a long head, with a pointed muzzle; its ears are soft, long, and pendent, fitted to gather the sound of footsteps from the ground; its hair is silky and waving, and either of a red liver color, or black and white; the tail bushy. Its scent is very delicate, and guides it in the pursuit of its prey. It is exceedingly docile, intelligent, and affectionate. Many instances are on record of its attachment to its owner. It has been known to preserve the recollection of its master, and to recognize him after an absence of so long duration that his friends had forgotten him. There are several varieties of the spaniel. Some, as lap dogs, are very small; others are larger, and are employed in field sports. One species, from its mode of marking its prey, is called the *setter*. The following account well describes the characteristics of this dog: "A setter dog should be a fine land spaniel that will range well, and yet at such absolute command, that when he is in full career, one 'hem' of his master shall make him stand still, gaze about him, and look in his master's face, as it were expecting directions from him whether to proceed, stand still, or retire. But the main thing he is to be taught is, when he sees and is near his prey, of a sudden to stand still, or fall down flat on his belly, without making any noise or motion till his master comes up." What a lesson does such a dog teach children! What is there in this animal they may imitate? His prompt obedience; his desire to please, and to do his appointed work; his self-denial, giving up his own pleasure to that of his master.

The *pointer* is another dog also employed by the sportsman. It resembles the spaniel, but it has less hair, nor is its hair waving. This dog is trained to stop and to point to the spot where game lies hid. Its natural instinct is to approach its prey stealthily, and then, pausing for an instant, to spring upon it with an unerring aim derived from this pause. Education has converted this short rest and rapid spring into a fixed and deliberate rest, which has been thus quaintly described: "This semicolon in his proceedings, man converts into a full stop."

The dogs called *hounds* are used in hunting the deer, fox, hare, and otter. They are keen of scent, and are kept in numbers, called a *pack*. Their fleetness is so great that the swiftest horse alone can keep pace with them. The tone of their cry is deep and mellow, but the neighborhood of a dog kennel is not very agreeable, as they make a sad howling when fed. The feeding of a dog kennel furnishes a proof of the complete obedience to which these animals can be trained. "They are hungry, and know that they are about to be fed, but they manifest no rebellious impatience. The feeder stations himself at the door which separates the outer kennel from the feeding room. On his arrival, a cry of joy is set up by the whole pack, but it is instantly silenced at his command. He calls, 'Juno'—Juno passes out; 'Ponto'— Ponto follows; and so on through the pack, even should there be as many as thirty couples. If a young dog should attempt to move out of his order, he is sent back; he recollects his punishment, and seldom transgresses again. The pack is brought to this state of perfect discipline by gentle correction."

The *greyhound* is remarkable for the great beauty and elegant lightness and symmetry of its form, peculiarly fitting it for fleetness and agility. Its head is very pointed, ears short and erect, but pendent at their tips. Its limbs are slender, its body thin, and standing high; its fur smooth, with short hairs. In disposition it is gentle and affectionate. It is principally used in hunting the hare, which it pursues chiefly by sight, not having so keen a scent as other dogs of the chase.

The *terrier* is another of the sporting dogs. Two of these dogs usually accompany the fox hounds. They are also most useful in catching rats. The terrier is a thick-set, brisk-looking animal, with rather short legs, its muzzle not projecting so much as that of the spaniel. Its short legs enable it to creep under the grass and through brakes and bushes. There are two species: one, the Scotch terrier, has very rough and wiry hair; the other has a smoother coat, and altogether is more delicate in appearance. It is supposed that the terrier is the native dog of the British Isles. It is remarkable for the eagerness and courage with which it makes its way into the earth after those animals, from the fox to the rat, which are usually called *vermin*. It possesses great sagacity, and is most daring in its attacks upon larger animals. It is used as a guard to the house, as well as in the chase.

These lessons on the sporting dogs may be useful as exercises for the children in drawing out a description of the various dogs they may see in pictures, or with which they may be familiar, the teacher supplying whatever escapes their observation. They should be led to observe the education these dogs receive, and the improvement it produces, and draw the inference that they should themselves value education, and be thankful for being taught. Not only are the senses of these dogs rendered more acute by their being used in the service of man, but they are also wonderfully trained to forego the indulgence of their own natural propensities, and to use their powers, not for their own gratification, but for that of their master. Their carnivorous appetites would prompt them immediately to devour the animal which their scent has discovered, were they not trained to obey their master at the sacrifice of their own inclinations.

Dogs—(*continued*).

In what service are those dogs employed, upon which you have had lessons? What organs are most useful in the chase? How would you characterize their motion? How are their feet adapted to fleet motion? Why, for instance, can they run more swiftly than the bear? In what respect are their bodies better fitted for motion than that of the bear? They are light and slender, and their muzzle pointed. Now repeat together: "The dogs of the chase are fitted for rapid motion by being digitigrade, and by having a light, slender body, and pointed muzzle." What sense is very important in directing their pursuit? How has the Creator wisely provided for this necessity? What do they need in addition to the power of pursuing their prey? The power of catching and eating it. By what organs are these actions accomplished? By the teeth and claws. How are their teeth and claws fitted for seizing and eating animals? What is essential to the life of animals? What is the chief food of dogs? How are they fitted for their flesh eating propensity? What are the lessons which their history affords you? Tell me some other uses of dogs other than that of the chase. They guard our houses, our property, and our lives. Here is a picture of two dogs which are especially useful as guards to our dwellings and property—the bulldog and the mastiff. What do you observe when you compare these with the spaniel tribe? The head is thicker, the muzzle short, and the aspect very fierce. They are bold and ferocious. How does man make use of this disposition? He turns it against those who would injure him or his property. There is another very useful dog, which perhaps some of you may have seen, which is much used in the old countries in watching and guarding flocks on the mountains, and in driving them from one place to another. What dog is this? The shepherd's dog. What does the shepherd's dog do? Yes; he drives the sheep along the streets; he keeps them together, and allows none to straggle. Looking at his master, he receives his directions, and then faithfully and sagaciously executes his will. The dog you see thus employed in the streets is called a *drover*. The dog that guards the mountain flocks is a much finer animal, and it is very beautiful to see how he can keep a very large flock of sheep within their proper bounds, bringing up every straggler without any violence, and knowing the sheep of his master from those of every other flock. Do you think that it is natural to these dogs to take care of sheep? No. How, then, do they become such a valuable help to the shepherd? You remember what we remarked as to the dogs of chase, how their natural instincts were turned to man's account. What, then, is done, should you think, with the drover and the shepherd's dog? They are educated by man, who teaches them their lesson, and that which they thus learn becomes a second nature to them. How do these dogs carry out the lessons given to them? What virtues do they display? What may children learn from them?

Is the dog useful to the rich only? No; he is also the poor man's friend. Can you tell me how? Yes; he will guard his clothes while he is at work, and will lead about the poor blind man. The following is a remarkable instance of the docility and sagacity of the dog: One of these animals was in the habit of conducting a blind beggar through the streets of Rome. This dog, besides guiding his master in such a manner as to protect him from all danger, learned to distinguish, not only the streets, but the houses where the blind man was accustomed to receive alms. Whenever the dog came to any one of these streets, he would not leave it till a call had been made at every house where his master was usually supplied. When the beggar began to ask alms, and was received, the dog would lie down to rest; but the master was no sooner served or refused, than the dog rose, without either order or sign, and proceeded to the other houses where the poor man generally was successful. When a halfpenny was thrown from a window, the sagacious animal went in search of it, carried it in his mouth, and placed it in the beggar's hat. Even when bread was thrown, he would not take it unless he received a portion from his master's own hand.*

* A story renders the subject under discussion very attractive. There are

The Fox.

The most obvious characteristics of the fox may be discovered by the children; as, its pointed head, its long narrow pupil, and its long bushy tail. They may be told that the shape of the pupil marks it as a nocturnal animal; and they may be led to understand why its eye should be so formed, by considering the effect that light has upon eyes accustomed to darkness, and to admire the goodness which, by thus enabling the eye to contract and take in but few rays of light, provides for the comfort of the animal, and affords another instance of the kind care that the Creator bestows on his creatures.

The fox is distinguished from the wolf and dog by its longer and more bushy tail, its larger head and more pointed muzzle, its long body and short limbs, its triangular ears, and the form of its pupils, which contract under the influence of light to a mere line. The odor emitted by the fox is very disagreeable. The usual length of the animal is about two and a half feet;* the height, one foot. The color is fawn, intermixed with black. The fox digs out holes under ground, to which our Saviour refers in Matt. viii. 20. It is a cunning, wily animal. In the dusk of the evening it steals from its burrow with noiseless step, to prowl about for prey. Its sense of smell and of hearing are very keen; it listens, and snuffs the breeze, attentive to every sound, and observing every odor. With a crouching attitude† it advances on its prey; it surprises the rabbits gambolling near their burrow, the hare in her form, and the poultry on their perch. It slaughters all it finds; and when its appetite is satisfied, it buries the remainder in the earth, to supply future necessities. It is exceedingly particular in the choice of its quarters. When it has selected the spot for its

---

many very interesting narratives illustrating the fidelity and sagacity of dogs. The beautiful story of the dog at Bethgelert is well known. There is another in the "Library of Entertaining Knowledge, Menageries," vol. i., p. 79.

* When the children are told the size of an animal, they may be required to mark it on the board; and also when told the color, they may point to some specimen of the color named.

† Attitude marks character. The wolf is bolder than the fox, and is more erect.

abode, it explores the country to see what advantages it may afford, examining every spot likely to prove a safe retreat in the hour of danger. Its excessive suspicion and caution render any new object a source of distrust and inquietude; it is uneasy until it has discovered what it may be, and approaches for the purpose of observation with slow and hesitating step, and by circuitous paths. It passes the day at the bottom of its hiding place, and sallies forth in search of prey during the obscurity of twilight or the darkness of night, gliding along stealthily to surprise the partridge. When it cannot find game, it contents itself with field mice, frogs, and even snails. It is very fond of honey, and its liking for grapes is the subject of a well-known fable, and is also alluded to in the Bible, Song of Solomon ii. 15.

The young are playful, and remain with their parent about four months. She is tender, watchful, and most resolute in their defence. The children may be told these facts, and then be questioned upon them, being required also to draw up from them a sketch of the character of the fox; and to say what in the animal we may imitate, and what avoid.*

There is an instance on record of the great sagacity of the fox. The Earl of Thanet had a seat at Hothfield, in Kent, and another in Westmoreland. At the former place an extraordinarily large fox had been taken, and the earl ordered it to be conveyed to Westmoreland. The following year, in Kent, a fox which had run into the earth was dug out, and declared by the huntsmen to be the very individual that had been taken to Westmoreland. Lord Thanet was incredulous, but having earmarked the animal, it was again removed to Westmoreland. In the following season a fox was killed at Hothfield, which proved to be the one in question, and it is evident that it must have found its way twice from Westmoreland to Kent, a distance of about 320 miles.

The Wolf.

The children should first determine to which of the animals already examined the wolf bears the closest resemblance, and in

* Teachers should especially avoid having one plan for all their lessons. Variety gives interest, and draws out different intellectual powers.

what respect it is like the dog, as in its general form and appearance, its teeth and claws, &c. Which are the organs that mark the habits of an animal? If an animal have claws and sharp-pointed teeth, what might we expect to be its food? And if it feed on animals that it catches, for what kind of motion must it be fitted? How is an animal fitted for pursuing its prey? Let the children then consider the wolf, and say what they think its habits must be. Its claws, sharp teeth, and light, pointed form, indicate that it lives on animals which it pursues. What sense guides carnivorous animals in the chase? The wolf has a very keen scent. Let them compare the erect, forward ears of the wolf, with the thrown-back ears of the pursued hare, and find out the reason for those of the one being directed forward, of the other backward; and acknowledge in this the wisdom and the goodness that fits each animal in every respect for the habits that are special to it. Having determined the points of resemblance between the wolf and the dog, the children should discover in what respect they differ, and so arrive at the characteristics of the wolf. The wolf is stronger and larger than the dog; it possesses great muscular power; its height at the shoulder is about two feet six inches, and about two feet four inches behind; the length, from the tip of the muzzle to the root of the tail, three feet eight inches;* its coat is very rough and coarse, of a grayish yellow color, with a black oblique stripe on the fore legs; its eyes are placed obliquely, and its tail hangs down. In character it possesses none of the noble qualities of the dog; whilst it is ferocious, cruel, and sanguinary, it is also cunning, wary, and cowardly. In former times this animal was the dread and terror of Great Britain. The month of January was then called wolf month, because at that season the wolves, not being able to find their usual food, used to come forth from the forests and attack man. King Edgar did much to rid the land of these pests, by changing the tax levied upon the Welsh into an annual tribute of 300 wolves' heads. In the early settlements of some portions of this country they were also quite troublesome. How thankful should we be that we are not now exposed to such dangers! (The children should draw the com-

* The children should mark the size on the board.

parison, and say what feelings our improved condition should inspire.) There are many allusions in Scripture to the ferocious character and nocturnal habits of the wolf. (See Matt. vii. 15; Ezek. xxii. 27; Acts xx. 29.)

Though the wolf is in general a solitary animal, it unites in troops for the purpose of securing its prey, and shows its cunning in the stratagems it employs. When wolves attack the deer, which is greatly their superior in swiftness, they arrange themselves in the form of a semicircle, and creeping slowly toward the herd, they either completely hem them in and surround them, or urge them by hideous yells over some precipice in the only direction they leave open to them.

This course may be completed with reference to the list given at the end of the Step.

MISCELLANEOUS SKETCHES.

For the sake of variety, occasional lessons may be given on animals belonging to various classes. Variety secures interest. For sketch on a bird, see "The Ostrich."

1. *Sketch of a Lesson on the Ostrich.*

Adaptation of its structure to its mode of life:

1. The size of the head is adapted to its long and slender neck.

2. The eye, furnished with an additional lid which can be drawn down at pleasure, is peculiarly protected against the intense heat of the sun, and the fine sand of the desert lands in which it dwells.

3. The feathers of the wings, being loose, and not furnished with barblets, aid the bird in running.

4. The great strength of its large legs enables it the better to take those long journeys which it is obliged to travel in search of food.

5. The membrane of the foot, and the pad which it incloses, give this bird lightness and buoyancy, and fit it for its passage over sandy deserts.

6. The pad on the breastbone constitutes a safeguard against injury from any hard substance when the bird is resting on the ground.

The lesson should conclude by drawing the proper inference from such complete adaptation of organs to the peculiar wants of the bird.

Birds, as a class, are referred to the Fourth Step. It would prolong the Third Step too much, did it include a full course on birds as well as on mammals.

Moreover, children, when they make the advance of a Step, like new subjects, as well as new plans.

A class of students might construct "The Lion," "The Camel," or "The Eagle," as "The Ostrich."

2. *For Sketch on a Reptile—The Tortoise.*

1. *Habits.*—The tortoise lives either on land or in water. It moves slowly on the ground, but swims beautifully. It comes on land to deposit its eggs, of which it lays a great number; scrapes a hole in the sand, and leaves them to be hatched by the heat of the sun. Creatures that come from eggs are birds and reptiles. How their eggs may be distinguished? The eggs of birds become hard by boiling; those of reptiles become soft. The eggs of the tortoise become soft. What, therefore, it must be?

2. *Parts, &c.*—The tortoise has a small head like that of a serpent; four legs; a tail. Children to decide how it defends itself. Name means of defence possessed by other animals. It has no horns, no sharp teeth. Children to infer that it cannot fight. Reference to the hare and the mouse; also other creatures that cannot. What these do when an enemy approaches? But the tortoise cannot run away. How, then, kept in safety? It has a hard covering. Describe shell: Very strong, thick, and hard; formed of many pieces. (Draw on the board, to show how these are joined.) Draw a diagram representing the shell of the back. There are *thirteen* large pieces in the middle, and *twenty-three* round the margin. Let the children count the number of pieces which compose the shell. Under part also covered with

shell. Tell children that all creatures covered with this sort of armor are called *reptiles*. What they can call the tortoise, and why? Compare with crocodile, &c. Children to name the parts the shell does not cover. Tail has a scaly covering of its own. Head and four legs uncovered. How protected? Can be drawn into shell. Picture out the tortoise on a bright summer day, floating on its back in a calm sea, and enjoying itself. No enemy able to hurt it. How kind it is in God to create this creature for happiness. After floating for some time, it will want to swim. With what? How fishes swim? How the tortoise will be able to swim without fins? Show how beautifully its feet are formed as "paddles" for this purpose. After a while it will have to come to land to lay its eggs. Whether likely to go far inland, and why not? Care it takes to find a safe place for its eggs. Who enables it to do this? What would happen to the eggs if this were not done? It scrapes away the sand: how formed for doing this?

Summary.—The tortoise is a reptile. It is protected by a hard, strong shell, which covers its body, and underneath which it can draw its head and legs. Its feet are formed into "paddles," to enable it to swim, but furnished with nails hard enough to scrape away the sand where it wants to make a hole for its eggs. If time allows, tell the children that the shell is used for making combs, &c.; that men catch tortoises by turning them on their backs, with spikes, when they are on land; that they cannot get up; they then take them away, and hold them over a very hot fire; the upper shell loosens from the lower one, and falls off. The poor creature is then set free, and in another year a new shell appears.

Students may construct a sketch on "The Frog," as "The Tortoise."

For a sketch on an "Invertebrated Animal," see

3. *The Earth Worm.*

MATTER.—I. Habits. II. Parts. III. Uses.

I.—1. Worms live under ground. They come to the surface when disturbed; also in search of food.

2. Worms, when they appear above ground, keep their tails firmly fixed in their holes, that they may retire on the least alarm. Even when altogether on the ground, they adhere to the surface, and are not easily removed.

3. Worms feed on a very fine mould, which contains particles of putrid matter. They sometimes eject their food. What they throw up is called *worm casts*.

II.—1. The worm is boneless, and covered with a thick skin, which is formed into more than a hundred little rings.

2. Every ring has four sharp, hooked bristles on the under side. These the worm can lift up or press down at will.

3. The head is sharp and pointed. It has a mouth with two fleshy lips, but no eyes, nostrils, ears, nor brain.

4. The worm has a large stomach, which runs along the body to the end of the tail.

5. The worm has four holes down the back, by means of which it breathes.

6. It has reddish blood, which is cold.

III.—1. It removes and consumes decaying vegetable matter.

2. Worm casts are a fine manure for grass.

3. It loosens the ground.

4. It serves as food to various classes—birds, moles, and fish.

METHOD. I.—1. Where the children have seen worms? Where they hide? Disturbing causes likely to bring them to the surface; as, digging, uprooting of trees, &c. Necessity of the worms moving about in order to obtain food, brought out by comparison of animals with plants.

2. Refer to previous observation and experiment.

3. Children to judge what food worms are likely to find under ground—roots, slugs, grubs, &c. Why such food is unsuited to the worm? It has no teeth, therefore its food must be soft. Give information, and explain *putrid*.

II.—1. Bring out *boneless*, by comparison with the arm, or by letting the children feel the worm. Illustrate by means of a piece of spring wire with a long needle put through the ring, to show that while a boneless body can contract and lengthen, a body formed with a skeleton cannot do so. Show the use of this contraction and expansion, by explaining how the creature moves. To show that the skin should be tough, refer to the effect of digging the ground with the hands.

2. The difficulty of lifting the worm from the ground. The advantage of this to the worm. Refer to the condition of a worm on a street pavement, or in a stone quarry. Why, in such a place, it must perish?

3. *Head.*—Why no eyes and ears? Refer to its habitation. No nostrils. Finds its food by touch of lips. Compare animals having brains, with brainless animals. Children draw conclusion from examples.

4. Refer to the character of the food; whence children judge of the small amount of nutriment it contains, and what difference this makes as to the quantity consumed.

5. Refer to the holes in our face. Absence of nostrils rendering some other means of breathing necessary.

6. Refer again to the habitation of the worm. Compare it with warm-blooded animals living under ground. The mole. Its covering. The exercise it takes. The worm has no covering, and no power of taking rapid exercise; but these are not needed by it.

III.—1. Refer to the nature of its food. Effects, if not removed.

2. Tell this.

3. Compare garden beds with garden paths, to show that in loosened soil the rain penetrates. The fibres of plants expand.

4. Refer to previous observation.

IV. *Summary.*—Children write out what matter they can remember under each head.

Students construct "The Dor-Beetle," as "The Earth Worm."

4. *The Fish.*

I. *Habits.*—Found in water; some in salt, some in fresh; some emigrate from one to the other; some frequent shallow, some deep water. Usually they move with great rapidity, and in direct lines, discovering their prey by the sense of sight, darting on it, catching it, and instantly swallowing it alive; red blooded, though cold blooded; breathing air found in water by means of gills; dying when taken out of the water; young produced from spawn; hatched by the heat of the sun.

Let the children condense what has been found out. Classify the actions of the fish under three heads:

       1. Moving (swimming).
       2. Preying.
       3. Breathing. (W. B.)

II. *Adaptation of Parts to Habits.*—1. How adapted to swimming?

(*a*) By its shape: Pointed muzzle; head set on shoulders, without a neck; shoulders rounded; body rounded and tapering; tail set edgewise. Why?

(*b*) By its covering: Scales—strong, light, smooth, water proof, often varnished. Why? Refer to the artificial flies used by anglers—formed of many pieces. Refer to a suit of armor.

(*c*) By its limbs. Fins—light, strong, flat, undivided. Why? Compare with position of the fingers when swimming, and with the webbed foot of a water bird. How the fin offers resistance to the water; also its use in balancing the fish. Refer to the instability of the element in which the creature moves.

Tail compared with the fins as to size and position. From the difference in position, lead the children to infer that the use would be different. Use of the tail in guiding the course of the fish described and simply illustrated.

2. How formed for preying.

(*a*) Eyes—size, position. Absence of eyelid. Why?

(*b*) Mouth—its width. Teeth—compare with teeth of mammals, and refer to the food of the fish. Number of rows, shape, direction.

3. How formed for breathing in the water? Refer to the human lungs, as a spongy substance, pervious to air, and full of veins, filled with blood, to which the air penetrates. Examine the gills. How they differ. External organs, consisting of a suc-

cession of plates. The skin wrought into fringes at the end of each, so as to expose the greatest possible quantity of blood to the air. By experiment with a piece of sea weed, or of a buffalo robe, show that the blood is brought into contact with the air only when the gill is under water.

III. *Summary.*—Children write out what they can remember under each head and sub-head.

Students construct a lesson on "The Whale," as "The Fish," and then draw up sketch on "Comparison of Fish and Whale."

Lessons on Parts of Animals are sometimes advantageously given.

EXAMPLE.

5. *Horns of Animals.*

Get the children to name any animals they know having horns. Show the picture of a cow, a goat, and a deer. Let them find out the difference in the horns of these.

1. *As to Position.*—The horns of kine are placed in front of the head, and extend upward and outward. (W. B.) The horns of goats slant backward. (W. B.) The horns of stags branch in different directions. (W. B.) Bring this out by drawing the outline of a head, and let children represent the three kinds and directions of horns.

2. *As to Form.*—(*a*) The horns of kine are round, broad at the base, and tapering toward the point. (W. B.) (Compare with cylinder and cone.) They are curved. (W. B.) (*b*) The horns of goats have the same general form, but are larger than those of kine, and less curved. (W. B.) (Compare them.) (*c*) The horns of stags spread out from the base, like the branches of a tree. (W. B.)

3. *As to Substance.*—Horn is a stiff, hard, semitransparent, yellowish-brown substance. The horns of kine and goats have a bony core, that fills up the interior space of the horn. Stags' horns differ, in being solid. (W. B.) Children observe and describe the material of which horns are composed. Are told that the cow's horns are sometimes used as drinking cups. Why?

That goats' horns are the same in substance. How stags' horns differ?

4. *As to Uses.*—Horns are given as a means of defence to creatures that would otherwise be defenceless. (W. B.) (What cows do with their horns? goats? rams? Refer to the poor hunted stag when it stands at bay.) Why God has given horns to these animals? (Compare the teeth and feet of horned animals with those of carnivorous animals.)

Students construct a lesson on "The Teeth or Feet of Animals."

LISTS OF SUBJECTS.

Class Mammalia.

I. Monkey.
    Ourang-outang.
    Baboon.

II. Bat.

III. Mole.
    Hegdehog.
    Porcupine.
    Ant Eater.

IV. Weasel.
    Stoat.
    Ferret.
    Sable.

V. *Domestic Dogs.*
    Spaniel.
    Pointer.
    Hound.
    Terrier.

    Fox.
    Wolf.

VI. Cat.
    Lion.
    Tiger.
    Leopard.
    Panther.
    Hyena.

VII. Brown Bear.
    Polar Bear.

VIII. Seal.
    Whale.

IX. Hippopotamus.
    Rhinoceros.
    Elephant.
    Tapir.
    Pig.

    Horse.
    Ass.
    Zebra.

X. Buffalo
    Cow.
    Sheep.
    Goat.
    Antelope.
    Camel.
    Giraffe.
    Deer.
    Reindeer.

XI. Beaver.
    Squirrel.
    Hare.
    Rabbit.
    Rat.

XII. Kangaroo.

MISCELLANEOUS SUBJECTS.

Boa Constrictor.
Rattlesnake.
Viper.
Common Snake.

Shark.
Dolphin.
Torpedo.
Cuttlefish.

Lobster.
Starfish.
Bee.
Ant.

Alligator.   Salmon.   Housefly.
Turtle.   Cod.   Beetle.
Tortoise.   Sole.   Spider.
Frog.   Herring. Earth Worm.
Toad.   Pike.

FOURTH STEP.

CLASS OF BIRDS.

The teacher should begin by procuring a full set of pictures; specimens are still better. The children give the name that applies to all; then, as far as they can, the name that applies to each. Are told that it is the object of the lesson to put all these birds into classes, or groups. Children exercised in finding points according to which a classification may be made: According to color; according to size; as wild or tame; according to habitation, food, or structure. Children led to decide on the best basis for classification—structure. The best points on this basis are *beaks* and *feet*. They may then begin to classify. If they need guidance, teacher may direct their attention.

I.—1. To the eagle—the king of birds. Why so called? How characterized? Size, beak, claws. Children to infer the habits indicated by this structure. Select birds with similar characteristics; as, condor, hawk, owl. W. B. in column under title of "Birds of Prey."

2. Children to find a distinct group of birds. They choose, say the hen, turkey, peacock, on account of their resemblance, having blunt beaks, strong legs, heavy bodies. W. B. in column. Give the term *Ground Birds*. Children say how this name applies.

3. A third set of birds to be found. Children select, say stork and heron, for their long legs, bony beaks and necks. Form column under "Stilt Birds." Name—why given?

4. Children may perhaps next select the duck, goose, &c. May be told that all birds that frequent large bodies of water, whether fresh or salt, have one important characteristic, which

they must find out (webbed feet). Write column under "Web-footed Birds."

5. To lead them to discover another class, they must be told to compare the feet of the birds that remain unclassified. They will soon distinguish the climbing birds. Name given, and column made.

6. Children to be told that all the remaining birds are classed together as Perching Birds.

II. Children mention various birds, and decide in which column each name is to be written. The blackboard may appear as follows:

Birds of Prey.	Ground Birds.	Stilt Birds.	Web-footed Birds.	Climbing Birds.	Perching Birds.
Eagle.	Hen.	Heron.	Goose.	Woodpecker.	Raven.
Condor.	Turkey.	Stork.	Duck.	Parrot.	Magpie.
Hawk.	Peacock.	Flamingo.	Penguin.		Pigeon.
Owl.	Quail.	Ibis.	Gull.		Canary.
	Partridge.		Frigate Bird.		Lark.
	Ostrich.		Albatross.		Nightingale.
					Thrush.
					Wren.
					Robin.
					Kingfisher.

In recapitulating, the orders should be arranged as given by naturalists, and the term *order* given. Whether or not to give scientific terms, as *Raptores*, may be left to the discretion of the teacher. The English terms would seem to be as good as the Latin; thus,

1st Order.	2d Order.	3d Order.	4th Order.
Raveners.	Perchers.	Climbers.	Scratchers.

5th Order.	6th Order.
Waders.	Swimmers.

When the teacher names the order, the children should be able to give examples. Examples given by the teacher; they refer to the order. Lessons need to be given on the subordinate groups; as,

LESSONS ON ANIMALS.—FOURTH STEP. 351

Raveners { Diurnal. { Feeders on fresh flesh.
{ Feeders on carrion.
Nocturnal.

Perchers { The Crow tribe.
The Swallow tribe.
The Finch tribe, &c.

Refer to any good work on Natural History. For example of Method, see sketch on

1. *The Swallow Tribe.*

I. Teacher tells the children that they are about to inspect a species of bird which spends almost all its time in the air, and hardly ever touches earth. Requires them to tell, first, what organs will be in constant use (wings). Of what general character these must be (large and strong). Secondly, which organs will hardly be used at all (legs). Of what character these (probably) will be (small and slender). Thirdly, what kind of food the birds will be able to find in the air (insects). Fourth, what birds will do when the cold winter comes, and no insects are to be found? (go to a warmer climate.) Fifth, whether they (children) can name the species they have thus far described?

II. Teacher produces specimen of the swallow (also a specimen of a bulfinch for comparison). Children will tell the structure: Long, slender, tapering, and light body (compared with bulfinch); very long wings (compared with the body); broad and forked tail; very wide mouth; very delicate beak (compared with that of bulfinch); short, slender legs; delicate but long and curved claws; thick plumage, smooth and glossy.

Children required to explain the adaptation of this structure to habits. If they have been previously trained, it will no longer be found necessary to question them on separate points. They will at once give the required explanation. Thus: Body light, that it may be easily sustained in air; long, slender, and tapering, that it may pass through air more swiftly and readily; thickest just below the neck, where the muscles of the wings are developed, that the muscles may be large and powerful enough to move them; tapering, for lightness; tail expanded, to help to support the body; length of wing, indicating the immense power of flight; very wide mouth, for catching its prey on the wing; delicate beak, corresponding with the general delicacy of the bird, indicating the soft character of its food; slender legs, not required for walking; thick plumage, to meet alteration of temperature; glossy plumage, that little friction may impede its flight. Teacher directs attention to habits, which children do not so readily discover: That of keeping insects in the mouth till many are collected; that of clinging to roofs, &c., when resting for a moment in flight.

III. Teacher presents specimens of swift and marten. Children compare these with swallow. Find swift the largest; can fly farthest; marten the least. Swallow distinguished by the peculiar beauty and burnish of its plumage. Information given as to the number of hours these birds pass in the air daily. Character of their movements. (Exercise the conceptive faculty.) Kind of nest. Special kind of food. Time of their appearance and departure. Countries to which they migrate. Scripture and poetical reference.

Summary.—Children write out lesson under heads:
I. Birds of swallow tribe. How distinguished?
II. General structure.
III. Habits, and adaptation of structure to them.

2. Incidental Lesson on the Habitations of Birds.

I. *Introduction.*—Get a list from the children with reference to the various habitations and localities of birds. (W. B., supplying their omissions.) The list may stand thus: Eagle, owl, lark, rook, magpie, ostrich, hen, swallow, heron, sea gull.

II. Let the children say what they know about the eagle. What sorts of places it frequents, or where it rears its young? Give any information required, and help the children to form a vivid conception of the craggy mountain top, far above the distant village; the few sticks that indicate a nest, &c.; the owl in the church tower, covered with ivy, looking forth at night like a sentinel; the lark, hidden in the meadow, springing up, soaring, singing; the rook, with its companions in the tops of the tall trees near the mansion house; the magpie on the apple tree in the cottage garden; the ostrich, with even pace, faster than the gallop of a horse, scudding over the interminable expanse of sand; the hen in the farmyard, by the barn door; the swallow circling above the pond; the heron on the edge of the marshy pool in the hollow of the dark moor; the sea gull cresting the white waves, or resting on the cliffs that border them. The children will recognize the goodness of God in peopling the world with so many beautiful and happy creatures. They will be ready to say: "O Lord, how manifold are thy works; in wisdom hast thou made them all; the world is full of thy goodness."

CLASS MAMMALIA.

1. The children, having finished the course on birds, may be required to draw on their previous knowledge of mammals, and to make a classification of them on the blackboard. A record of their work should be kept.

2. Next time teacher offers some help, directing their attention to the points which should guide them in classifying; as, limbs, teeth. They make a second list.

3. Next time the teacher gives them the number of orders. Children make third classification, which is compared with the proper one. Where this differs from theirs, and why?

The separate groups of mammals may now be taken up, but usually with brevity. Example:

1. *The Dog Tribe.*

I. Origin of dogs. Other animals of the dog tribe. Animals of the dog tribe named. Their general characteristics. Origin of the domestic dog. Whether from the jackal? the fox? the wolf? or an original dog? Resemblance in habits to the jackal, and in structure to the wolf. Point of difference in position of the eyes, and possible reason for this. Comparison of the wolf and dog as to disposition.

II. Domesticated dogs. Different groups, and characteristics of each. European dogs compared with those of the East. Scripture illustrated. European dogs divided into three groups:

    1. Arctic dogs.
    2. Hunting dogs.
    3. Watch dogs.

1. *Arctic Dogs.*—Where found? From the name, children decide in the north of Europe and Iceland, though also in Kamtchatka and China. How distinguished? Very sharp muzzle; pointed ears; shaggy hair, long at the neck; elevated curled tail; color black, white, or black and white. How connected with the second group (by the Newfoundland.)

2. *Hunting Dogs.*—Where found? In all the temperate regions, but especially in Europe. How distinguished (large pendulous ears; large jaws; long legs; thick tails). What the group includes (fox hound, stag hound, pointer, setter, terrier, and Danish dog—spaniel a cross).

3. *Watch Dogs.*—Found in all temperate climates. Physical characteristics not so marked as in the other groups. Greater variety in all respects. Reason for this. Includes all shepherd dogs; also mastiff, bulldog, and greyhound; the two last at first sight dissimilar, but nearly allied, having delicate feet, slender tail, good sight, imperfect smell, ferocious disposition. Irish greyhound called *wolf dog*. Anecdote of. How the third group is connected with the first? By the shepherd's dog. How with the second? By the greyhound.

III. Conclusion drawn as to the general characteristics of each group. The first are nearest to a state of nature; the second show in the highest degree the effects of physical cultivation; the third have most intelligence. Anecdotes proving this. Use of the dog to man, in every state. Goodness of God in giving him such a friend.

2. *The Cat Tribe.*

Animals of the cat tribe compared with those of the dog tribe. (Terms *feline* and *canine* given.)

1. Compared with respect to structure: Body, limbs, feet, shape of head, eyes, and teeth, covering, feelers.
2. With respect to habits: One found in packs, and the other alone, or with its mate. Character of food. Methods of securing their prey, &c.
3. With respect to appearance: Beautiful markings, spots, &c., on the glossy fur of the one; shaggy hair of the other.
4. With respect to distribution: The canine tribe is found all over the globe; the feline tribe chiefly in torrid regions, thinly inhabited by man. Wisdom of this arrangement. Species of each tribe distinguished. What species are found in the Old World, and what in the New?

INCIDENTAL LESSONS.

3. *Animals Used in Hunting.*

I. *Animals of the Dog Tribe.*—Draw from the children the fact that animals hunt as well as men. What kinds of animals hunt? Dogs. Children to say how the dog is adapted for hunting. Refer to the wolf as a natural hunter.

II. *Animals of the Cat Tribe.*—Tell the children that in Eastern countries animals of the cat tribe are used for hunting. Let them compare these with creatures of the dog tribe, and find out which make the best hunters. Creatures of the cat tribe (*a*) cannot run far; (*b*) are less docile; (*c*) are more bloodthirsty. Give account of the chetah, and, from the facts before discovered, let the children say why it must be brought in a cart to the field? Why blindfolded? Why allowed to drink the blood of its prey?

III. *Animals of the Weasel Tribe.*—Produce picture or specimen of a ferret. Refer to its tribe. Kind of animals it hunts (rats and mice). How adapted to this kind of hunting? Tell children that it is often muzzled, and set to hunt rabbits. Compare the cat, dog, and ferret, as *tameable* creatures. Refer to the otter and ichneumon, creatures of the ferret tribe, as employed in India and Egypt. Conclude with reference to the power given by God to man over the inferior creatures. How it should be used?

4. *Sketch on Rodents.*

I. *Order.*—Present stuffed specimen or picture of the squirrel, rabbit, hare, rat, mouse. All or any, with a picture of a beaver. Children, who name each, are told they are grouped together, and required to find the basis of classification. It might be *size*, for they are small animals; or *disposition*, for they are timid; or *character of food*, for they live on hard substances; but the children know that animals are classed according to structure, especially the structure of the feet and teeth. Examination of the feet presents no special characteristics. We must look to the teeth. These creatures are named from the manner in which they use these. They gnaw, and are therefore called *rodents*.

II. *Structure of Teeth.*—Teeth of specimens examined, and diagram placed on the board.

1. Incisors: Sharp at the edge, chisel shaped, meeting the opposite teeth in a semicircle ◡. Tell children that the front surface is of the hardest enamel, the inner surface of softish bone. What must happen to teeth that are constantly working against very hard substances? They must wear away rapidly. How this is provided for by constant growth of teeth, &c. Which surface will wear away the sooner? (The inner surface.) Effect of this arrangement on the shape of the teeth—securing always a sharp edge.

2. Grinders: Ridges—their direction, from side to side. Children find in what direction the rodent must move its mouth to grind its food. Are told the creatures are furnished with a strong muscle, which gives great power to the movement of the jaw.

3. Canine teeth absent. Rodents have no weapon of defence. Children to find five means by which they are protected.

  1. They are small.
  2. They are very timid.

3. They have large eyes.
4. They have ears pointing backward.
5. They have long bodies.

Use of each point to the rodent?

III. *Summary.*—Substance written on the board as dictated by the children; the teacher, however, leaving ellipses for them to supply in reproducing the lesson on paper.

Gnawing animals include ———. They are so named because ———. They have sharp ———, which enables them to ———. The front surface is ———, the under merely ———. Constant feeding upon ——— causes ———. This is remedied by ———. The soft bone wears away, while the ———. The advantage of this is ———. The grinders are ———, so that in masticating the food the jaw must be ———. The jaws have great power, owing to ———. Canine teeth are ———. The rodents have many enemies; cannot ———, but often escape, because ———.

5. *Clothing of Animals.*

I. *Introduction.*—Let the children know the subject of the lesson. Get them to name animals having different clothing. If they are slow in giving examples, suggest the animal, and let them say how it is clad. Put down each answer on the board, thus:

The cat is covered with fur.
The herring is covered with scales.
The horse is covered with hair.

II. *Classification.*—Help the children to classify the facts, putting them on the board, asking where each creature lives, and marking those that live on earth with fig. 1; those that live on air, with fig. 2; those that live both on land and in water, with fig. 3; give the term *amphibious;* and those that live in water only, with fig. 4. Children state the clothing of each set (W. B.) from dictation. Mammals are clothed with fur, hair, wool, or skin only. Birds are clothed with feathers; some have an undergarment of down. Reptiles with a thick skin, scales, or shelly plate. Fish, with thin scales.

III. *Adaptation.*—Let the children imagine a creature like a horse, with a covering of feathers. Why they would not suit him? They would be much too warm. With a covering of scales not warm enough, yet would check perspiration. Refer to the condition of horses after a gallop; the structure of their skin, &c. With a shelly covering; this, by its weight and stiffness, would impede motion. The horse has a skin just suited to it. But feathers are the covering for the eagle—why? Scaly plates for a crocodile—why? A thick, hairless skin for an elephant—why? Scales for a mackerel—why? Why jointed? Go over the list, leading the children to see the adaptation in each case. One cannot do this without reference to the infinite wisdom and goodness of God manifested in this adaptation.

A series of lessons corresponding to the last should be given, thus:

1. Limbs of animals, and their movements.
2. Localities (general) in which animals are found.
3. Breathing, and circulation of blood.
4. Form in which the young first appear.
5. Finally, the children should be led to distinguish vertebrated animals from others, and to put them into the four great divisions:

Mammals.   Birds.   Reptiles.   Fishes.

The teacher can proceed in the same way with invertebrated animals. It is evident, however, that the later courses must become less full, and more general, than the earlier ones.

In conclusion, the scholar should be led to recognize all the groups as component parts of the one great system of animated nature. See Mrs. Redfield's "Chart of the Animal Kingdom."

LESSONS ON PLANTS.

DESIGNED AS THIRD STEP LESSONS.

On the Nature of Plants.

THE teacher should be prepared with an object for the lesson selected from each grand division of the natural kingdom; as, a plant, an animal, and a stone. Call upon the children to observe that the three are very different. Tell them to find out something which may be said of all of them, but which could not be said of a hat, a knife, or a watch. The plant, the animal, and the stone, were made as they are by God; man did not make them. We call them *natural*.* To which of the three objects are *you* most like? In what respect do you and the plant differ from the stone? What will some day happen both to you and to the plant, which never can happen to the stone? We and the plant shall die. (See that the children understand, that when we speak of death, as applied to plants, we mean that they cease to live, and then decay.) In what, then, does the stone differ from animals and plants? The stone has not life. What can you say of a vegetable? That it has life. What do living things need to support their life? Food. Where do animals take in their food? By what organ? By the mouth. Where do vegetables take in their food? By what organ? By their roots. In what, then,

---

* It is not expected that the children will so immediately arrive at this conclusion, but the question is suggested in order to show that the idea is to be drawn from them, their minds being stimulated and directed by the questioning of the teacher. The answers are inserted in order to indicate the point to which they are to be brought.

do animals and vegetables differ from stones? Animals and vegetables require food to support life; but stones have no life which might need support. In what do animals differ from vegetables? Animals take in their food by the mouth, but vegetables by the root. What other benefits do these derive from food? Besides that of being kept alive by it, it makes them grow. What are animals able to do, that cannot be done by vegetables? What does a lion, when he is hungry? What a hare, when pursued by dogs? What do you in the playground? For whose pleasure do you run or jump? You move about when you like. Thus you find that animals can move at pleasure from place to place. But is this the case with vegetables? Suppose a plant drooping for water, and that there was water near, could it get at it? Why not? Because it is fixed to one spot in the earth.

Tell me all that you have found out regarding plants, by comparing them with animals and stones. Vegetables are made—*by God;** we therefore call them—*natural;* they have—*life;* their life is supported by—*food;* this they take in at their—*roots;* food makes them—*grow;* they are fixed to one spot in—*the earth,* and cannot—*move about*—as—*they please.*

There should be a simultaneous repetition of this by all the children, to fix it well in their memories.

The Several Parts of a Plant.

Commence with questions on the preceding lesson, as to how a plant is distinguished, with a repetition of the summary; then lead the children to find out the principal parts of a plant. These are, the root, stems, leaves, blossom, fruit or seed vessel, seeds. The names of these should be written down, and frequently simultaneously repeated. The relative position of the different parts, and the period in the existence of the plants at which they severally appear, might form the subject of conversation.

---

* The words in italics are to be given by the children. The ellipsis is very useful in maintaining attention and interest in the summing up of a lesson.

THE ROOT.

1. *The Use of the Root to the Plant, as an Organ of Nourishment.*

The children should have several roots and pictures of roots to examine. They should be led to observe that they all have fibres, and they may be informed that these fibres are the true roots, and that at the end of each of them there is a substance like sponge. If questioned as to the properties of sponge, and as to the use of such a substance to the plant, they may be led to discover that these *spongioles*, as they are called, suck up from the earth, as so many mouths, the moisture which nourishes the plant. The class may be led to observe how very suitable such a substance is for the office it has to perform, and that, while God has withheld from plants the power of moving about to get their food, He has provided a beautiful compensation by furnishing them with a multitude of mouths, each of them placed at the end of a long fibre, and that these stretch out in all directions. The observation of this fact, and the proof it affords of the providential care of the Creator, should be drawn from the children. They may also find out the reason why gardeners, when they transplant roots, are careful not to injure these fibres. If all the fibres of the root were destroyed, the plant must die, for it could not obtain nourishment.

2. *The Use of the Root in Fixing the Plant in the Earth.*

The children, having considered the root as an organ of nourishment, should next consider it as to its office of supporting the plant while growing in the earth. Its position is under ground; it is the lowest part of the plant. When a seed begins to grow, it sends downward a root, avoiding light, and seeking moisture. The children should find out of what use the root is in consequence of its position. They may be led to see that things will not stand firmly, if the top be not well balanced by the base. How is a plant balanced and fixed firmly? The roots extend in the earth in proportion to the size of the upper part. The roots of large trees branch out in all directions, and spread to a very great distance.* Draw upon the board a tree with its roots, that the children may perceive that the wide-spreading branches of the root act as a counterpoise to the head, and even extend beyond the boughs. Lead them to see that there is a reason why the mouth of the roots should stretch beyond the foliage, for they are thus enabled to obtain the moisture which the earth receives from the rain, which does not penetrate generally through the foliage near the trunk. How wise a provision for the plant is this extension of its roots! Let the children gather from this where a large plant should be watered; not, of course, just at the stem, but at a short distance, that the water may reach the spongioles of the roots.

3. *The Use of the Root in carrying off Waste and Injurious Matter.*

The plant not only receives suitably nourishment, but also throws off waste and hurtful matter by the root; it is not, therefore, desirable to continue sowing the same seed year after year in the same spot, because the soil has been rendered unfit for the growth of the new plants by the matter rejected at the roots of former ones. Some different kind of seed should be chosen for each spot under cultivation, for it has been found by experience, that matter which one kind of plant rejects as injurious, is often suitable for the food of plants of a different species.† The system of agriculture pursued by the Israelites might here be mentioned, and the law as to land remaining fallow every seventh year might be read to the class. They might be led to see the value of this law to this people, who knew neither the advantage of a rotation of crops, nor the mode of enriching the earth by manures. This law, also, conveyed to them a spiritual lesson, for they were taught by types and shadows.

* Teachers may give great interest to their lessons by drawing on the board before the children diagrams of the subject of them.
† This fact is beyond the sphere of the children's observation; it must, therefore, be told them; but the observation on the consequences may be drawn from them, as a reason for a rotation of crops.

DIFFERENT KINDS OF ROOTS.

The Globose Root.

The children should be shown specimens of different kinds of roots, and pictures of others. What have all roots? What is there at the end of the fibres? What is the use of the spongy substance? Why do plants require so many mouths? Attention should now be drawn to the different forms of roots. First give a lesson on the turnip, for instance. The children will observe its two principal parts—the fibres, which are the true roots, and the thick part, like a globe, from which the root is called the *globose root*. The children already know the use of the fibres and spongioles, but what is the use of this globe? It contains a store of nourishment for the plant, by means of which it brings its flower and seed to perfection. Where are turnips cultivated? Of what use are they? What part of the plant is eaten? When are the roots fit for food? Before the store of nutritious matter which the globe contains has been exhausted in maturing the flower and seed. All farmers and gardeners are aware of this, and act accordingly.

The Tapering Root.

Let the children examine the pictures of the various roots; then tell them to select a root of a very different shape from the turnip—the *carrot*—and let them describe this root, its parts and shape; and when it has become familiar, tell them its name—the *tapering root*. They will at once see why it is so named. Which are the true roots? The fibres and their spongioles. This root, though of such a different shape, performs the same important office to the plant as the globose root. The children can tell what this is, and also determine when carrots should be dug up. Let them give a list of the tapering roots which are usually cultivated, describing the peculiarities of each of them, and how it is distinguished from others. The list should then be written on the board. The more common tapering roots are **the carrot, parsnip, radish, beet, mangel-wurzel, and horse radish.**

Tuberous Roots.

Let the children next examine the roots of the potato plant and of the dahlia, which are similar in kind. What are the two principal parts? The fibres and the knobs. How do these roots differ from those already considered? They are composed of several knobs joined together. Yes; and these knobs differ from those of the turnip and parsnip. Find out in what respect they differ. Ask the children if they know in what way farmers and gardeners plant potatoes? If they do not, they should be shown the little specks on the potatoes, called the *eyes*. These are buds, of the same nature as the buds we see on trees in the spring, and at that season they begin to sprout, and the potato in this state is not fit for food, being full of black spots. Question the children as to the cause of these black spots, and why potatoes at that season are not good to eat. They ought to be able to reply, that the nourishing matter which made the root a wholesome vegetable, is expended in the shoots. The gardener, when he cuts out the eye for planting,* takes a portion of the potato with it, which affords nourishment to the bud till it has formed roots to obtain nourishment for itself. The children will now be able to find out the use of the knob (called a *tuber*) to the plant, and in what state the potato is best for food. These roots are called *tuberous roots*. Describe a tuberous root. The dahlia root is of this kind. In the spring the tubers send out sprouts, which the gardener cuts out, and from these new plants are raised. What a beautiful provision it is that the nourishing matter stored up for plants in their roots, should be so pleasant and so good for the use of man! What a blessing to the poor that so wholesome a vegetable as the potato is so easily cultivated, and that it multiplies so very abundantly! †

---

* A teacher would greatly increase the interest of the lesson, by putting into practice what is here described; planting some potatoes and dahlias, allowing some of the children to give assistance, and then observing their after growth.

† These observations should be drawn from the children. It is the art of the teacher to lead them to draw right conclusions and moral reflections from facts observed.

Bulbous Roots.

The children should mention the different roots upon which they have had lessons, describing and pointing out each several species.* Does the picture contain any root like those on which lessons have been given? Yes; the onion. Show them also a tulip, crocus, and snowdrop root. In what respect do they seem like the turnip? Though they appear to be like it, they are really different; for these knobs of the onion, tulip, &c., which are called *bulbs*, contain within them during the winter season the young † plant, though of course it is then very small. These bulbs have been compared to a winter cradle, as they keep the plant shut up snug and warm within them during cold weather. This root is called a *bulbous root*. Describe it.

Fibrous Roots.

Let the children say what they observe all roots to have— fibres. Let them give examples of roots that have fibres *only*. Let them find a good name for such roots—*fibrous roots*. Some trees have a large tapering root, called the *tap root*. It descends straight into the earth, and from it proceed great branches, terminating in fibres. A root of this description should be drawn on the board, and the children, from what they have before learned, will be able to say why such a root is necessary for a tree.

The concluding lesson on roots should be recapitulatory. The children should tell the names of the different roots on which lessons have been given, and these should be written on the board;‡ then they should be questioned somewhat as follows: What are the two principal parts of the globose root? Of what use are the fibres? Of what use to the plant is the globular part? When is it best for food? Describe the tapering root. What are its principal parts and uses? In what does it differ from the globose

---

* In the first lesson the roots should be brought in and shown the children; but in the subsequent lessons, when they are only referred to, the teacher should draw them on the board.

† In the spring time, if a root of a tulip be cut longitudinally through the middle, the plant may be seen within the bulb.

‡ The questions might form the subject of a home exercise.

root? Of what is the tuberous root formed? What is the use of the tubers? How are plants raised from them? What is the most common of these roots? What is a bulbous root? What use is the bulb to the plant? What are the different uses of roots to plants? How are they fitted for their different uses? When any one makes an instrument well fitted to perform a difficult work, what do we say of him? And if, in addition, we find that he has made it for the use and benefit of others, what more do we say of him? But who made plants, and gave them different parts, fitting them to perform different offices, to contribute to the comfort of man? What, then, must we acknowledge God to be? Wise and kind. What does the Bible tell us of the work of God? Do you remember what God said of everything when first made? "Behold, it was very good."

STEMS.

The children should be shown various kinds of stems; as, a piece of a tree, a straw, and a succulent stem—that of a geranium, for instance. Let them arrange stems under three heads, describing each, and finding examples of it. A name should then be given by which they may distinguish each division, and these should be written on the board.

1. FLESHY OR SOFT STEMS, as in herbaceous plants and annuals.
2. STRAW, as in grains and grasses.
3. WOODY STEMS, as in trees and shrubs.

Show the children several specimens of these different stems, and encourage them to bring others, and to say to which of the three divisions they belong. Draw from them what difference they perceive in these stems.

THE FLESHY STEM is soft, full of juice, generally of a green color, and lies down on the ground in winter. What stems of this description do we eat? Celery, rhubarb, sea-kale. Some of these stems are very fibrous, and are very useful on this account, the fibres being manufactured into articles of dress and furniture. This subject should be enlarged upon. A stem of flax and hemp should be produced, together with a picture of the plant, the manufactured fibre, and the various substances made from it. The children should find out what qualities in the fibre make it thus useful.

STRAW is stiff and hollow, having hard joints at regular distances, which give it strength, so that while it bends to the wind and rises again by its elasticity, it is also able to support the ear. From the possession of these properties the grain is continually brought under the drying influence of the air, and the ripening influence of the sun. Straw is used for bonnets, baskets, mats; for thatching, litter in farmyards, &c.

The sugar cane is a kind of straw, full of a sweet juice, which is squeezed out, boiled, and made into sugar.

WOODY STEMS.—The children should have some specimens to examine, that they may describe this stem, and tell its parts. It is hard, dry, strong, and stiff; its parts are bark, wood, pith.* Let them describe a tree. A tree has an upright supporting stem, called a *trunk;* this is of cylindrical form, tapering upward like a pillar, and is admirably suited for supporting a heavy weight. From this trunk proceed smaller stems, called *branches*, and from these others still smaller, called *twigs*, upon which the leaves grow. The children should see pictures of the various trees and their parts, that they may observe the different manner in which the branches grow. After having had lessons on form, they would of themselves observe, that the boughs of the oak form nearly a right angle with the trunk, whilst in the poplar they form a very acute angle; and they will perceive that it is this which causes the great difference in the form and appearance of trees. Let them give a list of the names of forest trees, to be written on the board, describing also the use of each; and then give a list of

* It is needless to point out exactly what the children will be able to tell from their own observation, and what must be communicated: well practised teachers will find but little in these lessons which they will not be able to get from their elder division of pupils, provided they bring in the necessary specimens, and direct rightly their attention, commencing with questions upon what is familiar to them. Whatever information is given should be well engrafted upon what was previously known, and the latter should be reproduced by questions, answered either *vivâ voce*, or at home on paper.

trees that furnish us with eatable fruit. Lead them to observe the comfortable shade afforded by trees in the summer, and their exceeding beauty. Let them next describe the different parts of the woody stem.

BARK.—Its qualities: Rough, hard, and fibrous, fitted to act like clothing to the stem, and to protect it from the effects of the weather. Try to discover what the children know of the uses of different kinds of bark. Specimens should be brought before them, that they may point out the difference in their appearance. Show them some tan—it is the bark of the oak. They know its use—to tan leather. What effect has it upon the leather? It draws the fibres closer together, causing the leather to keep out wet. Some barks are used as strengthening medicines, and affect the human frame something in the same way that tan strengthens the leather. Cork is the bark of a peculiar kind of oak. A piece of the bark in its natural state should be produced, and the qualities of cork elicited.

WOOD.—Its qualities: A new circle is formed every year in the wood of a growing tree; this is seen by the rings; its uses for fuel, for buildings of all kinds, and for furniture; the qualities that fit it for its various uses.* Different woods used for differing purposes; as, oak for ships, posts, &c., on account of its durability and hardness; mahogany for furniture, on account of its beautiful color; pine for housebuilding, &c., on account of its lightness, softness, cheapness, and abundance.

PITH.—A branch of the alder tree should be shown the children, that they may examine it, and give its qualities. Rushlights are made of the pith of rushes dipped in tallow. The poor people of England often make their own lights by dipping pith obtained from reeds in tallow. Sago, of which nutritious puddings are made, is the pith of a palm tree.

CIRCULATION OF SAP.

The children should be questioned as to the circulation of the blood, its journey from the heart throughout the body and lungs,

* It is to be recollected that these lessons are only hints for the assistance of teachers.

supporting life. They may then be told that plants also have a fluid which in a similar manner flows through them, supporting and nourishing the life of every part. The root absorbs moisture from the ground; this ascends into the plant, and reaching the leaves, undergoes a change, becoming suitable food for the plant; it then descends again, this fluid supplying nourishment to every part in its course. It is called *sap*.

In addition to food for the plant, juices, which vary in their nature in different vegetables, are produced from the sap, some of them very useful to man. The children should be questioned whether they ever saw juice oozing out of a tree? They may have seen this in fruit trees, or in the oozing of turpentine out of deal. The chief of these vegetable juices are gum, resin, vegetable milks, acids, oils, tar, turpentine, and water.

Gums.—Some gum, soft from the tree, and some gum arabic, should be shown to the children, and they should say all they know of gum, and the trees which yield it. How does it appear when oozing out? What effect has the air upon it? What qualities distinguish it? Its adhesiveness; its solubility in water; its use as a cement.

Resins are vegetable products, which ooze out of pines, firs, &c. The more common resins are pitch, tar, turpentine. The children should see them, and describe their qualities and uses. Resins are distinguished from gums by dissolving in spirit of wine, but not in water, as the gums do.

Frankincense—mentioned in Scripture, and used as an incense, a type of that intercession of Christ which makes our prayers acceptable to God—is an aromatic resin.

Balm of Gilead, also mentioned in the Bible,* and celebrated for its healing properties, is another resin.

Oils are also vegetable liquids, peculiar to some plants. The perfume sent forth by various plants is caused by volatile oils. These, when pressed out of the plants containing them, afford us fragrant scents. The oils in common use are chiefly obtained from

---

* The teacher should refer to the Scriptures, in which these substances are spoken of.

seeds, in which they exist as nourishment for the tender plant, when it first begins to shoot forth. A great deal of oil is obtained from nuts, and much also from the seed of flax; the latter is called *linseed oil*. The oil we use in food is pressed out of the fruit of the olive. Lead the children to observe how all nature contributes good things to promote the comfort and pleasure of man. It is our duty to receive all these as God's gifts.

The children should have some oil to examine. They should find out those qualities which distinguish it from other substances, and make it so useful; no information being given till all they know or can discover has been drawn from them. The mind having been thus brought into an active, inquiring state, they will be interested in hearing anything new concerning any object which may be the subject of instruction. Lessons should always conclude with a summary, in which, by means of the ellipsis, the children should reproduce all they have heard.

VEGETABLE MILKS.—The children may form some idea of the milky substance which is found in many plants, by breaking the stem of a spurge. In this plant the milk is of a caustic nature, and used to remove warts. The milky fluid of plants is often poisonous, producing fatal sleep. It is so in the case of that obtained from the poppy and lettuce, from which are prepared opiates, which are used in small doses to relieve pain and to cause sleep.

INDIA RUBBER is obtained from a kind of laurel tree. When it flows out of the tree it is a milky fluid, but it soon becomes thick, and hardens in the air; it is then dried over the smoke of a wood fire, which makes it black. The children should name the qualities and uses of India rubber. This vegetable substance has of late years been extensively used in rendering cloths impervious to air and water, and also in the formation of instruments in which elasticity and flexibility are required.

There is a liquid that flows out of a tree in America, which very much resembles the milk of the cow, and the tree is called the *cow tree*. It is a great blessing to the people of that country, for it grows in rocky, dry, and barren places, which would not produce herbage for cattle. During many months no rain falls there, but the tree has dry leathery leaves, which live very long without any moisture; and when the branches look quite dry and withered, if the trunk be pierced, there will flow out a sweet, nourishing milk; and at sunrise the natives may be seen hastening with their bowls, which are generally the shells of some fruit, to obtain this nice vegetable milk. All this must be told the children; but having previously seen what a vegetable milk is, they will be the more interested in the subject. The use to be made of the history is the leading them to see how beautifully God provides for His creatures, and how exactly He adapts both animals and vegetables to the countries in which He places them.*

HONEY.—This is a familiar vegetable juice. The children well know how the bee obtains it, and treasures it up in waxen cells, and they will be able to tell its qualities. A reference may be made to the promise given to the Israelites in the wilderness, that the land which God would give them was to be a land flowing with milk and honey. They may be led to see that this involved its being a land rich in vegetation, possessing abundance of flowers for the bees, and herbage for the cows, to make both honey and milk abundant. We are told that Palestine abounded in these aromatic flowers which produce the best honey.

THE STINGING POWER of such plants as the nettle, resides in a poisonous liquid contained in a little bag at the bottom of a sharp hollow bristle. When the bristle is struck, this fluid is pressed up through it, and flows out through it into any wound the bristle may have made in the skin, causing the pain and irritation of the sting.

The children should now name the peculiar juices of plants

---

* These facts must be communicated to the children, but the reflection should be drawn from them. They should be trained to perceive and acknowledge the goodness of the Creator in his works. We are all ready enough to find out defects, and to express discontent at blessings withheld, whilst our innumerable daily mercies are received as a matter of course, without a thought. What we have to encourage in children, is, a quick perception of the wisdom and goodness manifested in the creation and providence of God, and the habit of gratefully acknowledging these; for feeling is increased by expression, and it is also thus communicated to others.

which they have learned, and, by the help of questions, recapitulate the lessons on this subject. They may also be reminded that all that would be injurious to the plant is separated from the sap and thrown out at the root, and that this, though bad for the plant producing it, may not be so for another; indeed, in some instances, that which is injurious to one kind of vegetable, is beneficial to another. Thus leguminous or podded plants, such as vetches and tares, prepare the soil for corn and grasses. How this variety in plants shows the wisdom and goodness of our Great Creator!

BUDS.

A variety of buds should be placed before the class, the children being helped to describe what they are. They are little bodies which are formed on the surface of vegetables, sometimes containing a future shoot, sometimes leaves, sometimes flowers, and in some cases leaves and flowers together. They preserve the new parts of the plant from the severities of winter, and, therefore, are sometimes called *winter cradles.*

The leaves are often curiously folded within the bud, where, as the children may discover by examination of each on the outside, are generally hard scales. These are only the outer leaves, which, having been chilled and checked in their growth, become stiff and hard, and curve inward, thus forming scales that protect the inner leaves. This occurs only in cold climates, where such protection is necessary, and thus a simple yet beautiful provision is given the plant for self-preservation. Besides this, the young leaves are often surrounded within the bud by a cottony substance, which resists the cold. They are also sometimes covered with a clammy varnish, which protects them from the rain, as is the case in those of the horse chestnut. In what position are buds formed? The children may discover that it is at the angle formed between a leaf stalk and a stem. The reason of this is, that here the sap, when passing from the leaves, does not flow so easily. It is stopped, and a little accumulation is formed, which is the cause of a bud being produced. This takes place in the summer and autumn. In spring the warmth of the sun causes the bud to expand, and to draw up the sap from the parts below, which are again supplied by the parts still lower, and thus the sap in the plant is set in motion, and this is what is called the *flow of the sap.* This might be made clear to the children by drawing on the board a plant with buds, and pointing out the course taken by the sap.

The Use of Buds.—They are not only useful in keeping the future shoots alive during the winter season, but they afford also the means of multiplying plants. Each bud is a complete little plant in itself, having within it everything necessary for the existence of the plant that springs from it, together with the power of sustaining life under favorable circumstances.* Gardeners know this, and cutting off the bud from one plant, they place it in a cut upon the stem of another, the sap of which flows into the bud, causing it to grow. This operation is called *budding.* Plants are also raised by laying a branch under ground, that the buds it contains may send roots downward and shoots upward; then, when the branch is cut off from the old plant, it becomes a new plant. It is from this power of life in the buds that plants can be raised from slips. Vegetables, indeed, are full of buds, and this is a most wise provision for their preservation. They cannot defend themselves, or flee from their enemies as animals can, for they are fixed to one spot. How has God made up for this? He has furnished them with a multitude of buds, each of which is capable of reproducing life, so that a plant may be cut in every direction, or stripped of all its branches, and yet, if any bud remain, there still is left a source of life, from which new shoots may be produced. When a shrub has been cut down to the ground, it will often spring up vigorously the year following, because some buds have been left on its stump. How beautifully has the all-wise Creator suited everything to the situation in which it is placed, and to the work it has to perform! Each leaf and each bud proclaims His wisdom and goodness. When we see His wonders of creation, shall we not praise and glorify him? Yes. He has declared that

---

* Some of these facts may be rather difficult for the children to understand; anything that may prove to be beyond their capacity may be omitted; but it is very desirable to give them a reason for the common operations they may see practised by gardeners and farmers.

His praise shall come even out of the mouth of babes and sucklings!

There are three kinds of buds: those which produce the flower only, others that produce only leaves and branches, and a third description which develop both leaves and flowers. A good gardener knows how to promote the formation of the flower buds, which afterward produce the fruit. When the sap flows through the tree rapidly, it forms the most leaf buds; but when it flows more slowly, it becomes richer and thicker, and forms flower buds. By training the branches of the tree horizontally, the gardener causes the sap to flow more slowly than it would do were they upright, and thus he obtains more flower buds, and, consequently, more fruit.

The picture of the garden will be found useful in explaining and illustrating these and other occupations of the gardener.

LEAVES.

The children should examine some leaves, and find out the parts of a leaf; as, the upper and under surface, the leaf stalk, the limb (that is, the whole expansion), the point or termination, the edge, the mid-rib, the veins. They should next be led to observe, from some well-selected specimens,* how these parts are characterized, and in what they differ in different plants. The upper surface of the leaf is generally smooth and bright, and of a darker color than the under surface, which is dull; the middle rib is furrowed or grooved at the upper surface, and keeled or ridged at the under surface. The course of the veins is sometimes direct from the leaf stalk to the termination; in other cases they form quite a net-work. Whenever a vein pushes out very strongly, it forces out a part of the limb, and in this way is caused the variety in the form of leaves.† All this, under a little guidance, may be discovered by the children themselves. The edge of a leaf is sometimes

---

* The children's interest will be increased if they are encouraged to bring specimens for their lesson.

† The more of these facts the children discover themselves, the greater will be their pleasure in the lesson; in this way also an inquiring habit of mind will be promoted.

quite plain or entire, sometimes very finely toothed, and sometimes the teeth are large; sometimes it is scallopped, sometimes jagged, sometimes hairy. The shape of leaves varies greatly. The children should determine, as nearly as they can, the shape of different leaves.

Leaves are curiously arranged on the stalks which bear them. Each of them has generally a leaf stalk, but sometimes they grow on the stem without this, and are then said to be sessile, or sitting. Sometimes they sheathe the stem, as in the grasses; sometimes two leaves are joined together, and the stem pierces through the pair; sometimes they grow in opposite pairs on the stem, sometimes on alternate sides, sometimes scattered, sometimes they surround the stem in a circle or whorl. The knowledge of these facts is of very minor importance, but such subjects furnish teachers with the means of calling out the observation of their pupils, and of encouraging habits that tend to render all nature interesting, thus putting the mind in possession of cheap and improving pleasure.

THE USE OF LEAVES TO THE PLANT.—Ask the children what effect exercise in hot weather produces upon the skin? Plants also perspire, and it is by means of their leaves that this healthy operation is carried on. Plants thus lose two thirds of the moisture absorbed at their spongioles. The fluid they perspire is nearly pure water; the thicker and more nourishing portions of the sap remain in the plant. Vegetables perspire the most in the sunshine; it is on this account that gardeners always protect newly transplanted plants from the rays of the sun, because, as the roots are not at such a time in a state to suck up much moisture, it is desirable that the leaves should not be giving off much fluid; for if the plant part with its moisture more rapidly than it is able to replenish it, it will wither and die. The children will be able to give the reason for this when they are told the fact.

Leaves perform to the plant the same office which the lungs perform for animals; they draw in that particular air which is good for their support, and throw off that which is waste and injurious. It is in the leaves also that the sap is made fit for nourishing the plant; just as in the stomach, food is rendered suitable for the sustenance of animal life.

Use of Leaves to Man.—The children will be able to find out much on this subject. It is the leaves that make trees so beautiful and so valuable for shade and protection from the weather. Our gracious Creator has given to trees such differing leaves as adapt them to different climates. On mountains where the snow is constantly falling, grow the firs and pines, the clusters of whose needle-shaped leaves allow the snow to fall between them; for the weight of the snow would soon break down boughs that were covered with broad leaves. Again, Ceylon, which is a country at one season deluged with rain, and at another parched with heat, has a tree called the *fan palm*, a single leaf of which is sufficiently large to afford shelter for twelve or fifteen people.

Leaves useful for Food.—Many kinds of leaves are good for food, as those of the cabbage, spinach, endive, lettuce, parsley, turnip, mustard and cress, &c. The leaves of the tea plant produce an agreeable drink; those of the senna, and others, are used as medicine. Tobacco and snuff are formed of leaves. Cattle feed upon grass, clover, turnip leaves, &c.

THE FLOWER.*

Lesson 1.

A variety of flowers being produced, the teacher takes up one of them, and asks, What is this? It is a flower. A perfect flower has four principal parts; try and find them out. What do you observe in these flowers? The teacher holds up a wall flower and a primrose. The colored leaves. These colored leaves of the flower form what is called the *corolla*. What is the first part of the flower that I am to write down on the board? The "corolla."

What else do you see as I hold up these flowers? Some

---

* The two following lessons on the flower were drawn out fully at the request of the teacher, and may serve to show the mode in which it is intended that such instruction should be given.

green leaves at the bottom of the corolla. Are they green in the wall flower? No. What is their general color? They are most frequently green. Of what use do these little leaves seem to be to the corolla? They hold its colored leaves together. What vessel do you think these leaves at all like? They are something like a cup. Yes; that part of the flower that holds the blossom is called *the cup.** What shall I now write under the word "corolla"? "The cup."

Now observe what I do to this flower, and tell me. You have pulled off the corolla and the cup. I did this that you might see what was within them. What do we find there? A little thing in the middle, with a round ball at the top. That little thread-like thing in the middle is called the *pistil*. Repeat this word together. What shall I write down? "The pistil." Now we will look for the pistils in the other flowers. Where shall I find them? In the middle, within the blossom. The pistil is a very important part of the flower. We will talk a little more about it some other time.

Do you see anything besides the pistil within the corolla? Yes; several little things like threads round the pistil. These are called *stamens*. Repeat the name together. Let us find out the stamens in the other flowers. What shall I write on the board? "Stamens."

Of how many parts of a flower are the names now written down? Of four parts. What are these four things which I have written on the board? The four principal parts of a flower. Repeat them over together. Name each part as I touch it. You shall tell me now where each part is placed in the flower. Where do you find the pistil? Within the corolla, in the middle of the flower. Where do you find the stamens? Within the corolla, and round about the pistil. Where is the corolla? It surrounds the stamens and pistil. Where is the cup? On the outside of the corolla, at the bottom of it; the corolla rises out of it.

What part of the flower seems to be the most carefully protected? The pistil. How is the pistil protected? By having all the other parts of the flower placed around it. Why is it so

* Calyx.

carefully guarded? You said that it was a very important part of the flower. Can you tell me when it is that the blossom and cup still more carefully guard the pistil and stamens, by being folded close around them? When the flower is in bud. When do your mothers take the most care of you, and are most afraid of any harm coming to you? When we are little babies. Yes; when you are young and helpless, then your mothers take the most care of you, and try to keep you from all harm; and so when the pistil and stamens are very young and tender, they are beautifully covered and folded up within the corolla and cup. Look at this bud. See how nicely the leaves are folded around the pistil, sheltering it from cold and rain.

Who made this pretty flower? God. Do not use that word lightly; think of what you are saying, and speak with reverence. The great God, who made the world we live in, the sun, and the moon, and the stars, made also this little flower; and what does the examination of this little flower teach us about the great God? That He takes care of that which He makes. And what does the Bible teach us—if He takes care of the flowers, what will He do for us? Much more will He care for us. Now tell me what you have to-day learned about a flower? We have learned its four principal parts. What are these? The corolla, the cup, the pistil, and the stamens. What more have you learned? We have seen where the several parts are placed. What did you learn from the consideration of the flower? That God takes care of all His works.

Lesson 2.

What are the four principal parts of a flower? Where is each part placed? Each of these principal parts of a flower has also some smaller parts belonging to it. Look at the corolla of this wall flower; of what is it formed? Of leaves. In what do those parts of a plant which are generally called its leaves differ from these? They are generally green, and are larger and thicker than these. And what can you say of these in the corolla of these flowers? They are of different colors. Where are *green* leaves placed? On the stems of plants. Where those of different colors? On the flower itself. These leaves that form the corolla are called *petals*. Write the word on the board under the names of the other parts.

The teacher shows the children several flowers, and says, Tell me in what other respect these petals vary, as well as in color. They vary in shape. Find out something more in which the corollas vary, besides in the color and shape of the petals. They vary in the number of their petals. How many petals has the wall flower? Four. How many the heart's-ease? Five. (The teacher pulls the petals off one by one to show the number.) Now observe when I pull off the corolla of the primrose or that of this periwinkle. These flowers have each but one petal. The primrose has but one colored leaf, but does it look like one petal? No, teacher; it looks as if several petals had been joined together. Yes; the petals are so joined together as to form one.

Then you find that a corolla may consist of—*petals*—that are —*joined together*,—and form only—*one portion;* of—*petals*—that are—*separate*. I shall be pleased with any one who will bring me to-morrow a corolla with its petals joined together into one piece, and another with its petals separate. In what respect have you found out that a corolla may vary? In the color, form, and number of its petals, and in their being joined together or separate.

What is that part of the flower which is outside the corolla? The cup. Of what is the cup formed? Of small leaves. These little leaves you may call *leaflets** of the cup. Repeat this name together. What shall I write down as another part of a flower? "Leaflets of the cup." Where shall I write this name? Under the word "petals." What is the general color of the leaflets? They are green. Now observe these cups, and you will find out in them something like that which you remarked in the blossom. In some of these the leaflets are joined together, in others they are separate.

Tell me the name of another part you noticed in the flower. The *pistil*. And what did I tell you was a very important part of the flower? The pistil. Now observe its parts: here is the large pistil of a tulip; but as, perhaps, you will scarcely perceive

* Sepals.

the different parts, I will draw one on the board. How many parts do you observe in the pistil? Three. Which are these? There is something at the top of it. That is called the *stigma*. Repeat the word together. What more? A kind of stalk. You may call it the *stem** of the pistil. What is the other part? A thicker part at the bottom. That is the seed vessel.† Now tell me the names of the three parts of the pistil, that I may write them also on the board. The *stigma*, the *stem*, the *seed vessel*. Now can you guess why I said that the pistil is a most important part of the flower? Because it contains the seed vessel. Where do we learn that God provided for the continuance of plants, by giving to each of them its own seed? In the first chapter of the Book of Genesis. God tells you this in His Word, and by examining His work you find what care He has taken to preserve the seed vessel. How is it protected? By its being placed within the corolla and the cup. Which is the more delicate of these two parts? The corolla. And where is the corolla placed? Within the cup. All the works of our Heavenly Father, from the smallest flower up to man himself, display His wisdom and goodness. Now repeat the names of the several parts of the pistil. The *stigma*, the *stem*, the *seed vessel*.

Which of the principal parts of the flower have you not yet examined? The stamens. Where are the stamens placed? Round the pistil. Here is a stamen taken out of this tulip; but see, I draw it on the board. What several parts do you observe in this? A thick part at the top. This is called the *anther*. Repeat this word together. The anther is like a little bag. Did you ever notice, that when you shake a flower, something comes out of it? Yes; some yellow dust. This dust or powder, which is very often yellow, comes out of these little bags; it is called *pollen*. Repeat this word. What is the pollen? It is a kind of yellow dust. Where is it found? Upon the anther. The use of this pollen is to perfect and nourish the seeds; as it falls from the anthers, it is caught upon the stigma of the pistils, which is always a little sticky, and porous like a sponge. The children should try and find out the reason for its being sticky, and also for its being

* Style.   † Germ, or Ovary.

porous. But there is another part of the stamen you have not mentioned; what is this? The *stem*. What, then, are the three parts of a stamen? The anther, the pollen, and the stem.

Now you shall repeat all you know about a flower. How many principal parts has a flower, and what are they called? There are four principal parts of a flower, called severally the *corolla*, the *cup*, the *pistil*, the *stamens*. How are they placed? The cup outside everything, the corolla within the cup, the pistil in the middle of the flower, and the stamens round about the pistil. Of what is the corolla composed? It is composed of petals. How do petals differ? They differ in form, color, number, and in being joined or separate. Of what is the cup formed? Of leaflets. What did you learn about leaflets? They are generally green, and, like the petals forming the corolla, are sometimes united and sometimes separate. What are the parts of the pistil? The stigma, stem, and seed vessel. What are the parts of the stamen? The anther, the pollen, and the stem. What did you learn about the stamens and pistil? That the pollen falls on the stigma of the pistil, which is sticky and like a sponge, and the use of the pollen is to perfect the seeds. What did you learn of God from examining a flower? That even a little flower shows His wisdom and His goodness.

FRUIT.

What law was made by God in the beginning of all things, to provide for the reproduction of vegetation? That herbs should yield seed, and the fruit tree fruit after his kind, whose seed is in itself. Each plant, by the law of God, is to produce its own seed, that it may be continued on the earth, and the seed is contained in a seed vessel. When are the seed vessel and its seed found on the plant? After the flower has been perfected, and has perished. It is by means of the flower that the seed is brought to perfection. The children are to be led to perceive, that when the different parts of the flower have performed their work, they wither and fall, and are succeeded by the seed vessel and seed. The former is the increased germ of the pistil; when matured, it is properly called the *fruit*, though that name is generally confined to such seed vessels as are eaten. The children should be shown a variety of seed vessels. They will see that they vary much in different plants. They should try to describe them. In many plants the seed vessel is nothing more than a dry case to contain the seeds, as in the poppy, the violet, the convolvulus. In the pea plant it is a *pod*. The particular pod of the cruciform flower is called a *sillicle*. The *drupe* is a fruit or seed vessel, formed of a soft, pulpy substance, which incloses a nut with a kernel, as the cherry, plum, peach, &c. The *nut* is a hard shell inclosing a kernel. The *pome* consists of a fleshy substance, inclosing a core containing cells in which the seeds, called *pips*, are placed; as, the apple, pear, &c. The *berry* contains the seed inclosed in a soft pulpy substance; as, the currant, the gooseberry, &c. Sometimes a number of berries are joined together to form the fruit, as in the raspberry, blackberry, &c. The *cone* consists of hard stiff scales, each covering a seed, as in the fir. Let the children name all the fruits that are eaten.

THE SEED.

What seems to be the most important work a plant has to accomplish? To bring its seed to perfection. Let the children try to find out the means taken to accomplish this. The richest sap goes to the production of the blossom. The parts of the blossom that form the seed are beautifully protected; the seed is inclosed in a case; the pulp of the fruit is for the nourishment of the seed, as well as for its protection. There are many beautiful contrivances for scattering seed over the face of the earth, in all of which the careful providence of the Almighty is manifested. The children will be able to recollect instances of this in the dandelion, groundsel, and thistle. The down that surrounds these seeds acts like wings, and the wind wafts them over the fields; they also adhere to the shaggy clothing of sheep, and other animals, and are carried to other spots by them; and also by birds, and even by insects. Though these plants are considered only as weeds, they form the food of many birds and quadrupeds, and when they decay they prepare the earth for more useful vegetation. The seeds of some trees are furnished with a thin scale, and the wind easily wafts them here and there. Everything in creation manifests the contriving wisdom of the Almighty, and His care for all His creatures. What should this teach us? To praise Him, and to trust in Him. The children should name all the seeds that are useful to man. The growth of the seed. What part has man in making it grow? He prepares the earth, and puts in the seed. What more does it need? Warmth and moisture. Who alone can send these? Whose blessing, then, should we seek when we sow our seeds? Whom should we thank, if they yield a plentiful supply? The seed, when it is placed in the ground, begins to swell and decay; it then sprouts, and its own decaying matter at first feeds the young shoot; this sends a root downward and a stem upward. Through the porous earth it receives the air and moisture it requires, and is kept from the light, which would prevent its growth.

In all the above lessons, the parts spoken of should invariably be presented to the class.

It would be desirable that the children should learn to distinguish a few of the principal families of plants; as, the corns, peas, the cruciform, rosaceous, liliaceous flowers, and others, which should be taken up in the next grade or Step.

MORAL INSTRUCTION.

THE axiom enunciated by Pestalozzi as the basis of his system, is, that "education has to deal with the *heart*, the *head*, and the *hand;*" and therefore, to be complete, it must be *moral, intellectual,* and *physical.* He wisely gives the *heart* the first place; the wise Solomon also says, "Out of it are the issues of life."

All moral instruction must be founded on the truths of the *Gospel.*

In the First Step, the teacher seeks to awaken the moral sense; to lead the child to distinguish right from wrong; to make *moral impressions,* thus preparing for religious impressions.

In the Second Step, the child learns to distinguish, appreciate, and name *moral qualities.*

In the Third Step, the child is led to consider moral conduct, and to distinguish *moral character.* He continues to observe moral qualities, not as isolated, but as constituting character.

In the Fourth Step, the child proceeds to consider the relations of moral qualities, the basis on which moral conduct ought to rest; its results. In short, he commences the study of *moral principles.*

FIRST STEP.

MORAL IMPRESSIONS.

1. *Sketch on Habits of Order.*

I.—Bring before the children several objects; as, a cup, saucer, spoon, chair, tray and snuffers, candle and candlestick.

Let a child arrange them properly; *i. e.*, the cup in the saucer, the spoon in the saucer toward the right hand, the chair against the wall, the candle in the candlestick, and the snuffers in the tray.

Show them, that if the cup, spoon, &c., were placed on the table instead of in the saucer, the table would not look tidy. Show them how disorderly it is to leave chairs in the middle of the room; also how untidy it appears, if, instead of finding the candle in the candlestick, and the snuffers in the tray, we find them on the table. S. R.: "Things used in the house are to be kept in their places."

Teacher mentions different things; as, broom, tea kettle. Children mention their places.

II.—Exercise the children in folding different articles; as, dusting cloth, papers. Ask what they do with their clothes when they go to bed? Some children drop them on the floor, and leave them in a heap; some fold them up; others smooth them, and hang them over the back of a chair. Children say what ways are wrong, and what right; also where clothes not in use ought to be kept. S. R.: "Clothes not worn are to be folded up and put away." Children name articles they can fold.

III.—Exercise the children on the proper way of sitting in their seats. Lead them to observe how much nicer they look when sitting with their hands folded, each child behind another, than when they are spread over the seat irregularly. S. R.: "Children to sit upright and evenly in their seats."

Children show what is meant by sitting uprightly; by sitting evenly.

Students construct sketch on "Habits of Obedience," as "Order."

2. *Sketch on a Bird's Nest, and Bird-nesting.*

Object of the Lesson.—To illustrate the cruelty of robbing a nest.

First, exhibit the picture, and let the children point out the various objects represented in it, and tell the name of each of them.

I. *The Nest.*—What is it? The place where the bird lays her eggs, and the home of the young birds when they are hatched. What kind of a home is it, and of what shape? Why is it hollow, and why so soft inside? By whom is it made? How does the bird make it; has it hands? How is its beak fitted for making a nest? The nest is made of moss, hay, pieces of wool, straw, hair, leaves, feathers, &c. Why is it not built of stone, or of wood? How is the bird able to make its nest? It is taught by God how to build it. It obtains the materials for the nest by flying here and there to seek them, and then weaves them together with its beak. It places its nest between the branches of a tree, or in a hedge, or against a house, or sometimes even on the ground.

Tell the children that a little bird once built its nest in a lofty tree, and laid five eggs in it. When the eggs were hatched, the young birds came out of them. At first they had no feathers, and were very, very small. The old bird used to fly away to get them food, and when she returned, she found them all with their mouths wide open to receive it. Then this good mother used to cover her little ones with her wings, and keep them warm. One day, while she had gone to seek a meal for her hungry little ones, two boys, who were seeking for birds' nests, came to the tree in which this nest was, and soon perceived it; so they climbed up the tree, and just as one of them had seized the nest, and torn it from its place, the poor mother bird returned. What sorrow must she have felt, when she saw her little ones carried away by cruel, thoughtless boys, who did not leave her even one to nurse and watch over! And the poor little birds, taken from their mother's tender care, what will become of them?

II. *Application.*—Question the class as to the conduct of the boys. What did they do? What was there in their conduct that was wrong? What disposition did they manifest? If any child should ever feel tempted to take a bird's nest, what should such an one remember?

Students construct a sketch on "Saving Crumbs, and Feeding Birds," as "Bird's Nest, and Bird-nesting."

3. *Matter of a Sketch on Behavior in Different Places and Circumstances.*

I.—Children are sometimes in schoolroom, sometimes in playground, at home, at church, and sometimes in the streets.

II.—At school, it is right to sit still and pay attention to what the teacher says, or to speak when questioned; to put out the hand before answering; to keep one's own place. It is wrong to play, to talk to each other, to eat apples, &c., to be in any way inattentive.

III.—In the playground it is right to have a good game; also to go immediately into the schoolroom the moment the bell rings. It is wrong to push another down, or to keep the swing all the time, when others want it.

IV.—It is right to be very quiet, to kneel during prayer; to repeat prayers, and to sing aloud; to pay attention to what the clergyman says; to try to remember something of what they hear. The opposite of these things is wrong.

V.—At home, it is right to listen to parents, and elder brothers and sisters; if any one be sick, to wait on her (or him), and to make as little noise as possible; to help mother; to fetch a chair for father when he comes home from work. The opposite of these things is wrong. It is wrong, also, to keep the best chair or the warmest place by the fire, to make a noise in bed, &c., &c.

VI.—In the streets, it is right to go straight on; it is wrong to loiter, to throw stones, call people names, or shout after them.

Students construct matter of sketch on "The Kindness shown by Parents, Teachers, and Companions, to Children," as sketch on "Behavior."

4. *Sketch on Picture of "Saturday Night."*

I. *Point Examined.*—Get the children to mention what they see in the picture—several people. Their number, sex, and relationship—there are father, mother, and four children; viz., a little boy, two girls, and a baby. What each is doing—the mother is nursing the baby; how tenderly she holds it; how careful she is of it. Refer to the kindness of their mothers when they were babies. The elder sister is washing the younger; in what manner she would do this—*kindly*, so as not to be rough, or hurt the little one; *neatly*, so as not to make the room untidy. Who is coming into the house? Who runs to meet him, and why? What the father does to the little boy? What this shows? How the girls look? These children love their father, and he loves them. What the father has been doing all day, and the day before, and all the week, ever since Monday morning? But now his week's work is done, and he will have a day's rest. On what day he will rest? What day comes before Sunday? This picture shows what people do on Saturday night, to be ready for Sunday. What the mother has prepared for the father (shown by reference to the two cups and saucers on the table). She will take tea with him; she has waited till he came home. What else is on the table? What on the fire? What in front of the fire? (the cat.) How she looks? How the children will treat her? Refer to the bundle the father brings in with him. Children will say what they think it contains—food for their dinner on Sunday. How the father has prepared for Sunday? How the mother? Refer to the appearance of the room. She cleared it up before she sat down at the fireside. How the children are preparing—they will be nice and clean when Sunday comes. How pleasant it will be when they have their clean things on, and are ready for church.

II. *Application.*—From this, try to impress the children with a conviction that no work should be done on Sunday that can be helped; and that everything that can be done on Saturday to provide for Sunday, ought to be done. Let the children enumerate all the things they can do on Saturday, to prepare for Sunday.

Students construct sketch on "Picture of Sunday Morning," as sketch on "Saturday Night."

5. *Sketch on Picture,* "*The Blind Girl.*"

I.—Exercise perception, in letting the children describe the picture. How many persons drawn? In what alike? Both girls. How they differ? One is older than the other. What the elder girl is doing? Walking on a narrow piece of wood placed across a stream. Let them look at her face; her eyes; they will see she is blind. What the *little* girl is doing? She takes the other's hand, and guides. What would almost surely happen to the elder girl, if the younger did not guide her?

II.—Exercise conception, by calling out one of the children, bidding him shut his eyes, and walk to the door, &c. Why he could not go directly and quickly? Another child sent with closed eyes to some other place. Let them all shut their eyes, and by such exercises try to lead them to conceive of the nature of blindness. Lead them to recount things they could not see, if they became blind—the sun and moon, the green fields, the beautiful flowers, their kind mothers, fathers, sisters, or brothers. Whether, in such a case, they would be able to play, and run about as they do now? If they did, what might happen to them? What they would want, whenever they wished to go out? How sad to be blind! Having excited their feelings of sympathy and compassion, let them think of circumstances under which they can help poor blind people; as, when they are crossing a street, where they might be run over; or going along a bridge, where they might fall into the water. Whom would they then imitate? (The little girl in the picture.) Who would like to imitate her? Whom does such conduct please?

Students in training construct sketch on picture, "The Little Pilferers," as sketch on "The Blind Girl."

Plan. I.—In giving a lesson on a picture, it is necessary first to exercise the perceptive faculties. Let the children note,

1. Objects—whether persons or things.
2. Actions—what each person is doing, &c.

Children to determine the character of the actions delineated.

II.—Then deduce the story from the observations made, in such a manner as will excite interest, and call out sympathy.

III.—Apply the lesson to their own conduct and circumstances.

LIST OF SUBJECTS.

1. Duties to parents: To love them; to do all they desire; to try to keep in mind their counsels when absent from them; to try to please them; to speak and act properly toward them; to pray for them, &c.
2. Duties to teachers: These are to a great extent the same as those to parents, with the additional duty of attention to their instructions, and of seeking their forgiveness after ill behavior.
3. Duties to brothers and sisters. Particular acts of kindness to schoolfellows and companions.
4. Duties to the poor, the aged, the infirm, the blind, &c., or to those whom they can help in any way whatever.
5. The duty of doing as they would be done by; this called the "Golden Rule."
6. The duty of being careful to avoid injuring the property of another.
7. The duty of children to refrain from taking for their own use anything, however small it be, that is not clearly their own property.
8. That of avoiding quarrelling and fighting.
9. The duty of refraining from calling ill names, and from using wicked words.
10. That of being ready to forgive any unkindness done to them by another.
11. The duty of respect to superiors, with conversation as to the various occasions on which this is called for, and the mode of evidencing respect.
12. That of not returning evil for evil.
13. The duty of avoiding selfishness and greediness.
14. That of behaving rightly and suitably in different places, and under different circumstances.

It is essential to right moral training, that the instruction bearing on these several points should be based on the Scriptures; the Word of God being ever made the standard by which to estimate good and evil.*

SECOND STEP.

MORAL QUALITIES.

1. *Sketch on Industry.* (*Watts' Hymn,* "*The Busy Bee.*")

Question the children on each verse, endeavoring to make them feel the force of each epithet; for it is on the appropriateness of such expressions that one of the chief beauties of poetry depends.

Verse 1 (read).—What creature is here spoken of? What is a bee? Here the children should describe it, as to its color, the form of its body, legs, and wings, and its humming noise. What is here said of the bee? How does it show that it is busy? What are the hours it improves said to be, and why are they described as shining? When does the bee work? What is its employment all the day?

Describe the honey. Where does it get the honey? How are the flowers here described? Why does the bee choose the fresh-blown flowers?

What is the character here given of the bee? It is active, industrious, and never idle. How does it prove itself thus industrious? What instincts does it show in thus storing up honey for after use? Those of prudence and forethought.

After such questioning, call upon some of the children to relate in their own words all that is said of the bee in this verse, and to decide what those good qualities are of which it is an example.

The force and beauty of this verse consist in the qualifying epithets—" the *little busy* bee "—" the *shining* hours "—" the *opening*

---

* A set of twelve prints, suitable for this step of Moral Instruction, may be bought at the publishers.

flowers," those just unfolding themselves, and as yet unrifled of their sweets.

By such questions the children will be enabled to form a vivid conception of the little active bee, humming as it gaily flies from flower to flower, busily collecting sweet honey while the sun shines.

Verse 2.—What is the bee here spoken of as doing, in addition to gathering honey? Of what does she make her cells? What does she manifest in building her cell? What is a cell? What does she do with the wax? What does she show in the manner in which she spreads the wax? What two qualities, both of them necessary to a good workman, does she display in her work? How does she work? For what purpose does she labor? How is the food described? What does she exhibit in making this provision for future wants?

The beauty of this verse consists in the appropriateness of the epithets, *skilfully, neat, hard, sweet.* The children should here describe the character and work of the bee; as active, employing every bright hour in collecting honey; forming its cells in regular order with *skill* and *neatness,* and laboring *hard* to fill them with suitable provision. The children may be asked what those points are in which they may imitate the bee? They should strive to be as skilful and neat as this little insect is.

Verse 3.—In this verse some good little child is supposed to speak. What does he say he will be? In what kind of works will he be busy? What will he then imitate? Who will tempt, if we are idle? What will he tempt us to do? What other fault generally accompanies idleness? The children's experience may be appealed to on this point.

Verse 4.—How should little children employ their time? What should they be when at their books and work? What is here said of play? What advantage do the young gain from play? What dispositions should children manifest when at their play? To whom must every one give account of the manner in which each day is spent? Of what should this make us careful?

Students in training construct sketch on "Honesty," as "Industry."

(*Subject-Matter.*)   "*The Honest Woodcutter.*"

(1) A man, with many a hearty stroke,
Was cutting down an ancient oak,
When, as he smote, his axe's head
Far from the handle sped,
And, to the woodman's great dismay,
Into the river found its way.

(2) "Now tell me why," the rustic cried,
"Thou couldst not on the stick abide?
Thou surely mightst have stayed with me,
At least till I had felled the tree."

(3) Thus did the man his thoughts express,
And sat him down in great distress;

(4) But had not long reclined himself,
Before appeared a sprightly elf,
Who asked "the reason of his grief,"

(5) And said, "I'll quickly bring relief."
The man explained; the sprite withdrew,
Intent his magic power to show.
Forthwith he dived beneath the stream,
Full many a fathom, to redeem
The woodman's hatchet. (6) But, behold!
He found one made of solid gold.
"Is this the tool you lost?" said he.
"Oh, no; that ne'er belonged to me,"
The man replied. "Then," said the sprite,
"I'll try again to get the right."

(7) Again he plunged, again emerged,
And now a silver hatchet urged
On the poor rustic. (8) He, though lone,
Too honest was even that to own.
"Well," said the fairy, "I'll persist,
Till I obtain the one you've missed."
Again withdrew, again returned—
The man with joy his axe discerned.

(9) Said he, "Thou art a friend in need;
This is my very axe indeed."
"Pray, take it, then," the elf replied,
And gave the other two beside.

2. *Sketch on Keeping the Sabbath.*

MATTER.

I.

Hâste! put your playthings all away;
To-morrow is the Sabbath day;
Come, bring to me Noah's ark,
Your pretty tinkling music cart;
Because, my love, you must not play,
But holy keep the Sabbath day.

II.

Bring me your German village, please,
With all its houses, gates, and trees;
Your waxen doll, with eyes of blue,
And all her tea things, bright and new;
Because, my love, you must not play,
But holy keep the Sabbath day.

III.

Now bring your Sunday pictures down—
King David, with his harp and crown;
Good little Samuel on his knees,
And many pleasant scenes like these;
Because, you know, you must not play,
But learn of God upon His day.

IV.

Here is your hymn book; you shall learn
A verse, and some sweet kisses earn;
Your book of Bible stories, too,
Which dear mamma will teach to you.

I think, although you must not play,
We'll have a happy Sabbath day.

METHOD.

1st Stanza.—Read by paragraphs, leading the children to see, (1) the particular meaning of the words; (2) general meaning of the poem.

(*a*) "Haste," "playthings," "to-morrow," "Noah's ark," "music cart."

(*b*) Question why these are to be put away? Meaning of Sabbath. Who appointed it, and why? Read each stanza over after explanation.

2d Stanza.—(1) German village to be shown the children, if possible; if not, drawn on the board. "Waxen doll," "bright."

(2) Why the playthings are given to some one else to keep?

3d Stanza.—(1) "Harp," "crown," "holy."

(2) Who David was? What he did with his harp? Whom he used to play before? What he was when a boy? when a man? What he wrote? Why pictured with a crown? Draw from the children what they know of Samuel. Why pictured on his knees? How they may imitate him? Where we learn of David and Samuel?

4th Stanza.—(1) "Hymn book," "earn."

(2) Why mamma should read a Bible story out of a book? Why not the child herself? What this shows about her? What sort of a Sunday such a child will spend, with mamma reading, and the pretty pictures to look at? Try to impress the children with the idea of the peace and happiness of such a Sunday. Let them repeat any portion of God's Word which shows how He would have His day kept. Text: "Remember the Sabbath day to keep it holy."

Students in training construct sketch on "The Little Ship on the Waves," or "Looking to Jesus in Difficulties and Dangers" (Hymns and Poetry), as sketch on "The Sabbath Day."

3. *Sketch on Reverence.* (*The Athenians and Spartans.*)

I. *Introduction.*—Ask the children to name any nations of whom they have heard that lived a great while ago. If they mention the Jews, tell them that there were others of whom we have no Scriptural account; among these were some people who lived in Greece. Point out the country on the map, and then its relative position with respect to Palestine. Explain that it was divided into several States. One of these States was called Athens. The people who lived in Athens were called Athenians. They were lively people, fond of games and shows of all sorts. Another of these States was called Sparta, and the people were called Spartans. They differed from the Athenians, being very plain in their way of living, and plain in their habits. They used to take their meals altogether in the open air, that no one might have good things which others could not share.

II. *Story Told.*—1. One day the Athenians were going to have a play performed at their principal theatre. All the seats were soon taken. When the theatre was full, an old man came in, and looked round for a seat. He was old and infirm; could not stand long. (Picture out his distress.) He looked first one way, and then another. There were several *young* men seated. (What they should have done?) At length the old man saw a party of young Athenians beckoning to him. (What we mean when we beckon?) He tried to get to them, but had to climb over seats, and push through crowds; and when at last he reached them, they sat down, and instead of giving him the seat he had expected, took up all the room. The poor old man was still left standing. How he must have felt? What can be said of the young people? Who they were? (Athenians.)

2. In this theatre were some seats fitted up for strangers. These were filled by young Spartans, who, when they saw the behavior of the Athenians, were much displeased, and beckoned to the old man to come to them. When he was near, they all rose, and received him with the greatest respect. The Athenians, seeing this, could not help bursting into a shout of applause. (Mean-

ing of "applause.") The old man heard, and said, "The Athenians know what is right, but the Spartans practise it."

3. Contrast the conduct of the Athenians and Spartans. Who behaved rightly? In what respect the Athenians were wrong? in what right? What feelings actuated the Spartans? What Bible rule, though heathens, they fulfilled?

III. *Application.*—Get from the children various ways in which they can show honor and respect toward persons who are older than themselves: Giving up a place; standing; bowing; speaking in a quiet tone. What we call this behavior? Refer to God's approbation at seeing the young honor the aged, and His displeasure at seeing the aged treated with disrespect. Text: Lev. xix. 32.

Students in training construct sketch on "Filial Piety," or "Self-devotion of the Servant," as sketch on "Reverence."

Subject-Matter for Filial Piety. (*Chambers' Moral Class Book.*)

Anecdote.—Etna is the principal volcano in Europe. Hundreds of years ago, an unusually violent eruption took place. Burning matter poured down the sides of the mountains in various directions, destroying whole villages. The air was thickened with falling cinders and ashes. The people fled for their lives, carrying with them their most valuable goods. Amongst these were two young men, named Anapias and Amphinomus, who bore a very different burden on their backs. They carried only their aged parents, who could by no other means have been preserved. The conduct of these youths excited great admiration. It chanced that they took a way which the burning lava did not touch, which remained verdant, while all around was scorched and barren. The people, who, though very ignorant, were possessed of good feelings, believed that this tract had been preserved by miracle, and ever afterward called it the "field of the pious."

Subject-Matter for Self-devotion. (*Chambers' Moral Class Book.*)

Anecdote.—In the winter of 1776, Count and Countess Podotsky were travelling in the Carpathian mountains. The cold was very severe, and the wolves were more bold and savage than usual. These came down in hordes, and pursued the carriage. Of two servants, one had been sent on to the next town to procure post horses. The other, seeing the wolves come nearer and nearer, proposed to leave his horse to satisfy them, that so the travellers might gain time to reach the town. The count consented. The servant mounted behind the carriage, leaving the horse, which was seized and torn into a thousand pieces. Meanwhile, the party proceeded with all possible speed toward the town, which was not very distant. But their horses were tired, and the wolves, with appetites sharpened by a scanty meal, had almost reached the carriage.

In this extremity, the servant said, "Provide for my wife and children; I will go and meet the wolves." He got down, and was devoured. While the wolves were feasting upon him, the count and countess reached the town in safety.

4. *Sketch on Faithfulness to Promises.* ("*King John of France.*")

I. *Story Narrated.*—The relative position of France and England, and the wars between King Edward III. of England, and King John of France, to be spoken of. Mention the battles fought, dwelling especially on that of Poictiers; the success of the English; defeat of the French, with the capture of their king; his removal to England, and imprisonment. Endeavor to make the children realize the sad change in King John's condition: *before*, a king over a large country and a great people, possessed of riches and power, surrounded by every luxury; *now*, deprived of all—his house a dungeon, his fare that of a prisoner. What would be his feelings under such circumstances? What his grief? What his great desire? Liberty. His proposal to King Edward, and the conditions upon which he was released. His return to France; the effort to collect the money fixed upon as his ransom; its failure. What this might have led him to do? What he did? His return to England, and to prison. Why? Let the children give their opinion on his conduct, and learn the term by which it is expressed—*faithfulness to promise*. What is there to admire in the conduct of King John?

II. *Application.*—Do you ever make promises? How should they be regarded? What should you do before making a promise? In what way should you act when a promise has been made? However much may be the inconvenience, whatever trouble it may give, still a promise must be kept. Why? First, and mainly, because God requires this; secondly, because such conduct will give satisfaction and peace of mind in the end, though it may produce temporary suffering, as it did in the case of King John; thirdly, because of the effect such conduct will have on others.

As the lesson proceeds, the principal points of it may be written on the board.

Students in training construct sketch on "Candor," as "Faithfulness to Promises." Subject-matter, "Story of George Washington and the Cherry Tree."

5. *Sketch on Patriotism.* (*"Siege of Calais."*)

I. *Story Narrated.*—Begin by referring to the last lesson. What was said of the battles fought in the reign of Edward III.? Point out the importance of Calais from its position: it was like a key to open the way into France and the Netherlands; it was well fortified, surrounded by strong walls. Edward encompassed the city with his brave soldiers; none of the people of Calais could therefore get out to obtain provisions. When they had consumed all their store, what must follow? Still they fought—still they resisted Edward's demand that they should yield their city into his hands. At last, when nothing but starvation awaited them, they submitted. But Edward, instead of admiring their bravery and patriotism, was so angry at their long resistance, that he demanded the lives of six of the principal inhabitants. The suspense and anxiety of the people! How must their joy and gratitude have been mingled with deep sorrow, when six of their greatest men freely offered themselves to save the lives of the rest by the sacrifice of their own!

What virtue did these men show? Of what qualities do they

set us an example? They held not their lives dear, so that they might save their poor countrymen. What would you say of such men? They were generous, and loved their country. Imagine these brave, generous men, brought with halters round their necks before the angry king, who was so determined to punish them for the trouble that had been given him. O how sad is anger! Happily, there is one of a different spirit there—Edward's wife, the gentle Queen Philippa; she pleads for the noble sufferers. What feeling led her to do this? Compassion. This made her plead their cause, and with power. She succeeded. And how do you think she must have felt, when these brave warriors were set free? She felt the luxury of doing good.

II. *Application.*—What evil dispositions are manifest in the circumstances brought forward in this lesson? Anger and revenge in the king. What good dispositions? Generosity and patriotism in the six citizens; compassion in the queen. Which of these would you desire to imitate?

Students in training construct sketch on "The Galley Prisoner of Toulouse" (see Cowdery's "Moral Lessons," page 75), as sketch on "Siege of Calais."

6. *Sketch on Gratitude.* ("*The Lion and the Mouse.*")

Point.—To develop the idea of *gratitude*.

I. *Introduction.*—Bring before the children a picture of a lion and of a mouse, and lead them to draw a comparison between the two as to size, strength, and habits. The peculiar disposition of each: the one wild, fierce, strong; the other gentle, timid, and weak. Speak also of their food, and the manner in which they obtain it.

II. *Fable Related.*—Read or relate the fable of "The Lion and the Mouse," and help the children to realize the story. The forest; the thick, shady oak, under which the lion, faint with heat, is resting; the little insignificant mice running over the back of this king of beasts; the anger of the lion at being thus disturbed; the escape of all the mice but one; the lion's intention;

the distress and supplication of the mouse; effect of these upon the lion; the feeling thus excited in the mouse toward the lion. When the children have gained the clear idea, give the name for this feeling—*gratitude*.

Continue the subject, telling the children the danger in which the lion was afterward placed; his voice of distress heard by the mouse; the manner in which the mouse proves its gratitude; its readiness to repay the kindness of the lion. In what way can the mouse help the lion? In one way only, but this is sufficient; he gnaws the net with his hard, sharp teeth, and sets the lion free.

III. *Application.*—What lesson may be learned from this fable? That we should be grateful for kindness shown to us, especially if we have deserved otherwise. That none are so small or feeble but that they may be able, in some way or other, to return a kindness. That none are so great or so powerful, but that they may at some time need the service of their inferiors, and be helped by them. Of what virtue does this little mouse set us an example?

Students in training construct sketch on "Affection," as "Gratitude," taking for subject-matter, "Jackdaw and Pigeons." (See "Æsop's Fables.")

7. *Sketch on Ingenuity and Perseverance.* ("*The Crow and the Pitcher.*")

I. *Story Related.*—A crow, suffering greatly from thirst, perceived, with much joy, a pitcher at a distance, and flew to it, but found very little water in it. The children should determine what then was its difficulty—its beak was too short to reach the water at the bottom. The crow, however, does not fly away in despair. What can it do? Here the children should endeavor to think of plans by which the crow might accomplish its object; their practicability may be canvassed. First, the crow endeavors to upset the pitcher, but this it cannot accomplish; next, it patiently sets to work to fill the pitcher with pebbles. What is the effect of its doing this? The water rises to the top. Why? The pebbles are heavier than the water; they sink to the bottom, and cause the water to rise to the top. The crow is rewarded for its labor by getting a draught of water, of which it stands so much in need.

II. *Application.*—The children should determine the merit of the crow. What was its conduct? and then, how they can imitate it? When they have some work to accomplish which appears to them difficult, they must not say they cannot do it, but consider what means they can adopt. If the first plan fails, as that of the crow did, try another; find some new and better plan; persevere till they succeed. Consider, first, what to do, and spare no pains to succeed in what they feel is right to be done. Ingenuity and perseverance will have their reward. This to be repeated, and the children to sing, " 'Tis a lesson we should heed."

Students in training construct sketch on " Discontent," subject-matter, " The Frogs who Wanted a King," as sketch on " Ingenuity and Perseverance." (See "Æsop's Fables.")

8. *Sketch on Self-Reliance.* (" *The Lark and her Young Ones.*")

I. *Introduction.*—Commence by asking the children what kind of bird the lark is, and showing them a picture of it. Its habits: building its nest on the ground in a corn field, and soaring over it; ascending very high; singing most joyously.

II. *Fable Narrated.*—A lark had a nest of young birds in a wheat field. When the wheat became ripe, they were still unable to fly. What was likely to be the consequence? The men would come with their reapers, and the poor little birds would be trampled on by them, or they might even be cut in pieces by the scythes. How would the mother bird feel, when she expected that the farmer would commence reaping? She told her little ones to listen attentively to all he said, and to tell her every word. Whilst she was away procuring them food, the owner of the field came to look at the grain, and seeing it so ripe, told his son to go and call his friends and neighbors to come and cut it on the morrow. The young birds were greatly alarmed, but the old one thought there was no cause for fear. Why? If the farmer depended upon others to do his work, it would not, she thought, be done. She gave again the same command to her young ones; and the next day they reported that they heard the farmer tell his son to invite his cousins to come and cut the wheat. What would the wise old bird say to this? No cause for fear. Why? The next morning the birds heard the farmer say to his son, "Since neither our friends, neighbors, nor cousins will do our work for us, go, get a reaper, that we may do it ourselves." When the old lark heard this, she said, "We must be gone without delay; for when a man undertakes to do his own business, then it will surely be done." So she removed her little ones, and the field was reaped.

III. *Application.*—Draw from the children the lesson which the fable enforces—that if we wish our work performed, we must not depend upon others to do it, but set about it ourselves. Question them as to what disposition it is which leads us to give up our proper work to others.

Students in training construct sketch on "Mockery," subject-matter, "The Shepherd Boy and Wolf," as sketch on "Self-Reliance." (See "Æsop's Fables.")

A LIST OF MORAL QUALITIES, AND SUBJECTS FOR THEIR ILLUSTRATION.*

Obedience	The Rechabites. Jer. xxxv.
Disobedience	Absalom. 2 Samuel xv.
Kindness	David and Mephibosheth.
Respect	Solomon and his Mother. 1 Kings ii.

* In the various series of books published by the Educational Societies, many excellent and appropriate stories of useful tendency will be found; and also in the "Simple Lessons" and the "Moral Class Book," published by the Messrs. Chambers, of Edinburgh. But teachers should be prepared to supply the appeal to religious motive, and constant reference to the revealed will of God as the rule of action, in which most of these are defective. "A Kiss for a Blow," is a little work written in an excellent spirit, from which teachers may select several pieces. In Mrs. Tuckfield's "Book of Proverbs and Maxims," and also in her "Evening Readings," there are many interesting anecdotes, written in a Christian spirit. Some stories may likewise be selected from "Evenings at Home;" but the same caution is necessary here, as in the little work of Chambers. "Aids to Cate-

Generosity	King Alfred and the Beggar.
Covetousness . . .	Achan. Joshua vii. Gehazi. 2 Kings v.
Cruelty	Murder of the Innocents.
Envy	Joseph and his Brethren. Gen. xxxvii.
Gratitude	Fable of the Lion and the Mouse.
Diligence	Song of the Busy Bee.
Perseverance . . .	The Fable of the Crow and the Pitcher.
	Story of King Robert Bruce and the Spider.
Faith	The Little Girl and the Beads. Cecil.
Honesty	The Woodman and the Axe.

FABLES.

The Vain Jackdaw.	The Tortoise and the Hare.
The Dove and the Ant.	The Wolf and the Kid.
The Husbandman and his Sons.	The Ant and the Grasshopper.
The Dog and the Shadow.	The Dog in the Manger.

THIRD STEP.

MORAL CHARACTER.

1. *Sketch on the Errand Boy.*

HEADS.—I. Duties. II. Qualifications. III. Making application.

I.—Require the children to define the work of an errand boy.

1. Taking letters, messages, and parcels.

2. Lighting fires, sweeping, dusting, cleaning windows, taking down shutters, &c.

3. Tending the store. (W. B.)

II.—Draw from the children, that whoever enters a situation

chetical Teaching" contains a number of stories founded on right principles, and which may be used without fear, as may also Cowdery's "Moral Lessons."

For appropriate hymns and pieces of poetry, teachers are referred to the third edition of "Hymns and Poetry," published by the Home and Colonial School Society.

There is a selection of fables published by the Tract Society, which is cheap and good.

must possess qualities which will fit him for it. Tell them these qualities which fit us for our situations, are called *qualifications.* Refer to what is written on the board. What a boy must have before he can find out streets, or know how to leave a parcel at the place to which it is directed, or how to give a receipt. *A knowledge of reading and writing.* (W. B.) Speak of the advantage of going to school. How much they owe their parents and teachers. How a boy should listen to a message he has to deliver. *He must be attentive.* (W. B.) Show, by example (anecdote), how necessary it is to give the exact message, to prevent mistakes. *He must be exact.* (W. B.)

What plans might be adopted to help him to remember what he has to say? After listening attentively, to repeat it over to himself. Refer to a boy doing something else first, when told to be quick. The probable consequence. *He must be punctual.* (W. B.)

Contrast the appearance and behavior of two boys, one dirty and idle, the other tidy and quick. Which boy would people wish to employ? What objections would they make to the dirty and idle boy? He would be likely to soil what he had to carry, and to fail to bring it in time. The errand boy must be *clean* and *industrious.* (W. B.) Refer to the money or goods he may have intrusted to his care. He must be *honest.* (W. B.) Children to decide on the way he should speak to his employer, or to his employer's customers. He must be *obliging* and *respectful.* (W. B.)

III.—Remind the children that some of them may be errand boys, or girls. Ask what situations they would like to fill? Let them decide whether any of the qualifications written on the board can be dispensed with in the situations they select. Lead them to see that in all positions these qualities are needful. Ask what will help them to acquire these qualifications? Try to inspire them with a wish to possess these, not only to please employers, but that God may say to them, "Well done, good and faithful servant." S. R.: "Servants, be obedient to your masters; not with eye service."

Students in training construct sketch on "The Factory Girl," or "The Kitchen Girl," as sketch on "The Errand Boy."

2. *Sketch on "The Fisherman."*

I. *Introduction.*—Ascertain who of the children have seen men and boys fishing. Question, so as to bring out the particular mode adopted; *i. e.*, How many fish caught at a time?

II.—Tell them there are some men who get their living by fishing. They are called *fishermen*, and they catch fish in a different place, and in a different way, from those last spoken of. Where, and how? Show a picture of the net. Children say how used. Different proportion caught by net and line. Lead children to contrast and calculate this.

1. The angler fishes for amusement.
The fisherman fishes for bread.
2. The angler fishes with a line.
The fisherman fishes with a net.
3. The angler fishes in the river.
The fisherman fishes in the sea.
4. The angler stands on shore.
The fisherman goes out in a boat.

III.—Question as to the different kinds of fish caught. Herring, mackerel, cod, soles, salmon, &c. (W. B.) Tell at what parts of the coasts the most common fish are found. Herring and mackerel come in shoals at certain times of the year. Who sends them, and why? The salmon is caught in some of our rivers, and is plentiful off the coast of Scotland, and off the north coast of Ireland.

IV.—Refer them to the waves of the sea. Height to which these swell. Picture out the fisherman in his little boat, in the midst of the waves. What they would do in such a situation? The fisherman must be a *good sailor*. (W. B.) What often happens at sea? Dreadful storms. Kind of man he must be to face such—*bold*. (W. B.)

Picture again the uncomfortable little boat in which he has to sit. How often he gets drenched with rain. The effect this would have on themselves. The fisherman does not mind it at all; he shakes his wet jacket, and works on. People who can bear such hardships, we call *hardy*. (W. B.)

Tell them that the fisherman carefully examines the weather before he ventures forth. Of what use this is. He must understand the signs of the weather. (W. B.) And if he is a good man, he will ask God to give him His blessing and protection in his daily work.

V. *Summary.*—Children, from memory, contrast the fisherman with the angler. Mention different kinds of fish caught, and where found, and enumerate the qualifications of the fisherman.

Students in training construct sketch on "The Soldier," as sketch on "The Fisherman."

3. *Sketch on "Expedition of Sir John Franklin."*

I. *Introduction.*—Let the children name any countries they know. How different countries have been found out; as America, Australia. Bring a map of the world, and let the children find in what ways they would get to Asia by ship from New York. Either round Cape Horn, or round Cape of Good Hope.

Let them try to find another way of going by ship. If they fail, point out to them the northwest passage. Compare this route with the others as to length, to find the advantage of going by it. Refer to the climate, to show the disadvantage.

Picture out the Polar Sea. Immense masses of ice; a white bear, perhaps, on a peak of one of them; another mass floating toward the ship. The intense cold. So many inconveniences and dangers were there, that people did not know whether they could go that way or not. Who would be willing to try? What kind of men they must be?

II. *Story Told.*—A sailor, called Sir John Franklin, was asked to go. He went, taking two ships. Why two? He was not expected to return in a year. Perhaps there would be much ice in the winter, and he would have to wait till the next summer's sun melted some of it. His wife hoped to see him back in two years; at most, in three. Children to say how the ship must be provided for so long a journey. The ship sailed. One year passed, another, and another; still the people were not afraid. Why not? Then another year passed away, and again another. What people would think now? How would Lady Franklin feel? What Sir John Franklin and his crew would be likely to want now? They were kept out much longer than they ever expected. What could be done for them? The queen of England sent other ships, with plenty of food and clothes, to look everywhere for them, but in vain. The people, too, of other countries, sent ships to try and find them, but they could not. At last all parties said they must give up the search. It was useless to send more ships and men, to perish, too, in the icy sea. Could Lady Franklin give up? Could she rest, and not know whether her husband was dead or alive? She sent out ship after ship, till she spent so much money that she was only able to send one more. This went, and returned to tell her that she would never see her husband again. He was dead. He was taken ill in the ship, and died.

Would children like to know what became of the ships, and the rest of the men? The ice crushed the ships; so the men got out, and tried to walk over the ice, in hopes of finding some other ship. Of all those that were sent, they met none. It was terribly cold, and they had no shelter, no food, save what they could carry; so they perished one by one. Let us hope those poor men loved God, and are now with Him, safe and happy forever.

The children should be led to sympathize with the courage of Sir John Franklin and his crew. Who, with the affectionate perseverance of his wife?

Students in training construct sketch on "Dr. Kane's Arctic Expedition," as sketch on "Expedition of Sir John Franklin."

4. *Sketch on "Henry II. and his Children."*

Point.—To show the consequence of filial ingratitude and disobedience.

I.—Character of Henry II. as a father.

II.—Conduct of Henry's sons, and their punishment.
III.—Application.

I.—Children to name any eminent kings of England.* Select Henry II. as the subject of the lesson. Refer to the period of his reign; his descent. Give the names of his queen and children. Describe Henry's conduct as a father during the childhood of his sons. His love for them. How parents show their love? How Henry showed his love? 1. By his indulgence; the readiness with which he entered into their sports. 2. By the pains he took with their education, getting them the best teachers, that they might be ignorant of nothing befitting their station to know. 3. By the provision he made for them, appointing Henry to succeed himself; giving Brittany to Geoffrey, and Guienne and Aquitaine to Richard; making John, Lord of Ireland. *Chief points* put on the board, at the dictation of the children. Children to say what so kind a father might expect his children to be. To decide, from the fact to be given, whether they were dutiful, affectionate, grateful.

II.—1. Consider Prince Henry; his ardent wish to reign before his father's death; his disputes with his brother Richard; the part the king took in the affray; its results; Prince Henry's illness and death (the ring); effects of this on the king.

2. Prince Geoffrey. Narrate briefly his career and fearful end.

3. Note briefly the dissensions between Richard and John. The distress these caused the king. Henry's death; Richard's visit to the tomb of his father; his bitter repentance. Picture out the scene with reference to Mrs. Hemans's poem on the subject. His career as king of England.

4. John, king of England; his meanness; cruelty; tyranny; its results; his death. Write on the board, at children's dictation, how each son of Henry II. died.

III. *Application.*—Children to say to what the mournful fate of Henry's sons may be traced. What caused the remorse they felt? Let children find examples of disobedient children from the Bible,

* For account of this, see "Little Arthur's England."

and refer to texts which speak of this sin, and its punishments. In what respects they may be guilty of the same faults? What children must expect who persevere in acting thus? In disobeying their earthly parent, they sin against God, and God signally punishes such rebellion even in this world. Repeat together the Fifth Commandment.

Students in training construct sketch on anecdote, "Messrs. Adams and Quincy" (see Cowdery's "Moral Lessons," page 197), as sketch on "Henry II."

5. *Sketch on "The Gunpowder Harvest."*

1. *Story Told.*—A tribe of Indians dwelt near the Missouri River, in North America. These had but little intercourse with Europeans.

Ideas worked out. Point out the locality on the map. Describe the country—covered with forests. The people; their complexion, dress, mode of life—hunters. Explain *European* and *intercourse.*

2. A merchant went into their country; sold them muskets and gunpowder, taking fur as an exchange. Whether the man would be likely to give his muskets away? What he would expect? What the Indians would be able to give? Why they would particularly value firearms? Explain *merchant, musket, gunpowder,* and *exchange.*

3. After a time, a Frenchman came to the same country to sell gunpowder. The Indians had plenty—would not buy. What the Frenchman wanted? How the fact of the Indians having gunpowder affected him?

4. He told them gunpowder was a seed, &c. What seeds do? Motive of the lie? The sin of the lie? The effect of the lie? Try to make the children sympathize with the simplicity of the poor Indians.

5. So the Indians bought the gunpowder; sowed it; placed a guard to protect the field from wild beasts; waited for the harvest. What they expected? Why they placed a guard? When

they would find out the cheat? Lead the children to sympathize with their anxiety, while waiting for the gunpowder to sprout.

6. Next year the Frenchman, who did not choose to go again himself, sent his partner to the Missouri, with many things to exchange for furs. Why he did not go? Make the children understand he was afraid to meet the poor men he had wronged. Show that fear is a consequence of guilt. Explain *partner*.

7. Somehow the Indians found out that these goods belonged to the man who had cheated them. Straightway they gave him a hut, in which all his goods were set out. When this was done, they helped themselves, &c.

He demanded justice from the chief, and was promised the skins of all the beasts that should be shot with the produce of the gunpowder harvest. With what feelings the Frenchman displayed his goods? With what feelings he saw them disappear. Refer again to the manner in which the Indians had been deprived of their property. Refer to Exodus xii., and show that after the Egyptians had made the Israelites work without wages, God bade his people demand return.

Children to say whether, if a schoolfellow took something from them, it would be right to snatch something of his? What they can do? Appeal to the teacher. What a man who is robbed in the street can do? Appeal to the magistrate. Show the differences in the position of the Indians. There was no one to whom they could go for redress of wrong; they had a right to redress it themselves. Children to say what is to be condemned in the conduct of the Frenchman. What those who injure others must expect. "He that diggeth a pit, shall fall therein." Also Luke vi. 38.

Students construct sketch on the "The Moravian Farmer" (Chambers's "Moral Class Book"), as sketch on "The Gunpowder Harvest."

6. *Sketch on "The Shepherd."*

I.—Duties, and mode of life.
II.—The Shepherd of the lost.
III.—Character of a good shepherd.

I.—Children say if they have ever seen a flock of sheep. Where? What the sheep were doing? Who was with them, and for what purpose? The shepherd watches the sheep, to see that they do not lose themselves, and that no one steals them. He leads them to water, and to different meadows where they can find fresh grass. What he has to do every evening? Put them into a fold. Call on some of the children to describe this, and on others to tell its use. What he does every summer, when it is very hot, and the sheep can hardly run about under their heavy woollen coats? He takes them, one at a time, to a pond, and washes their fleeces, which are then clipped off. Why this is done? With what instrument? Whether the shepherd can do it all by himself? How the sheep behave? How they feel after it is cut off? What they will do in winter, having their wool cut off in the summer? What happens before winter? Who causes this to happen? What the shepherd always has to help him, and how? What we can say of his dog?

II.—Children name any shepherds mentioned in the Bible. Tell them that in countries the Bible speaks of, it is very hot, and there is little rain. What difference this makes to the sheep? So the shepherd has to look carefully for water and green grass. Refer to the fierce wild beasts that infest these countries. When they are most likely to come out of their dens? How to secure the flock? Luke ii.

III.—Let children picture a lion, first in ambush, then springing on one of the flock. What the *bad* shepherd would do? What the *good?* "The good shepherd giveth his life for the sheep." Again, picture out the shepherd during a hot summer's day, leading his flock to some shady place, and playing a tune to them, as David did. Tell them that David made songs referring to this subject, and repeat some part of Psalm xxiii. Children say what kind of a man a good shepherd must be: patient, tender, strong, courageous. Who is called *our* Shepherd? What he calls little children who love him? (his lambs.) Speak of his patience and tenderness; of the safety of his flock. Would not each child like to be one of Christ's lambs?

FOURTH STEP.

MORAL PRINCIPLES.—INTRODUCTORY TO MORAL PHILOSOPHY.

1. *Sketch on the Analogy of Spring and Childhood.*

I.—By questions, endeavor to draw from the children a description of spring. In what part of the year the spring comes? What they notice, when taking a walk in the country in spring? Flowers peeping above the ground. (Children give the names of some early flowers.) Buds sprouting on the trees; grass looking fresh and green. (W. B.) Everything is growing. Question as to the things done in spring. Laborers dig the ground; put seed into it; the gardener lays out his beds and plants; birds build their nests; bees collect honey from the early flowers; every creature is cheerful, and busy at its work. (W. B.) All are preparing for a future time.

Refer to the weather in spring. How the air feels? Warm, soft, and fresh. How the sky looks? Bright, though with some clouds scattered here and there. Children decide on the general state of the weather. To do this, let them compare it with the dry harvest time, the rains of later autumn, and the frost of winter. In spring, the weather is neither hot nor cold, neither wet nor dry; showers are common, but not long. (W. B.) Showers are soon followed by sunshine.

II.—Children read what is written on the board. In spring, everything is growing; all things are preparing for a future time; showers are soon followed by sunshine.

Tell them that wise men have compared spring-time to childhood, and help them to trace the analogy as to each point.

1. They are growing. Their bodies grow. They are taller and stronger than they were. (Refer to the babies at home.) Their minds grow; they know more than they did. Refer to the time when they first saw them. How little they knew then. What now?

2. They are preparing for a future period. As the laborer sows the grain in spring, so the seed of instruction is sown in youth. Children to say what is compared to the soil? What to

the seed? What happens, if the seed is bad? What will come up, if no seed is sown? Dwell on this point until the analogy is clearly traced.

3. Showers are compared to tears, sunshine to smiles. Refer to things that have happened to trouble them during the week. Let them notice how soon these things have passed over, leaving them as happy as before. The sun has shone out. Close the lesson with a few serious words, referring to the duty of being diligent and attentive in youth. Warn them, that where there are no blossoms in spring, there will be no fruit in autumn.

Students in training construct sketch on "The Analogy of the Course of a River and the Course of Human Life," as sketch on "Analogy of Spring and Childhood."

A course of lessons on Symbols, Emblems, &c., might advantageously be given here.

LIST.

Omniscience, represented by an Eye.
Adoration, " a Censer containing Incense.
Welcome, " a Hand stretched out.
Friendship, " Clasped Hands.
Royal Power, " a Rod, or Sceptre.
Military Power, " anciently, a Horn; recently, a Sword.
Immortality,
Life, } " a Serpent.
Health,
Eternity, " a Circle; often a Serpent, with its Tail in its Mouth.
Justice, " a Balance.
Hope, " an Anchor.
Faith,
Sorrow, } " a Cross.
Humiliation,
Victory, " a Wreath.
The Trinity, " an Equilateral Triangle enclosed in a Circle of Rays.

The two succeeding examples are not sketches, but *bonâ fide* reports of lessons given by two of the principal teachers in the Home and Colonial Model Schools.

1. *Report of Lesson on "The Nightingale and Glowworm."*

I. *Point.*—To work out the moral lesson; *i. e.*, God gives to different persons different talents for their general good.

II. *Heads.*—1. Introduction. 2. Stanzas read, questioned on, and explained. 3. Moral lesson and application.

III. *Plan of the Lesson.*—1. Lesson introduced, by drawing from the children such points in natural history as will bear on the subject. (*a*) Account of the nightingale, and its habits. (*b*) Of the glowworm, and its habits.

2. Stanzas read in separate paragraphs. (*a*) Questions put on each, to bring out the general meaning. Examples: What had the bird been doing? Why was he hungry in the evening? What effect was the glowworm's argument likely to have on the nightingale? Whose task was it to beautify? Whose to cheer? (*b*) Questions put on the meaning of the more difficult words, which the children were allowed to explain, either by definition or by synonym. Words explained: *Keen, demands, eagerly, hawthorn, crop, admire, power.* (*c*) Questions put, to call out a sense of the exact appropriateness of certain words, and their superiority over their synonyms. Children led to see that no synonym would have the force of *spied, right* (as an adverb), *harangued, minstrelsy, warbled.*

3. The children, being told that this is a fable, and not a mere narrative, concluded that it contained a moral lesson. To help them to find it, teacher bade them name the subjects of the story, and put the names on the board. Children decided that these meant different people.

What the nightingale possessed, and what the glowworm possessed, discovered, and put upon the board. Children decided that these meant different gifts or talents.

By comparison of the nightingale's full power of song, with the glowworm's little twinkling light, children decided that talents differed in character and in importance. Gave, as examples of talents or gifts, riches, mental ability, bodily strength. Relative value of these gifts touched upon.

4. Teacher next put on the board the heads of the glowworm's argument, as discovered by the children, thus:

(*a*) The glowworm states that he admires the nightingale's song.

(*b*) He argues that the nightingale ought in like manner to admire his lamp.

(*c*) He states that God gave to each his separate gift.

(*d*) That these gifts were bestowed for the general good.

The propositions, *a, b, c*, having been clearly made out before *d* was worked out, by special reference to the pleasures and benefits we derive from the labors of the highly gifted. (Eminent men, and their works, named, including the poet Cowper himself.)

IV. *Application.*—Made chiefly by reference to the different points in which they succeed or fail. How those who make much progress may be tempted to feel toward those who are slow? How those who are slow might be tempted to feel toward those who are more talented? What considerations would tend to prevent wrong feelings on the side of the more advanced? of the less advanced? Reference to "the Parable of the Talents."

In giving this lesson, the teacher exercised the conceptive faculty in the introductory descriptions, and the reasoning faculties in drawing out the analogy.

2. *Report of Lesson on "Strife."*

I.—Definition of the term. Draw from the children its various meanings; as, contention, disagreement, quarrelling. Show the origin of the word, in connection with *strive*. Show the difference implied—one may strive; for strife, there must be two. Show the senses, good and bad, in which the term may be used. Write on the board, from dictation of the children, "Strife is the effort to obtain victory. It requires two for strife. The word implies disagreement, opposition, and contention."

II. *First Example.*—1. Refer to Exodus ii. 13. Touch on what we know. The similarity of race; faith; condition; sorrow. Touch on what we do not know. Who was strong, and who was weak? who was right, and who was wrong?

2. *Cause of Strife.*—Refer to Proverbs xvi. 28. Define *froward*, as *contrary*. A froward person is one bent on having his own way, right or wrong; inclined to contradiction, and always ready for a quarrel. Compare this with Exodus ii. 13, to show that the violent man was the one to blame. General conclusion drawn.

3. *Consequence.*—The flight of Moses, who had come down at that time seeking to free them from their bonds. So far as it depended on the combatants, the result was an addition of forty years to the length of Israel's captivity.

Second Example.—1. Strife of Jacob and Laban. Account given by the children. Progress of Jacob from Padan-aram shown on the map.

2. *The Cause.*—Covetousness of Laban.

3. *The Consequence.*—As Laban was stronger than Jacob, Jacob, his wives and children, were in danger of being brought back, never permitted to go to the land of Canaan, or meet Isaac; deprived of their property; forced to become servants. To prevent such injustice, God himself interfered.

Third Example.—1. Strife between the servants of Abraham and the servants of Lot. Example drawn from the children.

2. *Cause.*—Rivalry. Compare this with the strife amongst the disciples, when they strove who should be greatest.

3. *Consequence.*—The separation of chief friends.

Fourth Example.—1. Strife between Jephthah and the Ephraimites. Account given as before.

2. *Cause.*—Pride and jealousy.

3. *Consequences.*—(Threatened) ungrateful murder, dreadful massacre; (actual) civil war and slaughter.

III. *Causes of Strife.*—1. The causes already discovered summed up, and written on the board.

2. Other causes found. Whether mentioned in Scripture, or drawn from observation?

LIST.

Frowardness.　　　Jealousy.
Covetousness.　　　Envy.
Rivalry.　　　　　　Tale-bearing.
Pride.　　　　　　　Foolish Jesting.
　　　Drunkenness, &c.

IV. *Consequences.*—Drawn from the children.

LIST.

Loss of Time.
　"　　Property.
　"　　Life.
　"　　Peace.
　"　　Power of Doing Good.
From St. James, "Confusion, and every evil work."

V. *Application.*—How to avoid strife? Consider who is the author of strife. Consider the conduct of those who refuse to be disturbed by it. The conduct of Abraham, and its effect. The conduct of Gideon. Compare this with that of Jephthah. Refer to texts: "A soft answer turneth away wrath," and "Blessed are the peacemakers."

INVENTIVE DRAWING.*

INTRODUCTION.

Principles of this Course Developed.

PESTALOZZI, the great and successful advocate of more natural methods of teaching, considered that form, number, and sound supplied materials for the development of the principal faculties of the mind. Moreover, he considered the communication of knowledge of little importance, unless tending to the development of the mind on the basis of given facts.

Drawing, the subject of this treatise, belongs to form, and presents means for the most elementary instruction. In its first stage it may even be preparatory to writing, as letters are mere compositions of straight and curved lines, for the performance of which the hand should have previously attained a certain degree of firmness and dexterity.

Let us now consider what are the faculties that are developed by drawing. In consequence of the way in which this art is usually taught, many think that it only exercises the faculty of *imitation*. We admit that imitation cultivates the hand and the eye, but doubt whether it cultivates or draws out talent and ingenuity. For even in copying the products of masters, we ought to be able to appreciate their merits, not merely in the aggregate, but also in detail.

Schelling, the great German philosopher, expresses himself thus: " In a time when people believe it possible to proceed with

* By Hermann Krusi, the inventor of this system.

one leap from the first to the last step of the ladder of knowledge, the sentence may appear hard, that art, like everything possessed with vitality, must go back to the first elements. We must see how every original product of art rises from the depth of imagination, branching out into an infinite variety of forms, and combining at last into a graceful whole. This power of invention cannot be communicated, for it is the pure gift of Nature, reflecting herself in the mind. A true artist can only follow the law which God and Nature have implanted in his mind. There is but little help from outside; every genius ripens by its own strength."

Thus Schelling, in this noble passage, recognizes the power of Invention as the principal mover and creator of art.

In the present elementary treatise, we intend to trace the progressive steps on which this important power may be cultivated, and to associate it with its natural ally, Taste; which latter is not such an arbitrary ruler as is generally believed, but subject to fixed laws.

But the object of this method, far from tending only to amusement, is an eminently *practical* one. Whilst acknowledging that the principle of invention is vastly encouraged in this country in all the improvements which administer to gain and comfort, we find occasionally a woeful absence of taste, and are obliged to borrow the finest patterns for ornament from France and Germany, in both of which countries drawing is introduced as a popular branch of instruction.

If the schools of this country will admit drawing as the most elementary, the most distinct and pleasing branch of instruction, they will become more practical than they have hitherto been, and apply more to the wants of the present generation.

The first exercises belonging to this course are of such an elementary character, that they may precede the knowledge of letters and of writing. Even geometrical forms may be introduced at this step, because the increase in the number of lines in every succeeding exercise, leads necessarily to all the forms on which the science of Geometry is built. Since, however, the elements of *form* have already been described under a separate head, the teacher is referred to it whenever she finds definitions necessary.

In case the children have already an idea of the geometrical forms which arise from the combination of several lines, the teacher must not neglect the opportunity of putting appropriate questions, by way of repetition. There are, no doubt, many combinations of lines which cannot be designated by any name, and which, as a product of the children's invention, must be received as readily as those which have been adopted as symbols of form. In order to show the plan of teaching, the first exercise will be introduced as a model lesson. It is supposed that the children are already acquainted with the ideas of *vertical, horizontal, slanting, parallel,* &c. Although it was stated that this knowledge was not absolutely necessary to begin this course, it cannot be denied that, at the age at which children are required to possess the power of drawing lines with tolerable accuracy, an acquaintance with the most prominent geometrical forms may be expected, or, at any rate, will be very desirable.

FIRST STEP.

EXERCISES WITH STRAIGHT LINES.

Exercise 1.—*Combinations with Two Lines.*

The teacher provides herself with two thin sticks, and asks the children what they see? Two sticks. Placing them vertically against the wall, she asks, How are the sticks placed? They stand. If you wished to represent these sticks by means of lines, what kind of lines would you use? Straight lines. Very well; and what direction would you give the straight lines? They must be vertical.

The teacher then may place the sticks horizontally on the floor, and ask, How are they now situated? They *lie* on the floor. What lines would you use in order to represent them thus? Horizontal lines.

The teacher then places the sticks so that they are parallel to each other, and incline to the right, and asks the children what they can say about their position, and what lines they would use to represent them. She inclines them to the left, and asks similar questions. After this she makes them incline toward each other, and draws from the children, that they approach each other at one end, and are further apart at the other. By making the sticks meet, an angle is produced, which the children name, and tell by what kind of lines they would represent it. If the end of one stick is placed against the side of the other, two angles are produced, which can be either right angles, or one angle acute and the other obtuse. By making the sticks cross, four angles are produced, which must be either all right, or two angles acute and two obtuse. This exhausts the combinations which can be made with two sticks or two lines. (See Plate I.)

The children, having thus obtained a clear insight into the forms they will have to delineate, are told to draw upon their slates the combinations which the teacher forms with the sticks. In doing this, they should be instructed not to change the position of their slates. When each has drawn one or more figures, the teacher, selecting a number of those exhibiting the most taste and ingenuity, puts them on the blackboard. She then calls their attention to them, making such suggestions or remarks as may occur to her. The figures should now all be erased, both from the board and from the slates, and the children called upon to reproduce them from memory as far as possible, thus cultivating the conceptive faculty.

Plate I. represents all the combinations with two lines.

PLATE I.

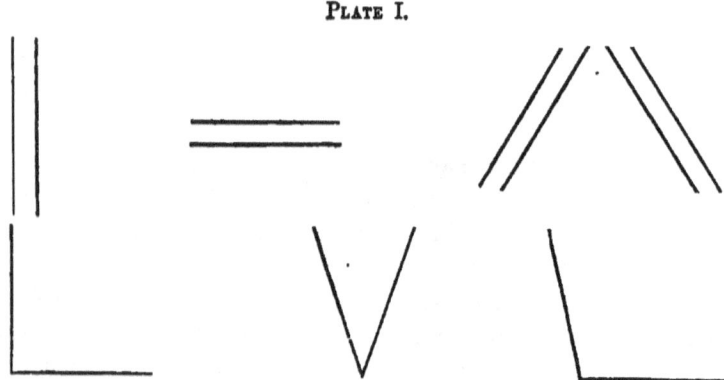

INVENTIVE DRAWING.—FIRST STEP.   423

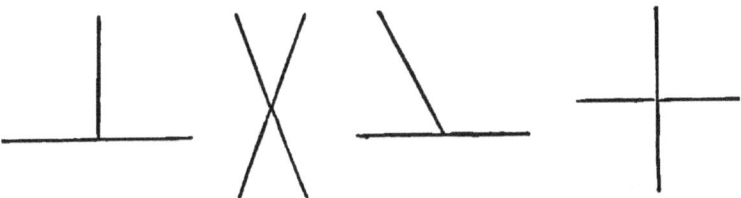

EXERCISE 2.—*Combinations with Three Lines.*

Although the first exercise was conducted entirely under the direction of the teacher, this was only done for the sake of making the children aware of the variety of positions which two sticks or two lines can assume. Now the children will be able to make these combinations for themselves. It is, however, advisable, not to dispense with the sticks as yet, but, placing *three* of them in the hands of a child, request him to arrange them on the floor, or against the wall, in as many ways as he can. When his power of combining them is exhausted, another child is called upon to arrange them in some other way, the teacher all the while repeating questions like these: What form do these sticks represent? What lines would you use to copy it? &c. Occasionally the teacher may infuse new life into the exercise, by suggesting a new application. For instance: combining the sticks in the following manner,

she may ask whether they recognize this form? As a consequence of this hint, several other letters will probably make their appearance, suggested by the children themselves. If the children make a combination of the triangle, it is for the teacher to suggest some varieties of triangles produced by the difference in the angles. The question may occasionally be brought up, whether, for instance,

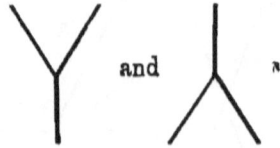

have to be received as different combinations—the one being only the reverse of the other. The answer to this is, that, geometrically considered, they are the same, but different as objects of drawing. Nevertheless, considering the immense variety of forms which the combinations of even a few lines afford, the teacher would do better to dispense with designs which are merely the reverse of others, or are simply modified by having their lines somewhat shorter or longer.

After the combinations have been made, by means of sticks, before the eyes of the children, they are required to draw them from memory upon their slates. After this, the teacher goes round, selects the best ones, and draws them on the blackboard. If she finds some that are wrong, she may submit them to the criticism of the class, by asking them in what they are wrong?

Plate II. contains combinations with three lines.

PLATE II.

EXERCISE 3.—*Combinations with Four Lines.*

The use of the sticks will not be found any longer necessary, in order to illustrate this and the following exercises. The teacher may simply tell the children to combine four lines in as many ways as they can, and collect their best productions. The blackboard will soon be filled with little designs. As before hinted, the teacher would do well to suggest occasionally a four-sided figure, or a letter formed of four lines,

or give a rough outline of an object,

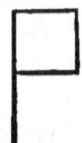

since these designs will be productive of others.

Plate III. contains combinations with four lines.

PLATE III.

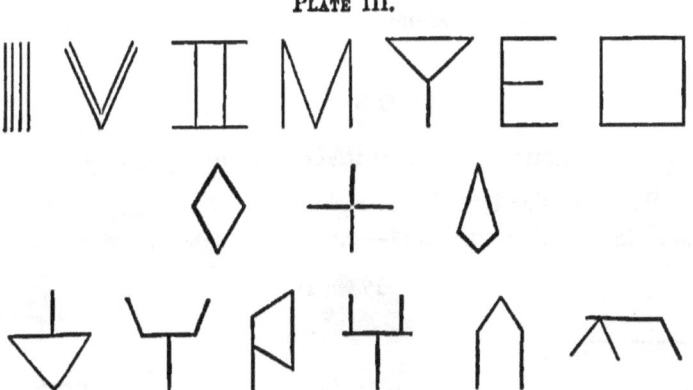

These exercises should be extended to figures composed of five, six, seven, and eight lines successively.

Before leaving the method of conducting these exercises entirely to the discretion of the teacher, we will make a few suggestions:

1. The principle of combination is that of *invention*. The inventive power is not, in the strictest sense, a creative power,

426 INVENTIVE DRAWING.—SECOND STEP.

but simply the power of forming a new aggregate by the different application of the same elements. The feeling with which the child regards his productions, which probably he never saw before, and which, perhaps, never existed, is one of intense joy and gratification. This gratification is shared by the teacher, who sees, in many instances, combinations arise which surpass her expectations, and which surprise her as an entire novelty.

2. Invention, at this Step, will not thrive in a healthy manner, unless the teacher gives occasionally some useful hints and suggestions, by indicating the directions in which the inventive talents of the children may be exerted to the greatest advantage. Again, she must discourage tasteless combinations, and contrast those that show unity and distinct arrangement of parts, with those that are loose and disjointed.

3. It will be seen, that in the combinations of angles, triangles, four-sided figures, &c., the number *four*, and its multiples, eight, twelve, sixteen, &c., will be the most appropriate for regular and tasteful combinations.

SECOND STEP.

Exercise 1.—*Combinations of Four Right Angles.*

The combination of four right angles will suggest two principal forms of arrangement—that of the *square*, and that of the

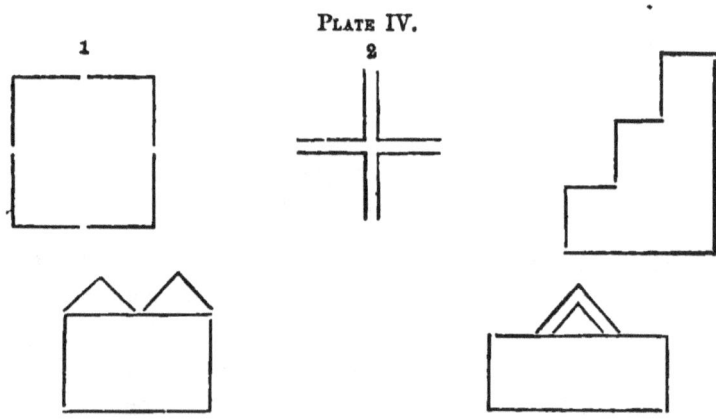

Plate IV.

cross—as seen in Plate IV., figs. 1 and 2. Besides these, other forms of a mixed character may be produced. After the teacher has collected a great number of designs of the children, and drawn them on the blackboard, she may make an interesting examination as to their innate feelings of taste, by asking which of these designs they like best? She will generally find their answers in accordance with the judgment of educated persons. Without reasoning, at this Step, upon the laws of taste, she may nevertheless practically let them see, that in all the good designs, the removal of but *one* part would destroy the unity and beauty of the whole; whilst in those which are disjointed, the effect is hardly perceptible. For instance:

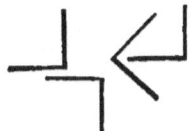

Such combinations hardly deserve the name of *designs*, and must be rejected, not on the principle of combination, but on that of taste.

EXERCISE 2.—*Combinations of Four Acute Angles.*

PLATE V.

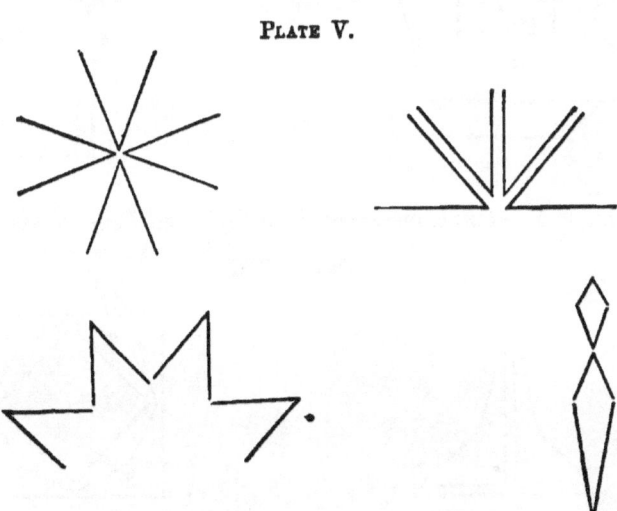

428 INVENTIVE DRAWING.—SECOND STEP.

EXERCISE 3.—*Combinations of Four Obtuse Angles.*
PLATE VI.

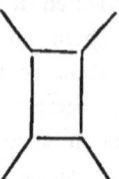

EXERCISE 4.—*Combinations of Four Right and Four Acute Angles.*
PLATE VII.

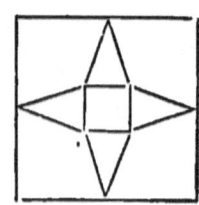
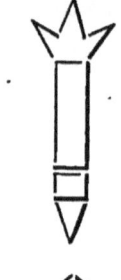

EXERCISE 5.—*Combinations of Four Right and Four Obtuse Angles.*
PLATE VIII.

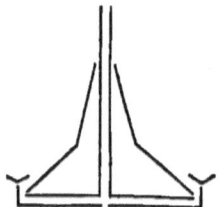
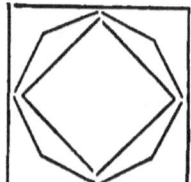

INVENTIVE DRAWING.—SECOND STEP. 429

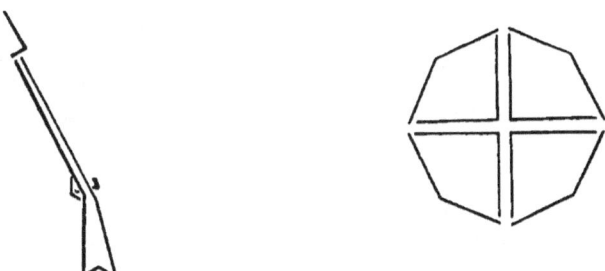

Exercise 6.—*Combinations of Four Right, Four Obtuse, and Four Acute Angles.*

Plate IX.

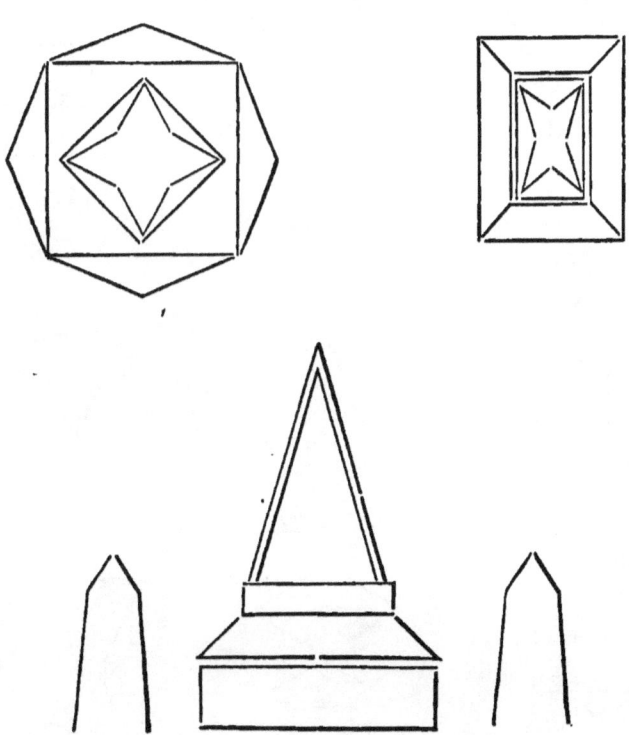

430   INVENTIVE DRAWING.—SECOND STEP.

EXERCISE 7.—*Combinations of Triangles.*

We will only allude to the order of these combinations, without giving diagrams, since the children can produce them now with ease:

(*a*) Combination of four rectangular triangles. (Plate X.)
(*b*) Combination of four acute-angular triangles. (Plate XI.)
(*c*) Combination of four obtuse-angular triangles. (Plate XII.)
(*d*) Combination of all the above kinds of triangles, indiscriminately united. (Plate XIII.)

PLATE X.

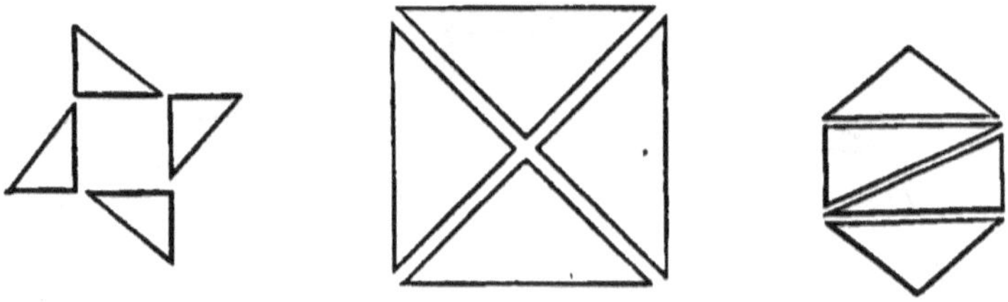

PLATE XI.

PLATE XII.

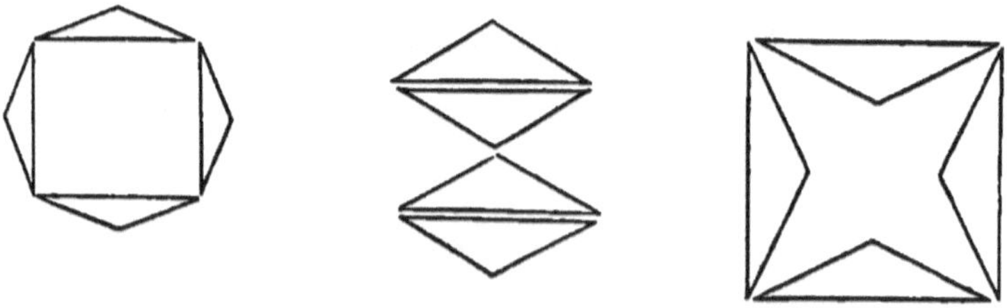

INVENTIVE DRAWING.—SECOND STEP. 431

PLATE XIII.

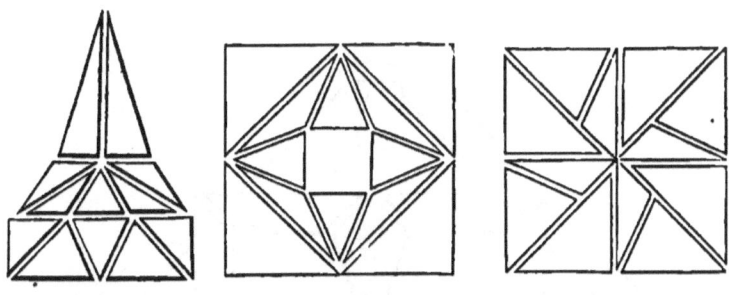

EXERCISE 8.—*Combination of Quadrangular Figures.*

(*a*) Combination of squares. (*b*) Of rectangles. (*c*) Of rhombs. (*d*) Of rhomboids. (*e*) Of trapeziums. (*f*) Of trapezoids. (*g*) Of all the above kinds of quadrangular figures, indiscriminately united.

NOTE.—Some of the above-named forms are less adapted to combinations than others. Of those that are very applicable to architectural designs, we will name the rectangle, in connection with the trapezoid, as seen in Plate XIV. All, however, can be used for ornamental purposes, as seen in Plate XV.

PLATE XIV.

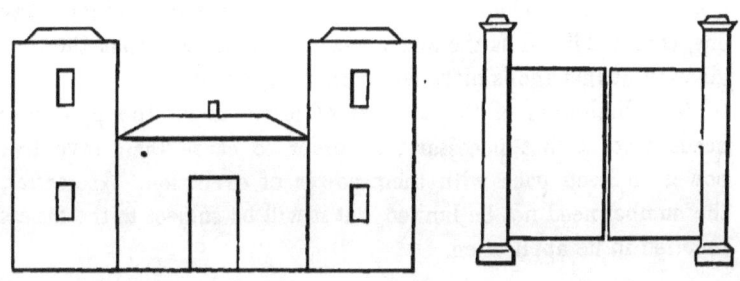

PLATE XV.

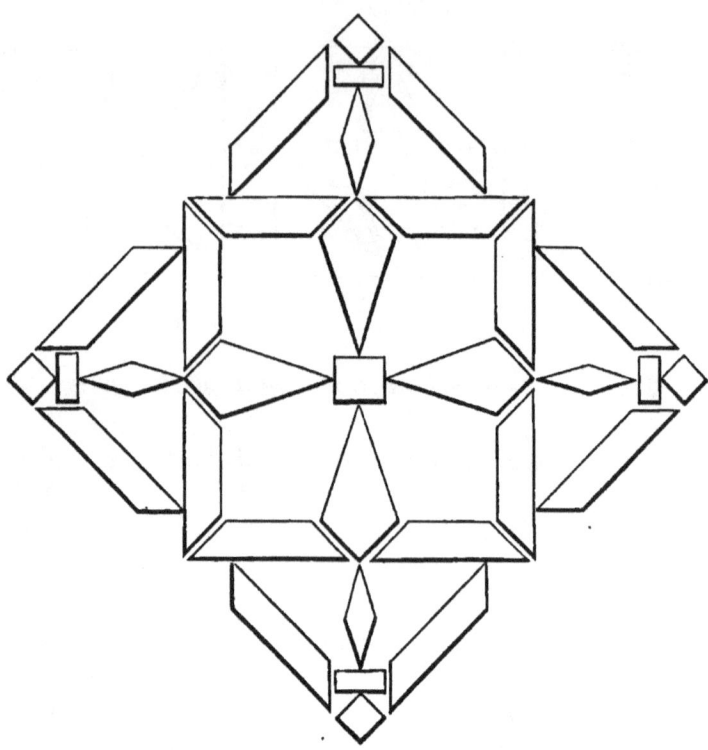

We have only shown a few designs that can be obtained by each exercise; but any observing teacher will be astonished at the multiplicity and beauty of the designs that may be obtained from children of even medium capacity. It will convince any one, that childhood is the age for combinations, and that the imagination at this age is more fertile than in the adult.

The limitation of the number of forms under the preceding heads was at first necessary, in order to cause their inventive power to keep pace with their power of execution. Hereafter, the number need not be limited, but it will be subject to the fitness required in its application.

THIRD STEP.

COMBINATIONS OF CURVED LINES.

EXERCISE 1.—*The Idea of Concave and Convex Developed.*

The line which is used in all the exercises of this Step, is a part of the circle, called an *arc*. (See exercises on "Form.") Some properties of the curved line have already been discussed under the head of "Form." There remains, however, one property to be developed, namely, that of *concave* and *convex*, which the teacher can do somewhat after the following plan:

The teacher presents to the class an object in the form of a hollow hemisphere, and asks whether they see any difference between one side of the object and the other? The children will probably say that one of its sides is *hollow*, whilst the other is not. If the teacher wishes to illustrate the subject in a still more striking manner, she may show that the hollow side acts as a cup, and is capable of holding other objects, whilst they would roll off from the other side. She may show them a solid sphere, and ask them whether the surface they see is hollow, or not? A watch glass

PLATE XVI.

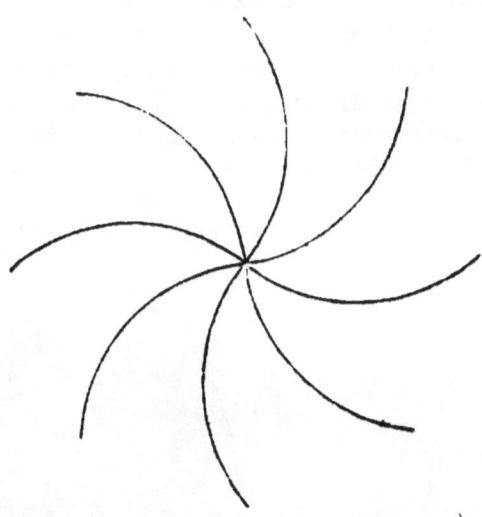

may also serve as an illustration of the idea of *hollow*, and its opposite. The teacher may then draw an arc on the blackboard, and ask them to point out its hollow side, and the one which is not hollow. She then gives them the name of *concave*, instead of hollow, and of *convex*, to designate the opposite of the line.

After this, the children might draw the arc in different positions, as seen in Plate XVI.

Exercise 2.—*Curvilinear Angles.*

Whilst the different sides of straight-linear angles are based upon the width of their opening, we shall find that the distinctive feature of curvilinear angles is based on the concavity or convexity of its lines. In order to develop this idea, let the teacher draw the angles (see Plate XVII.), and ask the following questions: Suppose, in fig. 1, you were placed in the inside of the angle, viewing the sides of its arcs, which sides would be turned toward you—the concave, or the convex sides? The concave sides. Let us view fig. 2 in the same manner. What sides of the arcs do you see? The convex sides. And in fig. 3? One arc shows its concave side, and the other its convex side. The teacher then gives the name of *concave* angle to fig. 1; fig. 2 is called the *convex* angle; fig. 3 would, according to its properties, be called *concave-convex* angle; but in order to have a shorter word, and on account of its *mixed* character, let us call it a *mixed* angle. The children may now draw these different angles in different positions, and with their openings of different degrees.

Plate XVII.

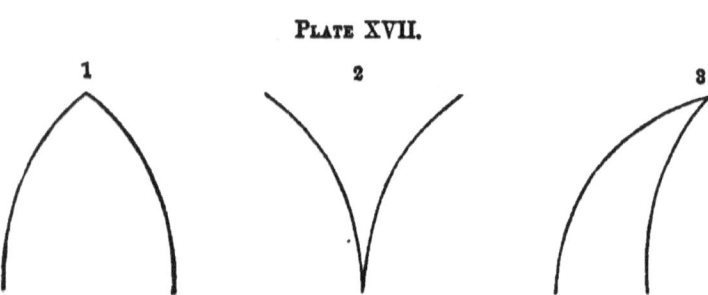

Curvilinear Combinations.

The curved line is in preference the line of grace and beauty, and offers a greater variety of pleasing designs than the straight line. The child will delight in the increased scope which its exercises will afford to his imagination. A curvilinear angle, for instance, will present to him the image of a cup, which, with the addition of some marginal ornaments, may branch out into the likeness of a flower. The effect of this discovery is twofold: it must lead the attention of the child toward nature's fairest productions—the flowers, &c.—and the treasures of art; and, on the other hand, he may easily be led to apply his inventive talent to the production of tasteful patterns, for domestic use as well as for the requirements of industry. The true educator cannot but approve of means given to him to develop that eminently moral power, *taste*, for which our schools have been unable hitherto to contribute even the smallest mite, unless by the slavish imitation of copies in drawing. This, however, considers taste but as an acquired faculty, whilst the means presented here propose to expand the innate germs of a divine power into evergreen branches of grace and loveliness.

EXERCISE 3.—*Combination of Four Concave Angles.*

PLATE XVIII.

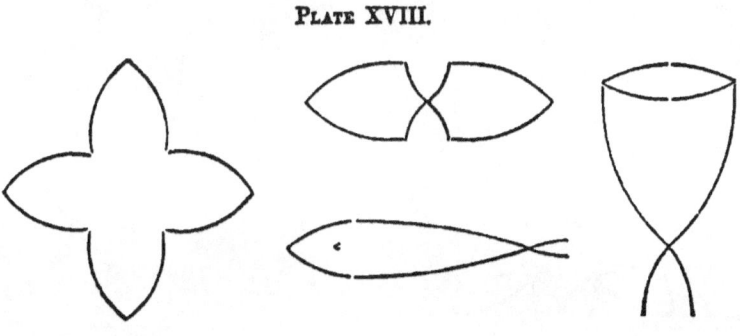

Exercise 4.—*Combination of Four Convex Angles.*
PLATE XIX.

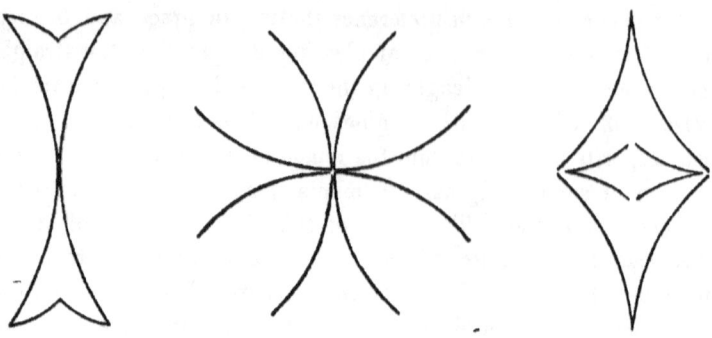

Exercise 5.—*Combination of Four Mixed Angles.*
PLATE XX.

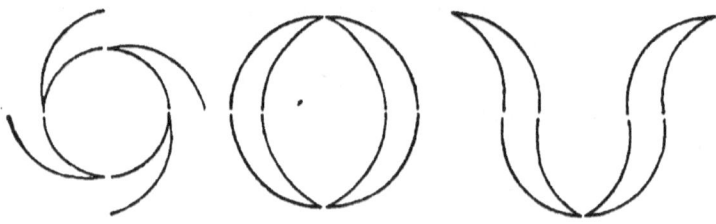

Exercise 6.—*Combination of a Certain Number of Concave, Convex, and Mixed Angles.*
PLATE XXI.

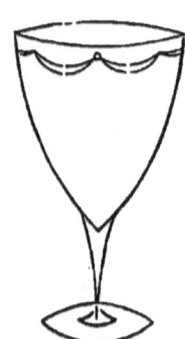

INVENTIVE DRAWING.—THIRD STEP. 437

Exercise 7.—*Combination of Two-sided Figures.*

There are three kinds of them, as seen in Plate XXII., figs. A, B, C, a definition of which must be made by the children themselves. The form of A is sometimes called a *double convex lens;* that of B, a *crescent.* Fig. C has a peculiar feature, in having both angles outside. These angles are called, in geometry, *re-entrant angles.*

PLATE XXII.

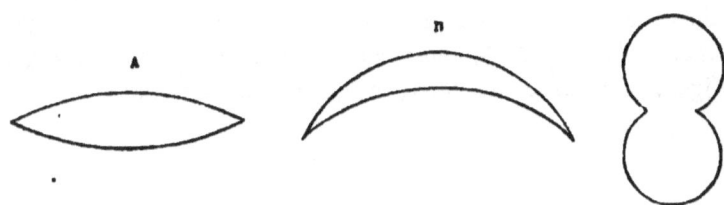

After this explanation, the pupils proceed to the combination of the above figures.

Exercise 8.—*Combination of Triangular Figures.*

We content ourselves with giving the different kinds of triangles which can be used for these combinations. (See Plate XXIII.)

The children will take pleasure in using them for the invention of many tasteful designs.

PLATE XXIII.

438 INVENTIVE DRAWING.—THIRD STEP.

EXERCISE 9.—*Combination of Four-sided Figures.*

We give, in Plate XXIV., a variety of four-sided figures obtained under this condition. Figs. 1, 2, 3, have all their angles inside. Figs. 4, 5, 6, those which have one re-entrant angle. Figs. 7, 8, 9, have two, three, or four re-entrant angles.

PLATE XXIV.

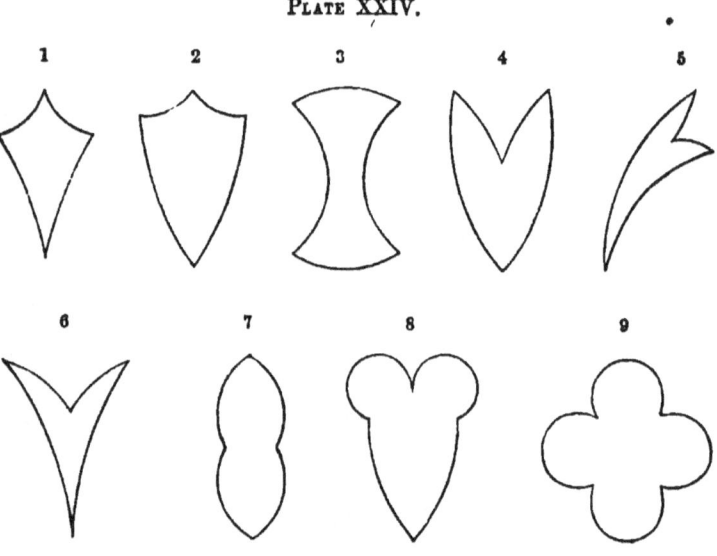

Of the immense variety of combinations which this exercise affords, we can only give a faint idea in Plate XXV.

INVENTIVE DRAWING.—THIRD STEP.

PLATE XXV.

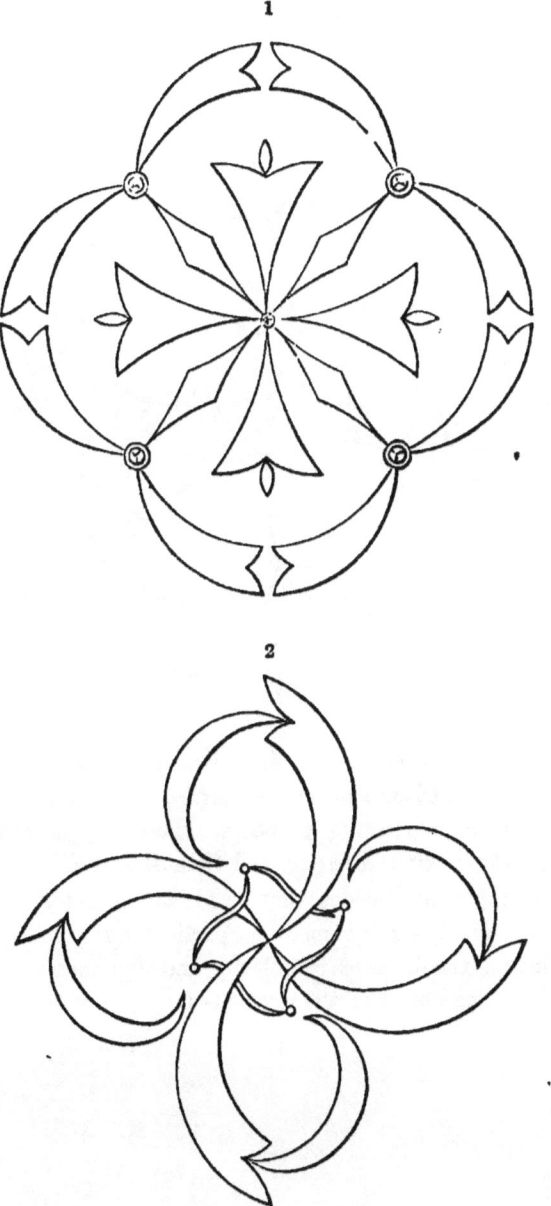

440   INVENTIVE DRAWING.—THIRD STEP.

The fig. in Plate XXVI. combines three and four-sided figures.

PLATE XXVI.

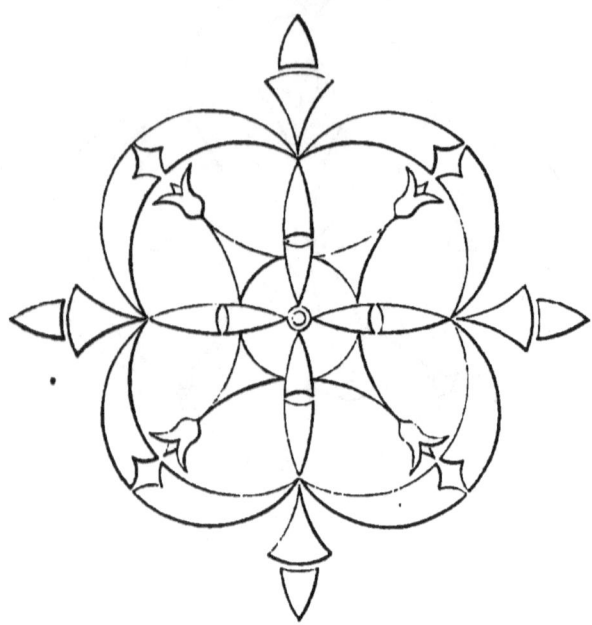

The design in Plate XXVII. shows how easily curvilinear figures can be shaped into flower-like forms, which are often found in patterns for manufacturing purposes. To draw, however, a design of the above kind *correctly*, and with the attributes of good taste, several powers besides that of invention must necessarily co-operate. Of these, we mention particularly a mathematical appreciation of the laws of Regularity and Symmetry, to supply which will be the object of the next Step.

PLATE XXVII.

FOURTH STEP.

DICTATION OF REGULAR AND SYMMETRICAL DESIGNS.

Introduction.

When we allowed the inventive faculties of the children a scope unfettered by exact measurement, it was done with the expectation that their sense of taste would guide them almost unconsciously to give to their designs the necessary exactness of delineation. It becomes, however, at this Step, the teacher's duty to develop, in a systematic manner, a mathematical conception of exact measurement, which will enhance the merit of the productions of her class. To do this, she must begin with the division of the simple line.

EXERCISE 1.—*Division of Lines into Equal Parts.*

The exercises under this head may be treated in the following order:

1. Let the children divide given lines into two, four, eight equal parts.
2. Into three, six, and nine equal parts.
3. Into five and ten equal parts.

NOTE.—The lines may be straight or curved. Exercises of this kind will also afford a practical illustration of the nature and relation of fractions.

Designs Based on the Division of Lines of Two or Four Equal Parts.

Some Laws of Taste Developed.—The object of this exercise is to fix certain points in a given square, from which other lines may be drawn, till we obtain a simple design.

In order to introduce the pupils to this new kind of construction, we advise the teacher to make them draw the first design under her dictation, as will be shown in the next model lesson.

EXERCISE 2.—*Dictation.*

Teacher (*dictating*).—Draw a square; then divide each of its sides into two equal parts, and draw from each of the points of intersection a line to the opposite point. How many squares have you thus obtained?

Children.—Four small squares.

Teacher.—Now draw two diagonal lines; that is, lines which are drawn from one corner of the square to the other. How many triangles have you now got? What kind of triangles? How do you like the design? (See Plate XXVIII., fig. 1.) Let us try to improve it somewhat, by removing some lines according to my further dictation. Rub out the right half of the upper horizontal side of the original square. Do the same with the lower half of the right vertical side; the same with the left half of the lower horizontal side; the same with the upper half of the left vertical side. (Plate XXVIII., fig. 2.) What have you now left? Do you like the design better than before? Why?

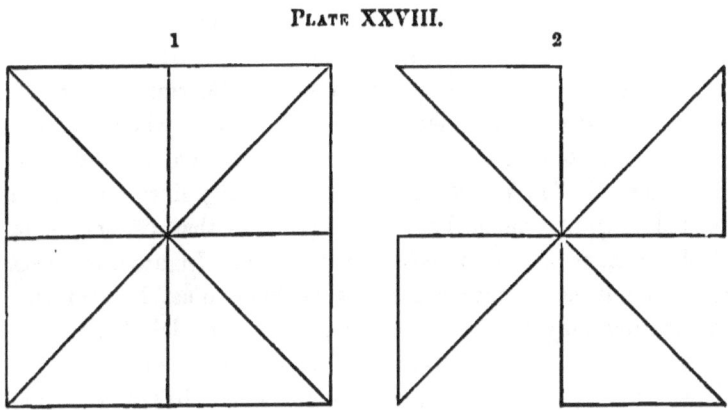

PLATE XXVIII.

The reason for liking a thing better, or for giving a preference in matters of taste, seems at first above the capacity of children. And yet such a question might elicit very sensible answers, and not the less true from not being scientifically given. Each child sees that the four remaining triangles are now more *distinctly* seen, because they have been separated from each other. Again, those triangles are all situated in different *positions* with reference to each other, which affords a pleasant variety to the eye. *Distinction of parts* and *variety of position* therefore form an important requisite of good taste.

EXERCISE 3.—*Dictation of Design in Plate XXIX., Fig. 2.*

Draw another square. Divide each side into four equal parts. How is this to be done? Next draw from all these points (except from those in the centre of each side), lines to points directly opposite. Describe the parts of the figure as it appears now. What form do you see in the centre of the figure? And what forms are situated on each side of that central square? What forms are situated at the corners of the original square? (See Plate XXIX., fig. 1.) Now draw a line from the left upper corner of the central square, to the centre of the upper horizontal side of the large square; next from the right upper corner of the central square a line to the right upper corner of the large square; after this, from the same corner of the central square, a line to the middle of the right vertical side of the large square; again, from the lower right corner of the central square a line to the right lower corner of the large square, &c. &c. The teacher will easily see how the dictation is to be completed, as shown by the light dotted lines in fig. 1. When all the necessary lines have been dictated, it will be found that the design lacks that distinctness to which we have alluded in a former dictation. In order to effect this, some lines, or rather portions of lines, must be removed. The teacher may now continue: " Remove the left half of the upper horizontal, and the right half of the lower horizontal side of the large square. Again, remove the upper half of the right vertical and the lower half of the left vertical side of the large square."

The children will now see more clearly the plan of the proposed design; but there are still some superfluous lines. In order to test their feeling of taste, the teacher might ask the class what lines they think should be further erased? Very probably some children will propose to remove all the pieces marked *a* (see Diagram). In addition to this, the teacher may tell them to erase all those lines which form continuations of the sides of the central square. It now stands as seen in fig. 2.

The design being now completed, the teacher wishes the class to describe all the portions of the design. Of what does it consist? Of one square surrounded by four rhomboids. Repeat this.

For the sake of improving their crude notions of taste, a judicious teacher may ask questions like the following, if her class is sufficiently advanced: Of what did you say the design consists? Are the parts all uniform, or is there some *variety* in them? Are the rhomboids all placed in the same manner? Before you erased some of the lines, did the rhomboids appear *distinctly?*

Did they afterward? When did they show to best advantage? If I removed *one* of the rhomboids, would the design look so well as before? Why not?

The teacher may also take occasion, if she finds a design badly drawn, from a want of accuracy in dividing the lines into four equal parts, or for other reasons, to contrast such a design, as seen in Plate XXIX., fig. 3, with one that is correct, and ask which they like best? Why?

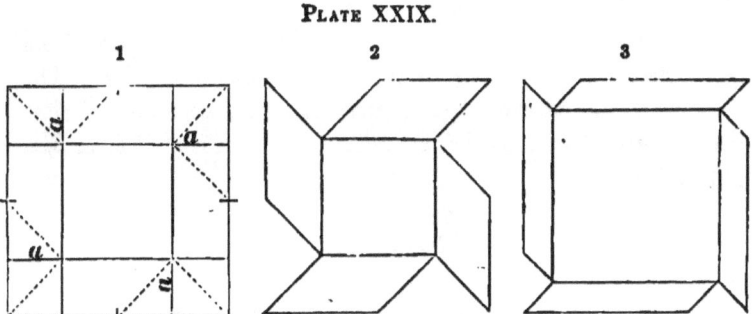

PLATE XXIX.

Without wishing to anticipate the answers of the children, we would remind the teacher, that the size of the central square in fig. 3 is too large, at the expense of the rhomboids, and thus prevents the design from being symmetrical.

It has already been suggested, that in these questions on taste, the teacher must neither reason nor lecture before the children, but simply ask questions, and lead them to discover the right principle, by using language which they can comprehend. But whether this is found practicable or not, one thing is sure: the teacher who would cultivate inventive talent in the children, as well as her own judgment about designs, must clearly comprehend that *unity, variety, distinctness,* and *symmetry* are the great leading principles of taste, as exemplified by all the works of the Creator.

It is not intended that the teacher should dictate *all* the designs of this kind, but that the children should ultimately be induced to invent others. The teacher may occasionally suggest a beginning, and allow them to finish the design. The next exer-

446   INVENTIVE DRAWING.—FOURTH STEP.

cise will render the path of invention so easy, that the children will not fail to enter upon it.

EXERCISE 4.—*Designs Based upon the Division of Lines into Three Equal Parts.*

To show the variety even in simple designs, let us assume each side of a square divided into three equal parts, and indicate these divisions by dots.

Now we will make a condition, that lines may be drawn from these dots to those opposite, or situated on some other line. The following diagrams show figures that may be thus produced after erasing portions of the original outline. (See Plate XXX., figs. 1, 2, 3, 4.)

PLATE XXX.

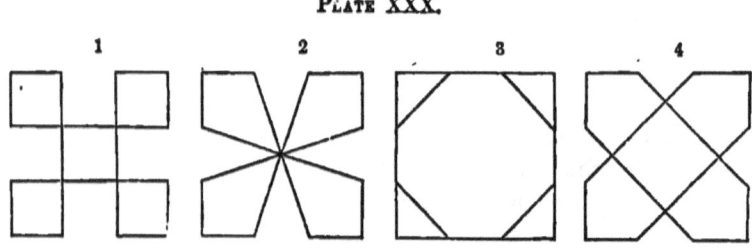

Suggestions in regard to Inventing Regular Designs.

If we wish to add more details to these simple designs, it can be done in two ways: (*a*) By the subdivision of the lines in the design. (*b*) By the repetition of the same design. We will give examples of each:

(*a*) *By Subdivision.*—By this method we consider the simple design as the one intended to receive the additional details, which are dependent on the division of its lines. For instance: selecting fig. 1, in Plate XXX., as the fundamental design, we obtain, by the subdivision of its lines, and the addition of new ones, the designs seen in Plate XXXI. Or, selecting fig. 2, in Plate

INVENTIVE DRAWING.—FOURTH STEP. 447

Plate XXXI.

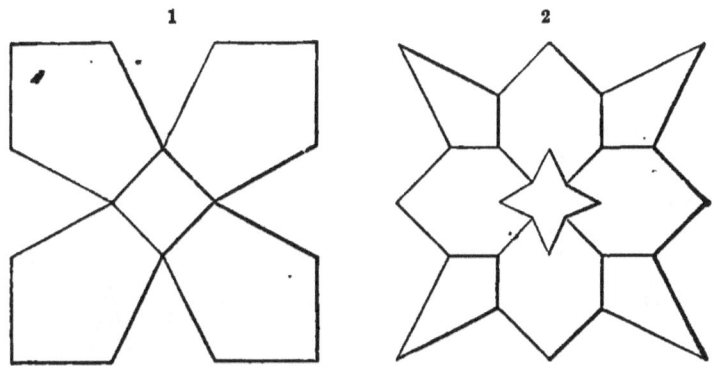

Plate XXXII.

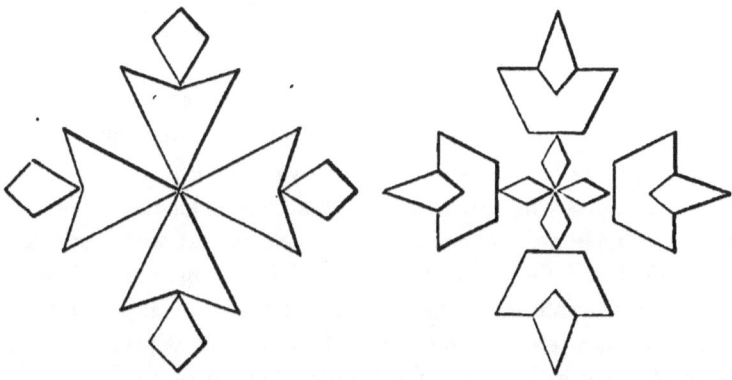

XXX., for a similar purpose, we obtain the designs seen in Plate XXXII.

(*b*) *By Repetition.*—By this method we repeat the same design a certain number of times, like a pattern. The object of such an arrangement is, to get an enlarged design round an apparently new centre, of which, however, some superfluous parts will have to be removed.

We have chosen fig. 2, in Plate XXX., to be repeated four times. (See Plate XXXIII., fig. 1.) But now the question arises, which lines are to be removed, in order to give the re-

PLATE XXXIII.

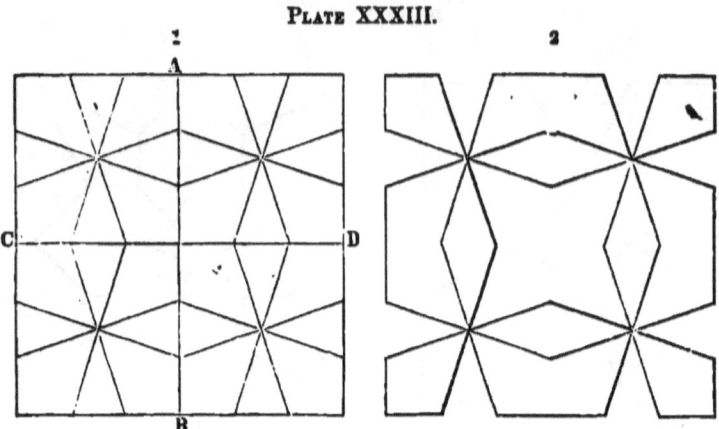

maining parts a more distinct and pleasing appearance. There will be three ways to perform this operation, namely:

1. We may remove the middle part of each side of one of the small squares (Plate XXXIII., fig. 2); or
2. The extreme parts of each side of the same squares.
3. The two middle parts of each side of the large square.

It may also be appropriate to remove the lines A B and C D. These examples will show what a scope there is for the variety of designs. They are innumerable, and each scholar with but moderate talent will find some new ones which he may call *his own*, and will appreciate the more as the result of his inventive power. It is always a pleasant feeling to invent; but when invention combines taste with utility, it will be doubly pleasant.

Care must be taken to change the outlines of designs, so as to produce more variety. Many of our patterns that are applied to practical purposes are within a triangle; others within a rectangle, hexagon, octagon. The latter of these figures, which is easy of construction, and affords much scope for variety, will here receive some consideration.

Construction of the Octagon.

The teacher dictates to the children: Draw a square with two diagonals, and mark the middle of each side of the square by a dot. Measure the distance from this middle to the centre of the square (where the diagonals meet), and mark off the same distance from this centre on the diagonal lines. Finally, unite the points obtained by the last operation with the points in the centre of the sides of the square, by lines, the sum of which constitutes the regular octagon. (Plate XXXIV.) The square may now be removed, having only served for the construction of the octagon.

PLATE XXXIV.

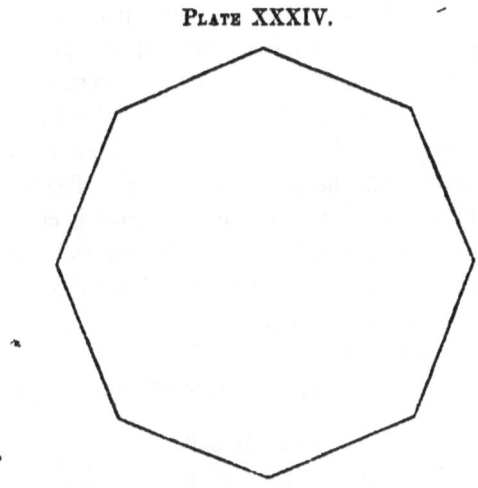

There is another method, which dispenses with the square, and only makes use of the bisection of the right angle. It is this: Draw a cross, by means of a vertical line bisecting a horizontal line of the same length at right angles. Bisect these right angles, by lines of the same length as the other two. Lastly, unite the ends of these lines, and we have the octagon.

The teacher would do well to point out to the class, that the four long lines alluded to in the second construction of the octagon, are in reality but diagonals of the same. These diagonals will be an important aid for dictating or making a design, since, from their equal distribution, it is possible to fix many other points upon them at regular distances.

In proceeding once more to the dictation of a design, in order to induce the class to produce others, the teacher will find that it is possible, by one well-applied remark, to produce the drawing

450　INVENTIVE DRAWING.—FOURTH STEP.

of several lines at once, instead of giving directions for the drawing of every separate line.

Dictation of a Design in the Octagon. (*See Plate XXXV., Fig.* 1.)

Draw an octagon, and let the four lines stand which were necessary for its construction. What are these lines called? How are they divided by the point of intersection? Now divide each half of the diagonals into two equal parts, as also each side of the octagon. Next draw from each of the points which are situated halfway between the point of intersection and the ends of a diagonal, two small lines to the centres of the two nearest sides of the octagon. How many such lines have you to draw? Now let us remove all the superfluous lines. Erase the two extreme quarters of each diagonal, and the design is completed. Of what parts does it consist? What do we call the four-sided figures round the centre of the design? What those situated near its corners? Now erase your figure. Who could draw it entirely from memory, and better than before?

In Plate XXXV., fig. 2, there is another design, made by the

PLATE XXXV.

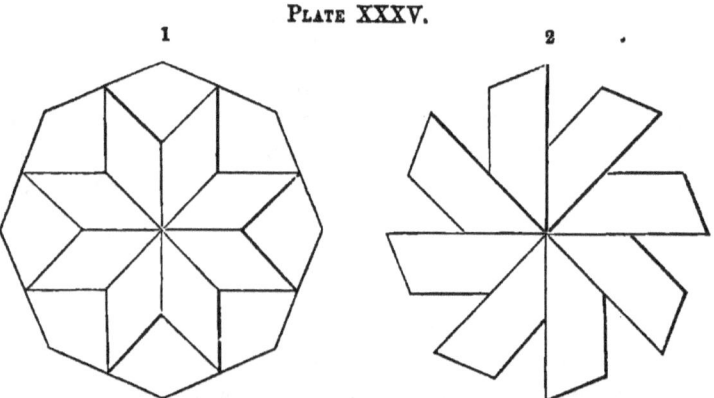

same construction, with a few modifications, and resulting in what the children might call "a wheel," formed of eight trapezoids. In Plate XXXVI., fig. 1, the design is based upon eight diagonals (different from those used in the former design), which, after intersecting each other, are slightly modified by erasing some of their interior parts.

INVENTIVE DRAWING.—FOURTH STEP. 451

PLATE XXXVI.

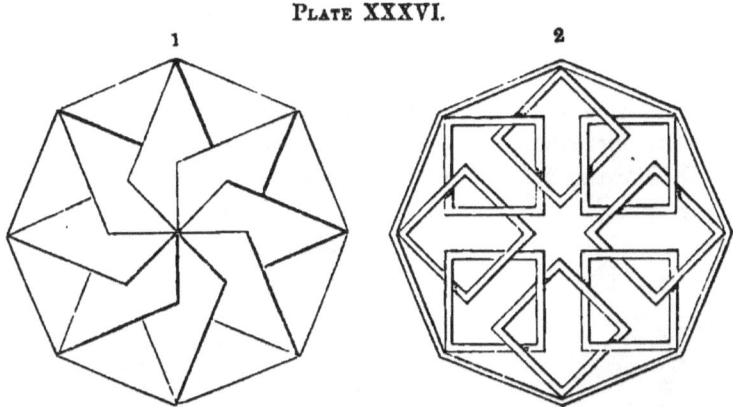

Eight diagonals, different from those used in the preceding diagrams, were necessary to obtain the ingenious design in Plate XXXVI., fig. 2. After drawing these eight diagonals, which will form two squares, a smaller octagon will appear, the sides of which are to be divided into three equal parts. After uniting the opposite points of these sides by parallel lines, and removing their central portion, we obtain eight small squares entangled within each other. Doubling these squares, in order to make them appear like solid frames, the effect becomes more striking.

The pupil will easily invent many more designs, by dividing the sides of the octagon into *three* equal parts, and drawing from the points of intersection lines to the opposite points.

CURVILINEAR DESIGNS, WITH DUE REGARD TO THE LAWS OF REGULARITY AND SYMMETRY.

Measurement of Arcs.

Since the invention of curvilinear designs has already been treated in the Second Step of this course, a few words only may be required respecting the measurement of curves, and their proper application.

In drawing or copying an arc in a regular manner, it will be found convenient to suppose it subtended by a straight line, from the middle of which a perpendicular is erected, as seen in the following figure. The straight line which forms the base, indi-

452 INVENTIVE DRAWING.—FOURTH STEP.

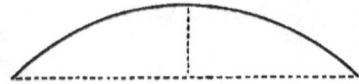

cates the direct distance from one point of the arc to the other, whilst the perpendicular measures the concavity of the arc.

In drawing, for instance, the shape of a cup or vase, a rectilinear triangle will be found of great advantage, to support the curves. (See figs. 1, 2.) If two of the lines are bisected, the

Fig. 1.	Fig. 2.	Fig. 3.
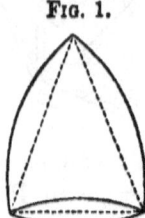	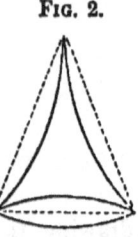	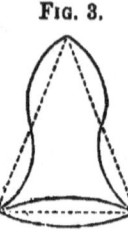

curves may assume a graceful waving character, as seen in fig. 3.

It is easily seen how the designs suggested in the previous Step may be used for the regular application of curvilinear designs.

The design in Plate XXXVII. is based upon the cross-shaped figure in Plate XXX., fig. 2. Let the class find others.

PLATE XXXVII.

Drawing of the Circle.

We conclude this course with the circle, which displays the greatest regularity and symmetry of outline, and which on this account it is difficult to draw correctly without the aid of a mathematical instrument. Since, however, the circle, or figures resembling it—the ellipse, oval, &c.—are often required in making illustrations, or in delineating artificial and natural objects, it is desirable to train the hand in drawing this difficult figure as accurately as possible.

In doing this, it is safe to support the circle by the same lines which were necessary for the construction of the regular octagon. Considering their point of intersection as the centre of the circle, these lines will form eight radii, over the ends of which the circumference may be drawn. (See fig. 1, below.)

Another method, which will at the same time be found convenient for drawing hemisphere maps with meridians, requires merely two equal lines intersecting at right angles. If we draw an arc erected on *d f* of the *height* of *a c*, and afterward others at stated distances, till the last one passes over *e* (the end of the radius *a e*), we have in the last line produced a semicircle. Repeating the same operation on the other side, another semicircle is produced. Thus we obtain the whole circle, intersected by arcs, which in a map might be termed meridians.

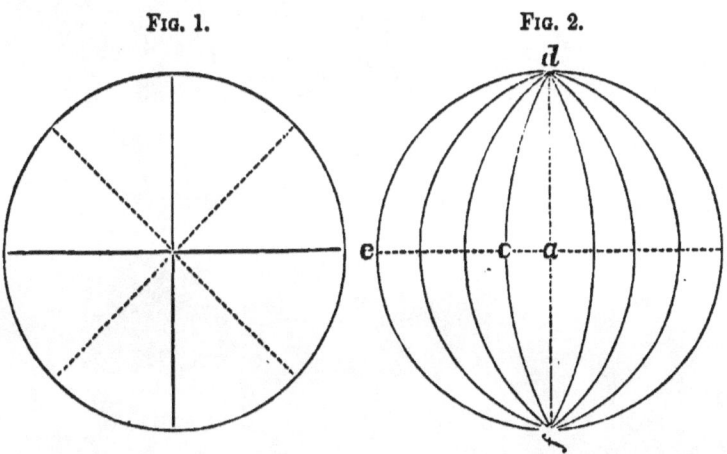

Fig. 1.   Fig. 2.

INVENTIVE DRAWING.—FOURTH STEP.

It need hardly be said, that many beautiful designs might be drawn in a circle, on the basis of its diameters, and assisted by a regular division of its quadrants, and hence of the angles round the centre. These designs must necessarily display an endless variety, since all the elements of form may be arranged around one rallying point, branching out in all directions.

PROGRAMME

OF

COURSE OF ORAL INSTRUCTION,

FOR

FIRST THREE YEARS IN THE OSWEGO SCHOOLS.

First Year, or C Class, Primary.

FIRST TERM.

1st *Fortnight.*—Lessons on Human Body and Mammals.
2d   "   "   Form and Color.
3d   "   "   Elementary Geography, or Place and Size.
4th   "   "   Objects and Inventive Drawing.
5th   "   "   Moral Instruction and Birds.
6th   "   "   Human Body and Color.
7th   "   "   Form and Geography, or Place.

SECOND TERM.

1st *Fortnight.*—Lessons on Size and Objects.
2d   "   "   Inventive Drawing and Moral Instruction.
3d   "   "   Mammals and Human Body.
4th   "   "   Color and Form.

5th *Fortnight.*—Lessons on Place, or Geography, and Objects.
6th   "   "   Inventive Drawing and Moral Instruction.
7th   "   "   Human Body, Fishes, and Reptiles.
8th   "   "   Sounds and Weight.

THIRD TERM.

1st *Fortnight.*—Lessons on Color and Form.
2d   "   "   Geography and Objects.
3d   "   "   Human Body and Mammals.
4th   "   "   Size and Weight.
5th   "   "   Sounds and Moral Instruction.
6th   "   "   Inventive Drawing and Geography.

Second Year, or B Class, Primary.

FIRST TERM.

1st *Month.*—Lessons on Form and Inventive Drawing.
2d   "   "   Mammals and Color.
3d   "   "   Objects and Geography.
4th   "   "   Sounds and Weight.

SECOND TERM.

1st *Month.*—Lessons on Size and Geography.
2d   "   "   Mammals, Insects, and Objects.
3d   "   "   Form and Color.
4th   "   "   Moral Instruction and Drawing.

THIRD TERM.

1st *Month.*—Lessons on Objects, Mammals, and Birds.
2d   "   "   Elementary Geography and Color.
3d   "   "   Form, alternating with Drawing and Moral Instruction.

Third Year, or A Class, Primary.

FIRST TERM.

1st Month.—Lessons on Objects and Inventive Drawing.
2d   "   "   Plants and Language.
3d   "   "   Color and Elementary Geography.
4th "   "   Form and Moral Instruction.

SECOND TERM.

1st Month.—Lessons on Geography and Inventive Drawing.
2d   "   "   Objects and Plants.
3d   "   "   Color and Language.
4th "   "   Moral Instruction and Form.

THIRD TERM.

1st Month.—Lessons on Geography and Language.
2d   "   "   Objects and Animals.
3d   "   "   Form and Color.

Exercises in Reading, Spelling, and Number daily, with each class. All new words occurring in Second, Third, or Fourth Step lessons to be spelled by the class. Any portion of the school not employed in recitation, should be occupied with their slates in printing or writing, inventive drawing, making out tables, or reproducing lessons. Some definite work should be assigned to all the divisions of the school for every hour in the day.

It will be remembered that all First Step lessons belong to the first year of the child's school-life, the Second Step to the second year, &c. This, however, can only be considered as a general direction.

Teachers may find it necessary not unfrequently to vary somewhat this arrangement, to adapt it to the varying ages and capacities of children. We cannot too carefully study the character of the children we have to educate, observing the effect of each lesson on their minds. If the lesson fails to interest the children, we may regard it as a very sure indication that the lesson is either not properly presented, or not adapted to them. It may be above, or it may be below them. The skilful teacher will carefully observe these things, and change the character of her lessons to adapt them to the children before her.

DAILY PROGRAMME

OF AN

OSWEGO PRIMARY SCHOOL.

C Class, or First Year.

A. M.

9:00 to 9:15.—Opening Exercises.
9:15 " 9:35.—Sub. 4, Phonic Reading.
9:35 " 9:40.—Physical Exercises.
9:40 " 10:00.—General Lesson.
10:00 " 10:20.—Sub. 3, Phonic Reading.
10:20 " 10:35.—Recess.
10:35 " 10:55.—General Lesson.
10:55 " 11:00.—Marching.
11:00 " 11:20.—Sub. 2, Phonic Reading.
11:20 " 11:35.—Recess.
11:35 " 11:50.—Sub. 1, Number, with Objects.
11:50 " 11:55.—Singing, and Dismissal of Youngest Children.
11:55 " 12:10.—Sub. 2, Number, with Objects.
12:10 " 12:30.—Sub. 1, Phonic Reading.
12:30 to 1:30.—Intermission.

P. M.

1:30 to 1:50.—General Lesson.
1:50 " 2:5.—Sub. 3, Number, with Objects.
2:5 " 2:10.—Physical Exercises.

2 : 10 to 2 : 25.—Sub. 4, Number, with Objects.
2 : 25 "   2 : 35.—Singing, Roll-call, and Dismissal of Youngest Children.
2 : 35 "   3 : 00.—Reading from Books.

Children not engaged in Class exercises, are occupied with their slates in printing, or drawing.

B Class, or Second Year.

A. M.

9 : 00 to 9 : 15.—Opening Exercises.
9 : 15 "   9 : 40.—Sub. 1, Reading. Sub. 2, Making Tables on Slates.
9 : 40 "   9 : 45.—Physical Exercises.
9 : 45 " 10 : 5.—Sub. 2, Reading. Sub. 1, Making Tables on Slates.
10 : 5 " 10 : 20.—Phonic Spelling, both Divisions.
10 : 20 " 10 : 35.—Recess.
10 : 35 " 10 : 55.—Examine Work on Slates.
10 : 55 " 11 : 20.—General Lesson.
11 : 20 " 11 : 35.—Recess.
11 : 35 " 12 : 00.—Sub. 2, Number. Sub. 1, Print Phonic Spelling.
12 : 00 " 12 : 5.—Singing, and Dismissal of Sub. 2.
12 : 5 " 12 : 30.—Sub. 1, Phonic Spelling from Slates.
    12 : 30 to 1 : 30.—Intermission.

P. M.

1 : 30 to 1 : 50.—General Lesson.
1 : 50 "   2 : 5.—Inventive Drawing.
2 : 5 "   2 : 10.—Physical Exercises.
2 : 10 "   2 : 25.—Sub. 2, Phonic Spelling. Sub. 1, Drawing, or Printing.
2 : 25 "   2 : 45.—Sub. 1, Number. Sub. 2, Drawing, or Printing.
2 : 45 "   3 : 00.—Examination of Work on Slates.

A Class, or Third Year.

A. M.

9 : 00 to 9 : 15.—Opening Exercises.
9 : 15 " 9 : 40.—Sub. 1, Reading. Sub. 2, Preparing Reading Lesson.
9 : 40 " 9 : 45.—Physical Exercises.
9 : 45 " 10 : 5.—Sub. 2, Reading. Sub. 1, Preparing Tables on Slates.
10 : 5 " 10 : 20.—Sub. 1, Phonic Spelling. Sub. 2, Preparing Tables on Slates.
10 : 20 " 10 : 35.—Recess.
10 : 35 " 10 : 55.—Sub. 1, Number. Sub. 2, Drawing on Slates
10 : 55 " 11 : 20.—General Lesson.
11 : 20 " 11 : 35.—Recess.
11 : 35 " 11 : 55.—Sub. 2, Number. Sub. 1, Drawing on Slates.
11 : 55 " 12 : 00.—Singing.
12 : 00 " 12 : 30.—Examination of Work on Slates.
12 : 30 to 1 : 30.—Intermission.

P. M.

1 : 30 to 1 : 55.—General Lesson.
1 : 55 " 2 : 10.—Tuesday and Thursday, Inventive Drawing. Monday, Wednesday, and Friday, Reading Stories to the Children.
2 : 10 " 2 : 15.—Physical Exercises.
2 : 15 " 2 : 35.—Sub. 2, Phonic Spelling. Sub. 1, Occupied with Slates.
2 : 35 " 3 : 00.—Examination of Slates.

The following Programme will show more minutely the work in Object Lessons. It is taken from the books in Model School, being a Programme for the Second Month of the First Term, from May 20th to June 9th.

C Class.

Birds.

REDBREAST.—Parts that distinguish. General conversation; cultivate humane feelings.

PEACOCK.—How distinguished. Moral lesson.

LARK.—How distinguished. Number of parts—Two eyes, two wings, one body, one tail, &c.

PARROT.—How distinguished. Names of parts.

STORK.—How distinguished. Position of parts.

FALCON.—How distinguished. Principal and secondary parts, or parts of parts.

DOVE.—Number and position of parts.

NIGHTINGALE.—Names of parts which are distinguished as principal and secondary.

PLACE.—*First Step.*

1. Objects placed in different positions by the teacher; children to imitate with minute accuracy.

2. As 1.

3. Objects placed in different positions; teaching the meaning of the term to express the position; as, *beside, between, under;* and the children imitate and apply the terms; then place the objects as directed, without a pattern.

4 and 5. As 3.

6. Objects placed; their position described, and represented on the blackboard.

7 and 8. As 4 and 5.

SIZE.—*First Step.*

1. Idea of *large* and *small.*
2.   "   *long* and *short.*

3. Idea of *wide* and *narrow*.
4. " *thick* and *thin*.
5. " *deep* and *shallow*.
6. " *deep* and *high*.

7 and 8. Various objects described with reference to all their qualities.

B Class.

Color.

1. Yellow, Red, Blue, Orange, Green, Purple, Citrine, Olive, Russet, distinguished, named, and matched.

2. Children form patterns with colored cards. *First*, like those made by the teacher, and then as they will. They are, however, limited as to the colors they put together, in order to accustom the eye to harmonious combination of colors merely.

>Yellow and Purple.
>Red and Green.
>Orange and Blue.

3. Orange and Purple.
>Green and Purple.
>Orange, Green, and Purple.

4. Citrine and Red.
>Citrine and Blue.
>Citrine, Red, and Blue.

5. Russet with Blue.
>Russet with Yellow.
>Russet with Blue and Yellow.

6. Olive with Red.
>Olive with Yellow.
>Olive with Red and Yellow.

7. Black with Red.
>Black with Yellow.
>Black with Red and Yellow.

8. Black with Orange.
>Black with Green.
>Black with Orange and Green.

Though the exercises in Color Patterning are not exhausted, and must be referred to again, it will be better now, for the sake of variety, to proceed to the Third Step in Color.

1. Re-calling Color.—Lesson on Red.
2. " Yellow.
3. " Blue.
4. " Green.
5. " Orange and Purple.
6. " Citrine, Russet, and Olive.
7. General Term.—Beauty of Color, &c. Color of Inanimate Nature.
8. General Term.—Color of Animated Nature.

PLACE.—*Cardinal Points.*

1. Idea of *East* and *West.*
2. Idea of *North* and *South.*
3. Idea of *Cardinal Points.*
4. Idea of term, *Cardinal Points.*
5. Exercises on the term, *Cardinal Points.*
6. Exercises on all the Points.
7 and 8. Necessity for having Four Points.

A Class.

BIRDS.

1 and 2. Eagle.
3. Condor.
4. Falcon.

PLACE.

Practice in drawing to Scale.
Schoolroom, adjoining rooms, school building.
Schoolroom with furniture, &c.

LANGUAGE.—*Begin the Course.*

Forming sentences with the name of an Object.

Forming sentences with a word expressing Quality.
Forming sentences with some part of the verb "to be."

>EXAMPLE.—*The Pencil is Sharp.*

Forming sentences in which different qualities are ascribed to the same object; as,

>Sugar is sweet.
>" white.
>" brittle, &c.

The different sentences afterward contracted into one.

Forming sentences in which the same quality is ascribed to different objects; as,

>Glass is brittle.
>Chalk is brittle.
>Coal is brittle, &c.

The different sentences contracted into one.

>THE END.

IN PRESS.

MODEL LESSONS ON OBJECTS.

BY

E. A. SHELDON,

SUPERINTENDENT OF PUBLIC SCHOOLS, OSWEGO, N. Y. AUTHOR OF "MANUAL OF ELEMENTARY INSTRUCTION," ETC.

The design of this work is to furnish a complete reference-book for Teachers, in giving "Object Lessons." It contains a number of detailed Lessons in each grade, together with a large list of Objects, with the names of such qualities as are suitable to be developed in each Lesson, and such information on the various Objects referred to as will be of assistance to the Teacher. It presents a complete graduated course of Developing Exercises and Instruction in Object Lessons, and is designed as a companion volume to "Elementary Instruction," &c., &c,

CHARLES SCRIBNER,

124 GRAND STREET,

NEW YORK.

GUYOT'S
WALL MAPS FOR SCHOOLS,

BY

PROF. ARNOLD GUYOT.

The large series, averaging 5 x 6 feet, contains the following:

1 Map of the HEMISPHERES.
1 " " WORLD (Mercator's Projection).
1 " EUROPE.
1 " ASIA.
1 " AFRICA.
1 " NORTH AMERICA.
1 " SOUTH AMERICA.
1 " OCEANIA.
1 " CENTRAL EUROPE.
1 " of the UNITED STATES.
1 " of the ROMAN EMPIRE.
1 " ANCIENT GREECE.

These Maps will be colored, either physically, politically, or physically and politically together, as ordered, and handsomely mounted on rollers.

☞ Any Map will be sold separately.

CHARLES SCRIBNER,

124 GRAND STREET, New York.

☞ AGENTS WANTED.

WALL MAPS FOR SCHOOLS,

BY

PROF. ARNOLD GUYOT.

The smaller series, averaging 3 x 4 feet, contains the following:

1 Map of the HEMISPHERES.
1 " EUROPE.
1 " ASIA.
1 " AFRICA.
1 " NORTH AMERICA.
1 " SOUTH AMERICA.
1 " OCEANIA.
1 " UNITED STATES (large).

These Maps are handsomely colored, and each set in portfolio.

☞ Any Map will be sold separately.

CHARLES SCRIBNER,
124 GRAND STREET, New York.

www.ingramcontent.com/pod-product-compliance
Lightning Source LLC
Chambersburg PA
CBHW022109300426
44117CB00007B/639